WHEN THE
DEVIL
SMILES THE
ANGELS
FROWN

MY LIFE AND TIMES IN ROCK 'N' ROLL

LEO ROSSI

When the Devil Smiles, the Angels Frown: My Life and Times in Rock 'n' Roll
Published by 20K Watts
Los Angeles, CA

Publisher's Cataloging-in-Publication data

Names: Rossi, Leo (1957-), author.
Title: When the Devil smiles the angels frown: my life and times in rock 'n' roll / by Leo Rossi.
Description: First trade paperback original edition. | Los Angeles [California] : 20K Watts, 2019. | Also published as an ebook.
Identifiers: ISBN 978-0-578-53980-5
Subjects: LCSH: Rock music. | Autobiography.
BISAC: BIOGRAPHY & AUTOBIOGRAPHY / Personal Memoirs.
Classification: LCC ML429 | DDC 920 ROSSI–dc22

Cover and Interior design by Victoria Wolf

QUANTITY PURCHASES: Schools, companies, professional groups, clubs, and other organizations may qualify for special terms when ordering quantities of this title. For information, email leo@knightsofrock.com.

TO MY CHILDREN:

Just Love It!

TO THE KNIGHTS OF ROCK:

There were about four billion people on this beautiful planet we call earth between 1970 and 1980.

There were one to two hundred of us Knights leading the way and assisting creative revolutionaries that became the voice of a generation that changed the world forever.

All you Knights of Rock still here and gone, you know who you are. Our lives are a one in a billion chance and we made the best of it, for ourselves and for millions of others who were inspired by what we helped create.

This book is dedicated to you.

LONG LIVE ROCK 'N' ROLL

THE LOAD IN

When you stay up all night
chasing your dreams your
punishment is seeing the sunrise
before the rest of the world.

FOREWORD

FOR LEO

At the age of 11 I was given my first camera and immediately became entranced with photography. It was more than just a hobby. It became my passion and all I cared about. Then in the virtual blink of an eye my life changed.

On a certain Sunday night in February of 1964, the ground shook under my feet. Rock 'n' roll music hit me with the ferocity of a Joe Louis right hook....a blow of staggering power and precision delivered by John Lennon. It knocked me out and I've yet to come to. My two universes of photography and music collided to define the rest of my life. By the time I had garnered my first photo assignment at 17, I had found my calling.

Sooner or later all professional photographers consciously or unconsciously gravitate to a specific area of photography because they love it and do it well. Some excel at fashion or sports. Some become great architectur photographers, and some globe-trotting photojournalis covering wars and other hard news. For me it was musi and the world around it.

Over 51 years. I've taken approximately 2 million photographs of rock bands and the universe they exist in.

Many people have told me I have a glamorous job. It couldn't be further from the truth. It's a job filled with pressure, deadlines, and constant jet lag.

I also learned something very important early in my career—to do a job like mine well, you don't leave your ego at the door—you leave it at home. You're not a member of the band and you never will be. The reality is, I'm just another guy on the crew, one of the Knights of Rock. And this is not fake humility. That's the way I've always felt and still feel to this day.

I simply cannot stress this strongly enough: I could never have had the career I've had, or created such a vast archive, without the help of every member of every road crew of every rock band I've ever photographed.

From the tour manager to the lighting crew and the monitor mixers all the way to the the house riggers and the bus drivers, every crew member is indispensible. They are the blood and guts of every rock show you'll ever see.

I always like to remind people that when you go to a rock show, whether it's in a club in LA, New York's Madison Square Garden, Wembley Stadium in London, or the Tokyo Dome, that show did not just end up there by chance. It didn't land there from outer space while you were paying for your Starbucks and swiping right. It took hard work and a fucking lot of it.

I'd describe a rock 'n' roll road rock crew as this: an amalgam of the Army Corps of Engineers, the offensive line of the Pittsburgh Steelers, the Egyptians that built the Pyramids, a couple of Sherman tanks , the writing staff of Saturday Night Live, and a dozen Swiss watchmakers.

No one on earth works as hard under conditions that are unimaginably difficult. They do it day after day, night after night, with little sleep and a boatload of stress. Even more astounding is they have to perform their jobs perfectly with a margin of error so slim it barely exists. It's a job that's not for the faint of heart.

There's little glory in being a member of a big rock 'n' roll road crew, and nobody on the crew is gonna get rich.

But the crew really holds the keys to the kingdom.

Leo Rossi and every one of the Knights of Rock knows what I'm talking about.

They are the ones who can welcome you with open arms or make you disappear—literally and figuratively. They are the fuel that keeps the rock 'n' roll tour engine running. Hell, they *are* the engine.

To get a great photo, I've had crew members allow me to go places on a stage where no one should have been allowed. They've saved my life by pulling me away from a flash pot I was straddling about five seconds before it was set to explode. I've had a crew member pay for my airline ticket when I'd lost my wallet.

And I've had a tour manager help me pick up a bag full of Nikons that had overturned getting into a limo, just before the loading dock door opened to reveal a near-riot outside the arena.

And like I always say—you'll have *much* more fun with the crew than with the band.

So when you go to a rock show, or remember the great ones you've seen, keep all that in mind, and when you read this book, just know that regardless of what anyone tells you, what you see on tv, read in magazines, hear on the radio or podcast—Leo Rossi is telling you how it *really* was and is.

NEAL PRESTON
Studio City, CA
August, 2019.

TABLE OF CONTENTS

INTRODUCTION 13

CHAPTER 1: Growing Up 19

CHAPTER 2: Rock 'n' Roll 31

CHAPTER 3: The Who (My First Tour) 47

CHAPTER 4: I Meet The Mac 55

CHAPTER 5: Leaving the Boy Behind 74

CHAPTER 6: Welcome to Your New Life 81

CHAPTER 7: The 1976 Bicentennial Bash:
"Look Out, World. Here I Come 93

CHAPTER 8: A Fall for Fall and Happy Holidays 105

CHAPTER 9: Love, Leo Rossi, Inc., and 1977 116

CHAPTER 10: Rumours 137

CHAPTER 11: Just Another Rainy Day in Florida 147

CHAPTER 12: Madison Square Garden 157

CHAPTER 13: Then There Was Light 167

CHAPTER 14: JC and Texas 171

CHAPTER 15: Million Dollar Beds 182

CHAPTER 16: Everyone Wants a Piece of Me 187

CHAPTER 17: Love at the Drive-Thru 193

CHAPTER 18: A Lesson in Loyalty 199

CHAPTER 19: Pallet Sixteen 206

CHAPTER 20: Home for the Holidays 236

CHAPTER 21: 1978 and the Summer Safari 243

CHAPTER 22: Leo Rossi: Stage Manager and All That Jazz 265

CHAPTER 23: A Very Busy 1979, And I Meet Rickie Lee Jones .286

Fleetwood Mac Entourage 1978

CHAPTER 24: *Tusk* 299

CHAPTER 25: *Tusk* Rehearsals 321

CHAPTER 26: *Tusk* Hits the Road 334

CHAPTER 27: The Angels and Devils in East Berlin 360

CHAPTER 28: Tusked and Done and Jazz Rehab Life Lessons ...368

CHAPTER 29: Old Friends Are Golden 375

CHAPTER 30: Stevie Nicks, Take One 387

CHAPTER 31: 1982 405

CHAPTER 32: One Word … Bette 437

CHAPTER 33: Stevie Nicks, Take Two 470

CHAPTER 34: 1984 the End of The World and the Start of Mine... 491

CHAPTER 35: 1985, Divas, Jazz, and Frequent Flyer Miles 511

CHAPTER 36: 1988 Back with The Mac, and Something
Completely Different 538

CHAPTER 37: Behind the Mask. The End of the Road 550

EPILOGUE 582

INTRODUCTION
ATLANTA 2015

THE BILLY IDOL TOUR BUS PULLED UP to the Ritz Carlton Hotel and was immediately surrounded by lots of younger fans. After a twelve-hour drive, I jumped off the bus like I'd done thousands of times before.

I incompassionately said, "Sorry, everyone, Billy won't be signing any autographs today."

I saw a number of faces flash: "Who's the old guy without a clue?" I noticed many were holding Fleetwood Mac and Stevie Nicks records.

Making my way to the front desk, I asked, "Hey is The Mac here?"

"Who?" The young worker asked.

"Fleetwood Mac."

"Oh yeah, they are, tonight—over at Philips Arena." My heart skipped a beat knowing I was so close to the family I had spent the majority of my youth with.

I called my good friend Marty Hom, the tour manager who took my place with Fleetwood Mac.

"Hey, Marty. It's Leo. I just pulled into town with Idol, and I'm at the Ritz. I hear you're in town. Wanna grab a drink tonight when you're done?"

"Wish I could, were on a hit-and-run and flying to Chicago right after the show, but come on down and say hello."

"Nah, I just got off a long bus ride. It's my only night off, and I have some catch up to do. Give everyone my love though."

"OK, in case you change your mind, I'll leave you a pass at the security gate backstage by the trucks and buses."

As I settled down in my room, knocking the road dust off myself, the familiar sound and vibration of a text message filled the room. Thinking it was the normal complaint from one of Billy's band, I just blew it off and continued my decompression. *Bing-bzzzt! Bing-bzzzt!* I finally gave in and read the text.

"Hey, Leo, you better come down. I told the band you're in town, and if you don't show, there may be some hurt feelings."

Reading the text out loud my heart went to my stomach, and my knees got weak. I wasn't sure I should go down and see the band, mainly because I didn't have the energy to manage the battle between my heart (saying "you belong there") and my mind (reminding me that was then, and this was now, and it would be impossible to be the same).

I decided to go, but only after the show started to avoid the awkwardness of reacquaintances before the band went onstage.

As I walked into the arena, The Mac was onstage—the familiar sound of its amazing thundering rhythm section combined with Lindsey and Stevie's perfect vocal harmonies—I felt complete ... I was home ... I was home!

As I awkwardly settled into the production office, watching various crew come and go out, I realized that other than the band, there were no other crew or staff from the original Fleetwood Mac gang.

Marty asked, "Is it weird, Leo?"

"Yeah, a bit. But I'm glad it's you, buddy, and not me."

Karen, Stevie's longtime confidant and good friend, rushed into the production office. We grabbed a quick hug as she said, "Stevie heard you were coming and really wants to see you, so don't leave."

"I can't promise, Karen, but in case I do leave, please give her my love."

Wanting to reflect and collect myself from my uncontrollable feelings, my body was on autopilot as I found a dark space backstage where I grabbed a road case and sat in the dark, where it would be easy to sneak out and be on my way.

It was the middle of the show, and I realized some things with The Mac just don't change. With Lindsey noodling the familiar tones and notes on his guitar, I knew that "Landslide" was about to begin.

I lay back and closed my eyes as Stevie began one of her nightly heartfelt dedications:

"This is a very special song that I dedicate to family and friends, and we have some family here tonight."

After a dedication to her godson and my friend Mathew, Stevie went on to say, "I'd also like to dedicate this to Leo Rossi who was Fleetwood Mac's tour manager and go to guy in the late 70s and 80s and into the 90s. He's here tonight and he's laughing backstage, saying I never thought you guys would make it out of the 80s. But we did, so he's very pleased, so I'd like to dedicate this to Leo Rossi. This is called Landslide."

Over the years and many dedications for my many birthdays on the road with The Mac, my guilt set in on how I took for granted all the sincere wishes from Stevie in the past.

Now, years later, this one was different. I felt special but couldn't help but think about all the many friends and fellow Knights of Rock who helped me along the way to deserve this love and dedication.

I also realized that for sure, I had to stick around and give Stevie a hug and see the rest of the band.

As the song ended Stevie went on to say, "Thank you, Leo, for all you did for us all those many years."

I teared up and just whispered, "No, thank you, Stevie. Thank you!"

That moment in Atlanta, and so many more like it, is the catalyst of the Knights of Rock; it's important for us to tell our story.

The Knights of Rock are those of us who—as a young group of pirates, renegades, rebels, rule breakers, and misfits—worked side by side with creative revolutionaries who transcended the culture, affecting and connecting the world like nothing else since perhaps the Renaissance.

It's a story about young people from different places with very diverse backgrounds finding each other to become the voice of a generation that gave people strength and hope to get on with their lives and realize dreams do come true.

This book will allow you to become part of the backstage crew of rock 'n' roll during an incredible time in history where the music created an everlasting love affair with people and their youth.

They say behind every great band, there's a great crew. The reality is, behind every great crew, there's a great band.

So, with a warm embrace, and the welcome-to-my-life attitude I inherited from my Italian family, I invite you to take this magical trip back in time with the ultimate backstage pass and share my life in the amazing times of classic rock.

As I pull the rope to open the curtain and shine the lights upon my journey with the artists and music that are the soundtrack of your life, just think: this could have easily been you.

My name is Leo ... Leo Rossi, and I am only one of the Knights of Rock.

CHAPTER ONE

GROWING UP

OFTEN, I'M IN LINE AT A COFFEE SHOP, restaurant, or grocery store, and I hear "The Chain" by Fleetwood Mac, "California Girls" from the Beach Boys, or "Rebel Yell" from Billy Idol, and I realize anew how lucky I was to be involved with one of the most important periods of music history: the Classic Rock era. During that time, normal, everyday life for me included days others can only dream about. Those days were given to me with a purpose, a reason, a gift ... a gift that became my fate to leave this world better than I found it.

I grew up in San Pedro, California. San Pedro was a blue-collar port town with transients sauntering down its narrow streets littered with dive bars and tattoo parlors with classic 1920s architecture. It's a town that was built by hardworking immigrants who came to America with all the dreams and fortunes it had to offer. It contained scenes right out of *The Godfather* but with less violence that played out on the sunny shores of Southern California.

I like to say I'm first generation American, and in fact, I am but only on my father's side. His Northern Italian family brought the hard-work-and-hide-your-feelings lifestyle to the "Little Italy" of the West Coast.

My mother was born in St. Louis, Missouri, where my grandparents settled with family who before them dared to take the journey to the New World. It really didn't matter where their feet were planted or where they rested their heads at night, they were still 100 percent Italian, thousands of miles away from a country healing itself from the ravages of World War II.

Story has it my mother's father escaped recruitment by the mafia in St. Louis, and in order to protect his wife and four children (that soon became seven), he fled to San Francisco to be a fisherman, like his father before him in Italy. My father's father came at the tail end of the Gold Rush only to find empty hills of the precious chemical element but still managed to survive and raise his family. Moving to the West Coast promised to give their children the best opportunities that America had to offer.

Dino Rossi and Mary Russo married and became the fruits of their parent's struggles and were the epitome of the American Dream. They met at Francisco Junior High School in North Beach, the Italian section of San Francisco. They worked hard to keep the peace between my father's stoic, close-fisted northern Italian family and my mother's jovial, life-loving, traditional Sicilian family that wore their hearts on their sleeves.

My father and mother: Captain Dino Rossi and Mary Russo/Rossi

When both sides staked claim for initiating holidays, weddings, or the annual Saint Giuseppe feast, it took time and homemade wine to realize they were in America now and needed to leave the Old-World *astio* (grudge) feelings behind.

The fourth of five children, I was born August 27, 1957, at 8:16 p.m. at St. Francis Hospital in San Francisco, California. My upbringing was very traditional Italian Catholic: Sunday gatherings celebrating life with family, friends, and food, lots of food. It was the kind of family where you better be home for dinner when Dad got off work and have a very good excuse if you missed Sunday Mass. He'd test us by asking, "What was the Gospel today?"

Overtime, us, the next generation crawled out of our cribs and grew with our strong Italian heritage but enlightened American way of life and became an even larger loving family with thirty-three first cousins, fifty-three great grandchildren, and a multitude of good friends we called cousins.

With the warm waters off Southern California perfect for the prosperity of fishing, the family moved to the safe haven of the multicultural city of San Pedro—the sea port of Los Angeles.

It was the early 1960s, and my father's desire to be around and provide for his family meant coming ashore from commanding merchant marine ships and taking a job managing a freight terminal at the growing port.

My parents did what they thought was right—not a mean bone in their bodies. They were perfect parents. A hardworking father with a stay-at-home mother and all the comforts of a loving home.

Rossi Family Front Row: sister Clara, mother Mary, sister Phillis, father Dino, brother David. Back Row: me, brother Joseph

My brothers and sisters were all overachievers. My oldest brother bore the pressure of the first Italian son: "Be a doctor, be a lawyer." My father would tell us, "You have to work hard, harder than the next guy. Life is under no obligation to give you what you expect. You have to live your life to the point of tears."

All they wanted for us was that American Dream, so much that they didn't teach us to speak Italian in fear we would be viewed as immigrants and not get our fair shake.

Growing up watching my two overachieving sisters and an older brother who was great at all he touched made me a child so curious about life that I hated to sleep in fear I would miss something.

Nine years into my life came the happiest of all accidents: my younger brother. My father, home from the sea, finally had a child he could be around all the time. I always felt like I was the forgotten child, born right in the middle of pride and joy, leaving me with some huge insecurity.

I saw my brothers and sisters getting attention and talking about their futures, so to me, attention was love and love was attention. I needed something. I needed to be noticed.

I was different from my siblings; I didn't have much of an attention span and had no capacity to stay on track, so I was destined for a life working on the docks. In San Pedro, that was the golden ticket: a promise of wealth and job security.

It just wasn't for me.

Back in grade school, I don't remember saying, "Hey, I want to be in the music business and work with the greatest rock stars of all times." It was truly a one in a billion chance, a one in a billion chance that happened to me.

I look back now and realized that my glass, it wasn't half empty, it wasn't half full. My glass was refillable, and there was an endless supply of this intoxicating liquid called life. I bought into it and just kept drinking, drinking, and drinking. And today, I'm still thirsty!

My life in showbiz started way back at Crestwood Street Elementary School, where for some reason I was selected to be the monitor of just about everything—raising the flag, setting up the auditorium, even ringing the bell. Most likely they chose me because I was so bored and fidgety, and I was always getting into trouble. It was their way of keeping an eye on me.

On one occasion, it was my job to work in the auditorium. I had to open the curtains for a choral show. It was midday, all the fathers took off work and mothers enjoyed a break from their family chores. Soon they all had taken their seats, ready to watch their cute little children strut their stuff and become the next Frank Sinatra or Barbra Streisand.

The show began, and when the choir had gotten to their places onstage, on cue, I pulled on the rope to open the curtain. The choir began to sing, but for some reason, I was under the impression that the curtain was not opening. Panicking, I began yanking as hard as I could on the other rope, which of course, caused the curtain to close. I didn't see anything happening, so I pulled the other rope again, and the curtain opened again. The audience started to laugh and holler—it was pandemonium. The teacher ran over to me with a look of horror on her face. She ripped the ropes from my hands and yanked the curtains open herself.

At that moment, I learned my first lesson about show business: Instead of being scared or panicked about what I had just done, I felt the exhilaration and the power I had at that moment. I can really affect how people think, feel, and see. WOW! That was cool.

I think that it was especially impactful to me because it made me someone. I was relevant. With relevance, "insecurity" is merely a word.

I thought about the curtain experience from time to time, but I didn't really know what to do about it. Then, on the first day of high school in 1972, circumstance, fate, and destiny stepped in.

I went to San Pedro High School in San Pedro, California. In high school, other than the core English, math, and science classes that were assigned, we had to pick out two elective classes that we wanted to take each semester. I was wandering aimlessly down the hallway, and really, I had no idea what I wanted to do with my life. Out of nowhere, a teacher came up to me and started pitching me on his class. He looked desperate. He told me he needed just one more kid to register for the Stage Theater Production class before he could get the hell out of there and get on home. He hurriedly explained to me that in his class, I would learn what went on behind the scenes during a play—the sound and lights. He also explained to me that there was no homework, it was really fun, and I would get out of class a lot to work all the assemblies for the school. Perfect! My kind of class.

More than appeasing this obviously desperate adult, the idea of an easy class with no homework sparked a definite interest. The thing that really sold it was the part about getting out of class to set up assemblies. So, in my freshman year, I joined the Stage class.

Lo and behold, the class that I had little initial interest in soon became my favorite time of the day, and I especially got into lighting. I really appreciated the ability that lighting had to create an atmosphere. I saw what could be done with different shades and different colors, intensities, changing the atmosphere. Here I was, this forgotten child who no one paid attention to screwing with people's heads, feelings, and perceptions—and them not even realizing it.

I fell in with a group of people who were dedicated to the craft of putting on great plays. They were older than me, mainly juniors and seniors, but they took the class very seriously, and therefore, so did I. Even though I was younger, we all had one thing in common: we were all artistic misfits with the same insecurities. They treated me as an equal.

In the summer, my teacher, Mr. Deemar—or as I would call him later, Richard—was also a stagehand for local television shows and theaters. He was a member of the Union 33, which is the International Alliance of Television and Stage Engineers (IATSE Union #33).

Me in high school stage class running the light board.

As far as I was concerned, he really knew what it was all about, and I started to realize for the first time that there may be something in life that I was not only interested in, but also good at.

During the course of the year, the class took field trips to the nearby Long Beach Auditorium to see plays. It was cool because we got to miss school for a whole day. The first one I went to was *Cabaret*. We took our seats, and the curtain went up. The actors read their lines and sang their songs, but I didn't like it. I was bored. During intermission, I had already checked out and was determined to make things more exciting. I noticed a door and was pretty sure it led backstage. I can't explain what force made me take the risk to sneak back there but I did—another decision that would change my life forever.

I found an out-of-the-way spot not far from the stage. The curtain rose, and I was enthralled. The sound, the

Long Beach Civic Light Opera crew 1974. I'm first row all
the way to the right.

lights, the set movements, the actors all running around;
I was even fascinated by the smell of hot lights and sweat
off the actors. All my senses were aroused, and to this day,
I remember the magic of that moment. It was definitely
more exciting backstage than in the audience.

The show ended, and the lights came up. Now my task
was to sneak back out. I saw an open door and made my
move. I thought I had made it when I suddenly felt two
big hands on my shoulder from the technical director.

"Hey, what are you doing back here?"

I was caught, and I was in trouble. I confessed I hated
the show but really liked what went on backstage. I guess
he could tell from my answer that I was enthusiastic and
appreciative about it. His attitude quickly changed from
antagonism to sympathy.

"Come on. Follow us."

The director huddled with John, the drama theater teacher filling in for Richard, and they came up with a plan. My punishment was to work with professional stagehands for one month. This led to an apprenticeship.

Mary Schlatter, my guidance counselor at San Pedro High School, saw my passion for working backstage. Her husband, George Slaughter, was the producer of *Rowan & Martin's Laugh-In,* the famous TV comedy show. She realized the pressure I was going through growing up under overachieving siblings. "Why can't you be more like your sisters and brother" was beat into my head daily! She knew I was a dreamer and that I used the part of my brain that most used for math, science, and English in a very different way. She found a work program that allowed me to work in the afternoons at the Long Beach Civic Light Opera and the Long Beach Arena to get school credit. It even would help me graduate early. Mary was a beautiful example of how one committed, passionate person who sees things as they are, and not as they should be, can make positive change.

For three years I worked hard, made contacts, and learned a lot.

At fifteen years old, I took the risk and snuck backstage, and it's like I never left.

My wisdom and success were born out of wonder and curiosity.

For all my years during high school, I was an apprentice stagehand. Over the course of those years, I ended up doing a lot of light operas—*Cabaret, Jesus Christ Superstar, Company, South Pacific* and many others. All the while, I was soaking up the collected knowledge of these union veterans who had been working stages and shows forever. I was learning how to build scenery, create lighting designs, set up lighting rigs, and track down and solve problems; all the general knowledge of how a show works—and I was good at it. I worked every afternoon and all weekend, and they would give me a T-shirt and tell me, "See ya next week, kid."

To them, I was free labor (well, not exactly free I did make twenty-five cents an hour). But to me, it was like Backstage University, and they were my professors. For three and a half years, I worked hard, learned a lot, and made amazing contacts.

My experience at Long Beach Auditorium gave me a privileged position back in high school. I was learning how to light a stage and how to work with directors. And, perhaps most importantly, for the first time, I knew what I wanted to do with the rest of my life. Show business!

During all my time in high school I focused on the plays, and I ended up winning a bunch of awards for lighting and set design. In the minds of many people, I was a techno nerd with the nickname Mr. Stage. I was on track to attend a theatrical arts college with one of the many scholarship offers I received, including to the University of Southern California. I even tried a three-week stint doing outdoor lights at the prestigious Los Angeles

City College's Shakespeare Theater. It was a hard school to get into, and it didn't take much to realize that circumstance, destiny, and fate were to dictate what school I would attend. It was the school of rock 'n' roll, and the whole world was to be my campus.

CHAPTER TWO
ROCK 'N' ROLL

IN MY FIRST YEAR OF HIGH SCHOOL, and while working at the Long Beach Auditorium, the stagehands told
me that, in addition to light opera shows at the auditorium, they also worked at the Long Beach Arena next door,
which did the ice shows, circus, and rock shows. These
were older union guys, and they absolutely hated to work
the rock shows. It was the counterculture of the time,
long hair, no structure, and they despised the make-it-up-
as-you-go attitude. They were glad to show young guys
like me how to do it, in the hopes that someday we would
take that work off their hands, keep the union going, and
feed the pension fund.

When they needed some of us younger guys to work the rock shows, we would head down to the arena, unload trucks, and set up the sound, lights, and band equipment. At the end of a long day of work, we'd get a T-shirt while the union guys were getting paid to play cards. They were there when we needed them, but they taught and trusted that we knew what we were doing. We were a group of young, hardworking guys who fast became a family and were destined to become the new face of the union.

During my high school years, I ended up working all the not-yet-mega classic rock groups that came through the Long Beach Arena—bands like Deep Purple, Led Zeppelin, and Jethro Tull that were shattering the establishment's control over America; they were empowering a youth culture to dare to ask "why," which created ever-lasting change.

As a matter of fact, I can still remember the day that rock 'n' roll possessed me, the day every cell in my body came alive connecting my mind, my heart, and my soul forever—Led Zeppelin.

It was March 11–12, 1975, and Led Zeppelin came through Long Beach Arena on one of their most iconic tours. I wasn't a big Zeppelin fan but was familiar and liked their songs. That morning, I started with lights. Zeppelin's lights show was massive.

There was one set of particular lights that we had set up that were the key lights for the lead singer, Robert Plant. We hung the lights and made them work. In

Long Beach Auditorium
Arena 1975

My crew pass for the
Led Zeppelin shows,
March 11 and 12 1975

the afternoon, I climbed up onto the truss hanging from the arena roof to focus the lights where Robert Plant was going to sing. We finished the lighting and moved on to sound, and then to the band equipment.

That day was the first time I met a real-life rock star up close. Over the three years at Long Beach, I had been physically close to many of them but never had any real interaction.

I had just finished helping set up the band instruments onstage and was outside the back of the arena taking a break. I was sitting on a wall, drinking a soda, waiting to see what was next. This English guy came out and sat next to me. We started having a casual conversation, and he asked me if I was from around the area and what it was like to live in California. We talked about my school, growing up in San Pedro, and a bunch of different things. He looked like a regular guy, and I never really asked him what he did. I figured he was on the crew or something. There were a lot of English guys around because Led Zeppelin was from England, and he seemed just like another one of the road crew working on the tour. I hung out with him for ten or fifteen minutes and went back in to help finish the load-in.

I finished up my work and waited for my dad to pick me up on his way home from work for the mandatory nightly family dinner. Sitting at the table, I excitedly inhaled my food, trying to get back to Long Beach as soon as I could.

I remember talking to my sisters about Led Zeppelin and what a big show they had. They, more into the Beatles and pop rock, said Zeppelin's music is about the Devil and drugs. It didn't matter to me. I was excited to see what it was all about and just wanted to get back to the arena and work the show.

After dinner, I drove the family's little yellow Ford Pinto back to Long Beach to work the concert. In my teen years, that was my life: one minute in school, the next minute working with rock 'n' roll road crews, the next minute at the dinner table saying prayers, and then hanging with the biggest so-called, Devil-worshipping band on the planet.

My main job at Long Beach Arena and Auditorium was lighting. One of the jobs for someone on the lighting crew was to stand at the foot of the stairs when bands went on and hold a flashlight so no one tripped getting onto stage. The house lights went out, and the roar of the crowd was deafening. It was dark, and it was an amazing feeling when the crowd broke into a loud endless roar of:

This is what it looked like from where I was standing that night in 1975.

"ZEPPE-LIN! ZEPPE-LIN! ZEPPE-LIN!" It was an out-of-body experience, like I was ten feet above, looking down at the whole scene.

I will never forget and from that night on I craved that feeling and knew I couldn't live without it.

In the darkness, my head was down as I did my job holding the flashlight on the stairs. I felt a tap on the top of my head. I looked up to notice the guy I was talking with earlier outside; he was now in a costume, holding a guitar, and going onstage. He gave me the thumbs-up and smiled. It took me a moment to recognize him with his stage wardrobe and the madness going on around us. I obviously didn't know it was Led Zeppelin's guitar player, Jimmy Page, who I was having a casual conversation with earlier; I gave him the thumbs-up and

36

felt like a million bucks because he acknowledged me.

After the band went onstage, I was so excited, I felt like part of the show. I went down to the front of the stage, and I stood next to the security guys ten feet from the band, marveling at what Led Zeppelin created. Near the end of the show, the band broke into their most iconic song: "Stairway to Heaven." Robert Plant was the amazing golden Rock God that Robert Plant was. In the middle section of the song, I looked a bit higher and saw the lights, my lights, the lights that I hung and focused on giving Robert Plant the halo that made him look like he wasn't even human.

That moment, when I saw Robert Plant drenched in the lights I hung, I got so excited, and my heart started to race. At seventeen years old, I helped Robert Plant of Led Zeppelin look good, and I knew there were no limits for what was to come and where I was headed.

Led Zeppelin was beyond music, and it was so loud, you felt every piece of your body immersed in the show. It was like you were out on a cold street and walked into a beautiful restaurant, not only feeling the warmth, but smelling the euphoric aromas.

Zeppelin created a chemistry that touched all your senses, not just your ears. They were four people in one body. I realized later in life that what I learned that night was something that I carry with me to this day: music is more than just a listening experience, it's all about sight and feel as well.

Great entertainers, straight or high, pour out their souls and connect with people in a way that is unique to each individual but creates relationships between millions of people. The power these special people possessed influenced the masses and literally changed the world.

It was easy to think that Zeppelin was all fabricated with equipment and effects, but when they came down to the front of the stage and stripped down to acoustic guitars to play one of the slow songs, "The Rain Song" or "Going to California," you knew they were real musicians—no gimmicks, no electronics, just shear talent. Robert Plant didn't just sing. His voice became one of the instruments, and as I watched Jimmy Page play acoustic, Plant focused on him and the two of them were one person.

After the show, I really wanted to see Jimmy Page and talk to him again. Maybe this time, I could have asked *him* some questions. But after the show, he was pretty protected backstage, and then they zipped into limos and took off. I had had my chance. I was embarrassed and felt so stupid. Most of all, I was hoping I didn't insult him by not giving him the respect I thought he deserved.

The next day, there was no sound check; the band came in right before the show. I did see Jimmy Page but couldn't get close enough to talk to him. He did see me and gave me nod of validation, and that was good enough for me.

I was too young to understand it then—rock stars are people. They're regular people who sometimes do some pretty extraordinary things.

In the early to the mid-70s, the music business was still relatively small. I ended up seeing the same lighting, sound, and stage guys coming through Long Beach show after show, and they started to know me by name.

I was so young that when they saw me, they called me The Kid. I got a reputation as this wonder kid who could fix anything. If it was broken, they brought it to me—lights, sound, musical equipment, anything; I fixed it.

So, all these familiar touring guys took a liking to me. I was young and energetic, and they were always looking for someone like me to go on the road and do all the hard work. I was taught by the best. The union guys were brilliant. Even while in high school, the tour offers were coming in.

Those years at the Long Beach Arena and Long Beach Auditorium were a time of amazing growth for me, not only personally but also musically. Those experiences gave me a passion for music, as well as confidence. When I think back over the list of bands I worked with and saw, it's no wonder: Led Zeppelin, Humble Pie, Deep Purple, ELO, Climax Blues Band, Ten Years After, Iron Butterfly, James Taylor, the Pointer Sisters, the Beach Boys, Diana Ross, Billy Preston—the list goes on and on. Some of these bands had a profound effect on me. After I saw Rory Gallagher—the great Irish blues guitar player—I went down to Redwood Records in San Pedro and special ordered a copy of his record, which was hardly known in the United States.

I guess you could say that I had a better musical education than the normal kid, who could only afford a show once or twice a year.

Somehow, that music gave me a sense of power. It gave me a sense of passion and pride. It made me feel more mature and more knowledgeable about the big world out there, and it also helped my insecurity. The day after a concert, back at school, people would come up to me and say, "Hey, I saw you onstage at the Zeppelin concert last night. How did you get up there? Do you know them?" I was someone—someone now getting attention. People wanted to be my friend. I was becoming more popular than the jocks and the cool kids on campus. All of a sudden ... I became the cool one.

It was during these years, at a very young age, that I learned how rock 'n' roll crews worked. The business was new and finding its way. These veteran road crews would come in like a team with this choreographed sequence of events. They would erect a small city every day and tear it down every night and move on to the next city and do it again—day after day after day. They weren't creating something permanent but rather something that would allow everyone in the arena to live intensely for a brief space in time. Then they would blow out of town, and it would be like they were never there. The only permanent thing the tours created were everlasting memories people would carry with them for the rest of their lives.

I also began to understand better how the groups worked, as far as the business side. For example, the first time I worked with Journey at the small Golden West Ballroom, a very small venue in Downey, California, I noticed that they were a bunch of musicians and crew from Carlos Santana's band. I understood that if you were talented enough as a backing musician or a sound guy or guitar tech, you could start your own band or crew. Little by little, I gained insights like that. I was only in my teens but was beginning to understand the music business. These experiences jump-started my career and gave me not only the knowledge but the insight, the gut, to make calculated right decisions.

And, finally, there were some big-picture lessons that would serve me throughout my life, no matter what I did. I was young, but I worked hard. I worked with people who were a lot older and more experienced than I was, and from that, I learned the ethic of hard work, of sticking with something, and of teamwork.

Over the course of time I worked those shows, I was tempted to quit school many, many times. In fact, in my senior year—I was asked to go on the road by a lighting company out of Memphis, Tennessee, and I made up my mind to actually take them up on it.

I went home and told my parents I wanted to drop out of school and go on the road, and boy, did that create a scene. My mom was actually calm and looked over at my father. His Italian face became stoic ... stony, and stiff, and he said, "You're not going anywhere. You're going to finish school." He said, "If they want you now, they'll want you next year. Just finish school."

Well, I was seventeen years old, and Italian guilt set in. I only knew to respect my father's wishes. But during my senior year, I kept working because I knew that it was eventually going to lead to something. And I did graduate—barely.

On my eighteenth birthday, after I finished high school, something happened that really summarized the difference between where I was and where my parents expected me to be. My parents did not understand what I was going through at all, nor did I expect them to. My dad thought I had no direction. Rock 'n' roll wasn't even on his radar. The counterculture of the youth in music was against everything he grew to believe. Music, long hair, freedom: to him these were all paths to the Devil's playground and a one-way ticket to hell. He had a backup plan, not only for me, but him to not have to feed me for the rest of his life.

On my eighteenth birthday, my dad sat me down, and with great gravity, handed me the paperwork for a longshoreman union card.

He wanted me to work on the dock and load cargo and do brain-dead work, and he was so proud of the fact that he had been able to get it for me. It's true: it would have been a good, steady, well-paying career with good benefits, but I loved what I was doing. When I rejected his gift, my father was very disappointed. I knew he was afraid I would fail. If I failed, that meant he failed, and with my overachieving siblings and my also brilliant younger brother, I would have been the only blemish on the Rossi dossier.

I tried to explain to him what I did in the world of music and lighting, but he couldn't understand. He was so frustrated. He just couldn't understand how I was going to make a living in this world of hedonism. When I talked to him about it, I heard enormous disappointment in his voice, and I felt incredible guilt for taking actions that he interpreted as turning my back on him. But I knew I couldn't be like my older brother, and I had to do what I needed to do for me. My mother, on the other hand, got it! For some reason, she knew I was going to be OK. She would tell my father, "He's going to be fine. Just let it be." I'm not 100 percent sure why she felt that way, but later in life, we had a conversation, and she told me it was my spirit, my determination, my passion, and that I was a good person. She said I was different, different than the rest, and good things happen to good people. She also said knowing there was a longshoreman backup plan helped her as well.

My fear of a normal mundane life, working nine to five with no daily doses of adrenaline running through my veins, drove me to the unknown. It drove me to take chances, and I realize then—and even today like back then—I'd rather be on to the next life before settling with no trepidation, excitement, and the feeling of knowing what's going to happen tomorrow.

Disappointing my father made me sad. I realized that my parents had done a great deal for me growing up, and I was thankful for the values that they imparted to me. But I knew in my heart that I could not live the life my father wanted me to live. I knew that I had found something that I was good at, and even though it was so different from the way I was raised, I was going to pursue it.

Things were rough between my father and me for a long time. It wasn't until the winter of the next year, 1977—when he saw a picture of me with Fleetwood Mac in *People Magazine*—that he finally started to get it.

I spent the rest of the 1975 doing shows in Long Beach and picking up local gigs throughout Southern California with the lights and sound companies while continuing to build my reputation and making friendships.

Then, one day in early 1976, I came home to find a message on my answering machine—the tiny red blinking light of fate. The message was from my friends at Obie's Lighting who had just moved down from Oregon. I had met them coming through Long Beach doing shows, mainly the British band Ten Years After, where I fixed a piece of equipment for them, and they had remembered me. They had a short tour going out and asked was I interested. Was I? It didn't matter who it was; I just wanted to get on tour.

I called them back, and they said I should have a bag packed because I was going to be gone three to four weeks. I was to meet them at their new lighting shop in Torrance, the next town over. I found that I was going to be fourth electrician and unloading trucks and doing all the shit work, like humping cable all day on The Who's West Coast tour. It was a run that included mainly stadiums and a few indoor shows.

Now picture this. Sitting around the dinner table: my sisters talking about college, my older brother talking sports and school, my younger brother at the end of the table, spilling something. When it was my turn to talk, I said, "I won't be at dinner for a few weeks. I'm going on a music tour tomorrow with The Who." My sisters perked up, and my father said, "Tour? Who? What?"

I said "The band is The Who."

He said, "Tour? What? Who? What are you talking about?"

I said, "Never mind, Dad, but I won't be home or at dinner for a few weeks."

That night, in my room with my brothers, I lay awake in my bed like many nights before, excited and realizing this was an amazing dream coming true. What I didn't realize is that it would be the last night I would sleep in that bed in that house—and how much my life was going to change forever.

The very next day, I showed up at the lighting shop, and we proceeded to load just about every spotlight in the whole place. Loading the sixth light into the back of the truck, I thought, "Damn. This is a big tour."

Then, they surprised me even more by driving to another shop in Hollywood. And, again, we loaded up every damn spotlight in the place. Then we went to a third place in downtown LA and a fourth place and a fifth place. We must have picked up damn near every follow spot in Los Angeles County. Finally, we got on the 405 Freeway and headed south toward San Diego.

Suddenly, it dawned on me. The Who! I couldn't believe it. "I was going on tour with one of the greatest rock 'n' roll bands on the face of the Earth!"

I sat back and looked down the long road. I was doing it. I was going out on the road. I was on top of the world. I had arrived.

The Who Anaheim Stadium
Poster 1976

The Who concert ticket
$10 General Admission

CHAPTER THREE
THE WHO (MY FIRST TOUR)

THE WHO WAS ACTUALLY MY FIRST tour with consecutive dates, and I was one of the lowest of lowest crew members when it came to importance. But I was a crew member, and I had a job that was important to the shows.

As a lighting grunt I was first in, last out. Loading in a show was layered. First the lights, then the sound, and then the band instruments. On the way out, it was the opposite, band instruments, sound, then lights.

The outdoor stadium shows had massive stages, roofs, and sound platforms that were ready for us to put our equipment on. The lighting and sound mixing boards that required the engineers to be in front of the stage were put on large scaffolding structures that always went in the day before and were also ready when we arrived at the stadium.

The lighting design and set up for this The Who tour was unique. The guy who designed the lighting for the show was kind of a genius—or at least way ahead of his time. He decided to use minimal stage lights and just light the four band members with follow spots. We brought twenty-four follow spots in all, so each band member had six follow spots on him at any given time—four on the stage and two in the house. It was elegant and easy to set up, and it really made the performers pop out from their environment.

Super Trooper Follow Spot. On the Who tour we set up twenty-four spots everyday.

My job was to work with the local union crews (that I had a lot of experience with) to put the follow spots up on scaffolding about 150 feet in front and seventy-five feet high of the stage. I also ran the power cables, made sure that the headphones to communicate with the spot operators worked—all that grunt work.

Remember, this was 1976, before modern machinery and big forklifts, so we put the follow spots up with the old block and fall pully system that had been around for hundreds of years. I was on top of the scaffolding (about seventy-five feet high) to receive the spots lights, anchor them onto the platform, and then run power to them and communi-

The spotlight tower in the middle of the stadium.

cation to the lighting designer to instruct the operators what to do.

After my job with the spots was complete, I volunteered my services to assist the sound and band crews to load-in and set up their gear. I was so excited to be there on the tour and just wanted to soak it all up and be a part of it.

There was no way I was just going to do my part of the tour and go back to the hotel like the rest of my team. I spent at least twenty hours a day at the venues, including standing right on the side of the stage for the sound checks as The Who tested their gear and the crew got their settings and levels.

The Who's primary crew (sound and lights and band) actually didn't know who I was working for and didn't really care. They were incredibly receptive to the idea that all I wanted to do was be a part of it and learn. My knowledge and ability to talk the talk and walk the walk meant they accepted me and immediately made me one of them, The Who's crew. I didn't know it at the time, but I was preparing myself to understand the whole concept of how a rock show works. Anything I didn't already know, I would ask, and I was soaking it up like a sponge.

My friend and one of the best crew mates ever, the late Alan Rogan.

They were an amazing talented bunch of English rebels and became good friends. Alan Rogan, Pete Townsend's guitar tech, was especially nice and was excited to share his experience with me. We remained good friends, and in fact, I hired Alan to work with me on future tours.

John Entwistle, bass player for The Who going onstage. The Who tour 1976.

I kept pestering Alan about guitar rigs, bass rigs, and keyboard rigs—anything that was there, and God bless him, he didn't mind. I asked why and how their stage monitors worked the way they did. I asked all about the sound boards, everything. Most of all, I was learning what it was like to be on tour. This was my new home, my new family, and unbeknownst to me, my new way of life for the next forty-one years.

The band was great the whole tour. It was really the first time I had seen one band play night after night, and I was blown away by their work ethic and the energy level of their performances. I loved the sound checks where the band would come in and be able to be themselves, natural, no pressure to perform. They could expand their talents with no pressure of making mistakes. We witnessed their true talent, a private show for all of us—the special few, their crew.

At the end of the set every night, they went into the last part of the rock opera "Tommy." Watching Pete Townsend and Roger Daltry sing, "listening to you I feel the music," and seeing Keith Moon jump out of his stool every time he hit a drum fill was unbelievable. There I was, eighteen years old, sitting high in the scaffold structure, onstage watching Keith Moon of The

Keith Moon 1976.

Who play the magic he played. It was mesmerizing, and I couldn't take my eyes off of him. I didn't want to miss a lick, not a beat, and I was afraid if I took my eyes off him, I would miss some magic moment I would never get back. I was so excited I couldn't control my senses.

After growing up listening to The Who, and especially Keith Moon, the drummer, you can imagine that I was totally in heaven. For four weeks, the tour took us to San

Diego, Anaheim Stadium in Los Angeles, San Francisco, Portland, Seattle—all over the West Coast.

By the time the short tour was over, I had decided that rock 'n' roll lighting was actually easier than working the light operas I did at Long Beach. I was confident that I would be able to take a lighting rig out on my own and be a key part of a tour. That was a big thing for me. I was only eighteen years old, and I already had a great deal of responsibility. I had entered a world where I had to act older. Luckily, because I was Italian, I was able to grow a mustache and a beard, and that helped me be perceived as older than I was.

And I acted that way. I'd get the light rigs up and running right and quickly. I would help troubleshoot band equipment and solve sound problems, even if they weren't my responsibility. Whatever needed to be done, I knew how to do it. I continued building the reputation from Long Beach as the kid who knew a lot and could fix anything. I kept learning and kept meeting people. It got to the point where people would come to me with problems that none of the other guys who had been out on the road for years could figure out. I was proud to hold my own with the gnarly old veterans who supposedly knew everything. I took it as a kind of challenge. I was really confident, sometimes not for my own good. I knew what I wanted, and I meant to get it.

Having that much power at that age was dangerous. My big head could have easily gotten me ousted from the business in no time. But, at that time, I never really lost my small-town values. I never cheated, lied, or stole. (With the help of drugs, that would come later.) And I attribute a lot of that to my parents, who raised me that way. I always treated people the way I wanted to be treated. I was always careful about how people viewed me and how I wanted to be viewed. Even when someone didn't know something, I wouldn't look at them like they were wrong. I learned if someone has an idea that sounds absurd, it's usually either one of two things: either they are very passionate about their idea or they really don't know or understand the whole situation. Either way, they are not wrong—just passionate or misinformed. If passionate, don't kill their passion, nurture it. If misinformed, do a better job educating them and try to teach them. This philosophy took me a long way and was one of the cornerstones of my professional success and formed my attitude while raising children and having my own family.

One week after the tour ended, I got a call from Obie's office that I needed to fill out some paperwork. I drove down to the office and filled out papers so I could get paid. It was a total surprise to me. Oh my God! We get paid for this?

I was so excited just to be on tour I totally forgot about getting paid for the tour. I filled out the tax forms, and they gave me a check, a big check! I didn't know what to do. I wasn't even sure if it was fair or not. My insecurity made me not ask. As I was driving back to San Pedro, my excitement surged, realizing what was in front of me. I understood that when you love what you do, it's not work. I'm proud to say, I've never had a job.

CHAPTER FOUR

I MEET THE MAC

I HAD BEEN INTO FLEETWOOD MAC for a while before I ever dreamed of working for them. As a matter of fact, I worked a show at Long Beach with a band that was calling itself Fleetwood Mac, but it was a completely different band. As soon as I saw them onstage, I knew it was BS. There was no Mick Fleetwood, no John McVie, no Christine McVie. I remember saying, "Who are these people?"

Fleetwood Mac's former manager, Clifford Davis, believed that he had rights to the name, and he put a bogus band on the road. In the end, they ended up working that one out in court but not without taking a toll on the band and knocking some wind out of their sails.

After the settlement of the bogus Fleetwood Mac, another variation with Bob Welch, an amazing guitar player and singer-songwriter, emerged. The band had now moved to California full time and put out several records with a contract in hand for more. Some to this day still think that, even though not as successful, this was the best version of Fleetwood Mac.

The poster for Rory Gallagher and the "new" Fleetwood Mac at the Long Beach Auditorium. Kiss was added at the last minute.

In December 1974, Bob informed Mick he was leaving the band to pursue writing and production. He just didn't feel the band was going anywhere. Even though there were decent record sales and multiple tours, Bob wasn't feeling any growth.

While Bob was still in the band, Mick was looking at studios to record the new Fleetwood Mac record. While at Sound City Studios in San Fernando Valley, just outside Los Angeles, Keith Olsen, a producer at the studio, had the song "Frozen Love" from the 1973 Buckingham Nicks record blaring through the studio speakers. "Frozen Love" was a high energy song featuring Lindsey Buckingham and his girlfriend Stephanie Lynn Nicks. They called her Stevie.

Mick remembered the sound and stylings of what he heard and had an idea. He called Keith and asked who the guitar player was he heard at the studio. Keith explained, "That's Lindsey Buckingham, half of the duo Buckingham Nicks."

Mick asked, "Is he busy?"

Keith said, "I don't think so."

"Think he would like to join a band?"

"Maybe, but I'm pretty sure you'd have to take his girlfriend too."

Mick contacted Lindsey and let him know they were looking for a guitar player. Lindsey made it simple for Mick, "We're a package deal. You want me you take her."

Mick explained they already had a woman in the band, but those were Lindsey's terms.

Mick asked Christine about adding another woman in the band. She was concerned that Stevie might feel competitive, and she was also concerned about the possibility of confusion over having two women in the same band, but she agreed to meet Lindsey and Stevie.

Mick, John, Christine, Lindsey, and Stevie all met New Year's Eve of 1974. Christine and Stevie immediately hit it off, and another version of Fleetwood Mac was born.

From my days at Long Beach, I met Dave Oberman (affectionately known as Obie) who owned Obie's Lighting, which was growing rapidly. The first time I met Obie was the mid-70s at the Ten Years After concert, where they were the lighting company Du'jour, along with Tycobrahe Sound Company. They were having some problems with a set of lights and asked me if

I knew how to fix them. I did and obliged, and they were not only grateful but enamored about how much I knew.

Ten Years After Long Beach Arena 1974.

Tycobrahe and Obie's were now all located in the South Bay of Los Angeles and everybody lived in Manhattan Beach. The area became a haven for rock 'n' roll road crews and was our stomping ground. The Manhattan Rectangle, named after the famed Bermuda Triangle, was born. At any time, day or night all around Hermosa, Redondo, and Manhattan Beach, there would be road crews from some of the largest bands in the world blessing the local establishments, not only with their presence, but the multitude of road stories meant to wow the local women.

Obie's was now doing light and sound package deals with Tycobrahe Sound.

In the summer and fall of 1975, Fleetwood Mac was on their first tour with limited funds, carrying a small Tycobrahe sound package and Lone Star lighting package with no trussing to hang the lights on. On that tour, The Mac was opening for Rod Stewart and the Faces, which were also a Tycobrahe account, and that's how Tycobrahe ended up doing sound for The Mac and introduced Obie to Fleetwood Mac.

Obie's was asked to supply trusses to hang the lights for the West Coast dates. It would be a separate truck and crew from The Mac's touring crew.

Obie needed to staff that crew and called and asked if I was available to go out with one of his guys to supply trusses for the light rig.

At eighteen years old, I was looking for anything to get my foot in the door and saw it as an opportunity, so I took the gig.

It was very small scale, but it was a job. We loaded in every morning, did our work, and went back to sleep all day because we had to drive the truck all night to the next show, so I never really saw the band, except for a song or two at the end. I did meet the crew but didn't realize then that they would become my family.

Through Tycobrahe, Obie befriended John Courage (JC), an Englishman who was the loyal tour manager for Fleetwood Mac for years.

JC relocated to Los Angeles along with Fleetwood Mac and was looking for a place to live. He moved in with Obie in beautiful Manhattan Beach. They were both characters but shared the same drive: working

John Courage "JC"

Dave "Obie" Oberman

relentless hours with a strong dedication to succeed. They became good friends.

Fleetwood Mac's Fleetwood Mac record released July, 1975

In early 1976, the Fleetwood Mac white album, simply called *Fleetwood Mac*, as zooming up the charts, and the band was getting a lot of attention, especially from Warner Records, who knew they had a winner. With all the touring in 1975 and the band getting tighter and finding their way with the new sound, Warner's saw that the table was set for Fleetwood Mac to take on the world.

The band was set to play two days at Studio Instrument Rentals (SIR) at Sunset Boulevard and Gower in Hollywood—not for a tour but a record. The band rehearsed the first day to play the new music live before recording it, and Warner wanted to film the now seasoned white album songs the second day for promotion footage and prosperity.

After my success on The Who tour, I was one of Obie's go to guys and part of his new crew. Obie called and said he got this gig and asked if I was interested in working with Fleetwood Mac again. I said, "Sure, I dug the shows we did in 1975."

He said, "The new version of the band is really taking off; if we do this, we will probably get the tour when they hit the road."

He also said, "By the way, there's no money in it. But when it hits, you're in and can do the tour."

I was bored just sitting around, had nothing going on, so I took the risk and decided to do the rehearsals for no pay. It was a small rig with two lighting trusses and just enough light for feel and the video.

I went to the shop, prepared the system, and drove to the Hollywood rehearsal hall.

It was a small dark space on Sunset Boulevard with cement floors, a short ceiling, and padded walls to absorb the sound. I walked in, and my first thought was, "Where are we going to set up the lights?" Although not a very big light rig, our rig was big for that space. The band's crew was there along with John McVie, the bass player, and Mick Fleetwood, the drummer. I met Rhyno, the de facto stage manager, Raymond, who converted from truck driver to guitar tech, and Mike, Mick's drum tech. They said they were figuring things out, "So just hold on, and we'll let you know where and when to set up the lights."

At the time, the relationships between the members of the band were changing tremendously. John and Christine McVie were in the middle of a divorce. Stevie and Lindsey were breaking up in dramatic fashion, and Mick and his wife, Jenny, were on the outs as well.

There was an immense amount of tension from these complex personal dynamics. There was a lot of angst in their songs and especially in their music. It was that "magical animosity" that helped the new record, *Rumours*, become one of the largest selling records of all times.

I put together a small light rig and brought it to the rehearsal hall. After I loaded in all the gear, I was looking for some direction and found out the band didn't have a lighting designer.

Mike, Mick's drum tech, stepped up to take over the lighting duties, as well as his daily job of setting up the stage. Mike was from Kansas and loyal to the band. He didn't know much about lights but really wanted a shot at it, so JC said, "Why not? You know the songs."

I set up the trusses and lights, and early on in the setup, it became apparent that Mike had no idea about the concept of lights—nicest guy in the world, but he just didn't know about lighting.

No one, including the band, was happy with Mike's work. What he put together just didn't look good, he missed cues, and it was way different from what they were used to with their old lighting designer, plus the film crew didn't have enough light to get the footage they needed.

The band was concerned and took a break to have a meeting to decide what to do about their lights. They all agreed that the creativity and look of the lighting was very important to The Mac, so they decided to bring back their old lighting designer.

The call was made, and I was told he would be in later that night. The film crew was put on hold, so I just turned on some light so the band could still play and waited for the new lighting designer to show up. Lindsey said, "Hey, since we're here, we should run down some songs." The rest of the band agreed and gathered on the stage, and what I witnessed next was a moment that would change my life forever.

The band broke into "So Afraid," an older song from the white album. Live, the song took on a whole new energy and feel that was very different from the album version that was good but somewhat subdued. Live, "So Afraid" kicked your ass. It was like someone came up and punched you in the face, and it took you a few seconds to realize what just hit you.

Lindsey's solo after the haunting verses and perfect three-part harmonized choruses was pure power. Lindsey was a million miles away, singing with his eyes closed so the sweat couldn't intrude. The words projected out with so much power and passion,

"*I'm so afraid*
Days when the rain and sun are gone
Black as night, agony's torn at my heart too long,
so afraid, trip and I fall, and I die."

Lindsey, Stevie, and John worked their way up in front of the drums for the finale, and it was electric. Christine set the melodic floor as her Hammond B-3 organ laid down the melody. Lindsey convulsed in time with Mick's

Lindsey Buckingham 1976 "So Afraid" from the video
shoot second day at SIR Studios.

high-powered drumming in perfect time with John's thundering bass licks. Then Stevie's tambourine and swirling movements took just the right amount of edge off to make it perfect! The whole band was in a zone, and the five of them became one.

When the song ended, I stood up in complete disbelief. Keep in mind, in my previous four years in Long Beach, I saw the best of the best, Led Zeppelin, Deep Purple, Jethro Tull, all the greats, but I never witnessed anything like I did at that moment at that rehearsal. Nothing compared, not even Led Zeppelin doing "Stairway to Heaven" had the energy I just felt.

Next, they broke into a very early version of "Go Your Own Way," a song Lindsey was writing to Stevie. To this day, I clearly remember Lindsey's haunted look at Stevie while singing the line "shacking up is all you want to do." Their eyes locked onto each other with intense pain connecting their tender souls.

Then the guitar, again the solo at the end, screaming with attitude. Lindsey's power and feel as Stevie, now with her back to Lindsey, worked right through it like it didn't bother her ... but I could tell it did.

Stevie Nicks and Lindsey Buckingham 1976 "Go Your Own Way"
from the video shoot second day at SIR Studios. These are frames
from the video with Stevie turning her back to Lindsey to look at
Christine as Lindsey sings "you can go your own way."
Stevie's looks in the last three frames tell the story.

I was blown away. They were amazing! I recall my mind being in some kind of state of unconsciousness lost in time and space. Music with a powerful feel, perfect harmonies, and they looked good. Man, they looked good!

Lindsey stage left, Christine stage right, Mick on his drum riser in back center stage, John a bit back between Christine and Mick (but closer to Mick for feel), and then Stevie center but just off to the right—away from Lindsey.

So much style, so much diversity: Mick the proper traditional English gentlemen, white shirt and classic vet waistcoat; John with his new, relaxed Hawaiian beachcomber look; Christine, the Bohemian style with flowing gowns and silk scarfs; Stevie with the tight blue jeans and halter top showing just the right amount of smooth skin; then Lindsey, the rocker look with styled shirt and bell bottom jeans with boots ready to kick in his speakers.

Next, Stevie sang "Thunder" (that became "Dreams"), her song that became the retaliation to Go Your Own way, singing, "there you go again, you want your freedom." followed by "Silver Springs." I sat back and continued to have my mind blown. I immediately heard the Fleetwood Mac magic and felt that Fleetwood Mac energy. I'm convinced the forces of circumstances, destiny, and fate are so unique that another band like Fleetwood Mac will never be heard.

The old lighting designer walked in, and lo and behold, it was Curry from Lone Star—the same Curry who saved my life back at the Humble Pie show in Long Beach a year earlier.

Curry and Lone Star came in one cold, windy March night in 1975 to do a show for the band Humble Pie. Humble Pie was at the top of their game with songs like "30 Days in The Hole" and "I Don't Need No Doctor."

The band was great, with a very charismatic singer named Steve Marriott. Most musicians or entertainers strive for the energy that came naturally to Steve. He was edgy with a strong voice and owned every stage he ever stepped on.

During the show, with beer in hand, Steve came to the front of the stage, letting his adoring fans know how good he was. That was Steve Marriott. He was way ahead of his time and was a punk rocker before punk rock was even a term.

Jimmy Page actually asked Steve to join Led Zeppelin before Robert Plant, but Steve said, "Why should I do that? The Pie is blowing up."

A young girl came down on front and gave Steve some flowers. He took the flowers and then took a big gulp of beer and spit it all over the girl and threw the flowers at her. The funny thing was she loved it. I stood, amazed, watching this take place.

This was my first experience of a real, drunk, fuck-you-in-your-face rocker. It was true passion, right or wrong, and the crowd loved it—and he knew it. He had total control of his audience and played it his way.

Humble Pie Stage pass 1975.

Anyway, after the show, I was standing in front of the drum kit helping the crew break down the band equipment when someone opened the arena's big back door.

The wind came off the ocean and through the open door, and it filled up the backdrop like a sail. I saw the whole thing happen right in front of me, like it was in slow motion. The whole rack of lights on the backdrop truss was going to fall right onto me. Suddenly, someone tackled me from behind and fell with me right next to the base of the drum riser. I felt like all hell was breaking loose around me with a roar like thunder before the backdrop settled down over us like a serene dream. The trusses had fallen. The band equipment laid in heaps around us. The sound gear that was stacked on the stage was knocked out into the first ten rows of the house. Luckily, by then the crowd had left, or I'm sure people would have died.

I mean, the gear was everywhere and smashed to bits: crushed amplifiers, broken guitars, smashed drums. It was a total mess.

We pulled ourselves up, and I turned around to thank the guy who had saved my ass and ask him his name. "Curry," he said in his iconic Texas drawl, and he walked away to finish cleaning up the stage.

So, there we were a year later, and I was so excited to see him. He was happy to see me and hear how much I had grown and how much I had my shit together. He later told me he was relieved I was at the rehearsal because he knew I knew what I was doing.

Now, while he had been serving as lighting designer for Fleetwood Mac from 1974–1975, Curry had hooked up romantically with the soon-to-be-divorced Christine McVie. This had led to no end of confusion and chaos. I learned later, as a matter of fact, that some of Christine's great songs, such as "You Make Lovin' Fun," were written for and about Curry. Some people even accused him of breaking up Christine's marriage to John, but I had heard that their marriage was over way before Curry. In the end, the band had felt it necessary to let him go.

Curry, Grant, and me at the light board figuring it out.

So, Curry came in, and we created the new design on scratch paper. He told me the band would be in full costume the next day, and we needed more light and colored gels to get the look that we needed for film. He described to me what he wanted, and I put it together, and soon we were done; Fleetwood Mac had lights. Curry knew the music and, living with Christine, knew all the all new songs as well, so he hit every cue for every song, including the new ones.

The next day, we brought in more lighting gear from the shop, and Curry and I expanded the design to accommodate the film crew that needed more light. For me, it was getting exciting, and the combination of the band, their music, and now? Working with Curry was something I knew I wanted to be part of.

The band and Curry were extremely happy, and when Curry found out I did this all for free with no pay, he let the band know, and they offered me the job of head electrician and production for an upcoming tour to continue to push the Fleetwood Mac record that was climbing the charts.

So, there I was, eighteen years old, as the head electrician on the 1976 Fleetwood Mac tour. I was on the fast lane to the moon.

To me, this episode stands out as a lesson that I carried with me for the rest of my life and what it took to make a band a success. Fleetwood Mac consistently put everything in their lives on hold to make the band work. They sacrificed more than most bands would ever think about. Hiring Curry back was an amazingly bold and brave act on everyone's part—but most of all John. They actually were willing to bring someone on the road with them who could potentially cause bad feelings between band members, just to make the audience experience the best it could be.

What finally made me decide to go out with Fleetwood Mac was the feeling I got when I really got to meet the band. Stevie was unbelievably beautiful—although, believe it or not, I was still too young and excited about being in the business to look at her sexually. Christine was the essence of class; she was pure elegance, with the voice of a goddess but the strength of a man. Lindsey was eccentric and talented, and sometimes, I swear he has six fingers on his hands. John was down-to-earth—almost like one of the crew guys—and a very solid bass player. John never made mistakes when he played, and he and Mick became one of the most famous rhythm sections in music history. Mick was the most amazing: tall, father-like, the most charismatic, confident figure you would ever want to meet; you just knew the minute that Mick entered the room that he was a star. He was, and always will be, the glue of Fleetwood Mac.

Then there were my new brothers ... the crew: Ron Penny "Rhyno," bass and key tech; Ray Lindsey, guitar tech; Kenny D'Alessandro, stage monitor; Mark Drale, sound engineer front of house; and Stevie's younger brother, Christopher, who picked up all the slack where needed. They remembered me from the short run on the West Coast in 1975. I was younger than all of them, and soon they learned how much experience I had, and how much I knew, and how I could assist them with some of their problems.

One thing we all learned over time was that we all shared the fear of a normal 9-to-5 life. We did whatever it took to succeed and not fail. We were all very proud and shared deep insecurities that drove us to go the extra mile, so as not to look like idiots.

We became a family, very quickly identifying our places and realizing we were becoming brothers in this extraordinary time in history. To this day, we still use our experiences and past with Fleetwood Mac to help others.

JC, John Courage, The Mac's longtime tour manager, was the band's go to guy for all things. After regrouping with Lindsey and Stevie, the band made a decision to manage themselves. No manager. Just a good friend and their girl Friday, Judy Wong, (who was with Mick and John since the 60s) and Micky, the lawyer to watch over all things legal.

When I look back, I know that for Fleetwood Mac it was not just about music. It was about feelings, and emotions, and how to reach everyone through all their senses and every fiber in their body and souls.

It was apparent that they cared about the people on their team. You just weren't their road crew; you were part of the Fleetwood Mac family. If you needed something, it was there.

As for me, I think they were intrigued that I was so young, and I was intrigued that they were so down-to-earth. That's the way it was with Fleetwood Mac. You wanted to help them; you wanted them to succeed because you succeeded with them—something that is so lost in today's sterile world of packaged sanitized music.

Mark Drale, Sound. Ray Lindsey, Guitar Tech. Ron "Rhyno" Penny, Keys/Bass. Mike Miller, Drum Tech. Leo Rossi, Lights. Kenny D'Alessandro, Stage monitors. Curry Grant, Lighting Designer.

When the five of them played music together, it was just pure, raw magic. In 1975–76 when I first met The Mac, they weren't really rock stars yet. They were just coming up to that point in their lives. But after I found out what they were like as people, after I saw and heard them live, after I felt their passion and drive to be the best musicians they could be—I knew that they were headed for super stardom, and I wanted to be part of it.

Fleetwood Mac, band and crew, all came from different places and were brought together to make the magic and give so much to the world.

I drove home from the rehearsals thinking, "I can't wait to tour with this band." I spent close to twenty years with Fleetwood Mac: started as a lighting tech, then moved on to stage manager, production manager, and finally, tour manager.

Call it circumstance, fate, destiny: in 1976, I took a risk and did a rehearsal for no pay, a decision that landed me right in the middle of an extraordinary time in music history that changed my life, and the life of millions, forever.

CHAPTER FIVE

LEAVING THE BOY BEHIND

THE DECISION TO GO OUT WITH Fleetwood Mac marked my entry into full-time touring. The schedule dictated that we would be out on tour all of 1976, with a new record coming out in the spring of 1977 that the band planned to tour on as well. So, it looked like the next two years of my life were mapped out for me. Fleetwood Mac was not a household name yet, but you just felt the energy, the magic, and knew it was inevitable. The earthquake had hit, and we were all preparing to ride the tsunami, not only into music history but history itself.

The 1976 Fleetwood Mac tour is where I grew my first road legs and really left home and was 100 percent

out on my own. I thought I was ready, ready to leave the safe haven of San Pedro and explore not only the world but the world through the eyes of rock 'n' roll. Looking back, it's hard to believe that I survived it. I was this small-town Italian Catholic kid that dove in headfirst to the uninhibited world of 1970s rock 'n' roll that was the rebellious devil child of the peaceful 60s music movement.

We were modern-day pirates. We came into a town, drank all the liquor, did all the drugs, and took all the money. All the women wanted to be with us, and all their men wanted to be us. For a twenty-four-hour period, we owned whatever town we were in.

Fleetwood Mac Crew on the bus 1976.

The funny thing was we were invited back every year to do it all over again.

So, at eighteen years old, with an angel on my right shoulder and a devil on my left, I was treading water in the turbulent sea of rock 'n' roll.

I found out what it was like to travel every day and be part of the camaraderie of a rock 'n' roll road crew. Back then, it was a family. We worked hard with common goals and bled for each other. We were family!

My first tour was 256 shows in 365 days! We traveled together, stayed at the same hotels, ate together, worked together, played together, dreamed together, succeeded together, failed together, learned together, grew together, and loved together. We did everything a family does.

It was an exciting time of my life, but it wasn't always easy. As a matter of fact, the first day of the tour, there it was, another fork in the road, with an impromptu initiation from my crew brothers that affected the rest of my life.

When I told my parents that I was going to go on tour for most of the year, my mom, God bless her, went out and bought me some clothes and a really nice new powder blue Samsonite suitcase. The case was top of the line—impervious even to gorillas, according to the famous commercials. I went over to their house the night before I left, and my mom made me a nice, home-cooked meal. She sat me down for a long, heartfelt talk after dinner and gave me a blanket that she had hand knitted. It was really terrific, and it represented everything I thought I was going to miss while on the road: warmth, protection, and security.

Down on 14th and Hermosa Avenue, there was a small hotel called the Grandview, right by the surfboarder restaurant we called The House of Tits because all the girls who worked there were big-breasted bombshells. We were all regulars, and all the guys who came in from out of town for rehearsals and prepping tours would stay at the Grandview, and of course, eat at the Surfboarder (hoping to leave with one of the waitresses).

We were all going to meet up and share one room so we could leave from there to catch the early flight to go on the tour. To my surprise, there were a lot of us and only one room, and I quickly figured out there would be no sleeping that night. My parents drove me to the Grandview, but I had them drop me a block from the hotel out of fear of being spotted by my soon-to-be crewmates. Wow, how cool that would have been! Mom and Dad are dropping me off to go on tour.

When I got to the Grandview, Mark, the head sound guy; Kenny, who was in charge of the stage monitors; and Ray and Rhyno, the band techs, were already there, They were excited to be heading out on the road, and of course, by the time I got there they were very high, extremely drunk, and raging. They took one look at me as I walked in with my brand-new powder blue suitcase. The room exploded with shouting and loud rants that I thought was my welcome until I realized they were looking at the suitcase. I could read it on their faces, "Oh my god! New guy!"

These salted road dogs started to raz and tease me and immediately grabbed my suitcase, and I watched them carry it up onto the roof of the hotel. Oh shit! This was not a good sign. By the look in their eyes, I could tell they were not looking for a nice, safe place to put it. I followed them onto the roof as they walked directly to the edge. I followed them, beginning to beg them not to do anything to my suitcase. They looked at me, pausing as if considering my request. Then they unceremoniously threw the suitcase off the roof.

It dropped the three stories and landed in the middle of busy Hermosa Avenue. Hitting the ground, the case exploded, spreading my belongings all over the street. Cars began skidding around and slamming into it. I just stood there, looking down. I was angry. I felt like crying. And there wasn't a goddamn thing I could do about it. They were all laughing and buckling over in hysterics, high fiving each other and celebrating their inebriated achievement.

It was another one of those life-changing moments; I truly believe what I did right there and then changed my life forever.

If I had complained, gotten angry, or showed I was hurt, I would have been seen as the uncool, crybaby, can't-handle-it pussy and probably would have been banned. I now realize the way I did handle it was the difference between being accepted for the duration of the tour or tossed aside as just another crew causality.

For some reason—call it divine intervention—I decided to just roll with it. I chalked it up as their way of initiating me onto the road. It was my turn. I asked for a beer, a line of cocaine, and a hit off the joint, and laughed it off with them and instantly became one of them, but inside, I was really upset. In many ways, I was still that little boy who was leaving home. Seeing all my stuff on the street was a representation of how my life was going to be turned upside down, and I was trying to decide if I was ready for it.

After a while, and totally high at this point, I went downstairs and started picking up my stuff. Shit was everywhere! Cars were dodging and honking at me, and the guys were up on the balcony laughing hysterically and throwing shit at me. The magnitude of their joke really hit me when I watched a car run right over and rip a whole right in the middle of the blanket that my mom had taken so much time and care to make for me. I heard them laughing, and my mind and my heart battled. My heart cried for my mother and my drug- and alcohol-hardened mind told my heart, "Grow the fuck up!"

I rolled with it and didn't complain. In fact, I joked right along with them, and I now know that was a big moment, not only in my career but my life. I have no doubt if I had complained or reacted differently, I would have spent the rest of my life working the docks of San Pedro.

There is no way I would have been accepted or fit into my new world.

From that day on, I became one of the guys, and many times throughout my young career, I was forced to live with the schizophrenia of the Italian Catholic boy and the rock 'n' roll pirate.

I had one more initiation to go through before leaving boyhood behind and settling into manhood.

CHAPTER SIX

WELCOME TO YOUR NEW LIFE

IT WAS APRIL 1976, and I was touring full bore with Fleetwood Mac. We did two shows called Day on the Green that were huge stadium gigs in Oakland, California. The Fleetwood Mac white album had sales of over one million copies and showed no signs of slowing down. The band was now able to headline arena dates, but being loyal to all the small promoters that carried them before they were big, they decided to keep playing the small theater, college gyms, and county fairs already booked. One day, we were playing a small gym, the next day an arena, and then stadiums with other large acts.

The famous San Francisco promoter Bill Graham had started the Day on the Green stadium shows where he would couple three or four large acts and sell hundreds of thousands of tickets per event. Each event had a theme where Bill would design a nice-looking set with ambience, and his backstage hospitality for bands and crew was first-class. Great food, endless supplies of alcohol, and comfortable dressing rooms.

Day On The Green.

One particular Day on the Green included Peter Frampton, who was at the end of an album run with the then bestselling live record of all time: *Frampton Comes Alive.* Bill had booked two stadium shows at the Oakland Alameda Stadium where the Oakland A's baseball team and Oakland Raiders football teams played.

With fledgling tickets sales for the Peter Frampton dates, Bill saw the Fleetwood Mac surge and offered the band more money than they had ever made to support and open for Frampton on both shows. The Mac was on a roll and brought in to sell the many unsold tickets and pack the stadium to capacity. Having Fleetwood Mac play right before Peter Frampton was a mistake for Peter because Fleetwood Mac literally blew him off the stage. The Mac was allowed to play their full set, which was uncommon for supporting acts. They played all their hit songs, including Stevie's new song

82

"Rhiannon." Energy shot off the stage with enough power to light a small city.

Both shows—April 25 and May 1 were deemed "The British Invasion" and included UFO, Status Quo, Gary Wright, Fleetwood Mac, and Peter Frampton.

The Day on the Green was a memorable event, not only for the quality of the performances but also for what happened next.

The day before the show, we arrived at Oakland Stadium to set up all our equipment. My job that day was to make sure that the stage band gear and the sound monitors had power. Because my equipment had to be laid down first, it meant that I got my work done very early in the day and had the rest of the day and that night off. I finished my work and went to the Hyatt Hotel where we were all staying.

When I entered the lobby, I ran into a woman whom I had seen around The Mac quite a bit over the last year. She was older, at least thirty, and was a friend of the band. She had an amazing body, like Cameron Diaz, and her face resembled a younger Diane Keaton. Real sexy in a classy way, but not shy at all.

I was so into my work and being on tour that the whole groupie sex thing was the furthest thing from my mind. Plus, that sure wasn't the way a good Italian Catholic boy behaved and did things.

She would always flirt with me, but I didn't really take it seriously, and I really didn't get it. I thought it was just a joke, and I was the brunt of it. She would spend a lot of time teasing me—telling me she wanted to "have her way with me and make me a man," and I thought she was kidding; in my mind, I never figured why an older, unobtainable woman like her would be attracted to me, this young, just falling off the turnip cart, boy.

We started small talk and made our way into the bar: me, eighteen with a fake ID and her with a mission.

We hung at the bar. I wasn't ever much of a drinker and was taught that drinking was something you shouldn't do. The rules weren't the same for her. We hung out for hours, and over time, her wandering hands began touching me in places hidden under the bar. It was clear to me that she hadn't been kidding after all. This was really going to happen. I was still in disbelief that something like this could be happening to me.

Many drinks and many inconspicuous toots of cocaine later, she asked me if I wanted to go up to her room. You'd think I would have had the answer at the tip of my tongue or the tip of something else, but I wasn't sure. I was taught that these things were only supposed to happen when you're in love. Plus, the drugs and the alcohol made me nervous. In any case, the whole thing was way out of my league.

Throughout the whole night, she was teasing me with some pretty specific requests, but when she asked me to go with her, I wondered who was I to deserve this attention. Then desire and curiosity hit me over the head, and

I figured, "Who was I to disappoint her?" She ordered a bottle of Jack Daniels to go, saying, "We could use this," and off we went up to her room.

The whole scene was very awkward, and I was trying to be cool, like I had done this all the time. I was nervous, apprehensive, and curious, like your first day at a new school, realizing that the total fantasy of sex with a hot older woman, with cocaine and alcohol, was really going to happen.

When we got to her suite (not just a room), I was nervous, strong, confused, happy, apprehensive, and every other emotion that is possible and impossible. We walked in, and she led me by the hand to the bedroom. She put both of her arms around my neck and mine around the small of her back. I was trying to be cool and take control but had no idea what I was doing. I was way out of my league. She started to kiss me, and being so young and with no real sexual experience, I was trying to totally get into it, but I was fumbling around like a blind man ... and then she took control. We ended up naked in bed in a matter of minutes.

We had sex, and it took less than a minute for me to finish. Soon after that, thinking we were done, I got up and began to get dressed. She said, "Ahhh, where do you think you're going?" I was perplexed, thinking, Aren't we done? I was new at this. What was she expecting? I had no idea and not a clue of what to do.

She gently patted her hand on the bed and said, "Come here." Then it was obvious; we weren't done. We drank some more Jack Daniels. Things slowed down a bit, and we talked. We talked about the tour, the band, her life, my life, and what had just happened. She was telling me a lot about the business and what to expect. She also told me how much the other crew guys liked me and how blown away they were with the talents I had. They couldn't believe I knew so much for how young I was.

She went to her bag and pulled out a bag of the white powder. We kissed again, and then she slowly started to draw lines and pour whiskey onto different parts of my body. She would then snort the cocaine and lick the Jack Daniels from places I had never imagined.

We took turns as she taught me to do the same to her. She took her time and taught me many things about a women's body that I had no idea about.

For hours, we took deliberate and slow turns of this ritual with interludes of long French kisses and more sex.

My heart was racing, and my mouth, tongue, and other parts of my body were numb. My mind (and other parts of my body) were being blown.

In the excitement and blurriness of the moment, she would stop and teach me how to pleasure a woman and slow down and really enjoy the sexual experience.

From the bed, to the sofa, to the bath, on the floor standing up, sitting down, in front, from behind, bending, contorting our bodies in every room.

Our encounter lasted the rest of the evening and all through the night to the early morning. I did things that were only seen in porno films or read on the pages of *Penthouse.*

In the early morning, our bodies silently agreed we were done; I was so spent I knew I couldn't go on any more. It was unreal. It was now light outside, and I knew I had to go. I stood up, stark naked, feeling like the biggest man on Earth. I just had a night that most guys could only dream of ... I had arrived, like Columbus finding the new world.

I walked over to the window and ripped open the curtains, like I was tearing out the pages of my old innocent life. It was one of those beautiful Northern Californian days with a perfect view of San Francisco Bay; it could have been storming, but to me, it still would have been beautiful.

I was a bit sober by then and remember this like it was yesterday: looking at the Bay, I said, "Wow! Welcome to San Francisco." There was pause with no response. I turned to look at her, and she was sitting on the bed. She was beautiful, wrapped in the sheet, and with a little Mona Lisa grin, she said, "No, Leo, Welcome to rock 'n' roll."

Yes, indeed. Welcome to rock 'n' roll.

I got dressed and gave her a hug and kiss goodbye. Feeling hungover, but exuberant and about ten years older, I went off to my own room to get ready for the Day on the Green Concert.

Our call time was ten a.m. at the stadium, and as I walked up on the stage, there were 70,000 fans starting to come into Oakland Stadium.

Not many people have had the opportunity to experience the feeling of being on a stage at one of these amazing events. I'm fortunate to be in that group of the lucky few for over forty years.

We would be onstage, people would look at us, and we would joke, "Look at them; everybody wants to be us, but us."

It was hard work ... long hours ... miles and miles of travel ... no sleep ... sacrificing things at home, taking a cold shower in some locker room ... sleeping on the bus for maybe three to four hours, if you had a bus. Waking up in another city, a cold coffee, choking down a stale doughnut and doing the show again—sometimes six to seven shows a week for months at a time

So, why did we do it? Why? It was the excitement. The passion, the adrenaline rush of hundreds of thousands of people chanting, screaming, and expelling their uncontrollable physical energy—aimed right at us!

At showtime, the stage was the center of the universe. You just didn't see it or just hear it. You felt it, the earthquake, like rumble from stamping feet. People screaming, singing, creating air pressure hitting us with the force of a hurricane. The familiar odors of pot, sweat, and charred plastic from the burning colored gel of the lights, that sweet oily odor from the smoke machines, and mostly, mostly the invisible scent of our own excitement.

The beams from the spotlights cut through the night, caressing the stage. We found ourselves at the end of the rainbow with new colors not yet invented. Massive, loud sound systems with frequencies refreshed our souls like a cool river running through a hot dry desert that gives life to all it touches.

Yes, we were part of it … a big part of this cultural collision … this phenomenon that was changing the world forever.

We were a family—a family in a story that wrote itself, wrote itself right into the history books.

The bands trusted us—trusted us to enhance their music, their careers, their lives. We took people to places they'd never been before and would never forget for the rest of their lives.

It empowered us, eliminated all our fears, our doubts. We took people away from their struggles and their problems, at least for a moment. We gave them hope, strength to get on with life, creating an everlasting love affair with their youth.

We didn't realize it, but we redefined the American Dream. It changed from white houses, picket fences, dogs, and children to doing what we wanted, when we wanted, with only one rule—use the gift we were blessed with to make positive changes and the world a better place.

To us … nothing was impossible.

So, there I was, onstage, no longer a boy but a man. The strength I was feeling was unexplainable. Muscles I never knew I had were aching, a good ache, an ache of victory and satisfaction.

I was checking my gear when Rhyno and all the other crew guys came up to me and said, "We all were hanging out last night. Where did you go?"

I said, "I just hung at the hotel."

"Did you have fun?"

At first, I didn't pick up on it, but then I noticed they were all there—and for a reason. I looked at them with a curious grin, like I was busted, and asked, "What do you mean?"

"I mean," he said, "did you have fun with you-know-who last night?"

Oh fuck! Do they know? It didn't take long until I figure out, they did. I said, "Hell yeah! And it was awesome!" They were all around me, looking like proud fathers.

"We all hoped you did."

I said, "We?"

"Yeah, we set it all up because we figured it was time you grew the fuck up."

They had convinced her (even though I think she didn't need much convincing) since I was only eighteen, and thinking I was still a virgin, I needed to be broken in and see what being on the road in rock 'n' roll was really like.

It was true; I had not been particularly interested in the whole "sex" part of sex, drugs, and rock 'n' roll. This was, in part, due to my overwhelming drive to succeed in this business and my old world Italian Catholic values: find a woman, fall in love, get married.

I was still in the mindset that I was going to find that special girl to settle down with and then live the American Dream. I was also learning very fast that those kinds of girls don't hang around backstage of rock shows.

Day On The Green 1976 The British Invasion. The stage and sound wings were an English Castle.

Even now, when I think back and relive that moment, my emotions are all over the place. I didn't know whether to be mad at my brothers or thank them for one of the most amazing nights of my life!

I wanted to think I did it all on my own. But I realize that it was good to have people look out for me and care about me and know that they

John and Christine McVie walking off stage at Day On The Green 1976. That's me, caught in the photo that was placed in a national magazine.

accepted me as "one of them, one of the crew." Even today, I carry this event with me and make it a point to go out of my way and make people feel accepted and loved. The worst feeling of all is loneliness and feeling that you

The gang at Fleetwood Mac Day On The Green Oakland California
April 25, 1976, opening for Peter Frampton.
Notice the small amount of stage space we had.

don't belong to anything or anybody; it's the one true poverty, and it taught me to reach out my hand, share a smile, and make a difference. There's one thing for sure, I'll never forget Lynn and the Day on the Green 1976.

CHAPTER SEVEN

THE 1976 BICENTENNIAL BASH:
"LOOK OUT, WORLD. HERE I COME."

THE 1976 TOUR WAS ROLLING ALONG and so was the band. Dates were getting bigger, and we were forced to increase the sound and lights to accommodate the larger venues.

The fight for truck space was a daily adventure, with the sound guys asking for more space than the lights. The argument was: "Do people come to hear a show or see a show?" The lighting guys used to say, "People can stay home and listen to the record, and the sound guys would come back with, "You never hear a person leaving a concert humming the color red."

In the first two months, we went from one forty-foot

semitruck to two, and by midsummer, we had three.

We started on the West Coast headlining our own shows, then headed into the Midwest for larger stadium shows, with other acts, such as Kansas, Jeff Beck, and bands like Loggins and Messina (that not long ago The Mac was opening for) but who were now opening for us.

We finally ended up on the East Coast embedded into the hottest, most humid days of summer doing monster big stadium shows with the largest bands out on the road.

On the Fourth of July 1976, we were in the middle of a twelve-show leg—the Bicentennial Bash—one of the biggest events of that summer or, for that matter, rock and roll. It was America's two hundredth birthday, and large celebrations were planned from the East Coast to the West Coast, so rock 'n' roll needed to represent.

The Bicentennial Bash included Dan Folgelberg, Loggins and Messina on their farewell tour, Boz Skaggs (on some of the dates) was coming out with his *Silk Degrees* album, Fleetwood Mac was riding high on the Fleetwood Mac album, and the Eagles were already huge and about to release *Hotel California*.

Five bands at the top of their game, and all this amazing talent and music for just twelve dollars and fifty cents a ticket. On July 2nd, we were in Greensborough for the first show with The Mac and the Eagles. There was always a competition between the Eagles and Fleetwood Mac, even all the way down to the crews, and we needed to figure out how technically we were going to make shows work.

We were constantly trying to outdo each other by adding more speakers to make it louder, more lights and effects to wow the crowds, and the best drugs.

On July 4, we ended up in Tampa Stadium in Tampa Bay, Florida, to celebrate our nation's two hundredth birthday with 100,000 of our closest friends.

Bicentennial Bash poster
July 4, 1976.

At that time in music's storied history, the record labels would give bands money to support touring to help sell records and generate interest and popularity. Back then, the bands were so great, with so much talent, that often the live performances outdid whatever a band could record.

There was no internet for publicity or promotion. Traditional radio and TV were used, but mainly records were sold because of touring: fans could see their favorite artist up close and personal.

The money was negotiated in the record deal that traditionally was a three to four record deal and was non-recoupable. Today, the band has to pay back their tour support out of the records they eventually sell. But back then, the bigger bands had money to work with to make their concert a kick-ass experience for the audience. Subsequently, the bands were able to be quite competitive about who put on the best shows and who had the best lighting, the best sound, and the best spectacle. The label just figured that if you put on a great show, then people would buy the record. And it was a fact that if you came through a town with a great live show, people would not only buy your new record but all the other albums in your back catalog as well.

The Eagles were a bigger band at the time, so they were headlining (playing last) the Bicentennial Bash. The Eagles and Fleetwood Mac had an intense but friendly rivalry over who had the loudest sound gear and the biggest stage show. The crew of the two bands were all friends. To outdo the Eagles, we needed to make a larger statement to overshadow the headlining Eagles. We ordered a huge inflatable 100-foot penguin—with "Fleetwood Mac" on the side of it to fly behind the stage. The bird would be flying there all day, including during the Eagles set. The cost of the massive penguin was around $150,000 (and these are 1976 dollars, mind you).

When we got to Tampa Stadium, we found an enormous box waiting for us. And inside, sure as shit, was an enormous inflatable penguin—a penguin the size of a house. There were other boxes nearby, in which we found huge helium balls. Instead of filling the whole penguin up, we were supposed to inflate the balls and put one ball under each arm, one ball in its head, and two in the body.

So great. We added the penguin, but who was going to set it up? We didn't think about that. We all had very specific and time-consuming jobs to do. Our merchandise guy Phil had nothing to do on the load-in day, so he volunteered to set up our new massive mascot.

Well, the half-assed instructions were there, and our new penguin tech dutifully read them and tried to figure the whole thing out. After many hours and input from the whole crew and local hands, it wasn't working very well. The whole time, he was struggling with this giant inflatable bird. He was doing his best, but the damn thing just wouldn't get off the ground. Like its real-life counterpart, the thing wouldn't fly. Maybe it was just too big; I don't know. It was painfully flat where it should have been round, and it was listing heavily to the right. There was no way we could bring that pathetic penguin out.

Finally, someone had a radical idea. "Let's fill up the penguin itself." We gathered all of the helium bottles that came with it and emptied all the helium into the massive penguin. We even used the helium from the balls. We tethered the thing down with some wires, and we got it to where it was looking pretty damn good. The band came on, and it was a nice effect, if I do say so myself.

Right on time, the show started and running order on July 4 was Dan Folgelberg to open, followed by Loggins and Messina, then Fleetwood Mac, and then the Eagles.

Dan Folgelberg was breaking his new album that was climbing the charts. Originally, nobody thought he fit on the bill. It was too slow, but at the end of his set, he cranked it up and proved everybody wrong.

Loggins and Messina were great. Out of all the bands,

they were by far the most talented music-wise, with a large ensemble with very talented musicians. They were also seasoned veterans who knew how to work a crowd with a good crew.

Then Fleetwood Mac challenged with something to prove. Lindsey mostly really wanted to prove The Mac was a better band than the Eagles for numerous reasons. One, The Mac was a new sound with more energy, and the show was just more exciting than a bunch of guys standing static in front of microphones, lackadaisically with no stage presence. The main reason was Stevie Nicks and Don Henley of the Eagles were now an item, and even though Lindsey and Stevie were over, it just didn't sit right with Lindsey, and in fact, not with the rest of the band.

Fleetwood Mac came out strong and never let up. I remember the band taking the set to a higher level, especially Lindsey and Stevie. They had something to prove, and they were not going to be denied. The solos and banter between songs tended to linger, and it became obvious that the band was making a statement.

Then, right in the middle of the set, the penguin started to move around, and inexorably, it started to wobble and fall side to side, like it had too much to drink because the helium was leaking out of the bird. Finally, it took its last breath and fell to its side, never to stand again.

Onstage, Mick Fleetwood said over the mic, "Like my father always said; penguins can't fly."

The legendary Fleetwood Mac Penguin July 4, 1976.
Photos courtesy of Mick's mother Biddy Fleetwood.

After Fleetwood Mac and the set change on came the Eagles—the seasoned pros with multiple albums and megahits under their belts. They were perfect! Every note, every harmony, every light cue and the sound, the sound was pristine and perfect. Listening to Joe Walsh's solos along with Don Felder's high-powered rock 'n' roll guitar and the plethora of hits, it was easy to figure out why they were at the top of the food chain in rock 'n' roll.

All of the crews from all of the bands got along, and we all respected each other, and some of us became lifelong friends working with each other on future tours and still talk today. We were all a big part of it; we knew then, and know even more today, that we made one of the quintessential rock 'n' roll events in history happen and no one ... no one ... can take that away from us.

The Bicentennial Bash finally ended; it ended July 24, 1976, in Pittsburg, in front of 70,000 people at Three Rivers Stadium—and it was a tour for the ages.

After the load-out sitting backstage, all the bands safe and sound at their hotels, all the crews from all the bands gathered, drank, got high, and still argued about which band was the best. We all knew it wasn't about which band was the best or who drew more, the parts were the sum of the whole. The whole tour worked, and each band made the others better, and they took each other to new highs none of them knew they had in them or existed.

In hindsight, it's amazing to think now, four and half decades later, that concerts of that size, that magnitude, and that much talent happened all the time in rock 'n' roll in the 70s.

Bicentennial Bash
last show pass
Pittsburgh
July 24, 1976.

No one could have predicted the true impact that all those artists on the Bicentennial Bash would have on the history of music and how it still resonates today.

At eighteen years old, it was just another day in my new life. Like the music, I was just a kid, and we were growing up together. We made the rules up as we went along to give everlasting memories to all who were fortunate to witness the Bicentennial Bash.

As Fleetwood Mac rolled on, so did my newfound rock 'n' roll lifestyle. We did more shows and were winding our way down to the south, where we had a planned break in Florida. The band had already laid down the basics tracks for the new record and needed some time to put on the finishing touches of vocal harmonies and instrument solos before the final mix. Their choice to do this was Criteria Studios in Miami. The band rented a giant house near the studio, and rather than sending the road crew all the way home, they put us up in a small hotel in South Florida. In the mid-1970s, South Florida was the home of big parties and the purest and finest cocaine you could get your hands on. For most of us (other than the crew that took care of band equipment that was needed for the sessions), it was game on. Along with the band's growing popularity, the crew had grown, and the team got bigger and braver. Every night, we went out and were hosted at the best restaurants, clubs, and of course, the decadence of the sex and drugs of discos. Everything you've heard and read about the 70s drug and free love lifestyle, multiply it by 100, and that was our life.

After my Day on the Green episode, I jumped in full force. My drug of choice was cocaine. The cocaine the band was getting was good, really good. It came in large quantities with no cut, pure and straight from South America. It's no secret, and the world knows, Fleetwood Mac was synonymous with cocaine. Even on the bottom of our tour passes it said GMAT that was our war cry, "Give me a toot." We all needed it, and couldn't live without it.

In the early days, the band shared it with us—their crew, their family. We used it to stay awake so we could keep pulling off the miracle of six to seven shows a week with twenty-hour days challenging our bodies and minds to do supernatural impossibilities. Like a sweet beautiful demon that constantly tempted your heart, the drug consumed us, leaving us in a state of total euphoria until we woke from the minutes of sleep our bodies forced us to take. When you woke, you felt like you were wearing a lead suit, but then a sniff and the new day began, and all was good in the world once again.

My chemically induced brain controlled my physical desires with no regard to right or wrong: Sex, drugs, and rock 'n' roll was not a saying. It was our way of life, my way of life, and there was no turning back. I was driving right off the map of my youth. The world was flat, and I was close to the edge. I was nowhere near ready for what had become my new life.

While in Miami, during the day, I went to the studio. The new songs that The Mac were playing at the sound checks throughout the tour were recorded, and they were good! I mean amazing! The songs became the Fleetwood Mac record *Rumours*, one of the bestselling pieces of music in history. When we all first heard the final mixes, we knew it was going to be big, but none of us ever imagined that forty years later—and for many years to come—*Rumours* would still touch people's hearts and souls and is passed down as a family heirloom and a rite of passage.

We finished the tour August 26, 1976, in San Diego. August 27, we headed home. The depression hit me hard as I faced the reality the tour was over. Now what? We were going warp ten all year, knowing what we were doing, where we were supposed to be tomorrow, with our lives mapped out for us. I was a sailboat with no wind. I just couldn't go home, I wasn't ready for that, and plus, I had nowhere to stay. Going home to my parents was out of the question, not like this! It was way too far down the path of my self-centered life to take a step back and go home.

I took a room at the Grandview Hotel with some of the other guys who were staying there to decompress. We had to load-in the old Universal Amphitheater in the valley of Los Angeles for a four-day run of sold out shows.

The Universal Amphitheater Los Angeles open to the sky.

At that time, the Universal Amphitheater had no roof, and The Mac was to play to their fans with the warm night under the beautiful stars of Los Angeles. Then it hit me, August 27 ... Hmmm, August 27. Fuck! It was my birthday! I forgot my own fucking birthday! I was nineteen years old and already living the life of a much older soul. I worked through the rest of show, and I kept thinking about my mother, my father, my family, my new reckless life verses my old austere life. Once again, the angel and devil appeared on my shoulders and were brawling, until something remarkable happened in the middle of the show. Whenever it was your birthday on the road, Stevie would dedicate one of her songs, "Landslide," to you. That night, she dedicated the song to me, introducing me as "Sugar Bear," a name that stuck to me with all the women on the tour, but as you can imagine was fodder for endless razzing from the rest of the crew. After that, I knew I was where I needed to be ... right where I was.

CHAPTER EIGHT

A FALL FOR FALL AND
HAPPY HOLIDAYS

IN LATE AUGUST 1976, I got home from The Mac tour. We cleaned up all the gear and stowed it, and I immediately felt the tour postpartum. It's a tremendous sense of let-down and depression. I was back home, and I had road burn big time. We call it road burn because when you get home it's burnt into your brain that you should be doing something or going somewhere all the time. Life becomes accelerated, and every day on tour was like a week of normal life.

My cocaine and drug use were going at a pretty good pace. On the tour, I started off doing cocaine just to stay up and get my work done.

My first experience with the beautiful demon: I was eighteen and had just started working with Fleetwood Mac. We were starting the tour with rehearsals at the Wilshire Theater in Beverly Hills. I thought we were leaving on the tour Thursday for a Friday show in Fresno and on from there. I drove up to the rehearsal Wednesday, with no bag packed or idea we were loading out and departing right after we were finished rehearsing that night. When Rhyno informed me, I was not only shocked but unprepared to depart on the tour. I phoned the shop, and a couple of my friends agreed to help me. They brought me up some clothes and picked up my car to drive it to the shop and keep it there for safe keeping while I was on the tour.

Rehearsals ended, and we began loading up all the gear. I saw a smaller truck pull up and was told we were loading the band's musical equipment into that small truck and sound and lights into the forty-foot semi. The band was getting more popular and the venues bigger, so we needed to bring more sound and lights, and we were going to add an additional forty-foot semitruck in Fresno.

As the last pieces of gear were loaded and we closed the truck doors, I caught the truck keys out of midair that Raymond had tossed in my directions with the words, "Hey, rookie, you're driving the first leg." Driving! That truck? These were before the days when trucks had automatic transmissions—they were manual shifts, and you didn't need any special license to drive. I'd been in many trucks but never drove one.

I explained to the guys, "I can't drive that truck. I've never done it, and I'm really not sure I'm ready."

Rhyno said, "Well now's a good time to learn. It's easy, piece of cake." We got into the truck, Ray in the middle, Rhyno by the door, and me in the driver's seat. Ray calmly instructed, "push in the clutch the pedal on the left outside." As I did, he took the shifting stick that went to the floor over to the left and down.

"That's first gear." Then he took the stick went up and over to the right and up again. "That's second gear." And then third, fourth, and finally fifth. Ray put the truck into first gear, "Now lift your foot off the pedal on the left and give it some gas." I did as instructed, and the truck violently started to shake and jerk until it stalled and made a noise like the engine had blown up.

Rhyno screamed, "More gas, Leo!" I was determined to get this. I started the truck, put it into gear, revved the gas, and slowly let out the clutch. We jerked along, but the truck started to move forward, and we were on our way. Ray, as always (like he is today) was calm and patient, the exact opposite of Rhyno.

"Stupid new kid," he muttered.

Ray said, "Now, the clutch!" and he put the truck into second. "Now the clutch! More gas!" Third gear I did on my own, and that night, I became a truck driver.

I was excited to have an additional skill in my repertoire, and we were on our way to Fresno. There was only one problem. I was fading, getting tired. Climbing the Grapevine on Highway 5 north of Los Angeles, Ray and Rhyno were sleeping. I managed to pull off at an off-ramp where there was just a gas station.

"Hey guys, I can't keep my eyes open; I'm dead out."

Rhyno called me a pussy and said, "Go grab some coffee, and get on with it." I jumped out of the truck and got some coffee as instructed, and when I got back to the truck, Rhyno said, "Here. Do this." There it was, a spoon filled with the white powder fix-all of rock 'n' roll: cocaine.

"I don't do drugs," I said.

Rhyno, in his midwestern heart of America forwardness said, "Well, you better start. This truck isn't driving itself to Fresno."

Ray said, "Go on; try it. It won't kill ya. If it doesn't work, I'll take over and drive." Peer pressure kicked in. I wanted to be accepted and not let my new brothers down; I didn't want to look like a loser. I took the spoon and inhaled the powder up my right nostril, then my left. I jumped back into the driver seat, grinded the gears of the truck on to Highway 5, and we were on our way.

As the horrible taste of mucus mixed with cocaine dripped down the back of my throat, a euphoric feeling kicked in. This was real cocaine (that The Mac always had) with no cut or filler. The feeling of strength overtook my body; I felt like there was nothing that could stop me. I was on my way until the angel-and-devil Italian Catholic thing creeped up again. Oh my God! I just did cocaine! Drugs! It was against everything I was taught. The guilt set in. If my parents knew or found out! This is wrong. Yeah, but that was then and this is now, and it feels good! My dream was coming alive: of being on the road, on the road with a band that was headed to the stratosphere. My mind was racing, and the words in my brain made no sense. I would laugh when I cried and cry when I laughed.

There I was on the US-99. With the help of the cocaine, I was pouring out my soul to Ray and Rhyno. "I love you guys ... Thanks so much for being here for me ... giving me a chance ... teaching me. I can't believe I'm here, living my dream." I was so lost in the madness and euphoria, I just babbled. I'm not even sure how long I was talking to them—could have been minutes, but it sure seemed like it was hours.

With my heart and soul on the dashboard, I looked over, and there were my brothers, my new family, passed out dead asleep, not hearing a word of my deepest most heartfelt feelings. Having no sense of space or time I made it all the way to Fresno. I drove the whole fucking way. I found the Selland Arena in downtown Fresno, drove to the loading dock door, and parked the truck. I curled up and went to sleep.

We were awoken with a knock on the window by the local crew ready to load the show in. I jumped out of the truck and stumbled into the arena, grabbed a coffee and a stale doughnut, and gathered my thoughts. Rhyno approached me from behind with a big bear hug, kissed me on the neck, and said, "Thanks for driving, Leo. And, by the way, I love you too!"

So, cocaine became a big part of my life, and in San Pedro, it wasn't as mainstream and popular as in my new world of rock 'n' roll. Being on tour without the vigorous hours of hard work, but ingesting the same amount of cocaine while at home, I was struggling. I needed downers and alcohol to get to sleep and more cocaine to wake up. My brain was screaming at my body, "Get up and do this, now! Now!" Then, in the next breath, saying, "But after you get some rest." It was a vicious cycle of insanity.

After the tour, and especially Florida, cocaine soon began making itself at home in all the corners of my life. The money was coming in and going out just as fast. I was making a good living at the time but wasn't planning to stay home for long, so I didn't want to rent a place, and for sure, couldn't go home. I took a small twenty-dollar a night hotel room at the Tasman Sea Motel, in San Pedro, that my cousin Frank owned. The Tasman Sea was not only a restaurant and motel but also where the local hookers would hang out and work their trade for the locals who needed the attention they weren't getting at home. I spent many late nights at the bar hanging with Judy, Roxy, Jill, and Candy, solving all the problems of the

This is a Postcard of my cousin Frank's place at the Tasman Sea. It was my home for most of 1976.

world. Between tours, I used the Tasman Sea as my home, but I never once partook in activities with the girls, not because I didn't want to but because they wouldn't let me. In their eyes, I was too young, and it felt incestuous and just wrong.

Other than cocaine and cars, I really didn't have anything else I wanted to spend the large amounts of money I was making on. I was nineteen years old, owned a 1969 Red Alfa Romeo GTV, and had just bought a new Lotus Esprit Series One two-seat rocket.

I would drive to the Hermosa Rectangle and get the good cocaine, not cut with crap. It was as easy to get as water out of the tap when you were in the music scene. I've always been the kind of guy who likes to have a good talk with people, especially now with my rock 'n' roll ego, so cocaine was definitely the drug for me. I was snorting cocaine and taking downers, chasing that perfectly balanced place, trying to get the high of being back on the road. Looking back now, I see it was dangerous, really dangerous.

One night in particular stands out in my mind: November 6, 1976—the night I almost involuntarily killed myself.

I picked up a little West Coast three-show tour with a band out of Boston named—Boston. Earlier in the year, I had gotten the record and was excited to work with them. They were screaming up the charts with a new style guitar sound that was high tech for the day, and it translated into a huge rock sound.

It was their US tour debut, and the dates I agreed to do ran from Santa Barbara, to Santa Monica, to Fresno. I had already known their crew from working with them on the East Coast portion of The Mac tour, where we were on some of the same festivals. I had promised some of my old friends from Pedro that they could come to the shows. Santa Monica was in Los Angeles, so tickets were hard to get because the comps were being used for music industry people getting their first look at the band live. But in Santa Barbara, being 100 miles north of LA, the show was wide open.

This was my time to shine, so I invited my buddies and their younger sisters up to the show at the Arlington Theater in Santa Barbara. Of course, I wanted to show off, so I scored about a quarter ounce of cocaine from a local dealer to celebrate the occasion. We loaded in, did the sound check, and around dinner time, my friends showed up. It was great to see them, and I was totally amazed to see how their little sis-ters grew up and were now totally hot—even more of a reason for me to strut my stuff. As we all waited for the show to start, we hung in the crew room and did line after line after line of cocaine. About halfway

Inside the beautiful Arlington Theater in Santa Barbara. The inside looked like a Spanish village. Being so close to Los Angeles, I did many shows there.

through the night, as Boston took the stage, I started to feel very weak and light-headed. Following my normal ritual, I started to chase down the cocaine with Jack Daniels, but this time it wasn't working. I remember my legs went numb. I couldn't feel my legs and got really weak, and it was hard to stand. I started to panic. Then I was dizzy and the room started to spin. I was seeing bright spots flashing in my eyes and hearing a high-pitched ring in my ears. I totally panicked. The only thing I could think to do was to find a dark spot, lie down, and try to come down off the seriously bad reaction I was experiencing. The band went onstage, and I found a stack of cases behind the curtain and rested on my back. I was really freaking out and thought for sure I was going to die. I started to pray, thinking my life was over. I floated in and out of consciousness, not sure if I was dead or alive.

I started making deals with God. "Please Lord, get me through this, and I promise never again." As I looked down toward my feet, I noticed my heart was pounding so hard my chest was vibrating, up down, up down. I was sure this was it and started thinking of my parents and family and how bad this really was. I hurt so badly and started to cry. Every muscle in my body was tense and felt like my blood was boiling and going to pop out of my veins.

Last thing I remember was feeling the music and big beats of sound, like all my senses were on overload, and I finally just passed out.

I have no idea how long I was out and was only

awakened by the fact that I had pissed my pants. I didn't care and was just happy to realize I was alive. As I lay there in the dark, listening to the music, I started to feel better. I was still afraid to stand up and really didn't know 100 percent if I was alive or dead. I hurt, every part of my body ached, especially my head.

Finally, the music stopped, and I somehow mustered enough energy to get up. I snuck back to the crew room, got some clothes, and cleaned up. All my friends and their sisters watched the show and came backstage after. It was noticeable that I was worked, and they asked, "What happened to you?" I told them that I needed to get some sleep because we had an early morning load-in and I wanted to be rested. All I really wanted was for them all to leave so I could load-out and go to bed. They all left, I made it through the load-out, and I promised myself (and God) I would never do cocaine again.

The next day, I found out that it wasn't only me but a lot of the other crew guys who got dosed by a bad batch of cocaine laced with speed that we scored from a local dealer. So, there was my excuse to keep doing it. You know, "Cocaine isn't bad; we just got a bad dose." I wish I could say I kept my promise to God, but cocaine has a way of being very persuasive; it consumes you like good sex.

So, I went into Thanksgiving, Christmas, and New Year's single and alone, except for my new mistress cocaine and the hookers at the Tasman Sea. All the people I grew up with, as well as my family, seemed so remote.

The drugs made it so I couldn't relate to their problems and experiences, which were so different from mine. As soon as I got home from a tour, all I could think about—and desperately wanted—was to go back on the road. The roles had reversed; the road had become my home and home was now foreign and hard to settle into.

I was also having a very hard time relating to my parents. At that time, my mother—God bless her—was overdoing it. Every time I went to their house, she would be in my face, cooking and cleaning like crazy. I can understand that my parents just really missed me. I have children myself and now realize what my parents went through.

When my children came home from school, I felt starved to see them—to be in their presence and drink them in. But at the time, with my parents and me, that was not where my head was. Every time I visited, I would literally count the seconds until I could get out of there.

CHAPTER NINE

LOVE, LEO ROSSI INC.,

AND 1977

I GREW A LOT AND LEARNED A LOT about myself in 1977, both professionally and personally. The things that happened to me in 1977 had a big influence on the way the rest of my life proceeded. I was doing less drugs; I finally got my own apartment in San Pedro, but I was still not managing my money.

Here's how it started:

Soon after New Year's, I cleaned up a bit, less drugs and alcohol and more sleep. I rejuvenated myself but still I felt I was missing something. Even though I was in a good space, something didn't feel exactly 100 percent right.

Looking back, I had everything going for me but

really had no one to share it with. There it was, that Italian Catholic American Dream thing creeping back up.

I ran into a girl I had known since high school. Her name was Kerin, and as much as I wanted to pretend we were just friends, the truth is that I had a mad crush on her from the minute I met her in high school.

Unfortunately, she always had a steady boyfriend. After graduation, she went her way, and you know how my life went. As much as we always said we would, we never really kept in touch after graduation—such is life.

Then I ran into her in one of the local hangouts where she happened to be working. We talked for a little while, and I found that all the feelings that I had harbored for her were still there—just waiting to be rekindled by a kind word and a telling glance.

After that night, I started asking everyone I knew if they knew what had been going on in her life since we had last known one another. It turned out that she had had it pretty tough. She had eventually broken up with her old boyfriend, and as a result, he had committed suicide. The small bedroom town of San Pedro made it more of a terrible situation with the rumors and false truths swirling around her.

Kerin and I started hanging out, and slowly but surely, we saw each other daily. She told me she had just left her current boyfriend and wasn't looking for another relationship but missed being with someone to care for and we could just be friends and be with each other. I agreed but immediately fell in love with her. Kerin wasn't my first love though. That happened in the fall of 1975.

I often wonder how and why I remember this part of my life so vividly. For me, it's a place and time that would change my life forever and shape me into who I became and what I am today.

They say you always remember your first love because it happens when our hearts are still innocent and pure and before that first inevitable heartbreak that influences all your relationships for the rest of your life.

In the fall of 1975, during my short attempt at attending LA City College's Theater Art's program, I needed a place to live to be close to the school and easy enough to get back to Long Beach. So, once again, I found the perfect solution, and as happened many times before, luck would step in again.

At the time, my brother Joe was attending USC in downtown Los Angeles, and he was living in the fraternity Theta Chi, right in the center of fraternity row. USC and Los Angeles City College were blocks apart. He told me that his fraternity was soft on attendance and that they needed to boost the rents. I asked him if I might be able to rent one of their rooms. All the brothers voted yes, so I was in. For sixty dollars a month, I got a room and three meals a day—you see, not at home but with my older brother not far from home. So, between spending my time at LA City College, Long Beach, and doing a lot of local shows, I was keeping myself very busy.

The hard part, for me was coordinating and making sense of the three different circles I was traveling in—once again, a very fragmented life. One day I was in the mega music biz onstage with legendary bands and rock stars. The next day I was hanging with sheltered college kids at USC. And the next day I would hang out with my parents and old buddies around home in San Pedro.

At USC, the preppy image was the height of fashion. I was a long-haired rock 'n' roll guy whose wardrobe consisted of a stunning variety of hockey shirts and flannels, which was a 180-degree shift from the image of a typical guy from USC with khakis and an IZOD sweater around his neck. I started to notice that the sorority girls were migrating toward me. Maybe it was because of the bad boy rock 'n' roll image I was portraying and being way different than the frat boy image. I used my rough rebellious look to cover up my insecurity about not being as smart or rich as them.

One night, I came home to the frat house to a raging party. That night, the American Dream that was beat into my head and heart for whatever reason walked into the frat house.

She immediately caught my attention, and I totally fell in love with her at first sight. Her name was Alexa, and her presence, like her name, was one of a goddess. It was obvious by her look and style she wasn't from California. As I focused in on her among all the masses of college prep kids, all I saw was Alexa and really didn't focus on anything else. Long brown hair pulled back so I could see her beautiful smile—she was wearing a short dress with wedge heels that revealed perfectly shaped legs that complimented her hourglass figure.

She looked at me, and our glance lasted more than the casual hello or "sorry not interested." After realizing I was mesmerized and staring at her, I looked away so as not to be so obvious. When I turned back around, she was gone. Again, my insecurity kicked into high gear. Oh well. Just another beautiful girl not interested in me.

A quick moment later, I turned around and wow! There she was—right next to me. Beaming with cautious confidence, I realized this was my chance. As I prepared myself to start a dialogue with her, I noticed she was standing with one of the frat brothers, and I realized she may be with him. Being a guest of the frat, it wouldn't have been right to cut in, but I was thinking, She with him? No, not possible.

Then it happened. She turned to me, smiled, and said, "I'm Alexa."

I said, "Hey, I'm Leo."

After a moment of awkward silence, and with a tone of obvious intuition, she asked, "Do you go here?"

"No, no, not me. I just live here."

With a puzzled look, she smiled, and said, "OK, explain that one."

As I started to explain my situation, the crowd was growing, and the music was getting louder, and we found ourselves shouting instead of talking. She asked if I wanted to go somewhere quieter and away from the crowd and the noise. I paused and pointed at the frat brother; she smiled, shook her head, and grabbed my hand, and off we went to the patio.

We spent the next few hours talking about our lives, our likes, and our families, and it seemed our different situations were attracting us to each other. She was from a very wealthy family and the heiress of a candy company from Wisconsin. I was infatuated. I felt she was really unobtainable for a middle-class guy from San Pedro. She was elegant and beautiful with class and a sex appeal you only read about or see on TV. She just wanted to get away from her home and her parents. Maybe it was my rebellious attitude and rough edges that Alexa was looking for.

Sex entered my mind, but assuming a girl like this would never be loose or easy, I figured it was definitely out of the question.

As the party wound down, we did what all young people do who share that "I feel like I've known you forever moment," and we said good night. As we went back inside, her roommate and friends from her dorm met us. I asked her for her number and, with no pencil or paper, I memorized her number, and we said goodnight.

I called her the next day, and she said she had class and lots of homework and let's try to get together later in the week. That was OK with me, I had some work in Long

Beach, including the Black Sabbath concert at the Long Beach Arena that I was looking forward to.

The next weekend, we finally connected and set up a time to meet and go eat and just hang out. We decided to meet at her dorm, and as I was heading out to see her, I had to ask my brother where her dorm was; I had never even been to the campus and had no idea where I was going.

I was excited to see her again. We walked around USC for hours, picking up where we left off at the frat house. She told me she was excited about coming to California and was looking forward to getting away from her hometown and that included breaking up with a long-term relationship with a boy back home. I told her I never had a relationship, and I used the music business as an excuse: "I have no time." We ended up at her dorm room, where I met roommates and friends, and listened to music until it was time for me to leave.

One date became two ... three ... four and so on, and our relationship was starting to get intimate. The hugs became embraces, and the embraces were followed by long kisses and heightened sexual energy.

Being from a different, high-class world than me, I couldn't wrap my head around having sex with Alexa. I was afraid that sex would be insulting to a girl of her caliber. Did girls like this even have sex? Was being intimate not in her makeup? Call it bizarre or weird, but it's how I felt, and I struggled to manage my feelings.

What started out as friendship for me very quickly turned into pure, 100 percent love. One day, she asked me to take her to San Pedro. After hearing so much about it, she wanted to see it. She said she would pick me up. "Pick me up?" Apparently, along with paying for college, her dad bought her a brand-new Ford Granada for her to use while in college. OK great! She came by the frat house, and I met her outside. She got out of the car, threw me the keys, and said, "You drive." OK by me; I jumped into the driver's seat, and we were off.

We got to San Pedro, and we drove around and ended up at the park where I hung out with my buddies from high school until we realized we were hungry. Funny, I don't remember where we ate, but I sure remember what happened next.

It was one of those beautiful, warm Los Angeles fall nights where the weather was perfect. I decided to take her to the Hollywood Sign with a breathtaking view of Los Angeles. We parked and looked at the city below with my arm around her and her head on my shoulder. We ended up in the back seat, where we shared each other like never before.

Alexa got really quiet, and then I heard her softly crying. I didn't want to ask what was wrong. Playing all the games in my head, I figured this wasn't the way she imagined our first time. Back of a car! I felt so guilty and was afraid to speak, but after some time, she put her arms around me, pecked me on the cheek, and said, "Thanks."

I'm not sure what she was thinking or feeling, and probably never will.

We became very close and started hanging out together every moment we could, and I started to share parts of my life with her. She would come to shows I was working, and it was turning into a relationship.

We took long, fantastic road trips on the weekends. We ran away every chance we could—San Diego, Santa Barbara, San Francisco, as long as we were back by Monday for school and whatever work I had, it was cool.

She was my first love, and I fell hard. I was ready to give it all up for her, the music business, the road, the whole enchilada. I even checked into working for the local stagehand union, just to be close to her and not leave home. This was the middle-class Italian Catholic upbringing, that angel on my shoulder pounding into my head to find a good job, get married, have kids—you know, the American Dream.

It was the other side of me, the rebellious fight-the-system-attitude part of me that I had learned from rock 'n' roll that was keeping me from getting that dream. Again, there was the conflict I was faced with every day ... what to do? I loved her, and that dream was all there for me, but I also loved music and being on the road.

One trip in particular stands out. We planned a trip to San Diego—to visit the zoo and just run away. We had an amazing day, and heading home, we found a small hotel in the quaint, little seaside town of Del Mar. We got a room and were excited, knowing we were going to get to spend a whole night together alone. I still had that higher image of Alexa, and our sex was pretty straight edge. I wanted to get more into it but was intimidated to do so for fear of doing something wrong or that she wouldn't like, embarrassing both of us and blowing the whole relationship.

The next day driving home, we were both unusually quiet. I'm not sure what Alexa was thinking, but I do remember I was facing a decision between two loves ... Alexa or music. Music was going to take me away from her, and I thought that she would take me away from my dreams. Which life to choose? As I later realized, I had no say in the matter because, once again, fate had stepped in.

We continued to see each other until it was time for her to go home for the holidays.

As the time came for her to go home for the holidays, she asked me if I could drive her and her sister to the airport. Alexa had a sense of excitement that I had never seen in her before. Something felt odd, and my gut told me something was wrong. I had this sick jealous feeling and knew when she came back, it wasn't going to be the same.

I remember hugging and kissing her goodbye, and it felt hurried and unemotional. Driving back to USC, I had this feeling like she was on loan to me and she was going back home to her boyfriend. I was truly devastated and realized as easily as she had walked into my life, she walked out.

I knew the first love of my life was gone.

Maybe she realized that I was going to be on the road, and I believe she had trouble with the idea of it. After all, it was not your normal job, and as much as I said sex, drugs, and rock 'n' roll was a myth, I think she knew it wasn't.

My feelings toward her made it difficult for me to know whether I was going to stick with a home life that included her or go back on the road. I knew I was never going to be able to live them both. It was hard for an eighteen-year-old kid to know what to do. Given that she had left for the holidays and the way we parted, I started building resentments toward her.

After the holidays, as I suspected, things did change. We were disconnected, spent less time together, and became distant. We stopped seeing each other. She told me she didn't want to leave one steady relationship for another and wanted more while in college. She began dating and seeing other guys. I was hurt, but what could I do?

I truly do believe fate stepped in and made the decision for me. If it had been another part of the year and she hadn't gone home for the holidays, or we were older, who knows? I used to wonder what would have happened if we had stayed together but realize it wasn't my choice.

It was right after that my career in music started to flourish. Having so much responsibility, which fed my power addiction and eased my insecurities about losing Alexa and making so much money, my decision was clear: stay in the music business, and don't fall in love, ever again.

The American Dream, as well as the little boy with middle-class values, was departing my body and soul. Alexa and I would meet again, but that's another story.

After my hurtful episode with Alexa, my first love, I was cautious about allowing a woman to get close to me. I never wanted to feel rejection from a woman, ever again.

Over time, because of my inbred values and my Italian instinct to nurture a woman, Kerin was swaying me back into that American Dream and away from the touring that I really wanted to do. All I wanted to do was be around her. Again, that middle-class Italian upbringing was resurfacing. I would leave Obie's shop early or turn down local shows so I could spend more time with her. Bands would ask me to go on tour or to Las Vegas for a weekend for a gig, and I wouldn't go. I wanted to hang out with her instead. Eventually, this behavior really started to hit my pocketbook. I mean, I wasn't exactly used to living on a budget.

Circumstance, fate, and destiny stepped in again. Kerin was spending a lot of time at the new apartment; you could say we were living together. I came home one day, and Kerin was getting ready to go out. I noticed she was spending extra time dolling up to look good. I felt something was different, and I asked her where she was going, and she said out with some friends and she would be home late. Not thinking much of it, I gave her a kiss and told her to have a good time and I'd see her when she got home.

I don't remember what I did that night, but Kerin never came home. I figured she went to her apartment, so I called, and there was no answer. After several attempts, I drove to her apartment, and there was no answer, and she wasn't there. I went back two or three times until early in the morning, with the same result. Kerin wasn't home. Not sure what was going on, of course, with my insecurities, my head went to the worst place it could possibly go. She found someone else. Back at the apartment, I eased my pain with cocaine and alcohol, and all was good in the world again.

I finally did catch up with Kerin later the next day at her place, and she was honest and said she had met up with her old boyfriend that she left for me and still had feelings for him. I knew then and there it was over, another hope of the American Dream down the drain, and I was truly starting to believe it just wasn't for me.

Kerin and I had great times together; we took long, intimate road trips dreaming about getting married, having a family, and living the perfect life. We shared special moments, intense life lessons that forever and profoundly affected the rest of my life. Kerin was and still is a good woman: always quiet and honest, and with a beautiful soul.

Kerin was put into my life at that moment in time to teach me lessons to get on with life. Kerin moved away from San Pedro, and we kept in touch over the years, but as life went on, so did the distance between us.

About this time, vowing to never to fall in love again, I was working with an Italian friend of mine at Obie's, David Covelli. David had also been a local promoter rep with Pacific Presentations, and we worked together a lot in Long Beach. We were so much alike—same upbringing, same work ethic. Just get it done! Covelli asked me to do a gig in Las Vegas with him for Obie. He knew if he brought me it would be done right; it was the Pointer Sisters, and he was begging me to do a show with him at the Aladdin.

It was actually a pretty big rig, and he was more into the concert promotion side than the lighting, so he needed me. Besides, he always had good drugs (cocaine and pot) around, and even though I thought I was done with all of that, I wasn't.

One night, over some good stuff and many drinks and talking about Kerin, he told me, "Dude, believe me. Chicks are going to come and go. She wasn't the one you are going to end up with. Do the gig for me, your fellow Italian, and I promise your life will never be the same.

Well damnit, I've always been a born sucker for the "Italian bro" thing, so with a good high going and despite my misgivings about Kerin, I finally relented. I committed, Dave built the rig, and I drove to Vegas.

Dave was what you might call a party animal. He was flamboyant and good-looking, and the ladies loved him. He was also a truly good friend and a very, very hard worker.

He was years older than me but gave me the respect that not too many people would give someone as young as I was. I spent a lot of time teaching Dave about lighting, and in turn, he taught me a lot about stage management—and mainly life. Years earlier, Dave had

Me (Left) Bobby O'Neal (Center) David Covelli (Right).

been busted transporting 600 pounds of pot in his van, and worked and maneuvered the system, and somehow got out of it. He was definitely a character.

He and I became good friends and working partners for a lot of events and tours. We were so notorious, and with both of us being Italian, people started calling us the Pasta Brothers. In hindsight, I knew that going to Las Vegas with Covelli was going to be a wild ride. How right I was, but it wasn't the sort of ride I had anticipated.

We did the gig for Obie, no problem, and Dave got the $5,000 lighting fee from the promoter before the show in cash. After the show, I was going to hang with a couple of buddies of mine who lived in Las Vegas and worked at the Hilton. David said he would stay at the Aladdin and hang out and when I got back, we would drive back to Los Angeles. It was only a couple of hours—what could go wrong? I went out, grabbed some drinks with my friends, and came right back.

As I was walking back through the casino, I saw David at the craps table. "Oh shit," I thought as I sauntered over to the table. But when I got to the table, lo and behold, the dude was on a roll. He had a huge pile of chips in front of him—all the colors of the rainbow. When he saw me, a huge smile broke across his face, and he said, "Man, I'm up!" He wasn't kidding. He must have had $10,000 or $15,000 spilled out in front of him.

I said, "Great. Let's take the winnings and get on back." But he insisted that since he was on a roll, it would be pure stupidity to leave right in the middle of it.

Then a terrible thought occurred to me. "Where did you get the money to bet all of this?" I asked him.

And he said something that made my blood run cold. "I used Obie's money."

I said, "Oh man, you're kidding, right?"

He smiled and said, "I'm on a roll; I can't lose."

"Are you crazy? Why did you do that? If Obie finds out about it, we're going to be screwed and never work again. Hell, we'll be lucky if we don't get killed." Like a man reaching for a life preserver, I picked up a handful of chips and stuffed them into my pocket. The pit bosses reacted, saying, "Back off. You can't do that," and it caused a small scene that soon subsided.

I went upstairs to pack and grab our stuff so we could get out of there. I told him I wanted to see him up there in ten minutes—no later—and, surprisingly, he agreed.

WHEN THE DEVIL SMILES, THE ANGELS FROWN

Well, after an hour, he opened the door. I was glad to hear it, but when he came in, I could tell from the look on his face that he had bad news. The truth was even worse than I feared. He had let it roll, all of it, and he had lost. He had lost it all: the winnings and the money we were paid for the gig.

"You lost everything?"

"Yeah, dude," he said. "We're screwed. I don't know what to do."

I said, "Well, we're going to have to tell Obie."

He said, "Yeah, but how are we going to get home, man? We don't even have enough gas for the truck."

I pulled the chips out of my pocket to see what I had. Luckily, I had grabbed a bunch of chips—about two or three hundred dollars' worth. So, at least we had had one problem solved. I went to the money cage and cashed in the chips, and we left the casino.

There is nothing in the world that's longer than a drive home from Vegas after a losing trip. What made it worse was it wasn't even our money. But this was going to be the longest ride of all. All the way home, he was scheming to figure out how he could get away with not telling Obie what had happened. I knew he was wrong, and this really didn't affect me, but we were a team, and I was going against my better judgment in trying to help my friend figure out a way to swindle money from someone else. All the way home, it was: "We could tell him the money got stolen" and "We could tell him we didn't get paid."

But I knew we had to tell him the truth. It was the only way. "Just tell him you screwed up. Tell him you were drinking; that always works."

We got back to Obie's shop early in the morning, locked the gear and the truck up, and went home. Then, the next day, we sat down with Obie, and after much hemming and hawing, Covelli told him the whole thing. When the story was out there on the table, there was a long moment of silence. I just sat there with my shoulders hunched, honestly not knowing what was going to happen next. I was scared shitless that I was going to lose my job, as well as my credibility.

Obie went crazy. He started throwing shit around the room. He told Dave that he was never going to work for Obie again. Then he looked at me. "How could you let him do this?" he asked me, and honestly, I didn't have much of an answer. I told him, without selling out Covelli, that I had no control over it; and Covelli, God Bless him, backed me up and protected me. I was lucky I saw him in the casino, otherwise we never even would have made it home. "Next time," Obie told me, "You collect the money." When Obie said that I remember thinking "well, at least I still had a job."

In the end, Obie took the money out of Dave's checks over time. But he never fired him. Covelli was just one of those guys who was born under a lucky star. He always landed on his feet. But in hindsight, Covelli and I together were really good for Obie's business. Bands would request the both of us not only because we were hard workers but together, we made everyone feel comfortable and no task was too hard or undoable. Together we did a Black Sabbath tour before I was called back to get the Fleetwood Mac tour together and I brought Covelli on that tour for the summer.

Las Vegas had a profound effect on me. I had been terrified to find out what Obie's reaction was going to be, and that's a horrible feeling—something that I never wanted to go through again. The whole experience made me realize that I had put too much of my life in someone else's hands—not just Covelli's but Obie's. But it also opened my eyes that I was in demand. Not getting fired taught me that I was a commodity for other people's businesses; people who were charging more for me than I was being paid. Cruel but true and good business for Obie. I realized that lights are lights, but a good crew made all the difference. Covelli and I even went as far as investigating buying our own lights and starting our own production company, not only for lights but full tour production. We knew we had the knowledge and the expertise. In the end we couldn't get the financing. Covelli didn't have the most perfect past and I was just too young for the banks' liking.

What the whole Vegas episode made me realize is that I had to go out on my own and not work for anyone else but me. I had to do my own lighting designs, be the stage manager, and handle my own production management. I needed to be independent and have people hire me separately and control my own destiny. I was only nineteen and soon to be twenty years old and realized this wasn't going to be easy. I remember talking to my father about it and for the first time felt he was starting to take me seriously and believe in what I was doing. He had advised me to call my cousin Ron who was a very successful attorney. He told me in his very loving but sarcastic way "don't go this alone, call your cousin or you'll end up screwing it up"

So, I called Ron and he suggested I start a corporation. He set me up as Leo Rossi Incorporated. And from that time forward, I had everyone pay me as a corporation. I was no longer on the payroll. I controlled my own destiny and could work for whom I wanted when I wanted and where I wanted. I felt so important: company minutes, yearly tax returns, I even had the title President with business cards and paper letter head. Pretty cool.

I think this was the shot across the bow for Obie; he realized that I didn't need him or his company in order to survive. I started making my deals directly with the bands. Fleetwood Mac would pay me directly instead of through Obie. That way, I gained a little bit more respect and made more money. That was the way I was able to make something good out of a bad situation. I became much more in demand and most of all had freedom and I never looked back.

The work started flowing in and I was in demand for a much higher price and I controlled my own destiny.

Looking back and reflecting I realize that freedom was more important to me than money and the fact that I succeeded to control my own destiny at a very young age gave me the confidence later in life to take chances and not be afraid to go after the impossible.

CHAPTER TEN

RUMOURS

IN FEBRUARY 1977, FLEETWOOD MAC was scheduled to go back on tour and I was so excited. I now had my own company, I was working a lot around LA but was ready to get back out on a full-length tour, especially with The Mac.

On February 15, Fleetwood Mac called me. We were going to rehearse for about two weeks in Hollywood and rehearse the new songs from *Rumours*, and the tour would start in Berkeley with a benefit for Jacques Cousteau and the Save the Whales Foundation. This sounded like a great way to start the tour and we were all excited, not only for the tour but the *Rumours* Record as well. With the continued success of the white album and prereleased reviews of *Rumours*, the band's touring entourage was growing. We had three forty-foot trucks, four buses, and the band travelled on a private plane. Curry and I designed a new lighting rig with trusses on all four sides of the stage, more lights, and we increased the sound to match the larger venues we were playing. A crew of six was now sixteen and my role grew from lights to head electrician and stage manager.

The first show of the *Rumours* tour. February 28, 1977. A benefit to save the whales.

The tour would go on from Berkley into the Midwest and then to the East with stadium shows, arena shows—including Madison Square Garden in New York City. Some of the shows were huge, with other major headlining bands like the 200,000-person Sunday Break in Austin Texas.

Rumours was and still is an amazing piece of art that not only notched its way into music history but history itself. The demented fairy tale of the band's dynamic relationships transcended into the songs that everyone could feel and relate to.

Stevie Nicks and Christine McVie. Two members of the biggest band in the world empowering women through music.

Rumours is a combination of Christine's, Stevie's, and Lindsey's writing along with Richard Dashut, Ken Caillat's and Lindsey's producing expertise perfect layered sounds that created a sonic orgasm. Richard Dashut was a longtime friend of Lindsey and Stevie and literally learned the business from the ground up. He started as janitor in the studios where they recorded, and he worked his way to a sound engineer. Ken Caillat on the other hand was the top mobile recording engineer in the business.

Big drums, laid back bass parts, driving guitars, soothing melodies and perfect vocal harmonies doing different things became a record you didn't just hear but felt.

The world was in dire need of a new diverse sound that made people feel that they were a part of something. All the tumblers of music and time lined and connected the dots and broke barriers of silence. The record had love, hate, fear, anger, resolution and most of all emotion. It let people know whatever you're going through, it's going to work out and be OK.

Women were empowered and fixated on the words that Stevie and Christine wrote telling them to fight back and fight hard using peaceful solutions. Songs like "Dreams" and "Gold Dust Woman" gave women a purpose and a voice to say, "we don't have to sit here and take it."

We went back to Pirate Audio in Hollywood for rehearsals for the *Rumours* tour. You could tell things were getting bigger and that the momentum was picking up. We built a new light rig and came up with a concept to have a rigid front truss (the structure that you hang lights on) be an arched shape like a rainbow. Keep in mind this was before we hung and suspended things from the roofs of the venues. It was very modern and aggressive for its time.

The first single, "Go Your Own Way," was an up-tempo tune that required Stevie to play the Acoustic Guitar. As they rehearsed the song it was very apparent that Stevie couldn't get it right. Lindsey was getting very frustrated and almost to the point that he wanted to slam the guitar over Stevie's head.

After many, many attempts Lindsey finally screamed as he threw the guitar at Ray, "fuck Stevie, Ray can play this better than you." Ray Lindsey originally was a soundman and with no work he picked up the job as the truck driver for Fleetwood Mac. Knowing more about guitars than Stevie's younger brother Chris, they traded jobs and Ray became one of the most respected guitar techs in the business. Ray caught the guitar, learned the part, and became another guitar player for Fleetwood Mac.

Here is Ray's accounts from his book "The Care and Feeding of Fleetwood Mac And Other Species" of how he became one of the longest-tenured guitar players in Fleetwood Mac.

February 1977: the Rumours album is released as well as the first single, Go Your Own Way. Months have been spent layering and doubling instruments, especially guitars, to achieve the rich, full, Grammy-winning sound. Fleetwood Mac with Lindsey, Ken, and Richard producing, have crafted a sonic masterpiece. It was time for one of the strongest live acts on the road to take it to the people. The next order of business was a couple weeks of rehearsals to put the new songs into the set.

The band was blessed with the ability of taking their recorded tracks to the stage with just their four instruments and three voices without losing anything in translation. The power of the group playing live took the already strong material to another level and The Mac faithful worshipped the group's stage chemistry. Having two distinct guitar parts in the same song presented a new challenge for Lindsey. The acoustic rhythm guitar that he added in the studio was not only the signature sound that started the song, but part of the foundation for the electric solo going out. Lindsey wanted both parts onstage and needed a second player. He set his sights on Stevie who wrote songs on guitar and accompanied herself when singing. This was going to be a tricky negotiation. Stevie already hated the lyrics about her "shacking up" and there was no clear reason for her to show any vulnerability to her on-again, off-again nemesis. Somehow Lindsey broke through and she agreed to give it a shot. The group took a break in their rehearsals for the guitar player to teach his ex-girlfriend her guitar part.

Magically, the two began to bond and share pleasant musical memories. An unexpected positive vibe took the

room by surprise and everyone welcomed the friendly spirits. After half an hour of private tutoring, Buckingham and Nicks returned to their places onstage with their bandmates. Mick slapped his kick while guitar and drums meshed to set the beat and start the intro. Lindsey locked eyes with Stevie and started the count for her cue to begin. For the next ten minutes the band executed one false start after another as the singer struggled to hit the entry point for her part. To Lindsey, finding the turned-around beat was second nature. The fact that it was a little weird is what made it good, but also not easily grasped by Stephanie. Lindsey's veiled patience was vaporizing, and Stevie was beginning to melt down in an uncomfortable way. A familiar tension returned to the musty room.

My outpost during this entire exchange was by the monitor mixer onstage left, about ten feet. away. As the final false start begins, Lindsey catches me trying to help his struggling guitarist count in and find the entry point. When the Stevie train leaves the track for the last time, LB takes the guitar from her, walks over to me and lays it in my lap. He turns back to Stevie and says, "Raymond can play this better than you!"

I knew this was more of a rebuke to Stevie than an endorsement of my musicianship. Lindsey was on a mission and he wasn't leaving until he got what he wanted. He sat down next to me and began to teach me the elusive part. The song was in the key of "F" but Lindsey put a capo on the eighth fret and showed me what to play starting with an "A" chord. It made the basic I IV V pattern an "A," "D," and "E" for the verses and "F#m," "D," and "E" for the chorus and solo out.

I could find the chords okay but strumming with a pick was another trip entirely. I played finger-style guitar. I had rhythm but not with a plectrum. I was sucking bad. In spite of what had just gone down in the room with Stevie, Lindsey was patient and cool with me. We sat together and he played me through my spastic shuffle-like strum and got me to feel the strident on top of the beat attack. He stayed with me and we played the simple figure over and over and over until I finally started to relax into it. Then, out of nowhere, Mick slid into place and the rest of the band joined in with him. It was primitive but cool. I held on all the way through to the end of the pass and even got an "All right Raymond" from Christine. The band called it a night, and everybody headed out as I sat in amused disbelief. Looks like I'm going to be playing guitar with Fleetwood Mac. I think ...

The next day we returned rested, fed, and filled with the promise of a new day. I had been practicing my four chords since we left the day before. As a folkie finger-picker, I had never played guitar with a band or played standing up. Nothing had been said to me by anybody about my new task so I approached it like another roadie chore. I set up a Fender Twin and folding chair by my tuning station and waited for further instructions. The band wandered in and rehearsals began quietly. They ran the set from the top *without drama and got to Go Your Own Way. I picked up my guitar, sat down next to the amp and steeled myself. Stevie asked if she was playing guitar and Lindsey informed her that she was not.*

"No. Raymond is," was the chilly reply.

"Congratulations," Stevie humorously offered in my direction. "I'm never speaking to you again." "Poor Raymond," Christine fake sympathized.

John McVie delivered his best Chuck Woolery Dating Game introduction. "This is Raymond. He's from the Midwest. He has blue eyes and likes lobster and brandy."

With that portion of the roasting completed, Mick set the beat and Lindsey chunked his guitar as he counted us in and started the song. My contribution was shaky but not a deal breaker. It was going to take a few shows for me to find the pocket for the beginning strums. However, the straight-ahead rocking part at the end fell right into place and LB jumped on his solo with a newly discovered abandon. We kept going and going until there was nowhere left to go and surrendered to a noisy finish. For me, it was indescribable. It was such a gas to be a part of the band for that moment and such a relief that I didn't fuck it up too bad. One thing about this group, no one held back when it came to voicing their opinions about anything and I would have immediately known if there were any dissenting votes. Lindsey gave me an approving nod and I knew it was going to be OK.

We all heard *Rumours* grow from the small dressing

room where Rhyno and I heard Stevie plunking on the keys of a small electric piano for the notes of a song she called Thunder that became Dreams, to one of the greatest selling records of all time.

We were there, right in the middle of it. For over a year, working the songs live from the many soundchecks, to the first tracks laid in the studio in early 1976, to finishing touches in Miami and the final tracks in rehearsals in the winter of 1977.

What I didn't realize was how fortunate that we all were to be involved in the making of this new piece of historic music that became *Rumours*. We all had our part helping this talented group of people, this band called Fleetwood Mac, create what would become the soundtrack for people's lives, then, now, and forever more.

CHAPTER ELEVEN

JUST ANOTHER RAINY DAY
IN FLORIDA

THE 1977 RUMOURS TOUR WAS ROLLING ALONG. We were now in festival season. The promoters figured out how to make more money by combining multiple big bands on one huge stadium show and charge more. We were smarter though and figured out a way to make more for ourselves, but the pittance left for the promoters was more than they were making in smaller arenas. The promoters were getting more devious and padding cost and making side deals: kickbacks with vendors such as porta-johns, fence companies, even the local police, to increase their profit. In any case the shows were bigger, and our crews were getting bigger as well. For the

stadium shows we were well over fifty crew on the road—a far cry from the six crew when the band first started in 1975.

The large stadium shows back then were much easier than today's large stadium shows. Less rules and regulations and less hands reaching out for money. There were no building or safety permits, very little engineering and quite frankly we made it up as we went along. We used a lot of common sense but then again, we did take calculated chances. We invented things on the fly and did what we could to get things done and put on a show. It was a new world and we were the explorers.

There was limited liability insurance. Our mind set was if it's dangerous then just don't do it! We knew our strengths and weaknesses, but there were always unpredictable forces like the weather.

May 28 and 29, 1977, were two incredible days. It was a festival stadium show with Kenny Loggins, Chick Corea, Bob Seger, and Fleetwood Mac at the Tangerine Bowl in Orlando Florida.

By this time, we had started flying the lighting rig and sound from the roofs of the arena's, so we had to bring two riggers on tour with us. A rigger was a guy who would climb into the roofs of the arenas and hang the chains and motors that would lift all the gear. There really weren't a lot of guys who were willing to get up in a roof and stand there on a three-inch beam 100 feet in the air, pulling heavy chains up to the roof. It took a special sort of personality to be able to do that work and I soon realized that all riggers were crazy.

When we got to Orlando in the morning, the promoter provided an outdoor roof to hang our lights from as well as a couple three story steel scaffolds on each side of the stage. Our riggers, Jimmy and Mike, immediately started lecturing us. They were really not being helpful but lecturing us on how unsafe the whole setup was. "This scaffolding that's holding up this roof isn't anchored and we are hanging to much weight and it's very dangerous. You guys are going to get hurt. And blah, blah, blah, blah."

One of us said, "Whatever, guys, do your job. Make it better and anchor them. Do whatever you need to do." We needed them out of our way so we could move on with getting the show loaded in.

They went to the truck and pulled out steel cable and supports and spent the rest of the day mumbling and groaning while they got what they needed to anchor the support towers to the ground so the scaffolding wouldn't fall in because of excess weight. They were right, and they did good work, even if they were annoying.

We hung the lights from the roof and placed the large and heavy speakers on large scaffold three stories high left and right of the stage.

The roof went up, and we set up all the band's gear under it. We set up all three bands, and then, all of a sudden about three o'clock, with the crowd already in the stadium, that hot Florida rain just started pounding down. It was one of those Florida inch-in-an-hour torrents. We all started run around covering up and protecting all the gear.

We looked up at one point, and we realized that the roof was not tilted back. Usually we would tilt the roof back a little bit so that the water would drain off the back of the roof and not collect. But not this time. We forgot. It was already anchored off the roof and with the rain coming down so hard so it was impossible to tilt and drain the water at this point. So, the water was sitting on top of this roof, just collecting and forming a huge bubble right in the middle.

The bubble was big, and it was getting bigger by the second. Water weighs a lot! We knew this, but we had no recourse for getting the water out. The riggers said, "Well you have to do something, because the weight of the water's going to collapse that roof." So finally, it was proposed that we go up and punch a hole in the roof to drain the water.

Imagine this: we got strong wood poles, and we tied and taped large buck knives onto them. Shark Boy and I got up on an air ladder that we were using for rear follow spots and began trying to punch a hole in the hard rubber roof with these primitive devices. We were kind of holding on to one another, trying not to fall off the ladder that had several stagehands around it holding it.

While we were in the middle of our primitive plan, we suddenly heard a creaking and bending noise. I said, "Shark Boy, this doesn't sound good."

He said, "Hell no. Let's get down."

Then, just as we got the bottom of the lad-der, the trussing that strutted across from scaffolding to scaffold-ing snapped in half. And the roof itself just tore, spilling hundreds and hundreds of gal-lons of water in a wild gush all over the stage and gear, including very expensive guitars and musical equipment.

Dave "SharkBoy" Richanbach. My best friend, roommate, and confidant through the early years with The Mac.

Bob Seger's road guys were on the stage while all this was going on. And when I heard the roof start to go, I screamed, "Clear the stage!" Guys ran in all directions. I jumped off the back of the stage and landed face down in a mud puddle with Shark Boy. I cleared the mud from my eyes, thinking, "Shit, those stage guys were still up there."

The roof had fallen down and come to rest, about five feet off the stage. It was like the hand of God grabbed the large steel structure and just closed his fist and crumbled it like tin foil.

I pulled myself back up onto the stage to see what damage had been caused, and I saw all the Seger guys belly down on the stage. All I could think was, "Oh shit! Shades of Humble Pie."—the show where Curry saved my life in 1975. As we looked around to assess the damage, our first priority was to make sure all the guys were ok. Everyone was accounted for and it was just a miracle that no one got hurt.

That's when we noticed that if it wasn't for the Riggers who anchored the roof structure to the heavy sound wings, the whole thing would have really come down, hit the stage, and crushed everyone under it, and we would have had some serious, serious problems.

Simple physics, weight and ballast. The stage structure weighed less than the sound wings that weighed more than the roof so the lights didn't fall down and into the audience and hurt numerous people.

This all happened with the crowd already in the stadium. When the roof came down, bending in half over the stage, water poured everywhere, even onto the crowd. I mean large quantities of fresh cool water. The crowd started whooping and hollering and they were loving it. It was refreshing and on a hot Florida day to be drenched with cool water was a dream. To them, it was the shit—what a show! It was a full-on party in the mud.

Once we had figured out that no one had gotten hurt, we needed to figure out what we were going to do next. Did we need to cancel the show? We got together and talked to the promoters. We all made a confident decision to go on with the show. After all, you couldn't cancel a Bowl show. A stadium full of disappointed fans? No way. From that point on, it became a challenge. The show must go on.

So, we sat down and methodically figured out how the hell we were going to pull this thing off.

First, we knew the sound towers weren't affected, and we had to make announcements and put on some music. Next, we had to get the band gear off the stage. While doing that we needed to get the cooperation of the crowd because we needed to move the crowd back off at least 100 feet to get equipment in front of the stage. Finally, we needed to resurrect the roof. So, we orchestrated this really cool emergency status plan.

The gear crews from all the bands went back to their dressing rooms and got blow driers and whatever else they could think of, because all their shit was completely drenched.

We had this giant forklift that we had used to stack the speakers up, and we needed it to pull off our new plan.

We made an announcement saying we needed to move the crowd back, and we rolled the forklift around to the front, where the crowd was. The crowd was receptive and cheering us on.

We used the large forklift to hoist up the front of the stage that was broken down from the weight of the roof. We pulled it up high enough to use a piece of the trussing that ran from the floor to the ceiling to hold it up right in the middle of the stage. Then we did the back of the roof. Soon the whole roof was back up and we salvaged together what lights were left that still worked.

This alone took us two hours. We then methodically went around to all the structural points and made sure there were no more breaks and the roof was stable. We then started putting the bands' gear back together band by band. After we set Kenny Loggings gear, we looked at the time. The show was supposed to start at four p.m. It was already eight p.m. and was so late at that point that the promoter just told Kenny Loggins to do an abbreviated set, about thirty minutes. We then told Chick Corea he didn't have to play but and he would still get paid. It would have been way too late to put on The Mac and it just wouldn't work. Chick said he had fans there and would play after Fleetwood Mac. We agreed, figuring he would just bail and not play.

Seger agreed to do a shorter set as well. Then Fleetwood Mac came on and did a full set—Fleetwood Mac was the band that most of the people in the crowd had come for, anyway. During the show, Stevie had to navigate around this truss dead in the middle of the stage. It looked like a stripper pole. She would put her arms around the truss and pull her body around it and even tried to climb it at one point. The whole band pulled it off and the fans loved it.

When Fleetwood Mac finished, it was really early in the morning but Chick decided he wanted to play. All the crowd quite understandably was bailing from the stadium as if it were a sinking ship except one hundred people or so in this now very empty huge stadium. We were trying to figure out how to get all the equipment out. It was late, we were all exhausted, but knew we had to load-out. Chick Corea played as planned. After we got all the Fleetwood Mac gear off the stage and he was ready to play, there was only about one to two hundred people in front of the stage to watch Chick Corea. Of coursed to reward his faithful fans Chick decided to play for hours, and who were we to stop him.

The show finally ended around four a.m. and as we watched the sunrise, we took on the daunting task of getting all the gear into the trucks.

We finished the load-out with all the gear in trucks around ten a.m. and went back to the hotel and a few well-deserved hours of sleep,

A few hours later we got messages to meet down in the hotel ballroom where the promoter had set up a party and served a real nice meal with steaks, seafood, and all we could drink and snort. With our bellies full, drunk, high, we were feeling triumphant and that it couldn't get much better, but it did. Before we knew it, we were surrounded by beautiful women, all shapes and sizes. We all felt like we had just won the big game, and these were our trophies and the party was on and lasted the rest of the day and night.

The spirit of the time of who we were, and our pride dictated our accomplishments. We were not going to be denied or deny the fans what they deserved: a good show from the bands they loved. We celebrated the feeling of getting it done and, most of all, of overcoming all our fears of failure.

If that kind of situation happened at a show today it would have been canceled with no questions asked and in the courts with lawyers and insurance companies for years.

This was truly an accomplishment and just another day on the road for a bunch or young guys living the dream.

CHAPTER TWELVE

MADISON SQUARE GARDEN

BY SPRING 1977 AND WITH THE SUCCESS of *Rumours*, the band had reached the point where they were staying at five-star hotels (but without the larger road crew). They finally made it and were booked to play the famous Madison Square Garden in New York City, not one but two shows. Playing Madison Square Garden is the dream of every band or artist that ever dared to take the road of uncertainty to stardom. Playing the Garden in New York, that some believe is the Capital of the world, is an important show where the whole world watches and judges you and if you're able to show you've got it, you've made it.

Along with the prestige of playing the Garden comes the fringes of your success. Staying at posh hotels and a fleet of limos. It wouldn't be good if the press caught one of the most successful bands in the world being picked up by a van at the Ramada Inn in Times Square where we, the crew, were staying. For image and perception, the band was staying at The Plaza, which was the plushest hotel in Manhattan. The choice of accommodations for the band worked. The press showed up in mass to lurk around and the frenzy added to the excitement that The Mac was in town.

The Plaza amenities were expensive. A cup of coffee was ten dollars, and a normal breakfast could run you up to fifty to sixty dollars (in 1977 dollars). It was not for your normal everyday traveler and not for John McVie who really loathed the attention and the cost of things that were inflated because of status. John was an amazing person who always took care of the crew and never forgot where he came from and how hard it was to get as far as they had come.

We, on the other hand, loved staying at the Ramada down on 42nd Street near Times Square with all the hookers, drug dealers, and homeless—it was the rough area of Manhattan but also the fun area and really where we wanted to be. If you're going to be in New York, be in the heart of New York, where you don't have to find fun, it finds you.

We all got settled in and were getting ready to go have some drinks and dinner somewhere, when out of the blue, a limo pulls up outside our hotel and John McVie gets out. He asked us—and this was so typical—whether it 'might be OK' if he hung out with us. He was so unpretentious, and we all knew he came because he didn't feel comfortable among all the splendor uptown attention at the Plaza.

Madison Square Garden show poster 1977.

We said, "Sure, John, It's no big deal. You can hang out with us. You're always welcome." Sure enough, he got himself a room at the Ramada on his own credit card.

He asked what we were up to and we told him just dinner and drinks and settle in for the night to be ready for the big gig. John asked if it was ok to tag along. We said sure and he said "give me a few and we'll take my car."

After a few minutes a bunch of us jumped in and joined John in the limo, and we all went out to dinner. Of course, John paid for everything like he would always do. As I mentioned earlier, John was so down-to-earth and the least noticeable of the band; few people recognized him. He really liked being part of the crew as well as being in the band; and in fact, during the first tour always picked a night or two to ride with Gilbert our truck driver.

Then, after dinner, we drove all around New York City. With drinks and of course other stimulants we were experiencing the New York we always read about and see on TV. The fast pace in your face lifestyle. Pretty stylish women telling you like it is and what they want and believe.

We were randomly picking up people. Women, hookers, anyone who wanted or had the nerve to jump on this magic carpet and fly around New York City. We stuffed that limo full of people, lots of people. We had massive amounts of cocaine. We were drinking. We were really flying high. It was something right out of a movie. At a certain point, reality sort of hit me. Being the guy who always had to be in control, I said, "Listen, guys. Madison Square Garden is a big date. It's a hard load-in. We should not be doing this." But guess what? Our instincts and pirate way of living life prevailed over sensibility or logic at that point. Take no prisoners!

After all the decadence went down, and at a very early hour in the morning of the Madison Square Garden show, we went back to the hotel took a quick shower, and rallied in the lobby to go Load-in for the biggest shows of Fleetwood Mac's career.

Not many people in the world can say they have done a show at the famous Garden. For a bunch of young rebellious guys, it was quite exciting and worth sharing.

The Garden is not just an arena and in fact it's one of the first entertainment centers constructed. The main floor of the arena is for hockey, basketball, the Circus and Concerts and is on the fifth level of this massive structure.

There are smaller theaters and event space below the arena floor; Penn Station, the hub of transportation for the northeast, is in its basement.

Madison Square Garden ramp.

All the sound, lights, and musical equipment is loaded off the trucks at street level and brought up the long ramp by a fleet of forklifts, big carts, and many people.

You needed a degree not only in logistics but psychology to navigate the Union labor and many departments it takes to run the Garden.

There was the Teamsters for truck loading on an off, then there was the stagehand union for the gear on and off the stage and show crew, then the IBEW electrical union for all thing electrical and other unions like SIU for food and beverage. It took you some time to figure out who was with what union and some were very nice, but others were brutally non cooperative and there only for a paycheck, doing as little work as they could. With me it was no problem, I grew up around all the union guys back at Long Beach and knew the system of how they thought and worked. I even fibbed and told them I was in the stagehand union #33 out of Los Angeles and was one of their brothers. They immediately loved me, and I knew the white lie would make the day easier for the rest of the crew.

Over the years I made good friends in the New York union IATSE #1 and worked with many of them at other venues like Radio City Music Hall, Carnegie Hall, and the Lincoln Center. Most were Italian and I even had dinners at some of their houses and met their families.

If you came in guns a blazing and thought you knew it all, crossed them, and tried to do all the work by yourself, you were in for a long day and those old salty stagehands had memories like elephant's and your future work at the Garden were in jeopardy.

Needless to say, going into the Garden hungover, navigating the sea of confusion, was not a smart thing to do. We were all feeling like shit, but I soon discovered that I wasn't in the worst position, others were far worse off than me. A couple of the riggers that had to go up in the roof and walk small thin metal beams and pull up the motor chains to hoist our gear, looked like they were hit by trucks. I asked them, "You guys ok? How the hell are you going walk 100 feet off the deck when you can't even walk on solid ground now?" They said no worries; we'll get it done.

We muscled through the load-in, the riggers did well and were lucky enough when done to go back to the hotel and sleep. We weren't so lucky and were unfortunately stuck at the Garden all day and night. The only saving grace was we were there for two nights, so the gear stayed set up and there was no load-out and we could go back to the hotel and sleep.

The gear was in and set up and things were going smooth, so we thought. About three p.m. our problems began. There was a scheduled sound-check for four o'clock and the band started to arrive. One by one they arrived at the Garden but John McVie had not shown up yet and was nowhere to be found. JC called us into the production office and asked, "John was staying at your hotel last night? Do you know what happened to him or where he is?"

We all looked at each other like kids being busted for ditching school and said, "No, but we did go to dinner together last night."

He said, "Oh dinner? Only dinner? With his English angry voice getting louder. Did you go out after dinner?" He knew us too well.

No one wanted to lie, we all looked at each other and somebody said, "Yeah, we ... did." And then trying to be as honest as we could without telling the whole truth for the fear of the known harsh ramifications, we sketched out what happened.

He blew up. He said, "Man, do you know how big this date is? I want everyone who was in that car in the production office, right now." We all gathered and went in the production office where JC completely flipped out on us. He said, "You know what guys? This is bullshit. This is the biggest show of this band's career and if it goes badly you guys are all going to be fired." He told us that the rest of the band was pissed, and they're coming down on him. The worst thing was that we all knew he was right—there was no way you could really feel good about our behavior and what was happening.

So, we all got together and tried to figure something out. There were no cell phones back in that day, so we sure as hell couldn't call him. But we had the riggers back at the hotel go through all the rooms to see if they could find him. No luck, so we just waited and waited and waited.

Four o'clock came and went, and John missed sound check. The rest of the band did the sound check without him, and everyone was on edge. It really was a bad vibe and we all felt like shit knowing that JC was right, and we should have used more common sense and realized why we were all out there. To do shows, not party and miss gigs.

After sound check, JC called us all back in the production office and told us, "You guys are all done. You're fired and going home. We will figure out how to move on without you all." We knew that probably couldn't happen because there were too many of us with important positions on the tour, but in the back of our minds, we also knew anything was possible with JC. He was in way to deep and the most loyal to the band.

Just when it seemed the room couldn't get more tense, it did. John came strolling into the production office, easy as you please. "What's going on?" he asked. JC was all wound up, and he began going off on John. "Where have you been mate? How can you do this? This is New York! Chris and Stevie are livid, and Mick is worried sick." JC went on and on like a coach scolding a player that was slacking off.

John was normally a very calm guy with not a lot of words but at this particular time he would have none of it. He said to JC, "What's your problem? Don't raise your voice at me and remember something. I'm in the band. You work for me, JC." Then McVie started going off in a way none of us had ever seen. He said, "good to see you're worried about my wellbeing!

JC said "you needed to be here for sound check and you should have kept in touch with me, not been out fucking off with the crew! These guys know better as well."

"I'm the one who did this," John Thundered back at him. "These guys didn't do it to me. No one forced me to do anything, and by the way, you can have all that rock star uptown bullshit, I want nothing to do with it. I decided to stay with the crew."

Looking back, what I had learned from the whole incident was, John never forgot why we were all there: it was about the music, not about the whole scene of what it was becoming with limos, high end hotels, and decadence.

John asked us what JC had said to us, and we told him we apologized and never meant to cause any drama, but we had all just been fired. John turned to JC and said, "If they're fired, then you're going to have a find a new bass player, because you're going to have to fire me too."

He stood up for his crew and that's the amazing man and friend John was and still is.

After being chastised all day for our behavior, those words were music to my ears. I could have hugged him. Watching JC back pedal and try to appease John gave us some vindication for all the abuse we were taking all day.

JC always had the band's best interest in mind and was damned loyal for many years and would have taken a bullet for anyone in the band.

In this instance we all knew we were wrong, and we all felt really bad for feeling the way we did, but in the end, the show went off as planned and as usual the band was epic and added another notch in the belt of success while heading for the stars.

The show went on with many high-profile actors and actresses and rock stars like Keith Richards and Ron Wood in attendance. The Mac solidified their place in Madison Square Garden history.

So, that was Madison Square Garden. We hung out with a rock star. We got wasted, got fired, got rehired, and learned a couple valuable lessons: know your limitations and it's great to have good friends.

Me and my Son Tristan at Madison Square Garden touring together on the 2008 Neil Young Tour.

CHAPTER THIRTEEN
THEN THERE WAS LIGHT

WE ALL WENT BACK TO THE RAMADA and got some sleep. As much as we all wanted to go out and party, we figured with one more show at the Garden, a load-out, and a bad reprimand, we better just lay low and get some well-deserved rest.

The second night at the Garden was just as important and we needed to be on our game. The show was much larger now with more sound and lights; it was a show instead of just a band playing music. For scenic effect we would use backdrops. Backdrops were large pieces of durable material with painted scenes on them. Some bands, like The Mac, would carry five to ten drops that would reveal through the show.

On today's music tours it seems most bands struggle with good songs and talent and so they barrage the audience with video content to distract from the mediocre music performance.

For the *Rumours* tour, The Mac hired very talented painters and set designers to create backdrops for all our shows. Curry and I met with the designers to discuss how we can use light to accent the drops to make them look 3-D in order to subtlety enhance the already great music.

There was this one particular really cool-looking backdrop that was a forest scene and the effect was for Stevie's hit off *Rumours* "Gold Dust Woman."

The forest was deep and dark, and way back in the woods. We would accent the front of the drop in blue lights to bring out the warmer colors and pop out the green in the trees. At the center of the drop in the middle was a space that looked like the forest. When it ended you felt you were in Heaven. When we lit the space from the back with a Frennel—a giant white light—the scene looked really spooky and three-dimensional. It looked as if a light really was shining back there in the forest.

During the day at sound checks we tested the light to make sure it was working and ready for the song.

The second night we never tested the light before the show because of no soundcheck and pure complacency.

The big white light had to share a circuit with another light on the dimmer rack so as "Gold Dust

Fleetwood Mac forest backdrop.

Woman" was coming up, I put on the headset, and I told Dave Richanbach—our tour carpenter nicknamed Shark Boy—"Don't forget to plug in the Frennel.

He said, "OK, make sure to bring down the dimmer to kill the circuit." I said, "OK," and reached over to pull down the dimmer. Well with everything going onstage and feeling the music, I accidentally pulled down the wrong dimmer which left the giant white light on.

"Gold Dust Woman" was right after the song "Landslide." So, as Stevie and Lindsey were on-stage singing "Landslide" the rest of the band went offstage to take a break, except for a small interlude piano part Christine played in the middle of the song that was a lovely, quiet moment in the show with just Stevie, Lindsey, and Christine onstage. To make sure we were ready for "Gold Dust Woman," Shark Boy plugged in the light, and KABLAM! A big arc of white light lit up the whole backdrop right in the middle of Christine's piano part. The crowd started to scream and cheer right at the slow part of the song, which was supposed to be very intimate. I looked up in horror realizing what happened. I slowly brought down the fader to turn the negative into a positive and make it look like it was a planned event, but not a chance. A big blunder at a very big show.

I looked over at Curry, and he just looked at me like, "You're a fucking idiot." I felt really bad but as they say, the show must go on.

By any measure, I blew the song, killed the moment of one of the most beloved Fleetwood Mac songs. But luckily, the band was on such a roll at that point that they didn't even react until the end of the song where Stevie said, "I knew I had power, but not that much."

The next day one of the New York papers wrote a perfect review saying, "The whole show was perfect, except for the botched lighting effect in 'Landslide.'"

I've been back to Maddison Square Gardens many times since my first time with Fleetwood Mac, and every time I step in the building and walk up the ramp it's still like the first time in the spring of 1977 when I lit up the night.

The large
Fresnel light.

A photo I took of JC raging.

CHAPTER FOURTEEN

JC AND TEXAS

JC WASN'T A BIG FAN OF TEXAS. In fact, he just plain right out hated Texas. JC, was a traditional Englishman holding values opposite of everything that was Texas. He was always bagging on Texans—how arrogant they all were and how they thought they owned everything and how they thought they were above the law. He used to call them Tex-ass-ians. Plain and simple JC had a wild spur up his butt about Texas and that was it.

In spring 1977, we worked down through the south, which included a stop in Houston at the Summit Arena. The band was gaining popularity and in turn, power.

There was a promoter down there named Don Fox

who owned Beaver Productions. Fox was very loyal to the band, even before Lindsey and Stevie were there. He consistently booked the band throughout the south. In retrospect, Fox had the foresight and the belief in Mick, John, and Christine, and it paid off. Later in life on the Fleetwood Mac *Tusk* Tour, the band even had Fox promote gigs in cities that were not his territory. Fox even promoted the band in San Francisco around the famous promoter Bill Graham. That's the equivalent of the US military doing a parade in Red Square.

Fox and JC were really good friends, and there was a strong but friendly rivalry between them. JC knew that Fox was loyal and respected that, but he still had to make as much money for the band as he could.

Fox was also a prankster and JC was his favorite target. In turn JC would reciprocate with some outrageous pranks and put him in very awkward and precarious situations. They would make bets and challenge each other to see who could be the most outrageous and most of the time ridiculous.

On this occasion at the Summit Arena, Houston's premier venue, JC got up onstage and looked out on the audience to see how much time we needed to start the show. As we stood there he said in his English accent "Look at all these goddamn Texans with their goddamn cowboy hats." The Urban Cowboy thing was in full rage, and JC, being a staunch English guy who never liked Texas, was really repulsed.

Then like the sun breaking through the clouds, a big smile came to his face. His idea was that since there were two ladies onstage in Fleetwood Mac, he was not going to start the show until every Texan in building, including those in law enforcement took off their cowboy hats.

As I looked out, I saw thousands of men wearing cowboy hats in Houston's Summit Arena. JC went to find Fox to tell him his plan

Fox said, "That ain't going to happen, man. This is Texas. People are going to wear their hats no matter what you say."

JC told him, "Make it happen or the house lights won't go down, and the band won't start."

When Fox realized that JC was serious, he summoned his righthand man Ray Compton, who was good friends with the band and all of the crew. (Ray is a Knight of Rock and sad to say we lost him the winter of 2018.)

This passage is from Ray Compton during a Knights of Rock taping in 2006.

Ray Compton: *Fox called me over the radios and told me to meet him in the production office. We were all there. Fox looked agitated and told me that JC wanted every male in the building to remove his hat. I thought it was just another JC—Fox thing and laughed and started to walk out. Fox at this point was yelling. "NO! NO! He's serious. He wants all the hats off, even the fucking police! Like yeah right, that's going to happen. Fox was done with it and just told me to work it out. I wasn't going to do it.*

*My main concern was I needed to come back to Houston to do more shows and feared what would happen if people recognized me. I had a different relationship with JC and really didn't care about his threats and deal with Fox. I suggested maybe we play the national anthem and start the show because I was sure that most would remove their hats. That wasn't good enough for JC. It was clear he just wanted to mess with Fox. I told JC, you make the announcement and I will alert the local authorities to fend off any possible problems. But there was no way I was going to get on that stage and tell all these Texans to take off their fucking cowboy hats. I told JC if you really want this to happen then you make the announcement. He called us a bunch of spineless punters, an English term for a friggin' loser and then he said "fine I'll do it." I went to building security and got the head of police and let them know what JC was about to do. Like everyone, he thought it was a joke and I let them know this was no joke. They asked about refunds if people wouldn't do it. I told them we would honor all refunds but didn't dare to wind up JC and Fox about that. I was at the bottom of the stage stairs as JC went up to make the announcement with one eye at the back **door, in case I needed** to get the hell out of there. He pulled it off, in that typical JC fashion. I'm sure to this day that's never happened again.*

So, JC went onstage and made an announcement in his best English accent. "Ladies and gentlemen, as you know, there are two ladies in this band—not to mention all the ladies in the house—and I need all of you cowboys out there to don your hats." And believe me, he put every ounce of vitriol he could gather into the word 'cowboys.'

In hindsight, I think it kind of made the band look bad—like they were pompous or something. Although in truth, they had nothing to with it. But at the time, we were all laughing and getting crazy with it. Of course, there was some hooting, hollering, booing, heckling and shouted obscenities from the audience, but that's Texas

JC's English accent made him a prime target for them as well. By this time what was happening filtered around to the whole crew and they all gathered onstage to watch this crazy moment unfold and I was ready for the place to go off!

But sure enough, the majority of the men in the crowd took their hats off but there were many who didn't. Fleetwood Mac fans were loyal, and I think the ladies in the crowd sort of dug it too.

Well, that night in Houston, JC was proud that he had gotten the Texans.

For years Fox and JC continued to haze each other, and in fact Fox got his revenge a couple of years later in San Francisco, but that's another story.

There was a twisted history with JC and Texas. About a year earlier, on Labor Day of 1976, The Mac was in Austin at the Steiner Ranch in for one of the biggest shows in rock history at that time. That was some night. It was magical, and it also turned out to be very scary as well as educational.

All the bands had to be shuttled in to the concert with helicopters. Due to some very poor planning, there was just a little two-lane road into the gig. And close to a half-a-million people were converging on Steiner Ranch. The lineup was England Dan and John Ford Coley, Firefall, the Steve Miller Band, The Band with Robbie Robertson, Levon Helm, Chicago, and Fleetwood Mac to finish the show. A huge great event, by any measure of musicianship.

That night, Fleetwood Mac was electric. As The Mac went on, it was just getting to be sunset, and a huge thunderstorm was rolling in from the horizon. They were playing "Rhiannon," and during the middle instrumental section of the song, Stevie would always do a kind of dance while Lindsey and the rest of the band played a perfect, slow, sultry accompaniment. She always had sort of a beautiful-witch vibe, but that night, as the band broke for this instrumental, the thunder came up as if on cue. For a moment, as usual Stevie was using her powers to summon the forces of nature. The whole sky just seemed to revolve around her as lightning and thunder crashed down with the movement of her hands and the band's music. It was Fleetwood Mac at the height of their powers.

After the show, all the bands got back out on helicopters, but since Fleetwood Mac went on last it was getting near curfew hour where the Helicopters were going to stop flying. On the last trip of the night, Curry, being with

Christine took the seat that was JC's and that just didn't sit right with JC as he knew he would be stuck spending the night with the crew backstage at the festival.

As always, the crews were the last ones out and we were used to it. Unfortunately, they called from the hotel to confirm "Sorry, but everyone who is there will have to drive out or to wait until the morning are done for the night." With a half a million people trying to leave with only a two-lane road JC faced the fact that he was staying the night with us.

JC was getting more agitated realizing he was really stuck, and he wasn't going anywhere. "Fucking Texas assholes! Look at this shit, one fucking road to get a half a million people out of this shithole"

Looking like a caged tiger ready to pounce, he hopped into one of the rental cars backstage. Lenny, one of the truck drivers—a jolly Santa Claus-looking guy said, "I'll go with him so he doesn't do anything stupid." They jumped in the car and JC drove the rent a car right through steel and wood barricade in front of the stage and it broke into a million pieces. Honking the car horn and shouting obscenities to what was left of the crowd, they began picking up speed. The problem was there were fans sitting around and some

Sunday Break Concert. The fence that JC crashed through.

with blankets and sleeping bags waiting for the crowd to subside. We could see JC with a look of terror on his face and big Lenny bouncing around the car yelling at JC to slow down. JC started doing donuts and the car was getting trashed and ready to die.

They pulled back into the backstage area and parked the smoking, dented up, oil smelling car right by the dressing room where Rhyno, Gilbert the other truck driver, and I were sitting. Then two real-life Texas Rangers came roaring up asking "did you see who was driving that car?" I knew this wasn't going to be good and sat silent and as calm as can be; Gilbert just pointed and said "he went that way." Rhyno laughed and the Rangers said, "You think this is funny, son?" Rhyno said "No sir, not at all sir." They were completely livid and you could see they were out to get whoever was driving the car. The Ranger was yelling, "Who was driving this car?" "Someone better speak up or you're all in a heap of trouble. There are people out there in sleeping bags and walking around, and someone could have been killed." There were other Rangers out in the field now, looking around, trying to make sure that JC really hadn't hurt anyone.

Somehow, they found out it was JC and brought him over by the trailer. JC was not the sort of man to be intimidated by anybody, especially a man with an oversized cowboy hat in a uniform. They were in his face, I mean really in his face, and it was obvious something bad was going to go down.

JC started blustering right back at the guy, in his cockney accent. Before long, the Ranger—who obviously didn't suffer fools lightly himself—grabbed JC and handcuffed him and began walking him into the trailer.

Me and Rhyno followed the whole group to the trailer, trying to talk everyone down, trying to defuse and take care of the whole situation that was escalating out of control.

Such is the mantra when dealing with anyone outside the crew on any tour I've ever been on. Rhyno said, "Officer, we'll take care of it. He manages Fleetwood Mac and just had a bad day." Rhyno's reassurances did not work. The Ranger planted a hand in the middle of his chest and pushed him out of the trailer. Uttering a rather ominous parting line, "You don't want any part of this," he closed the trailer door.

We all listened to the commotion—smashing furniture, stamping feet, and the obvious groans of pain coming from JC from inside the trailer. With increasing agitation, we were concerned. What the hell was going on in there? More screaming, yelling, and scuffling around. Jesus! I went and got some of the other security guys and tried to get them to go inside the trailer to try to stop the madness. It was obvious that the security guys knew about the Texas Rangers and their capabilities and said, "just let it be and hope it all works out, its best none of us get involved."

After about a half an hour, the trailer door opened, and the Rangers came out of the trailer sweaty with their chests pumped and their faces looking at all of us to say, "Anyone else wanna fuck around?" With a slow walk they jumped into their patrol car and drove away.

We went inside, and there was JC. The Rangers had beat the living shit out of him. We got him over to the first aid booth to get him cleaned up, and then we just waited for morning light so we could escape the negative atmosphere.

Morale was low that night, as me and the rest of the crew slept on couches in the trailers. As I was trying to go to sleep I was re-evaluating where I was and where I was going. The little boy was creeping up again; I was shaken and just witnessed something I only thought happened in the movies or on TV. I missed home. I missed the innocence of my youth and after what I saw that night, I was afraid. I couldn't sleep until Shark Boy came up with some valium that we washed down with some Jack Daniels. Morning came as it always does and I woke up sick and hungover. The fear and apprehension were subsiding. Amazing what drugs can do. Looking back, I can now see why we did drugs, it was a way to move on.

I went to find JC and he was gone and had gotten out at the first possible moment he could. JC was a strong and loyal man. What he did was wrong, and people could have been hurt or possibly killed. It could have gone really bad not only for JC but The Mac as well. We all dodged a bullet, a big bullet.

I did learn a lot that night. Don't screw with law enforcement officers, especially in the South. Don't think you can control everything, and anything could happen so keep your eyes and ears open at all times. Most of all I learned what I was taught as a child. It's not only about you, think of others and how your actions can affect many.

I shudder to think what would have happened to me if I had not lived through and learned from this edifying Steiner Ranch Sunday Break incident.

My day planner before computers. The Sunday Break show.

The Sunday Break ticket.

CHAPTER FIFTEEN
MILLION DOLLAR BEDS

IN 1977, THE TOURING BUSINESS was now a billion-dollar industry and still growing. At stadium shows we started to see tee-shirts with the Fleetwood Mac's name and logo being sold outside the stadiums filled with hundreds of thousands of people. There were no laws for trademark or copyright infringements, so the clever entrepreneurs were out in full force selling tee-shirts, hats, tour programs, stickers, anything they could. Seemed if you put Fleetwood Mac on dog crap the fans would buy it.

The band saw money slipping away right under their noses, so the decision was to make "Official Fleetwood Mac" merchandise and sell it inside the stadium to the band's fan's.

The whole operation was a perfect fit, like a rock star and a stripper. To handle the whole lucrative merchandise endeavor, we added an old friend of the band to come in and run the merchandise. His name was Phil. His nickname was Roachclip—figure it out. Phil was an old sound engineer and his personality and abilities to get things done allowed him to actually do whatever he wanted. He was the perfect fit for this new position to handle the merchandise.

Roachclip was a character. He would make announcements from the stage that the real merchandise was inside the stadium and not to purchase the bootleg items outside because they were ripping off the band and the official merchandise was better quality. He would say, "you don't want to buy that shit outside, its crap and will fall apart after the first wash. The ink's bad and will give you rashes." It was true, too, except for the rashes part. The official Mac merchandise was good. High quality material with good prints. Of course, the fans were loyal to the band, so The Mac was making more money.

The merchandise was produced in Los Angeles in large quantities and boxes and boxes of merchandise, now coined "swag," were loaded on the trucks with the gear. It grew to be so massive so fast that soon it took twenty feet of a forty-foot truck to accommodate all the swag that now included tee and sweat shirts, caps, stickers, buttons, scarfs and much more.

The piles of cash from the swag were coming in so fast and there was nowhere to put it so it ended up on the crew buses. Roachclip, with security by his side would do one constant loop to each of at least fifteen merch sights collecting piles of cash.

Remember, this newfound way to make money was all new and accounting practices and procedures were not in place until much later. Credit cards were a luxury that was unheard of so the only option to purchase the merch was cash. After shows, hundreds of thousands of dollars in five, tens, twenties, and sometime $100-dollar bills would end up on the tour buses and have to be sorted and counted. Roachclip recruited the truck and bus drivers to help count and sort out the cash because he could trust them. They were normally big burly guys and if anyone would have tried to get to Roachclip they had to get through mountains of driver muscle first. Also, the drivers were loyal and Roachclip would take care of them with cash for their help, and they appreciated it.

After shows and on the weekends, there were no banks open to deposit the huge piles of cash.

It was crazy! Roachclip now had a problem. What to do with all that cash? There was so much cash and nowhere to put it, but Roachclip was creative and had an idea. He decided that the safest place to hide the cash (since at that time the buses had no safes) until he could get to a bank was in the mattresses of each of our bunks. If for some reason someone broke into the bus the last place they would look would be in the mattresses.

The Fleetwood Mac crew Eagle tour bus 1976.

After one of the large stadium shows we all got on the bus and were excited to see we got new mattresses for our bus bunks. Well it seemed we all got a new mattress. They felt and looked new. As we looked closer, we realized it was just new covers, much thicker and with more padding. When we laid in the bunk a noise like crunching potato chips came out of each bunk. With our heightened curiosity we unzipped the mattresses and Lo and behold all the mattresses were filled with cash from the swag sales. I mean hundreds of thousands of dollars. Roachclip found himself sleeping on the bus a lot because of the fear of people breaking in and accidentally finding the cash.

It was truly the honor system; we were literally sleeping on piles of cash. We were such a family I don't think it ever came into anybody's mind to pocket any of the cash except for the occasional Roachclip stipend for stimulants to keep us all going or a good crew meal at a really good restaurant.

The swag business kept growing larger and larger. Everything was selling, the sweatshirts, hats, stickers, buttons, anything that had the band's name on it. It finally got so big every night and there was enough cash to take care of us for the rest of our lives. It became impossible to fit the forest of green paper with dead presidents printed on it in our mattresses.

The merchandise became a problem quickly and it was way too risky to carry so much cash, and something needed to be done. Roachclip finally had an ingenious idea to count the money after each show and give it to either the promoter or the venue in return for a check that you hope wouldn't bounce.

The show loadouts had now changed. Usually at the end of the night the rest of the crew was waiting for the riggers and the lighting crew who were always first in and last out, but now we we're finding ourselves waiting for Roachclip to finish the swag accounting before we could leave.

Merchandise became one of, if not the largest stream of income for many artists for years to come and on most tours It's now a priority and I'm pretty sure road crews today aren't sleeping in million-dollar bus bunks.

Ray and Rhyno in the tour bus. You can see the mattresses in the bunks where we stashed the cash.

CHAPTER SIXTEEN

EVERYONE WANTS A PIECE OF ME

RUMOURS WAS SO HOT AND HAD NOW SOLD over two million records since its release with no signs of slowing down. The tour kept winding its way through the country and into people's hearts.

In late August we finally ended up in Los Angeles, and were booked to play the famous Fabulous Forum, once again on my birthday, but this time I remembered.

So, symbolically, we had moved from the two thousand seat Loyola Marymount University gymnasium to the Universal Amphitheater to the Fabulous Forum in a little over a year.

Fleetwood Mac was now huge. Playing the Forum and being back in Los Angeles offered me time to strut my stuff, show off, and to my let my family and friends know I was a part of Fleetwood Mac and its success. This was my first taste of what was— for my local, San Pedro existence—fame.

One of my favorite shots of Stevie and Lindsey. From the LA Forum 1977. I can still remember the combinations of old school lights Curry and I used to get this look.

Thinking back, we all knew it was big but I had no idea that I would be a part of something so historic as Fleetwood Mac and Classic Rock.

It was exciting. I was proud of my accomplishments, I thought I would really dig the attention. But it backfired. Everyone I knew in high school and their mother called to ask me for tickets. My cousins, my aunts, uncles, everybody. I remember my message machine having so many messages from everyone wanting comp tickets.

I wasn't high enough on the totem pole to get all the comp tickets I needed to handle even my family, and there was no way to get enough complimentary tickets for everyone who wanted them. With a larger crew and now overall entourage the band was gracious enough to give us all four real good seats and an option to purchase seats in the upper sections. I was either going have to shell out the dough to purchase tickets for everyone, or I was going to have to disappoint everyone off by telling them, "sorry, no tickets."

I was so distracted by the whole prospect of being in LA and not disappointing people that it took some fun out of the big homecoming.

I still dearly wanted endorsement for my decisions from my parents. I desperately wanted them to understand the size and importance of the band; Fleetwood Mac was huge and they could come to LA and sell out three nights at a 25,000-seat arena. I felt that this was my chance to prove to them that I had made it, that I was OK, so I offered the four good tickets to my parents.

They didn't want to come to any of the concerts—or for some reason couldn't come. That was very upsetting to me and affected me and my childhood insecurity came blasting into my brain like an atom bomb. Why didn't they want to come? How could they not want to come? Didn't I matter? Was I not important? Oh well, nothing that drugs and alcohol couldn't cure.

On the first night, we didn't have to load-out, so we could stick around and party at the Forum Club that was on the loge at the Forum. The Forum Club was filled to the brim with The Who's who of rock stars, actors, politician and anyone who felt they were important taking credit for The Mac's rise to fame.

A lot of people I knew who bought tickets came to the lighting board that was dead center on the main floor of the Forum to say hello. I was still upset about my parents not coming and I was a little out of sorts indulging in cocaine and drink. I was trying to pay attention and focus on what I was really there for—to make sure that the band looked good and that all the equipment performed well. I was lost in a sea of emotions and too polluted to even enjoy the fact that the shows were some of the best Fleetwood Mac shows they played. It was stress coupled with ego and hurt. One thing I took with me from the 1977 LA shows was to this day I never give or pay attention to anyone for any show who needs or wants tickets. The reasons are simple. You can't take care of everybody and if you take care of a few the others get hurt. It's a no-win situation and it's better to draw a line with the no-comp policy. To this day people know not to ask because they know my answer, an answer I learned back in Los Angeles in 1977.

Opening night's in Los Angeles are always tense and stressful. As far as the band that night, there was some weirdness that went on while the band was onstage. During one of the songs I noticed that Lindsey was more animated and playing with a lot more angst. At one point during the set I actually saw him throw his guitar at Ray because a string had broken. From there it seemed to go down-hill. I also noticed that Greg (Lindsey's new security person) was on and off the stage bringing him messages. I knew there was something going on. I figured it was just another Lindsey/Stevie drama moment. Later after the show I saw Greg and asked him "what's up with Lindsey, man?" He told me that Rod Stewart had been backstage and made a pass at Lindsey's new girlfriend, Carol. Somehow during the show Lindsey had found out. Greg was the one who innocently told him. Greg was new and learning how to navigate the Fleetwood Mac incestuous world. He told me he thought that Lindsey would get a kick out of it. After the show there was no Lindsey, no Carol. Here we go again more Fleetwood Mac drama. At the forum club, Curry told me that during the show JC got a call from the Los Angeles Police that Lindsey's house was broken into and robbed while he was onstage.

All I could say was Oh My God. The fact that someone knew that Lindsey was at the Forum performing and took the opportune time to rob them was just sick and I was starting to see what the cost of success was doing to all of us at very different levels.

Me in 1977 JFK Stadium Philadelphia.

After Los Angeles, we headed up to Portland, Seattle, and Vancouver and across Canada to Calgary and then down through the Midwest again with three last West-coast shows in Santa Barbara and finished in San Diego. More trucks, more buses, and now private four engine prop planes that flew the band and crew.

Fleetwood Mac "Day On The Green." The largest show of 1977.

What was really exciting was the international shows and offers that were coming in. The band was offered dates in Asia, Australia and New Zealand in late November and through December. Fleetwood Mac was on a roll not only in the United States but now world-wide. We were all excited and understood that this wasn't going to be easy but there was no way we weren't going to take advantage of this amazing opportunity. Things were moving so fast we didn't even realize the opportunities coming our way and just went on with life doing what we loved.

CHAPTER SEVENTEEN
LOVE AT THE DRIVE-THRU

IN THE FALL OF 1977 between the US and Far East Tours, I stopped by McDonalds in San Pedro and fell in love. Even though I had sworn never again would I do this.

When I got home, I tried to return my life to some amount of normalcy. But there was some other force awaiting me—to throw me off balance in a different way. I ran across Lisa.

The first time I had met Lisa was when I was a senior in high school. I met her because I had had a problem in PE in high school. I never got along with the jocks. My brother was a jock, and the coaches associated me with him and assumed I would be a jock too. But when

I told them that sports sucked, they turned on me, for some reason. I ended up hitting one of the PE teachers after I overheard them making a decision for my brother without his consideration. He was an amazing athlete. Any sport he did he was great. He held several track records and was a fast runner but really good at baseball. Baseball and track were at the same time in the school year and I overheard the coaches fight for which sport he should do. These coaches couldn't figure out that I was his brother and overhearing all this ridiculous conversation. I told the coaches "why don't you ask Joe and see what he wants." They very abruptly yelled for me to stay out of it and mind my own business. Well when it came to my family it was my business and besides no one fucks with my family. A shouting match soon ensued and one of the mental geniuses finally figured out I was Joe's brother!

He got right into my face and made some bullshit comment that he didn't even think we were from the same mother. That was enough for me. I was blinded with anger and I pushed him. He fell over and the rest of the coaches stood up stunned and all of a sudden, the coach I pushed came after me with a look of rage. The other coaches got to him first and calmed things down and sent me to the office. I was suspended for three days and told never to go around PE or the gym for the rest of my stay at San Pedro High. No problem there except I needed the credits to graduate.

I went to my guidance counselor, Mary Schlatter. She understood where I was at and she understood some kids were made for school and some were not. Mary told me about a little end-run around PE class. She said that PE was required, but it was not required to pass, as long as I got the credits from any other class I could graduate. So, she set me up as a monitor to help her in the guidance office so I could make up the units I'd be losing from PE. So, I failed PE, but got the credits from her. Plus, she slotted the counselor position at sixth period. She also saw my passion for my theater arts over at Long Beach Arena and figured out a way for me to work over at the Long Beach Light Opera and Arena and get school credits. This gave me so many credits that my final semester I only had one class and spent the rest of my day over at the stages in Long Beach. Mary, bless her heart, was really pivotal to my finding my vocation and a huge part of my success.

One of my jobs in the guidance office was to help make sure that the students who ditched a lot got to their class. I would walk them to the class door if necessary. So, it was my job to walk Lisa, who seemed to somehow always miss class. Even back then she had great energy and she always had a smile. She was a little skinny sophomore, but the more I got to know her, the better I liked

Lisa Freels 1975

her. She had a big crush on my friend Nick, as did most of the girls in the school. Almost every day she asked me if I talk to Nick and when could she go out with him. Because of that I never paid much attention to her as a potential girlfriend.

But now I walked into McDonalds, and who should be working there but Lisa. And, my God, she was beautiful! More mature, filled out, and with her gorgeous smile. The attraction was instant and since I already knew her it was all the better.

We started talking and she said she had heard that I was on the road with Fleetwood Mac. I said, "Look, we're doing a show in San Diego. Why don't you come down and check it out?" I didn't think she would show but she did. She asked her mom and dad's permission and they agreed. She and her friend Debbie drove down to San Diego to see Fleetwood Mac.

Since we were all going back to LA two days later as this was the last show of the tour, Lisa and Debbie decided to spend the night in San Diego so they didn't have to drive home in the dark. They got set up in their own room at the same hotel where I was sharing a room with Shark Boy. After the show Lisa and Debbie came to our room, and we all proceeded to party our brains out—drinking and doing cocaine and listening to music. It felt really stupid, actually, being that a couple of years earlier I was walking this immature little girl to her class. But I do remember that I really liked Lisa a lot and felt we had a connection. But I still saw this skinny little sophomore whom I was asked to take care of, and I didn't want to treat her like some road-slut. It would have felt incestuous. So that night, we didn't have sex or even get close to any sexual situations. We just sat up all night and talked about music, home, and I realized what a different world I was actually in. We fell asleep together on a lounge chair out on the balcony. On the other hand, Shark Boy was on a full court press to get laid. When he finally got it into his head it wasn't going to happen, he took his bed and Debbie took mine.

I remember how good it felt to sleep and just hold someone and wake up with no attitude or weird vibe about if I did the right or wrong thing.

When I got back to Los Angeles, I started hanging out with Lisa almost every day. She spent a lot of time over at my apartment because she had left McDonald's and was now at HS Salt Fish and Chips which was close by. She would come over after work smelling like fish and shower at the apartment. And the one day after one of those showers it happened. She was very special.

We had a little over a month to get ready for Asia and Australia. It was going to be a total of six weeks, and I was really excited about not only going overseas but doing things that other bands weren't even thinking about. I was in love again, but still had no hesitation about going on tour. Perhaps I was growing up, or maybe I still just didn't trust women.

But I was in love, and the result of my love for Lisa gave me the five most incredible and important people in my life: my four sons and daughter.

CHAPTER EIGHTEEN

A LESSON IN LOYALTY

THE FLEETWOOD MAC US TOUR was over, and we had a month off before we needed to prep the Far East Tour.

I often stopped by Obie's lighting to see what was up. I ran into Bobby, who was now the general manager for Obie. Obie's was getting really big and he needed to focus on sales and get someone else to run the shop. Bobby and I knew each other from way back in the Long Beach Arena days when he came through with the Southern bands.

Bobby worked with Scott from Continental lighting out of Memphis. Being from the South, most of the guys from Continental worked with all the Southern bands. Bobby's main band had been Lynyrd Skynyrd, who became probably the biggest of the Southern bands with the exception of the Allman Brothers.

Bobby had a dream to move to California and work in music and stay off the road. He had just gotten married to a beautiful woman. His dream arrived when Obie asked him to be the general manager for his lighting company that was growing fast.

Through working at Long Beach, I also knew Ronny Eckerman. Ronny was the tour manager for the Humble Pie tour and now the tour manager for Lynyrd Skynyrd. Ronny and his brother Rodney were also Curry's best friends. One day while at Obie's meeting with Curry to go over The Mac Far East Tour, Ronny came by to say hello.

He told me they were looking for a new lighting director since Bobby was now in California working at Obie's. He asked if I would be interested in being Skynyrd's new lighting director.

To tell you the truth I was very interested. Who wouldn't be? Skynyrd had four guitar players, as well as keys, big bass beats, and pure Southern rock 'n' roll. It was a step in the right direction of where I thought I wanted to be.

I told Ronny I would sleep on it because I had already committed to Curry to do The Mac Australia and Asia tour. Australia, Asia, and Hawaii seemed to be more fun and who wouldn't be excited about six weeks doing the tour.

Now I had a decision to make, stay with Fleetwood Mac and go to Australia and Asia and always be behind

Curry, or be the lighting director and in charge of Lynyrd Skynyrd's lights.

I really wanted to go out and rock with Skynyrd and I knew it was going to be a big tour. Bobby had told me that it was real family, but the band could be very volatile and would have knock-down drawn out fist fights, even onstage. He also said that if I was going to be the lighting director I would be traveling with the band on a private plane and I would just show up to run the lights for the show. No load-in or load-outs, real rock star stuff. But I had already committed to Fleetwood Mac and was afraid to let them, and mainly Curry, down.

I did what I always did when I needed help; I called my friend Jerry for advice. Jerry was also good friends with Ron and Curry and in his father-like demeanor, he explained to me that I should try to find someone to replace me if I wanted to go do Skynyrd. He thought that I should be more of a production manager than a lighting designer. He also thought that going with The Mac to Australia and Asia would benefit me more in that area with room for growth and much more money in the future.

All his words made senses to me but the chord that struck home the most was when he said, "in this business you are only as good as your word." I struggled all night, knowing it was another one of those life changing decisions.

As always, fate stepped in. Curry called me to discuss the situation and there was no way that Curry was going to let me leave Fleetwood Mac. He said we were the first band to ever bring our own gear to Australia and Asia and I was just too important to the gig. I also felt obligated to Curry and The Mac since they were family.

It was sort of a relief. I didn't want to say no to the Skynyrd band and to Ron so this was the excuse to do it. In the end I called up Ron and explained the situation and he was cool and dug the fact that I was loyal to Curry.

Ron ended up bringing a friend of mine from Showco as a temporary until they found a new lighting director.

What happened the night of October 20, 1977?

I was driving home from Obie's and we were prepping the Fleetwood Mac Asia tour. I changed the radio channel in my little red Alpha Romeo when I heard that the Lynyrd Skynyrd plane had crashed in Mississippi en route to Louisiana. The reports were sketchy, but I pulled over in disbelief and found a payphone to call Bobby; I got no answer. I made it home in a state of shock and started to get calls from friends that weren't sure if I took the gig and wondering if I was on the plane. I remember saying to myself "Oh shit that could have been me." I started to think about Ron and the other people who were on the plane. I realized how a simple quirk of fate, or one career decision, could turn into the difference between life and death.

The next day I went to Obie's and saw Bobby. I was quite shocked to see how he was handling it. I know if it were Fleetwood Mac I would have been devastated. Wasn't sure if Bobby was in shock or what but his demeanor was a bit confusing to me.

In the end it came out that the plane had a bad fuel gauge and the pilots ran out of fuel. Ronnie Van Sant, Chris Gaines, Cassie Gains, and the Assistant tour manager Don McKenzie all died in the crash. Arty Pyle (Skynyrd's drummer) crawled over a mile in swamps and bayou with broken legs to get help. Then to my surprise, I found out it was the Convair prop plane owned by Jerry Lee Lewis that we had flown from Santa Barbara to San Diego earlier in the year with The Mac. That night the fog was so heavy in San Diego we finally landed after four attempts by coming in from the ocean instead of the land. A charter experience we'll never forget.

How lucky were we. As much as you want to believe in the "when it's your time theory," you have to wonder why them and not us and why not me. It could have easily crashed when we had flown on the plane and I would have crashed if I had taken the Skynyrd job. Another life lessons. Loyalty!

TECHNICAL REPORT WCUMENTATION PAGE

1. Report No. NTSB-AAR-78-6	2.Government Accession No.	3.Recipient's Catalog No.
4. Title and Subtitle Aircraft Accident Report -- L & J Company, Convair 240, N55VM, Gillsburg, Mississippi, October 20, 1977		5.Report Date June 19, 1978
		6.Performing organization Code
7. Author(s)		8.Performing Organization Report No.
9. Performing Organization Name and Address National Transportation Safety Board Bureau of Accident Investigation Washington, D.C. 20594		10.Work Unit No. 2365
		11.Contract or Grant No.
		13.Type of Report and Period Covered Aircraft Accident Report October 20, 1977
12.Sponsoring Agency Name and Address NATIONAL TRANSPORTATION SAFETY BOARD Washington. D. C. 20594		
		14.Sponsoring Agency Code
15.Supplementary Notes		

Abstract

About 1852 c.d.t., on October 20, 1977, a Convair 240, N55VM, owned and operated by L & J Company and transporting the Lynyrd Skynyrd Band from Greenville, South Carolina, to Baton Rouge, Louisiana, crashed 5 miles northeast of Gillsburg, Mississippi.

There were 24 passengers and 2 crewmembers on board the aircraft. The 2 crewmembers and 4 of the passengers were killed; 20 others were injured. The aircraft was destroyed by impact; there was no fire.

The flight had reported to the Houston Air Route Traffic Control Center that it was "low on fuel" and requested radar vectors to McComb, Mississippi. The aircraft crashed in a heavily wooded area during an attempted emergency landing.

The National Transportation Safety Board determines that the probable cause of this accident was fuel exhaustion and total loss of power from both engines due tu crew inattention to fuel supply. Contributing to the fuel exhaustion were inadequate flight planning and an engine malfunction of undetermined nature In the right engine which resulted in higher-than-normal fuel consumption.

17. Key Words Flight planning; fuel consumption: power loss; fuel exhaustion; lease agreements; operational control.	18.Distribution Statement This document is available to the public through the National Technical Information Service, SpringTield, Virginia 22151

19.Security Classification (of this report) UNCLASSIFIED	20.Security Classification (of this page) UNCLASSIFIED	21.No. of Pages 26	22.Price

NTSB Form 1765.2   (Rev. 9/74)

The FAA report on the Skynyrd crash.
If you look at the tail number you will see it's the same airplane as the one
in the picture we used with Fleetwood Mac earlier in the year.

Us loading on to the Convair 240, the plane that crashed with Lynyrd Skynyrd. I guess I dodged two bullets!

CHAPTER NINETEEN
PALLET SIXTEEN

IN THE LATE SUMMER OF 1977, we all knew Fleetwood Mac was invited to do a tour of Australia and Japan and then finish in Hawaii. Since we were down under it was also decided to play an intermediate stop in New Zealand.

Normally, if a band went on an international tour, they would just rent equipment in the countries where they were touring. But nothing about Fleetwood Mac was normal. Managing themselves, with only Mickey their lawyer and their long time Girl Friday Judy, who ran the day-to-day laborious task of keeping the band on schedule and in line, they asked all of us to look into bringing our full rig on the tour.

In the mid to late 70s the gear in the international markets, other than Europe, were not up to the standards The Mac now were financially in such a good position that they could pretty much control their own destiny.

Fleetwood Mac far
east tour jacket

I believe The Mac's decision and passion to have all of their equipment, their full rig—sound, lights, band equipment, scenery, and the crew, is why they became a legendary band. You don't see that in today's artists. Fleetwood Mac wouldn't settle or compromise and insisted on giving their fans the best sound, lighting, and show at whatever cost. The band trusted us to make it happen, knowing we would make it work not only for the best show possible but financially as well.

Getting the equipment to the other side of the Pacific was the first challenge. To containerize the gear and ship it by boat would have taken too long and we would have to pay rent on all the sound and lights while it was in transit. So, we knew that we were going to have to fly it over, but that meant dealing with airfreight that was way too costly and would be cost prohibitive for the tour to be possible.

Finding the right airline was our first priority. There was a friend of the crew who was a pilot. We gave him a call for some friendly advice. He was not as forthcoming as we thought and cautious with his message. Interested but very guarded he said "yeah, I can get this done for you, but it's a bit risky and I'll have to call in a couple of favors."

The Airline he worked with in his mysterious past was Air America, basically the CIA's airline. Air America had a line on many types of jets from airlines you never would have heard of that could work for our needs. We needed something long range with less fuel stops and configured so it was easy to load our gear. Our cargo was different shapes and sizes than the military gear they normally carried. The perfect jet for us was a stretch DC-8 cargo plane from Trans-International airlines. It had four engines, two on each wing, long-range fuel tanks, and it was made to hold tons of cargo.

Our trucking company Consolidated Freight was brought in to handle the transaction between The Mac and Trans-International Air. Our contact at Consolidated was a guy by the name of Bill—we used to call him Chief because he was a big Native American. Chief was our middleman and handled the charter jet through Trans-International Air.

The plan was, the gear would fly to Sydney, with stops in Hawaii and Fiji for fuel and Pilot rest, then on to Australia. Then Australia to New Zealand and on to Japan, then Hawaii and return to Los Angeles six weeks later. It was a lot of stops, but aviation wasn't as developed and refined back then and even though the DC-8 had the longest-range fuel tanks, it still couldn't make it all the way in one straight shot to Australia.

It was still very costly, and we weren't sure the tour income from shows and merchandise would outweigh the cost of the tour. So, what could we do? Well Chief and Trans International had an ingenious solution, and it was quite a clever one.

For the two weeks we were touring Australia, the gear would be in trucks and we would jettison the DC-8. The plan was to sublease the plane to an Australian beef company that would ferry cattle between Australia and India. The beef company got a huge discount on the jet to make as many runs as they could with the time allotted. It was a perfect way for us to offset our cost of the stretch DC-8.

Now that we established how we were getting the gear overseas, we had to figure out how much gear we were going to bring. The whole crew—lights, sound, band gear and set—put our heads together and came up with the plan. We calculated the maximum amount of our own gear that we could fit on the DC-8 and still produce the quality of show the band expected. For the large outdoor festivals that were booked, we made arrangements to supplement the shows with additional lights and sound from the local companies in each country. We decided to print and manufacture all of our merchandise swag, (that was a big part of the profit equation) in Australia and Japan, so we had more room for gear and avoid import taxes.

Each of us from lights to sound to band gear and all the other ancillary parts of what became the Fleetwood Mac technical puzzle put together with ingenuity, purpose and long hours of planning felt great about our accomplishments. We all knew in our hearts that no other band in history had figured out a way to achieve this kind of an undertaking. We were taking our full rig, our full production on a six-week international tour. With our careful plan in place it was time to execute it and start our adventure.

On November 7, 1977, we all met up at the Hacienda Hotel near LAX at midnight. The scheduled flight time was four a.m., but on this day, I was to get my first (and by no means my last) lesson in the mutability of schedules when you're traveling internationally. We all got to the Hotel as scheduled and loaded into a van for the short ride to Airlift International the freight terminal where our jet was waiting. We pulled through the gate and there it was—our Trans International stretch DC-8. It looked unreal, like a huge plastic model. It was green and white and with the light from the towers on the tarmac the white even whiter and the green even greener. With the whining of the auxiliary power generator getting louder and louder and the harsh smell of jet fuel, our excitement grew as we got closer to the plane.

The first thing we had to do was load up, and I gotta say, this did not look promising. When the trucks rolled up with all the gear, I kept looking from the equipment trucks to the plane to the equipment trucks. It really didn't look like it was all going to fit.

We off-loaded the trucks and laid all equipment out on the tarmac next to the jet. The door was closer to the nose on the right side and was as big as a standard garage door on a house.

We then proceeded to pile everything piece by piece onto fifteen big flat pallets secured by cargo nets to stop the gear from shifting in flight. One by one the pallets were lifted to the door and slid into the hold of the plane. Sure enough, it all fit. Just barely.

We loaded fifteen pallets. Yes, I said fifteen of the sixteen pallets. What about pallet sixteen?

Another clever and money saving aspect of this plan is that the crew would fly on the cargo jet to save airfare. Getting more excited by the minute I couldn't contain myself anymore. Me and Shark Boy raced up the back stairs of the plane and sure enough there it was ... pallet sixteen. Secured onto pallet sixteen were twenty-four first class airline seats. My heart was racing. It started to soaked in. This was it. Pallet sixteen! Our travel cabin, our primitive bare bone capsule for the next six weeks.

They erected a little partition between the gear and us and installed a little convection food warmer and two ice chest

for cold drinks. They did
stock us with plenty of
pre-cooked airline food
and drinks for our trek
across the pacific.

Pallet sixteen.

They were first-class
seats all right, but this
wasn't no passenger jet. No luxury, no ambience. We
were cargo.

All the gear was loaded, and we strapped ourselves in,
thinking that we were all ready to go, but unfortunately
that wasn't the end of it. We ran across a little thing called
avionics, weights and balance. With a DC-8, you have a
tail-stick, which measures the distance between the bottom of the plane and the ground. If the stick touches the
ground, then the plane is deemed to be too heavy in back
and can't lift off.

When the plane was loaded, none of us were in our
seats. When we all got on the plane and in our seats the
tail stick hit the ground: too heavy, we couldn't take off.
So, we all got out of the plane and they loaded us one by
one to try to situate ourselves so that the stick would not
touch the ground. After an hour of unsuccessfully trying
to make that work and them figuring out we would never sit in the same seats or maybe sit at all, they decided
to reload the jet and put some of the light stuff like the
backdrops to the back of the plane and the heavy speakers
over the wings and to the front. We all got off the jet and

assisted them to rearrange the load so we were safe and compliant, and we wouldn't crash.

When it was all done, the sun was up, and we were all very tired and just ready to get underway. We were now hours late for takeoff and concerned about our day off when we landed in Sydney Australia. This was not a great way to begin what was to be a long, long flight.

Finally, we got off the ground and on our way. First stop was Hawaii for fuel and pilots' rest. And naturally, the kick-off for such an exciting tour was an invitation to party. Right? Out came the pot, the cocaine, the alcohol; everything but the dancing ladies. Before we were off the ground we were ripped. For some reason we all felt that doing cocaine on a flight to Australia would be a good thing. We were amped up the whole flight, ready for something to happen. This, I can tell you, is not the right attitude to have when you're strapped into the hold of a cargo plane on a trans-Pacific flight.

We did have one flight attendant … and to our disappointment, it was a guy. Smart move by Trans International though. We got hungry halfway to Hawaii, and the flight attendant readied the food warmer to heat up some of the airline food supplied by Trans International. There was turkey dinners, steak and potatoes, fish, anything we wanted, and it was great we didn't have to stay seated and had the run of the whole cabin.

Unfortunately, every time the warmer was fired up, a bell went off and the food warmer blacked out. Damn! But, hungry and high, we were not going to be denied. We figured we could fix anything, so we set into a process of elimination mode to fix the food warmer. Every time we tried a new solution, someone inevitably said, "we're close." Yeah right, a bunch of drunk and high road technicians trying to fix a DC-8 *in flight*. Then we noticed that every time we tried to make it work and just before the bell went off the plane made a funny little swoon and dip with turbulence.

Oh well, no food so we reverted to more booze and drugs, and the more polluted we got, the more determined we became to fix the food warmer.

After about an hour of us trying to be airplane mechanics, the phone that connected the back of the plane to the flight deck rang. The pilot said, "What in the hell are you doing back there?" By our standards, I gotta say we weren't doing much of anything, and the flight attendant told them we were trying to fix the food warmer so we could eat.

The pilot said, "Well whatever you're doing, you have to stop! You've been repeatedly shorting out the tail rudder and stabilizers!"

After that we finally accepted that we weren't going to eat any hot food. We abandoned the food warmer repair project, ate what we could, drank more, got higher until we all passed out.

Jeez! How would it look to be killed on account of a food warmer?

We finally reached Hawaii where the pilots had to get eight hours of mandatory rest. With no accommodation except hot Pallet sixteen on the jet, we decided to explore the island and score more pot for the long haul to Fiji.

We ran across a moped rental stand right outside the cargo facility and took off on our trek to burn time and find substance for the rest of our flight.

Several hours later, with all we needed in hand and burnt out from the day's activities, we boarded our Jet. The ground handlers, for some reason, nicknamed our DC-8 *"Mololo,"* which means "flying fish" in Hawaiian. We liked it.

With our food warmer now fixed and our stomachs contentedly full, we settled into a comatose state of mind, winging our way to the South Pacific.

Fiji was an uneventful quick fuel stop; we bought a few tee-shirts and got our passports stamped. I for one did get off Mololo just to get my feet on the ground. The water was blue-green, and the humidity was actually welcoming after eight hours of breathing recirculated air inside the cargo bay.

Now another ten hours to Sydney. We realized we needed to be completely rid of all our stash from Hawaii. The Fleetwood Mac reputation of drug use preceded us and we were warned that they would be looking at all of us with a microscope to make sure we weren't holding anything. That wasn't a problem, as we were confident there wouldn't be anything left by the time we landed.

We finally got to Sydney two days after we had begun our journey. The Australian custom officials searched the

The tarmac in Sydney.

plane for drugs, for what seemed hours, but we had made quite sure we had consumed everything. We were high over the Pacific, indeed! We cleared customs and immigration and then we had the tedious task of off-loading our gear off the plane and into trucks. It was actually quite a relief to stretch and use our muscles after being cooped up on pallet sixteen for two days.

The Australian tour went by fast with all the shows completely sold out including fifty thousand people at the Rock Arena outdoor festival at Calder Speed Way outside Melbourne. Now we had the two shows in New Zealand, which meant getting Mololo back and loading her up. Experience is the best teacher and we had it down and the load went fast. We were on our way to Auckland New Zealand.

Now remember, in order to be able to afford the plane to get around the Pacific, we had worked out what

Rock Arena, Melbourne Australia 1977. Little River Band,
Santana, Fleetwood Mac.

at the time seemed like a real genius move. We had sub-
leased the plane to a cattle company while we weren't using it. Brilliant, huh? Unfortunately, we didn't think this
through very well.

When we stepped on the plane to go to New Zealand,
there was a bit of a stench that hit us like a wet smelly
blanket of cow piss and dung.

Before the plane was loaded, Trans International got a
cleaning company to clean the plane out with some industrial cleaner but there still was a bit of smell.

After we loaded the plane it seemed OK, but lo and
behold, once we got up into the air, the air ducts—which

Cows in the DC-8.

hadn't been cleaned—started blowing the stench of methane, cow shit and piss back in on us again. It was really, really bad. Then, condensation started collecting in the vents and dripping down on us: Cow-piss rain fell down upon us.

That 'piss-flight,' as it was soon dubbed, was a five-hour long flight that tested all of our patience and luckily, we had the four day stop so Trans International could properly clean the plane before we had to take the eighteen-hour flight to Tokyo.

On Thanksgiving we were all excited to get on the next leg of the tour—Japan! At the time that most people in the States were sitting down to have Turkey and stuffing, we were reloading the plane in a country where Thanksgiving is not a holiday. We were on our way to the next gig—Narita, Japan, with a fuel stop in Guam.

Much to our relief, the plane had been given a thorough

steam cleaning with all the air ducts and vents cleaned. It didn't smell like cow-piss and shit any longer. Now that was something to give thanks for.

With Mololo, we were always taking off and landing over water. It was so heavy that each time we took off we didn't think we were going to make it off the ground and would have to ditch in the water and each time we landed, we thought we were going to shoot off the end of the runway into the ocean. On the way up, Mololo's engines roared and whined, and we would all shake, rattle and roll our way along. Every time, it was an adventure and we had to pretty much grin and bear it.

It was early evening when we took off from Auckland, I sat, as I always did, next to Trip, the front of house sound engineer. He was fun to sit next to because he had been on a lot of tours and always seem to have the answers. I don't think he was afraid of anything, and if he was, he hid it well through humor. Every time we took off, he would say, "This is the one. This is the time we don't make it. We're never going to get off the ground, we're gonna die like rock stars."

He would look at his $2,000 Pulsar digital watch—which cost about $9.99 now—and time the take-off, saying, "If we don't get off the ground in fifty seconds, that's it. We're dead." We covered our fear with humor. If Trip's countdown actually got up to forty seconds, we would all count off the final ten seconds as if we were going to the moon or heaven itself instead of to the next destination.

Ten … nine … eight … Our voices rising loudly, daring death. … seven … six … five … Trip could have very easily been right, but we really didn't care … four … three … We figured that if we were going to go, this was the way we wanted to do it—in the service of the great god of rock and roll … two … one … And we were up and off the ground, weightless.

We were finally in the air on our way to Japan. About six hours into the flight, around midnight, I started to get antsy. I told Rhyno that I was going to go up and see the pilots. Rhyno said, "How are you going to do that? The jet has fifteen pallets of gear in front of us packed to the gills. There's no way to get up to the pilots."

"I don't know, but I'll figure it out," I said.

I climbed and squirmed through a little trapdoor in the partition between the gear and us. All the gear was piled up from floor to ceiling. It took about forty-five minutes of crawling, stretching, squeezing, and clambering through the sound, lights, music equipment etc. At one point I got stuck. I realized that there was no way to reach anybody and I may be spending the rest of the flight stuck there. I finagled my way and made it to the cockpit. The door was open, and I walked in.

"Hey guys, how's it going?" The pilots were shocked, and I think I totally scared the engineer sitting closest to the door, but they welcomed me. They were astonished that I had been able to get through all the cargo to get to them. Crazy what boredom and some drugs can do.

The cockpit was amazing, and being night time, was all lit up with the lights from the gauges and switches. The surreal soothing red glow of the control panel made me feel like I was on my way to the moon.

I asked the pilots where we were, and the engineer showed me on the map. I noticed we were getting close to the equator and asked them when we were going to cross it. I wanted them to shake the jet so I could joke with the guys "did you feel us go over the equator." Seemed funny then.

They told me it was going to be a bit longer because we hit some strong headwinds from a storm that was burning more fuel than planned. They told me to sit in the jump seat as they hit the fasten seatbelts sign because headwinds and turbulence were just ahead.

I looked through the windshield to the dark sky ahead; it was beautiful. Stars and a shimmer between the moon-lit thunderclouds glowing white and purple like I had never seen. Down below all the lights from island cities dotted the darkness like fireflies.

It was just one of those unbelievable moments that made me realize how far I'd come from my little town of San Pedro. Just think, I could be sitting around the park in San Pedro, drinking beer with my friends and working on the docks, but instead I was in the cockpit of a cargo plane jetting my way to Japan with one of the biggest bands in the world.

After a time, the headwinds stopped, it calmed down

and they turned off the fasten seatbelt sign. Then the engineer told the pilot that with the headwinds we had used a lot of fuel—more than they had expected and there was a small mechanical problem that needed attention.

We needed a place to land to get assistance. They started radioing around to figure out where they could get fuel, but they didn't come up with any definite leads. It was obvious that they didn't want to discuss this any more in front of me. The engineer said, "you better go back and strap in, we're going to have to stop somewhere and get some fuel and take a look at something."

I was too curious to just go back, so I asked the engineer, "What did you find?"

He had made arrangements to go west, out of our way and backtrack to get fuel at a Naval airstrip. The decision was to land at Port Moresby New Guinea at Ward Air Field, a long Navy airstrip that could accommodate a larger heavy jet like ours. It was right next to what is now Jackson Field, the main public airport In Port Moresby.

I was in disbelief as excitement overtook my body. I couldn't wait to tell everyone where we were going. I climbed my way back through all the stuff in about half the time, and I popped back out through the trapdoor. I woke up Rhyno and I told him, "Rhyno, we're going to New Guinea!

He wouldn't believe me at first. "What did you do," he said, "smoke some shit you found in the gear or something?"

Rhyno tells the story this way:

I woke up from a small stupor (that had not been im-posed ALL by me) to see Leo come thru the cargo door. He announced that we were going to land in New Guinea. I laughed out loud and asked him how the hell did he know that. The kid was good at his job, but he did not have ESP.

Leo said, "dude, I made it up to see the pilots and they told me we were running low on fuel and had to land to get more. WE'RE GOING TO NEW GUINEA."

In my head, I was sure he was screwing with us. The fact that he had to navigate a labyrinth of equipment pallets to get to the front was immense. However, within about three seconds after Leo stopped talking my assump-tions were proven incorrect by a call from the pilots. We were told to buckle up.

Bitching Boys, We're, going to New Guinea.

It was morning as we came down out of the sky over a beautiful, lush island. I looked down and could see a coral reef surrounding the island clear as day through the aqua blue green water. We landed on the long remote Navy strip by the hills. There was nothing but a couple scat-tered villages nearby and a small building no more than a grass hut.

The plane was coming in un-usually slow and it felt like we were going to drop straight down and as we touched down, the pilot full-reversed the four en-gines trying to stop Mololo with her engines screaming and her body uncontrollably shaking . We were all real quite but inside freaking out. Maybe this time we really weren't going to make it and we'd run out of runway. The shaking and rumbling made it easy to believe and we ground to a halt with the engines going full reverse like they were going to rip off the wings. We made it and we all wanted to cheer but held back out of fear of looking fragile to each other.

On the ground, even though it was early morning, it was hot and damp. One hundred degrees and very humid. With excitement and curiosity, we opened the back door to see what we could do about getting out of Mololo, but we realized that there was no way of getting out. There was no gangway, no stairs, nothing. But for Christ sake, when were we going to get to New Guinea again? We didn't want to just sit there plus we wanted to get our passport stamped.

As we looked out from the back of the jet, we saw that there were some natives in shabby clothes and loin-cloths standing against the fence of the airstrip. They were mud-men that came down to see the large jet that landed in their backyard. We were trying to get their attention when a neat, proper guy in khakis and an Australian bush hat looking like the guy *from Ace Ventura* drove up. He yelled up, explaining in a traditional English accent that he was a customs official. He said that he would try to find a gangway to get us off the plane but planes this big don't normally come to this strip and it was going to take some time to find something that would work. That wasn't good enough for us. After about an hour of no gangway we decided to figure out for ourselves how to get off the plane.

Chucky, one of the sound guys and Jimmy, the rigger on the tour, managed to get to his ropes in his rigging gear. He figured we could all lower ourselves from the plane to the tarmac.

But, then, just as he was figuring the whole thing out, an old, laughable, rickety truck with the words "Air New Guinea" painted on the side drove up. They positioned it next to the plane, under the door, but it was still about four or five feet short. It was obviously designed to service much smaller planes. One by one, we jumped down onto the platform, down the stairs and planted our feet on the ground in New Guinea.

The Custom guy told us that if we did get off the plane, we had to be very careful.

We really didn't know what he meant by that, but we weren't the kind to pay much attention to warnings anyway.

Once we all got off Mololo, and were standing, the waves of heat from the tarmac rising around us, the customs official returned and gave us another warning. "Whatever you do," he said, "don't give the natives anything. Try not to even talk or communicate with them."

So naturally, the first thing we tried to do was communicate with the mud-men. There was one guy who spoke very broken English who translated. He told us that they

These aren't the actual mud men but this is exactly what they looked like.

were amazed to see a jet this size land. They thought we must be extremely important people—virtually we were gods from heaven.

The customs official, seeing that his vague warnings had not dissuaded us, began to reiterate that we should not give the locals anything or take anything from them. In his nervous, halting sort of way, he was trying to tell us that if we gave them anything, it could create inter-tribal dissent regarding who was "special" and who wasn't.

But we were too arrogant to give a damn about anything that serious, so we immediately started giving out Fleetwood Mac T-shirts and hats, and in turn they gave us spears and a mask. We started making gestures like we were smoking pot, and, sure enough, they brought out their stash that looked like pot, but we weren't 100 percent sure. In turn, we brought our alcohol and the sweet taste of soda.

It was hours before the fuel truck and mechanics showed up to give us the fuel and the parts we needed, but we passed the time pleasantly enough. There was really no such thing as being stranded for us. Home was where we landed and ended up.

We all connected on all levels and soon, the natives were as happy and high as us. They were curious about Mololo and were cautiously waling up the stairs and going in and out the plane to take a look. We gave them cold sodas and rum drinks, vodka drinks that they really enjoyed. We and the Mud-men were having a full-on party.

We were all one happy family sharing our cultural differences, laughs, and love on the tarmac in Port Moresby New Guinea.

Finally, the Navy scored us fuel and finished gassing up Mololo. They also did all the repairs. It ended up being a faulty warning light. We were told that we should get back into Mololo so we could get on to Guam and on to Japan. We were so high it was ridiculous and the looking forward to moving on and getting to Japan.

We started to get all the natives out of the plane, but one big native guy refused to get off. We tried to explain that we were leaving and that he had to go, but he was sitting down and refused to budge. The customs guy, now extremely agitated, said "He says he is tired of this world and wants to go to heaven with you guys."

We all laughed and said, "Let him know that we're pretty sure we aren't headed in that direction."

His tribe was now all around as we had to pry his hands off the doorway to dump him (as gently as we could, but still rather unceremoniously) into the care of the custom official, who seemed very relieved to be done with us.

We got the door closed, and I went to sit down by Shark Boy and Trip. Trip seemed extra nervous. He was always flipping out, but this time he was saying, "You know how hard it was for us to stop? That was with almost no fuel. We've just taken on thousands of tons of liquid fire, how the hell are we going to be able to take off. How are we going to do it?" He was so sure and so desperate, and I was so high, that he even had me believing it this time.

He looked at his Pulsar. We taxied to the end of the runway for what seemed like hours. I remember I was trying to get to sleep so in case we crashed it would all be in my sleep, but I was paranoid and that turned into excitement. The pilots revved the engines full blast. And this time more than usual, they got those engines going and again Mololo was shaking, and the engines' high pitch sounded like women screaming. The smell of jet fuel and oil was coming through the vents. The noise was so horrendous it was a new sound to all of us. Just as it seemed that the whole plane was going to fall into pieces, the pilot let off the brake, and all of our backs shot against our seats and we were off and rolling.

We rolled and rolled and rolled. Sweat was dripping off of us. It was so hot that the air from the vents turned into white streams of water dripping on all of us. I felt that we really weren't going to lift off this time. I thought about the headlines in the local San Pedro paper reporting my demise in a remote landing strip in New Guinea on tour with Fleetwood Mac, and I figured at least that would be pretty cool.

Trip looked down at his watch and reported that we were at forty seconds, and we all started counting down, ten ... nine ... eight ... seven ... six ... five ... four ... three ... At two, the front of Mololo lifted her nose off the ground and soon I felt the relief of that familiar weightless feeling of being airborne. I looked out the window and could clearly see birds flying off the tops of the trees confirming we left the earth.

The air was so hot that Mololo shook violently left, then right, then up. and then left again; as long as down wasn't in the equation we were OK. After about a minute of strong turbulence the ride became smooth and we knew we had beat the odds and the Sky God was smiling on us.

I looked down at the lush green island and the beautiful blue-green water, I felt relieved and realized just how lucky and blessed I was. I couldn't wait to call home and tell everyone what we had just done.

We took on enough fuel only to make it to Guam, where we'd re-fuel for the flight to Japan. If we had filled up Mololo full we would have never been able to lift off out of Port Moresby.

We landed in Guam. The Guam airport was so Americanized with long runways with an unceremonious landing. We stopped at a private terminal and all walked over to a restaurant by the passenger terminal and had hamburgers and French fries—the first American food we had had since we left the states.

We saw the pilot in the restaurant and asked him about the take-off at Ward Field. "It was close" he said, "I'll give you that." He explained how pilots calculate take offs and landings with weights and balances, and we realized we were never in any real danger.

The flight crew were amused by our lack of knowledge and our fantasies of danger and fear and said "we would never do anything to jeopardize your safety. We want to live too!" All the pilots were Air America pilots during Vietnam, and they said they had done those kinds of take-offs and landings a hundred times. That made me feel a little better, but then again, their motto was "Any landing you can walk away from is a good landing."

We didn't need to stay in Guam for the mandatory 12 hours pilot rest because Trans International decided to swap out and give us new pilots for the remainder of the ride to Japan. We thanked them for a job well done and were on our way.

We finally landed at Narita International in Japan. The band members were flying commercial, so the authorities figured that there was no way they were carrying any drugs. But here comes The Mac crew with a DC-8 full of gear. For sure all the pot and cocaine were in there, right? The local representative from the Trans International company got to the plane before customs, and he told us what was about to go down. A complete drug search. He asked whether we had anything even remotely drug-related. We all said no, of course we didn't. Who, us?

When customs got there, they let dogs into the plane, and those Japanese dogs went frigging berserk. They smelled the residue of the pot that we had smoked in New Guinea, and they went apeshit.

So, the customs officials searched all of us, and they couldn't find anything. Then they made us sit on the runway while they unloaded the palettes one by one by one. They made us take apart every friggin' piece of gear. Every speaker. Every light box. Every wardrobe box. Everything you could imagine. And they wouldn't let us put anything back together after they had searched it.

After the search we were a mess. Everything was on the tarmac in what seemed like a million pieces. Being that the Japanese custom officials didn't find anything we figured they were just fine busting our balls.

They annihilated us. What would have normally taken thirty minutes took nearly twelve hours. It was a nightmare. Knowing that we would have to make some adjustments to our equipment in Japan and that the band needed to do press, we had built in a couple of days off before the first show, which was up in the hills of Japan in the small city of Nagoya. But here we were in the middle of the tarmac with every piece of equipment taken apart. We were going to need all the time we could get to put everything back together enough to get it loaded into the trucks.

We were all so tired and just wanted to go to the hotel and go to sleep. I remember saying, "What else is going to happen." Sure enough, the minute I said that, the Japanese rain began falling on us and all the gear on the tarmac.

At that point, the chaos really broke out. Everybody started running. We were trying to cover up all this exposed, sensitive equipment with tarps. Our backdrops were getting completely trashed. The gear got soaked. A true mess!

After we had, at long last, passed customs inspection, they hustled us into waiting taxis. It took four or five cars to get us all to the New Otani Hotel in Downtown Tokyo where we were staying. Japan, here we come.

Japan was as successful as Australia; every show sold out, including the Budokan, Japan's premier venue.

After the Japan tour, we flew to Honolulu for two shows, then on to Maui to do a show that would benefit the Maui orphanage. John McVie was living in Maui at the time and supported a lot of the Maui's charities, including the orphanage in Lahaina.

In the 70s, Maui, mainly Lahaina, was very small and not really developed. There was just a small basically short airstrip that only accommodated smaller jets from Oahu and the other islands.

It was so short, but by now we were used to dangerous landings with Mololo. The pilot assured us again that there was no problem. Looking out the window, the beauty of the island of Maui overwhelmed me as well as the excitement of being on another island in Hawaii.

Again, we came in slow and then we touched down, slammed on the brakes and reversed the engines with such force that I suspected the wheels were going to snap off. Everything that was not bolted down hit the front wall. We stopped at the very end of the runway, and we just all sort of sat there. And sat there. There seemed to be some sort of problem.

It turned out that we had gone so far down the runway that they couldn't turn the plane around. There was no taxi way that far down the runway to get to the gate. Finally, the pilots plan was to reverse the engines and back the plane up forty or fifty feet until they could get the plane to make a right turn to taxi to the cargo terminal. The feeling of Jet engines screaming at full force and going backwards was a feeling I'll never forget.

Anyway, we did the gig, no problem. It was a beautiful location—the Royal Lahaina Tennis Courts—on a magical, warm Hawaiian night. We had a lot of gear and there was no way it was going to fit on the tennis courts. We cut down the show to a small speaker sound system and only used about thirty percent of the lights. Most of the gear stayed at the airport. It was almost like a day off. The show was magical. I was in Maui, looking up at the stars in the Hawaiian sky and listening to The Mac do what they did best—touch people with their music. The post tour syndrome started to set in that night and I had the feeling of "I wish this would never end."

The next day we loaded the plane and the pilots were concerned about getting the plane out of Maui and over to Honolulu to refuel for the flight home back to Los Angeles. *Now* they were concerned!

As much as we loved Mololo we were so tired and burnt out and we all decided to fly home commercial, which was a welcome relief.

Over the years we've had adventurous flights and some close calls while flying around the world. The 1977 Fleetwood Mac Australian/Asian tour was the adventure of a lifetime.

Necessity is the mother of invention and ingenuity and imagination can move mountains.

While reconciling the tour profit and loss, it turned out that the band made more money by subleasing Mololo to the cattle company than the net profits from the actual tour.

I was twenty years old. I and I'm sure the rest of crew will never forget Mololo and the Fleetwood Mac air-circus of 1977.

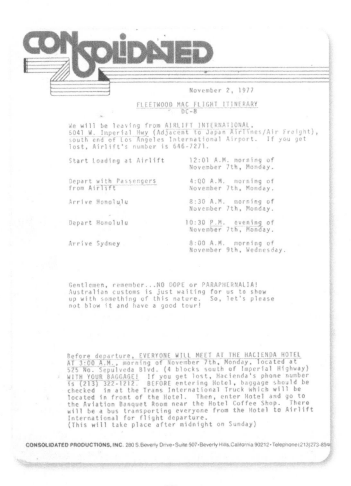

CONSOLIDATED

November 2, 1977

FLEETWOOD MAC FLIGHT ITINERARY
DC-8

We will be leaving from AIRLIFT INTERNATIONAL, 6041 W. Imperial Hwy (Adjacent to Japan Airlines/Air Freight), south end of Los Angeles International Airport. If you get lost, Airlift's number is 646-7271.

Start Loading at Airlift	12:01 A.M. morning of November 7th, Monday.
Depart with Passengers from Airlift	4:00 A.M. morning of November 7th, Monday.
Arrive Honolulu	8:30 A.M. morning of November 7th, Monday.
Depart Honolulu	10:30 P.M. evening of November 7th, Monday.
Arrive Sydney	8:00 A.M. morning of November 9th, Wednesday.

Gentlemen, remember...NO DOPE or PARAPHERNALIA! Australian customs is just waiting for us to show up with something of this nature. So, let's please not blow it and have a good tour!

Before departure, EVERYONE WILL MEET AT THE HACIENDA HOTEL AT 3:00 A.M., morning of November 7th, Monday, located at 525 No. Sepulveda Blvd. (4 blocks south of Imperial Highway) WITH YOUR BAGGAGE! If you get lost, Hacienda's phone number is (213) 322-1212. BEFORE entering Hotel, baggage should be checked in at the Trans International Truck which will be located in front of the Hotel. Then, enter Hotel and go to the Aviation Banquet Room near the Hotel Coffee Shop. There will be a bus transporting everyone from the Hotel to Airlift International for flight departure. (This will take place after midnight on Sunday)

CONSOLIDATED PRODUCTIONS, INC. 280 S.Beverly Drive • Suite 507 • Beverly Hills, California 90212 • Telephone (213)273-894

CHAPTER TWENTY
HOME FOR THE HOLIDAYS

THE FLEETWOOD MAC WHITE ALBUM and *Rumours* album tours were now over. In all we had done 291 days on the road. Eighteen countries. Close to every state in the nation. Millions of miles. Countless shows, countless amounts of alcohol, pills, and lines of coke. Countless laughs, countless tears. Countless memories and no regrets.

For almost two years we were running hard and now it was coming to an abrupt halt. I was packed down with souvenirs from the Far East Tour. Silk kimonos, small TV's, spears and a mask from New Guinea. And, of course, an ego that needed its own jet to fit on.

I was on top of the world. Two things became very apparent on the way home. First, where was I going to live, second, what about Lisa, were things going to be the same, a lot had happened since I was gone.

I was excited to see my family and my insecurity was still bubbling under my now confident rock 'n' roll persona and I needed to prove to them all that I was something, that I was OK, and most of all that I was successful. My heart and mind were battling again but together they came up with a plan. The best way to love and show love was to go crazy and spend lots of money on people. The perfect plan! Buy everyone expensive gifts to make them feel loved and at the same time show them I was rich and successful. Perfect!

New TV's and a refrigerator for my grandparents, new dining room set for my mother, new shortwave radio for my father, big stereo for my little brother, expensive jewelry for my sisters and on and on and on.

Money was no object. I was making a lot of it. I was never one for saving or investing because I loved what I did. It wasn't work; it wasn't a job. I was getting paid for having fun playing in this ecosphere called rock 'n' roll and the world was my playground.

Old habits die hard and to this day, I believe in living life like there's no tomorrow. I believe that because it's true.

First night home I decided to stay at my parent's house. I called my mother and of course, she did it up: breaded Sicilian steak, pasta, everything you could think of. The little boy in me came instantly back. As we sat at the table we talked about the tour, family, and what was next and what were my plans. I told them I wanted to keep on doing what I was doing and that I like the travel. I remember my father saying, "you look thin. Are you taking care of yourself?" Lying through my teeth I said of course, it was nothing but the best out there. "What are you doing with all the money you're making? "You know it's not how much you make but how much you save." "It's fine, Dad." Lying again. I never kept track of how much I made, what I spent, what I was owed, I did know I took a lot of advances while I was out. I never balanced my checkbook. One thing I did have, and not sure how I got it was a Gold American Express card. The worse thing in life, a karma card! I didn't even know how the damn thing worked. All I know is it made me a big shot and it worked everywhere I went. But reality was soon to hit hard. Very hard.

Then my mother looked over and said she was in the store and people in line were talking about Fleetwood Mac. One woman said "there's a boy here in San Pedro that works for them." Not knowing that my Mother was there and who she was, the other women responded and said yes, I heard it's the one of the Rossi boys, I hear he's strung out on dope."

"Is this true?" my mother asked me. I laughed and assured her all was OK. Now, later in life and with children of my own, I can only imagine how she felt and how it must have hurt. Again, I assured her "please don't worry." Lying again I said it's impossible to do my job and be high. My father looked at me and said, "look if there's a problem you can come to us, just be honest. We taught you the difference between right and wrong and you're a man now but you're never too old to talk to your parents." I promised them I would if I ever needed to.

I parked my Red Alfa Romeo GTV Spider coupe in my parents' garage. The next day as I backed it out, I noticed the front panel was damaged. I ran into the house outraged. Hey what happened to my car? Who drove it? "Oh yes," my mom said, "your little brother knew you were coming home so he wanted to wash it for you. He backed it out but as he was washing it the brake released and it rolled and hit the wall." I was pissed but how could I be? It's not like someone took it for a joy ride; he was trying to do something nice. When I saw him later after school, he told me what happened and how could I be mad. He felt badly. But what I realize is how easy it was to fall right back into the Familiga Italian Catholic forgiving role that was one hundred and eighty degrees different from my other life in rock 'n' roll. My good ole friend Covelli set me up to get the Alfa Romeo fixed and oh shit, I was forced to drive my new Lotus Esprit that was stored at the lotus dealer in Long Beach until the Alfa was repaired. All was good in the world.

I did get around to doing all my financing and to my surprise I had a lot of money.

I was twenty years old. Based on my old pay stubs I was making a base pay of $750 dollars a week and $250 dollars for every show. On top of that I was getting $30 dollars a day Per Diem for living expenses. For the Fleetwood Mac Far East Tour in November and December 1977, I made $7,500 dollars. That equates to $32,000 In 2019! I had very limited expenses like car insurance and yes that new shocking American Express bill. I soon learned about auto insurance when it cost me $550 to fix my Alfa with this new thing called a deductible. My American express bill was a bit higher than $2,000 and deciphering the charges was entertaining. One of the Geisha houses we frequented in Tokyo was billed as a noddle shop with a bill big enough to feed a village. I also had to learn about income tax. Since I set up my own corporation, I was responsible for not only corporate tax but my personal taxes as well.

Nonetheless, I gave myself license to spend, spend, spend—not only because I wanted to do nice things for people, but also it validated me. The underlying lesson that I did learn through all of this is that the gift of giving and seeing people light up was the greatest gift of all.

Of course, my father's lecture was stuck in my head: "It's not what you make but what you save."

Christmas was right around the corner—one of the holiest days of the year. Well, sacred wasn't my focus. Christmas became the grand stage for me to show I had arrived.

I was so looking forward to the holiday. My family's great food, all that was good when I was young. We usually gathered at my grandparents or one of the aunt and uncle's for the traditional seafood dinner Christmas eve and then somewhere else for Christmas day. The newest development now was Lisa. I decided to bring her into the family and she brought me into hers. Two completely different worlds. One very traditional Italian and one completely Americana: material possessions and it's all about money.

When I met her family, it was like the dysfunctional Brady Bunch on crack. *Nine* brothers and sisters! Her father was a Marine, very confident, rich, arrogant, and most of all protective, not so much toward Lisa but he had a strong "I'm in control and don't fuck with that" vibe. He wanted to make sure I knew who was in charge. He saw the cars, heard about the whole rock 'n' roll thing, and took a dislike to me. Looking back, shit, I wouldn't let my daughter date me either.

Her mother was nice but overwhelmed (who wouldn't be with nine Children). She was also very doubtful of our new relationship. When I first met them, I knew instantly this is not what they had in mind for their little girl.

The brothers and sisters were all very cool. It took me a while to get to know them. I only really knew Lisa's older brother Michael from school.

As I sat there at the HUGE eight-bedroom house in the prominent section of South Shores the rich part of San

Pedro, which was right on the water, I immediately wanted to let Lisa's parents know that I was ok, and she was going to be fine. The best way to do that? BRAG! Boy was that the wrong move, especially for her Dad. All the conversations became about money and stuff. Cars, Jewelry, material things, you know, manly things. He hated to see someone so young doing better than him and I loved to fuck with him. I would pull a wad of hundred dollar bills out of my pocket and ask if he had change and watch him turn green with envy. I always loved picking up his daughter in a brand-new red Lotus Esprit sports car.

But then I figured out where I could best him: travel. I started to talk about all the places I had just gone, Japan, Australia, New Guinea, and he couldn't top that.

Christmas came and went, and my big Italian family loved Lisa and we were cruising into New Year's and a brand-new 1978.

CHAPTER TWENTY ONE

1978 AND THE SUMMER SAFARI

WHEN I CAME OFF THE ROAD at the end of 1977, I was on the top of the world. I had earned a lot of money— beyond my wildest dreams. I had done things that I had never dreamed of doing. Gone places that I had never dreamed of going.

In 1978, there was one band pushing the limits of what lighting could do to express emotion, accompany the music, and create a spectacle in rock 'n' roll. Three friggin' words: Electric Light Orchestra. I mean, these guys put the concept of lighting stage and scenery right there in their name. They were one of the bands in the late 70s that put a lot of theatrics in rock 'n' roll.

Marc Brickman, who was the lighting designer for Bruce Springsteen and a friend who I saw around the industry since my days at Long Beach, told me that ELO was getting ready to put out a new record—a massive double record called *Out of the Blue.* Currently on the job was a young brilliant lighting designer from San Francisco, named Steve Bickford. Obie's had got the tour and everyone at Obie's was worried about how they were going to work with the guy. They needed someone to baby sit him, but it had to be someone who really knew lighting as well as someone who had a lot of patience. So, I got the call.

The first project on the table was to film a couple of videos, including the first single, Turn To Stone and the song Wild West Hero. They were going to rehearse for two weeks and get the lighting ready for the tour, and then they would shoot the video during the last days of rehearsals. They would then use the lighting set-up designed during those rehearsals for their world tour.

ELO's Wild West Hero video we filmed with
cowboy Monty Montana. At the end of the video,
Monty lassoed Jeff Lynn.

I worked with ELO back in my Long Beach days. They opened for Deep Purple and came through on their own headline show. I knew that working with ELO and Steven would be an incredible learning experience—intense and creative. I had to do it.

There were cellos and violins and the whole nine yards. I had been listening to ELO since high school, so it was a real gas to work with them. I was thrilled all over again to be working with one of my musical heroes.

ELO was going to Asia, but before that, they wanted to do a couple of warm-up shows, so the obvious choice was Hawaii. Sounded good to me. A couple of shows in Hawaii, just what the doctor ordered. They didn't want to take a lighting rig to Asia, but they did want to haul it to Hawaii. We put together a rig from Obie's that would work, and we put it on a ship to do the shows. From the fifth to the seventeenth of January, I was in Honolulu doing shows with ELO.

After the gigs in Hawaii, the band packed up and went on a two-week tour of Japan, and I went home to Los Angeles, waiting to see what was coming up next.

Then I got another call from Steven asking me to go and set up the lighting rig before he and the band got to London to rehearse. I knew the rig and design, and he knew if I were on the job, everything would be set up correctly. So, I was off to Europe.

I grew through the whole ELO experience. I was gaining knowledge, confidence, and mainly friendships. It was a self-discovery to the tenth power. I was climbing to the stars looking down at the world realizing it was mine for the taking. There was no stopping me.

My ELO tour pass.

While I was in Europe, I got a call from Obie. He told me about a gig called the California Jam 2 (the first one had been in 1974) at the Ontario Speedway in Southern California. On the bill were Aerosmith, Foreigner, Santana, and a bunch of other real big bands. I also heard that Stevie was going to play with The Mac's old guitar player Bob Welch who was also on the bill.

Cal Jam entailed installing high-voltage power lines for the spotlight and sound system sound delay towers that ensured people in back could hear, as well as power for the stage lights and sound and all the portable dressing rooms for all the band and crews. For me, Cal Jam 2 was a perfect way to be working in the business and be at home and make good money.

The first thing we needed to do for Cal Jam was a site plan for how the whole thing was going to lay out power-wise. For something this big and complicated, a plan was the key. They sat down with an aerial map of the

Ontario Speedway, and they figured out where we were going to put the stage and the trailers that would serve as dressing rooms. Then we worked out how we were going to power it. We decided to draw power from a high-voltage scoreboard and transform for the stage and dressing rooms. These were all pretty challenging tasks, and I guess that's why they called a lot of us guys including Covelli and Shark Boy. We all had a reputation for being hard workers and thinking on our feet. We worked hard, and all of us didn't require a lot of sleep, so we fit the bill. After careful planning and we were ready to power up the newest coolest city in Southern California, California Jam 2.

It was like a little tour. We had to be on-site at the Ontario Speedway from March 5 to March 20. Of course, setting up this gig demanded long days and long nights, but it wasn't much of a hardship. They had set up a bunch of really nice big motor homes for us to stay in. Catered food, lots to drink, and the drugs were flowing. Every night we would have a nice dinner, drink, get high, and tell road stories. The first version of liars club.

The show ended up attracting about three hundred thousand people. It was really the place to be if you liked Rock 'n' roll. The show was truly one of the biggest rock events of the 70s.

Experiences like Cal Jam 2 were just everyday life for us. We never thought about the historic value and that we were creating events that would end up in the rock 'n'

roll history books. There were no schools, no classes. All of us, the tech crews and people that perfected live music and tours in the 1970s were great at a lot of things, but we were masters at getting things done. We just went out and made it up as we went along and created industry standards that are still in place today.

Those first few months of 1978 had been pretty intense. ELO to Cal-Jam, Europe and back. After my coordination skills came to life at Cal Jam, I was being requested by bands not only for lighting but for stage management as well.

This was a big step up in responsibility. It was no easy task to be the head electrician for the California Jam at the

The sea of humanity at festivals in 1970's rock n roll.

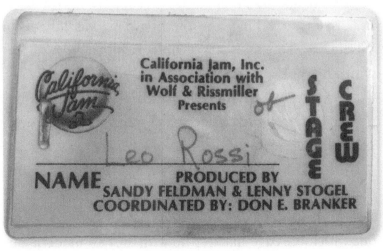

My Cal Jam II Pass.

age of twenty. I wasn't even old enough to legally drink.

The winter left and the spring was full of local gigs and time off to travel and spend money. There was talk about The Mac going to Russia and we all gave our passport and personal information to obtain visas.

Fleetwood Mac was in the middle of recording a new record at the Village Recorder. The record was supposed to take six months but that wasn't going to happen.

The Russia project fell apart after Bill Graham sort of punked our plans by offering the Russian Government Bob Dylan, Santana, Eddie Money, and a couple of other bands.

With touring on its mind Fleetwood Mac took a break from recording and decided to play some of the new songs live and make a little cash before the long break to finish the record. So, Fleetwood Mac's Summer Safari was booked.

We set up and prepped the tour in late May and re-hearsed in early June, and the first date was July 16 in Wisconsin. The tour was mainly large stadium shows with a few arena shows in between.

Rumours was pretty well played out at the time, but the tunes were so classic and so beloved that it was fine to keep playing them.

When the band came back together, Lindsey had changed his personal style a lot. It was obvious that he wanted to scrap the old Fleetwood Mac fashion for a new one with more edge and keep up with the new modern music trends. In my opinion his girlfriend Carol had a lot to do with it. He had sheared his hair short and was wearing more vibrant clothes. This, by itself, is not much of a big deal, but when I heard the new material, I began to understand that these external changes were symbolic of other kinds of changes he was going through. He was influenced by bands like the Clash and other edgy punk bands.

Musically, he was stretching out a bit and getting into what he believed should be the new direction for Fleetwood Mac. I remember when the band was meeting near the end of the *Rumours* tour, Lindsey was vehement saying, "at this point the scene around the band has become bigger than the music, and if we don't change it up, we will fail. We will never make or top *Rumours*." Being the driver of the production of the music for The Mac, there was a sensitivity to the way Lindsey was going to produce the songs and influence the writing style of Christine and Stevie.

So, rehearsals for the Summer Safari shows were pretty intense. The other members of the band didn't necessarily like the way it was heading. Mick was definitely into it, because he was into the idea of change and he had a lot of trust in Lindsey. John

Fleetwood Mac Summer Safari all access pass.

probably didn't think about it too much either way; he was busy with his outside activities—mainly sailing on his new yacht. But Stevie definitely had some ideas about it. She was questioning, "Where are we going with this band?" And Stevie wasn't quite about it and was showing her strength. So many big-time managers were looking for new clients and the dollars that came along with that were filling her head with the idea that she was the driving force of Fleetwood Mac and the band couldn't go on without her.

In my opinion and observation, the summer of 1978 is where the culmination of all the existing and new problems came to the surface and things got complicated. You can read all the truths and untruth of the many Fleetwood Mac stories. To me, I was witnessing the break op of a family, my Fleetwood Mac Family. Well maybe not a breakup but for sure the menagerie was shattered.

The Summer Safari was going well. The shows were sold out and even though the band seemed to be at odds. All the adverse energy empowered the music and they didn't miss a beat and the shows were amazing.

One date that stands out to me was July 28, Rich Stadium, Buffalo. It's when I witnessed my first real glimpse of the power a mega band like Fleetwood Mac had, not just on the

Buffalo Rich Stadium
ticket $12.00

stage but off. Music was like a bratty stepchild that had so much power and it pissed off big brother and the establishment.

It had been a long day. We loaded in, and we were taking a little break backstage. JC, Wayno—the band's head of security, and I were standing at the top of the ramp of the stadium between two of our trucks. Every once in a while, Courage would pull some of us aside and give a little hit of cocaine he carried around in a vial. It must have held at least an eighth ounce of cocaine. He pulled me and Wayno aside and said hey you want a toot. Of course, I obliged as he put the spoon up to my nose with a large quantity of the white powder.

All of a sudden, I looked up, and I saw a couple of New York State cops standing there. Seeing what we were doing they threw us all up against the trucks and handcuffed us. They started interrogating us about the cocaine, and searched all three of us, but no one was holding but JC. They told us we were under arrest and going to be taken in.

Naturally, JC was a bit belligerent. I was quiet. I was yet to hit 21, so I was still a bit scared thinking that we were going to be

Me and my good friend Wayne "Wayno" Cody in Maui 2015. He was head of security for Fleetwood Mac. We remained good friends until his passing in 2018.

locked up and how it would hit the news back home and how my parents would feel. When Courage chose to talk, he had a slightly different attitude. JC was a proud Englishman. As a matter of fact, he grew up as the heir to the John Courage Ale fortune. JC always felt he was above the law, even after what happened in Texas.

JC stood up to the cops and told them, "You can't arrest us. You're not going to do nothing to us ... .not a fucking thing." The cops looked at him and then looked at each other with a look like, "Who the hell is this guy?"

JC said, "You can run us in, but that wouldn't be a very smart idea."

"Yeah, why not?" asked one of the policemen.

"Look, here's the deal," Courage answered. "I manage this band; nodding at me he said "he's the production manager;" nodding at Wayno, "and he's the head of security, and they sort of need us to do the show. If you turn your back and take a peek into that stadium, you'll see that there are over 100,000 people waiting for the show to start. Now, if you arrest us and take us all in, who's going to run this show? I guarantee you, if you run us in the band won't go on. And if this band doesn't go on, (in his bad American accent to mimic the cops) you better call in all your buddies cause you're going to have the biggest fucking riot this county has ever seen."

The cops said, "Yeah, you think so, huh?"

JC said, "I guarantee it, because we'll just have someone go onstage and say, 'Due to police action, the band will not be able to perform tonight.' Fleetwood Mac has very loyal fans. They will not take kindly to this news."

He was just being the typical cocky Englishman. I was kind of thinking that he was only making it worse for himself and us by threatening the cops like this. The policemen huddled, and I felt a glimmer of hope. I looked at Wayno and said are we going to get away with this?

When the police came out of their conference, they went back over to JC and said, "So you're in charge of this whole mess, huh?"

He said, "Yep I am."

They took the big vial of cocaine, threw it on the ground, and stomped on it. Then they looked at us and said, "Look, we're going to let you go, but you know what? When you're done here, leave this town, and we never want to see you again, and if you so much as run a red light, you're dead."

JC, arrogantly with English pride said, "thanks officers, and we'll make sure we're on our best behavior."

As the police were walking away one looked back at us and shouted, "Don't be so goddamn stupid next time, you aren't always going to find guys who are so lenient." Boy was I relieved. My adrenalin was racing through my body and I felt like I'd just ran a marathon. JC took it like just a bump in the road of his day.

You can bet that for the rest of the day I was looking over my shoulder. I told the rest of the guys what happened to us and told them to flush and get rid of

everything, even an aspirin. We were all on our best behavior for the rest of the day and night.

We did the show. Everyone was happy. We loaded the
gear out and as promised they followed us all the way to
the state line until finally their lights faded out of sight.

Now flash forward thirty-five years, and I am the tour
director for the Beach Boys 50th Anniversary Tour. We
were headed to Calgary to play the prestigious Calgary
Stampede. For some reason I decided to ride with the crew
that night on the tour bus and instructed the driver to not
cross the border at the famous customs training crossing
at Sweet Grass Montana. But for whatever reason, he did
anyway. For years we had been making runs in and out of
Canada and one thing for sure was if possible, you never
cross into Canada by way of Sweet Grass. Sweet Grass is
a nonpopulated area where there wasn't much going on.
You may as well have been on Mars. Sweet Grass is where
all new custom agents were trained by a few veteran agents
who spent as little time in Sweet Grass as possible.

We arrived at the border at six-thirty a.m. with the
newest green Canadian border agents using us to train. All
three buses were lined up ready to do what we have done
hundreds of times before. I learned from one of the border
agents that luckily all the trucks with all the Beach Boy's
equipment passed through hours earlier and were cleared
so at least the trucks were cleared and on their way.

The agents brought out their drug-sniffing dogs and
lo and behold one dog hits an open bus luggage bay and

lets the agent know it's found something. Ordered to un-load and search the bay, the agent found some pot in a laundry bag of one of the crew. Game on!! All the buses were off-loaded, and all the crew lined up for interroga-tion to match all the luggage with its owner.

Now ten-thirty a.m. time was going on and on and on as the agents now boarded the buses and were doing their very thorough search under seat cushions, bunk mattress-es, any hiding place where the veteran agents found con-traband with previous bands.

Very concerned and conscious of time I suddenly had an idea. I asked to speak to the head Custom agent. They obliged, and I asked if I could speak to him in private.

Thinking back thirty-four years to that fateful day in Buffalo, I decided to pull a page out of the JC playbook minus the arrogance. I explained to the agent that if the riggers and lighting guys (first things in everyday) don't get moving soon I would be forced to cancel the show and there could be possible civil unrest and I'm sure riots that would affect a lot of innocent people in real bad way and blemish the Beach Boys 50th Anniversary Tour that they didn't deserve. needed the buses to move by eleven-thirty a.m., or I would have to make the call to cancel the show. Lucky the trucks were already through. If they were be-hind us, they would have stopped and searched the trucks too and we would have never pulled off the show.

I explained that I would stay behind with the one bus that was tagged and the perpetrator and we could handle

Me with the Beach Boys crew 2012. This picture was taken
right before the border stop in Sweet Grass.

this without any possible negative ramifications up at the
Stampede.

He got the logic and was very understanding. He
went to speak with the other agents and let me know that
three other crew members had violations that wouldn't
allow them into Canada. One for a DUI, one for an illegal
crossing into Canada on another tour, and one (believe
it or not) a pending attempted murder conviction in Las
Vegas. Now I thought with these new findings we were
done but to my surprise he agreed to let the two buses go
and keep the third and not allow the marked crew members in to Canada. We put all the legitimate crew on the
two buses and they were on their way.

After the third bus was cleared to go, I rode with the
four rejected crew members and got them a rental car to

drive and meet us in Seattle. I headed north to Calgary with only me and the bus driver to meet up with the rest of the tour.

Arriving at the Stampede in Calgary the rest of the crew had let all the band know what happen and what a genius move and how it was handled and they were appreciative although all four crew members were let go given the Beach Boys' zero tolerance policy.

I smiled and thought back to that fateful day in Buffalo, 1978, and my old friend JC.

After Buffalo, we went to Philly for some shows at JFK stadium. JFK stadium was actually a pretty cool smaller, older stadium; easy to work and was slated to be torn down later in the year and we were the last big stadium show before its demise.

We were setting up at JFK in Philly and, I don't remember who told me, but word was buzzing around that Lindsey had a stroke and was in real bad shape. We were told the show might be canceled but to keep working. As in all Fleetwood Mac incidents the rumor mill was spinning fast and hard. Late afternoon I was in the production office and I heard Rhyno say to the promoter that we need an ambulance and doctor on call all day and all night backstage. I asked what happen and he told me the Lindsey had had some sort of a seizure and had collapsed on the floor but he seemed to be OK for now and they ruled out a stroke and it was just exhaustion and lack of rest.

As the tour rolled on, Lindsey wasn't getting any better and we were now cancelling two shows at the Capital Center outside of Washington DC and Pittsburg at the Civic Arena. The shows were rescheduled and now it was anybody's guess how the rest of the tour was going to work out.

We ended up in Cleveland, where we were going to try to do two Stadium shows, one on August 5 at the Cleveland Municipal Stadium. We loaded in very early morning on the four, and that morning, we were still hearing that Lindsey wasn't feeling very

The Mac Cleveland show shirt.

well, but we set up anyway and tried to do the show.

We set up, and they opened the doors for the all-day event. All the bands including J. Giels and the Cars played. I went out to the soundboard to talk to Trip and make sure everything was OK, when we got the call through the intercom that said that Lindsey had had another seizure backstage and we may have to cancel the show.

Now, there were 80,000 people in the stadium. And, since both Trip and I had been through Cleveland before, we knew that it could be a pretty hostile crowd—especially some of the people that were there for J. Giels and the Cars.

Trip said that the worst place we could be was standing on top of the sound towers. The crowd could easily push the thing over if they got really crazy. We started to make our way off the tower and backstage before anyone got onstage to give the crowd the bad news.

We started walking through the crowd—which was difficult because the stadium floor was covered with 30,000 people huddling together. We got about three-fourths of the way there, and we started to get really nervous. Trip said, "Look, take off your stage pass and give it to someone. If they make the announcement, and someone sees us with our stage passes, we're going to be targets." Good advice!

I looked up and saw JC on the stage, and he made the announcement. The thing that had taken so long was the arrangements for when the band was going to come back to make good on the show. Without an actual date when they could come back, the crowd would have really gone apeshit. They figured out that the band could return on August 26, and JC went onstage to make the announcement.

Sure enough, the first thing I noticed was the crowd looking around for some object on which to take out its frustration. A hostile larger crowd is scary shit. Stampedes are like title waves of rock coming at you unexpectedly.

We got to the fence and stage door, and thankfully, the security guy remembered us, because we had been wandering in and out all day. He let us backstage, and as I went out onto the stage, I saw people in the crowd ripping up everything they could. They broke up the chairs and threw garbage as they screamed and hollered. They threw so much stuff up on the stage it looked like a dump. A full-on riot was breaking out and none of us knew how to deal with it. One thing for sure was if we were out in the house it would have been bad.

JC got back on the mic, and started telling the crowd, "Please stay calm. Let's not get crazy. This is a medical matter. It's not like we don't want to play. Lindsey is sick, we promise we will be back real soon, please stay calm."

But it was no use. The frenzy just kept escalating. I looked into the crowd, and I saw people going crazy. I saw people climbing up into the towers, now full of security to protect the gear. The thought that Trip and I had just been in the tower was truly chilling. I imagine that if Trip hadn't told me to take off my stage pass, we probably would have gotten beat to hell.

This behavior lasted for more than an hour before the police began to clear everyone out. We waited for a while longer—until we were just about sure that we were safe. But then, as we started loading out, I started to hear a lot of ruckus in back of the stadium. I headed to the ramp out back, and I saw a huge crowd on either side. They were throwing stuff and booing. Then they started actually shoving and rocking the buses back and forth like they were going to tip them over. They couldn't actually get the buses over, but they did end up tipping over a couple of small catering and utility trucks. They were lighting garbage cans on fire. I mean, it was a full-on, honest-to-goodness riot. It was truly demonstrative of the power of an angry mob.

After about two hours the stadium and its surroundings finally cleared out. It looked like a war zone. There was shit everywhere. Chairs were all broken up and strewn all over.

We decided to head back to DC to see whether we could pull those two shows off that we canceled. The morning of the sixth, we set up again in the Cap Center. The doctors wanted Lindsey to cancel the tour, but Lindsey said he was feeling better and wanted to do the shows. They came to an agreement that Lindsey would sit on a stool during the show and not exert energy so that's what he did. And you know what? He pulled off both shows pretty well.

This was what Fleetwood Mac did. They fought through everything to please their fans. And after the show, we all went back home for some well-deserved rest.

After the two weeks off to make up the show we went back to Cleveland. We added some more dates around Cleveland to make up the losses of the cancellations and pulled it off—making good on our commitment on August 26.

With the rescheduling we ended up on the road for my twenty-first birthday and I wouldn't have had it any other way. Were in Birmingham, Alabama, for one of the last shows of the Summer Safari. The crew took me out to dinner, and yes, I called my family to share this very special day. The only thing they didn't know was I called them from a strip club.

So that's pretty much how Fleetwood Mac finished off their 1978: with a bang!

In this day and age of sanitized packaged rock 'n' roll where the search for a trend to wrap a song around comes before the song is written has virtually killed the artistic process. TV shows like The Voice and American Idol where a person's story covers their non-sustainable wafer-thin talent has become the beacon for success. The worlds will never collide because big business and music have become the same.

Long live rock ... .rock is dead.

CHAPTER TWENTY TWO

LEO ROSSI: STAGE MANAGER
AND ALL THAT JAZZ

BY THE FALL OF 1978, I had kind of reached a plateau of sorts in the lighting field. As much as I enjoyed working with Fleetwood Mac, I knew that the band's lighting was Curry's gig and I would never want to try to take it over from Curry. Even though we co-designed The Mac's lighting , I knew he was there longer and he had all the experience with the bands politics, so he called the shots. But where was I supposed to go in lighting after Fleetwood Mac? The Mac's lighting was the biggest, best-funded, and most creative lighting gig in the world, and I had already experienced the best of what it had to offer and didn't feel it could ever be topped.

Just as the Fleetwood Mac tour was ending and I was trying to figure everything out. my old friend Jerry Levin came knocking. Jerry had always been a really close friend. I first met Jerry when he owned Lone Star Lighting out of Texas. He, Curry, Ronny, and Rodney all came through on tours when I was at Long Beach and they all became good friends.

Jerry was a father figure to me and he always believed in me and was amazed at how much I knew at a young age. Whenever I needed advice he was there and always gave me good advice. He had always been a kind of barometer for me and kept me in check. Whenever I had gone too far it was always Jerry who had the balls to tell me I was fucking up and reel me back in.

Jerry urged me to get away from lighting and more into production management. He knew that my vision and knowledge of the overall business was bigger than just lighting, and he said that he liked the way I handled people. Jerry was co-managing Al Jarreau, who was a classic jazz singer with a smooth, classically trained voice. Jerry's plan was to cross Jarreau, over a period of time, into pop rock sort of like what Earth Wind and Fire was doing. After all, that's where the money was, pop rock and Jarreau was talented enough to pull it off. Jarreau's voice was a virtual instrument and he could bend and create sounds to work with any band or sound. Truly one of the most talented artist I've ever worked with.

Jerry had a fall/winter tour planned for Jarreau. He needed someone who could both do the lighting director job and serve as a stage manager, so he called me. It was a perfect opportunity, really. It wasn't a huge tour, so it was a great place to start my production management career and get some experience. They were going to be playing theaters and other small venues with one truck and six guys. It was good money for the time: $1,000 a week, with a twenty-five-dollar-a day per diem. Back in the '70s, that was great money for a twenty-one-year-old kid. It was a crew of six but we still needed one more person to assist on lights and the set pieces. I hired my boyhood friend and roommate at the time Donald to come with us. Donald was in the middle of a problem with a DUI and needed to prove to the court he had a job so he wouldn't go to jail. He agreed to work for cheap which was good for the tour budget and it was going to be fun to tour with an old friend.

Jerry introduced me to the road crew. A guy named Gary was the stage tech and set up all the band gear. Gary's nickname was "Red" not only because of his bright red hair, but because every time he would drink or get high, he would get red, I mean beat-red. That was how you got a nickname on the road.

Gary "Red" Geller

Red was in charge of all the guitars, drums, everything that had to do with the band's instruments—it was a pretty big set-up; there were seven people in the band as well As Al. I used to help Red out a lot, which was easy because he was so much fun to be around. He was always joking, and when you're laughing, the time passes quickly. Like me, he always believed in turning a negative into a positive, so no matter what happened, he always kept his shit together, kept things happening, and you left feeling good. Red was from New York and the quintessential East Coaster. It was my first real experience with a typical shaker and mover. It fit perfect with me and I loved it. Always moving and going at warp speed, Red had been on the road for a long time, so no matter where we went, he knew someone—some guy who owned a restaurant or a bar or somewhere to crash. He used to come to my room and say "let's go man." I'd often reply "Red I'm tired. I just wanna sleep." "Bullshit" he'd cry, "you'll sleep enough when you're dead." For some reason I always gave in and found myself in the weirdest situations. Red always carried a feeling that no matter where we went you felt at home.

The soundman was Randy. I had met him before, early on in 1975. He had been working with Loggins and Messina as well as the Sanford Townsend Band, who opened a lot for Fleetwood Mac. Randy was one of those brilliant guys who could make any room sound good. Very versatile and low-key. Randy was brilliant, a true visionary.

Later in life Randy sold his house in Laguna Beach and set up one of the first mobile recording units where bands could go anywhere in the world, set up, and make a record. He would put a mixing board and tape players in road cases so he could fly them anywhere and he ended up recording musicians in some very strange places. He flew to Ghana, Africa, with Mick Fleetwood to record the Visitor in 1981 and also did the sound for U2's *The Unforgettable Fire*, which they recorded in a castle in Ireland. He ran his company called Effanel Mobile Recordings out of New York for years doing many live records and even the Grammy broadcast before selling the company and getting married and settling down.

After two weeks of rehearsals in Los Angeles, we started the tour in Kansas City at the Uptown Ballroom. Coming into town with one truck and a crew of really professional dudes,

There's only one Red Geller.

this tour was a real pleasure. Instead of the typical eight a.m. load-ins, we would arrive at noon and be done setting up by three. The band would be right there for sound check, and we'd be done. Soundcheck, show, load-out and back at the hotel by eleven-thirty p.m. This tour we had no tour buses, flew commercial every day, rental cars, and a bed every night. This was before airline security and you cold breeze in and out of airports in a matter of minutes.

The lesson I had to learn on the Jarreau Tour was that it was OK to throttle back and enjoy things a little bit. I also had to become more organized. My duties now included not only advancing the shows to make sure everything was there, I also needed to set up travel which was a big responsibility and half the job. I loved that part of the job. I took it as a challenge to get everything I could for the guys and me. I learned the gift of gab and how you can get anything you want as long as you try. It was a challenge to get us all upgraded to first-class as well as suites and deluxe rental cars. It was the most formative years in my quest to become a full-fledged tour manager. Red and I were a good team and between both of us the tour became first class. Also, when you toured with Jerry, there were a lot of perks. The best managers are the ones who used to be crew because they came up the ranks, so they appreciated what everyone was going through. Good hotels and great dinners were the normal when you toured with Jerry.

Most of the time during Jarreau's shows, Jerry would be doing all the tour manager business duties, so I also ran the lights. That was really fun for me. Jarreau is a tremendously dynamic singer and is very animated on the stage and the lights really accented what he did. I've never been the biggest jazz fan. I was more into rock and roll, you know, and I guess I considered jazz sort of boring. But Jarreau always surrounded himself with a group of incredibly accomplished musicians, and every night I

watched them play, I ap-
preciated their musician-
ship and their profession-
alism more and more as the
tour went on.

So, I soon got the feel-
ing for the music and Al's
personality. I figured out

Red, Me, Jerry Levin, and Al
Jarreau 1978.

that I had to use the lights with much more subtlety than
I was used to or they would be distracting. I really didn't
want to take the audience's attention away from Jarreau
hitting a beautiful clear low note. That was what the audience came for, and that was spectacular enough. Right
away, I started easing into a different vibe for this tour.
The music was different, the audience was different, and
the crew was different. But I was soon to learn that some
things never change.

After Kansas City, we traveled through Nashville, and
ended up in Memphis. During the Memphis show, I noticed
there was a gentleman sitting in a seat right behind the light
board. These were theater shows so we would set up the
sound and light boards in the center of the house over the
seats. Usually they don't sell the tickets behind the boards,
but they did and the guy behind me had paid for his seat so
I felt obligated to make sure he could see. During the show
I sat on the floor to run the light board so he could see.

Later in the show, while Jarreau was talking onstage,
the guy tapped me on the shoulder and as a gesture of

gratitude offered 'a toot.' I said I didn't mind if I did—I was never one to say 'no' to cocaine. He pulled out a little white envelope and a spoon and doled out two heaping scoops of the white powder.

About five minutes later, I started to feel very nauseous and sick. I took a couple of gulps of my Jack and Coke, but that didn't seem to solve anything. I called Red, who was backstage on the intercom, and told him that I was sick and going to puke and that I needed Jerry to cover the light board. Jerry came out, and said what's up? I told him how bad I was feeling. I said I needed to puke and that hopefully I'd feel better after a that. As I was making my way backstage, a weird feeling came over me. I almost felt as if I was floating and walking on air—it was almost an out-of-body thing where I saw myself walking backstage.

I did end up throwing up backstage and took a big drink of water. After that I felt a whole lot better. In fact, I started to feel positively euphoric. I felt like my whole body was being massaged. I went back out to the soundboard and was ready to take on the world. Jerry went backstage and I took over the lights. However, when I took my station and looked up at the stage, it didn't look the way it had before. Fuck! I was hallucinating! I was seeing things on-stage—lightning strikes, dancers that didn't exist, all kinds of weird shit. I started to get scared and thought I was going crazy. I closed my eyes and shook my head and then looked down at the light board, and nothing looked right. I was staring at the light board trying to focus. The board had a bunch of a little handles on it that controlled the intensity of the lamps. I looked at the handles and jumped off my knees like the floor was burning. The light faders had turned to little hands that were grabbing at me and trying to pull me into the board as if to capture me.

I turned around to the guy who had given me the drugs. He asked me if I was OK. I told he I was freaking out and he said good shit huh? "What the fuck did you give me, man?" "Good shit, huh?" "No man it's not good, what the fuck is it?"

"Duce man." (He pronounced it doo-che, like Mussolini's nickname "El Duce")

"Duce?" I said, anxiety beginning to rise from the euphoria. "What the fuck is Duce?"

He said, "Smack."

"Smack?

"Heroin, man."

"Heroin? Oh Christ," I said, freaking out a little bit. Heroin had always been such a bad word in the circle I was in. I started to really flip out. Heroin? Heroin? Shit! What the fuck? I remember thinking should I call Jerry or Red? But we were right in the middle of the show, and I knew that I had to try to hold myself together. I remember this vividly: I was standing in the aisle of the theater and looking at myself as if from a great distance, telling myself, "Hey, calm down, man. You're going to be cool. Don't worry about it. It's only your outer body having this experience."

I started to calm down, but running the light board was still mostly out of the question. I would sit there and try to concentrate on one light or one color at a time, but my lighting changes were sporadic to say the least. Randy was sitting about ten feet away at the soundboard. At one point, he looked over at me, and I must have looked kind of off in some way because he said, "My God. Are you OK?" "Yeah, why?" He said "Put some light onstage." I was so freaked out that I had blacked out the stage and the band was playing in the dark. Jarreau was talking to me from the stage. He was finishing a song, and he was asking for a little more light. I managed to comply, but I'm sure he was wondering what the hell was going on.

I just pushed up the faders, any faders. I went to Randy and told him " man, I'm wasted." I told him want had happened, and he started laughing. "This ain't rock Leo, this is Jazz, a different world. Do you want me to get Jerry?" I said no man don't, he'll kill me. Randy came over gave me some water and said "Dude, you gotta be careful, don't do shit from people you don't know."

I said, "Gee thanks for the advice." Anyway, somehow, I muscled my way through the rest of the show. I was even pretty much down from the trip by the end of the two hours, but during the load-out I was totally zoned. I told Red what had happened, and in addition to warning me very seriously about heroin, he laughed his ass off at my fate. All during the load-out, he would come up behind me and yell at the top of his lungs, "What's going on?!" And I would flip out. It figured: everything was funny to that guy.

In the morning my head pretty much felt like it had been hit by a sledge-hammer, but Red and Randy said that it was probably just a regular hangover from all the alcohol I had been drinking. I discovered that night that heroin was a dangerous high and I learned never get high with people you don't know.

The next day, we flew into St. Louis, which turned out to be the site of one of the most magical moments I've ever experienced in music. Al Jarreau pulled off something that I don't think any other artist could have done.

We were playing at George Washington University, and, fittingly, the show was held in a church on campus. All they did was take out all the pews and call it a multi-purpose room. All day the skies were threatening to open up and dump. It was getting cold and we were all worried about snow. In the middle of the show the thunder and lightning hit fast and hard. Right in the middle of the show there was a huge flash of light followed almost immediately by an earth-shaking clap of thunder. Every light in the place—hell, every light on campus—went out like a bomb had hit us.

There was a long moment when everyone just sat, stunned, in their seats. Then everyone started talking at once, and the audience began standing up to get out of the building. In the confusion, a couple of the security guards shined their flashlights up on the stage. Those beams were soon followed by more from the audience—it seemed that many of the people had flashlights with them so they could find their way back to their dorm rooms after the concert. Before you knew it, there were flashlight beams from all over the auditorium illuminating Jarreau on the stage.

When the lightening first hit, I started running around like crazy trying to get the lights on. Then out in the darkness, I heard Jarreau begin to sing one of his hits "Take Five" acappella. The crowd got very quiet. I had stopped what I was doing and looked up onstage to see what was going on. I saw Jarreau dimly lit as if he were a ghost. I stood in amazement like it was a dream.

Jarreau proceeded to complete the forty-five minutes that was left of the show all by himself, with just some occasional help from his drummer and percussionist. He sang a bunch of his own tunes. Then, since it was near the holidays, he led the audience in a bunch of Christmas carols.

There was one moment in particular that I will never forget. He walked out into the audience to where one of the audience-members was holding a child sleeping. He took the baby in his arms, and he talked about how "This is what life is all about." Then he sang a version of "Chestnuts Roasting on an Open Fire," while holding the baby in his arms. It was one of the most amazing, emotional moments I have ever witnessed. The crowd was dead silent and the whole scene was surreal, like something out of dream

The power never came back on that night. The power was all consumed by Al Jarreau and the energy he put into his singing. The show ended and not one audience member demanded a refund. Not one. Everyone stayed until the end of the show, and I would venture to guess that no one ever forgot that performance.

Personally, the whole experience and Al Jarreau's graceful, beautiful, simple reaction to it taught me not only that the show must go on but that the show *can* go on and an artist, a true artist is not fabricated, they are born with natural talents and abilities that normal people don't have. Seeing an artist like Al taught me to recognize true talent from fabricated talent and helped me all through my life to identify it and work with it.

As the tour moved on, I was looking forward to Chicago. It was always one of my favorite towns. It was bohemian and funky, and there was always great food. We were playing the Arie Crown Theater, which was one of the grandest, most beautifully appointed and upscale theaters in the country. It was not the kind of theater that most people were able to play. It was a privilege to do it. And it was definitely going to be a sold-out show. Chicago's a jazz town, so Jarreau naturally had fans there.

The beauty and history of the venue had a down-side, however. The stagehands were very protective about 'their' theater. They were used to doing opera and classical music at this place. I didn't get the feeling they differentiated too much between rock and roll and jazz, so they had quite a chip on their shoulders from the get-go. What's more, the unions were tough in Chicago, so I had to be extra careful how I handled them. The minute we started to move in, they warned us not to touch anything—like we were three-year-olds. They told us that they would move everything; we were to just point. It was kind of insulting to professionals like us. But I used it as an excuse to put into practice some of the principles that Randy had talked about. I jumped off my high horse for a change, and things went more smoothly than they often had before.

As predicted, it was a special show. Jarreau ended up doing some songs that he had never performed before—they rehearsed them during the sound check. The crowd ate it up and begged for more.

That show was a real turning point for me too. I was walking around backstage in my usual hockey jersey, and Jerry pulled me aside and handed me an orange-and-charcoal-colored Ralph Loren Polo sweater. I was a little taken aback—who was Jerry to tell me what to wear? But Jerry pointed out to the audience, and I noticed that they were wearing suits and tuxedos and dresses with class. He said, "Think about it." What Jerry was basically saying was you need to grow up and you're not only out here representing you, you're representing Al Jarreau as well.

I went backstage, put on the sweater, combed my hair back, and I looked at myself long and hard in the mirror. I felt … good. I felt as if I had jumped classes, somehow.

Somewhere along the line, my seats had been upgraded to first class, if you know what I mean. Since the last time I had been in Chicago, I had moved from Chicago Stadium to this gorgeous theater.

The schedule was pretty heavy around the Northeast, and I wasn't looking forward to the snow and cold weather—not to mention all the flying in it. At one point, we were scheduled to do seven days in a row where just about every day we would get up early, fly to a different city, rent a car, load-in, do the show, load-out, return to the hotel, get up early and do the whole thing all over again. December 2nd and 3rd we did two nights in Philly. The fourth and fifth were Boston. The sixth was Pittsburgh. The seventh was Hartford. The ninth was Edenborough, Pennsylvania. And the tenth was Washington DC. We were really hauling ass, which was a shame because I really wanted to hang out in some of those cities.

In Boston, we played the Boston Opera House that was a great, beautiful old theatre from way back. The seating boxes went straight up like a traditional opera house and were covered in gold leafing. I was thrilled to work in an elegant and beautiful historic theater. The Opera house still had ropes and sandbags and a traditional stage that I had only read about in the history books. To actually see that—and work with it—that was a real honor. It was incredible to realize it went back to the days of the birth of the United States. So many amazing people had blessed the Opera House with their presence.

We were having a good time, but there's a time in every tour where the days run together and it feels like one long day. With all the plane trips, hotels, load-ins and load-outs, time fly's faster than you can imagine. When you're on a tour your life is accelerated so fast, everyday becomes a week.

After Boston we a had very early flight the next morning. We were playing a gig the next night in Washington DC, and it was at a tough old historic theater called Daughters of the Revolution Hall.

I remember looking out the window in the morning—two hours before we had to get on the plane—and it was snowing ... hard. We were all wondering how we were going to get to DC and knew it was going to be a long day.

Jerry called the room early and said that despite the snow we should get over to the airport. I guess he figured that we could always keep the rent a cars and drive all the way to DC if the planes weren't flying. This was truly the thought of a man who had been on the road for a long time and who had the show must go on attitude.

We got to the airport, where they were preparing a small two engine DC-9 for takeoff. We got on the plane. They sprayed it down with deicer. Then we taxied out onto the runway. We waited, and we waited, and we waited. The pilot came on the speaker and said that we were waiting for a weather front to go by. And there was nothing to be alarmed about. So, we waited and waited and waited some more. When it was finally time to take off, we needed to be de-iced again so more waiting. It was a blessing because most of the crew were getting much needed sleep, I was too impatient and fidgety and just wanted to get going. I was sitting next to Randy, and he was having the exact opposite experience from me. His eyes were closed, and there was a serene and peaceful expression on his face. I tapped his shoulder and he angerly looked at me. I said "Hey Randy, how can you stay so calm? You look so peaceful; how do you do that?" He said, "I'm meditating, it calms me down." I asked. "How do you do that?" Randy said, "I close my eyes, empty my head, and I take all my negative energy, my nervousness and channel it out of the engines' noise, and I visualize all of it flowing out of me into the engines and out of the back of the engines and it's gone. It really works. You should try it."

So, I sat back and made the effort to tune into the engine's hum. I channeled my impatience and my fear of imagining how glorious my death from a plane crash would look in the newspapers back home (remember, I wasn't exactly enlightened yet). Then the signal for take-off went "bing." The roar of the engines intensified and grew louder. We started to move, and we were off—down the runway and in the air. I looked out the window, and all I saw was pure white snowflakes going by the window. I closed my eyes and realized that it was working. There was a calmness I've never felt before. I was tuned in and turned on. Then we popped out above the

Me and Randy Ezratty

cloudbank and surrounded by the brightest blue I had ever seen. I looked down at all the white clouds below and felt a moment of supreme clarity. I felt I had dodged a bullet. I had to stop fucking around. I had to chill out and focus more on my job. I had to be a better person. I had to figure out what I wanted. I still meditate today and when I do, I remember Randy, that cold day in Boston, and I smile.

It was December 9, 1978—a pretty big turning point in my life. That day I learned a lot about myself and never realized, until writing this, but that day was my dad's birthday. What do you suppose that means?

We worked our way south, ended the tour in Atlanta, and returned to Los Angeles for Christmas. I was really loaded. I saved all my money and had few bills. Again, I bought stacks of presents for everyone. This time it felt different though. This time I bought the gifts out of love. I was getting more solid with myself and didn't have to prove anything to them or myself. And in contrast to previous years, I wasn't mangled on cocaine or drugs, so I could really be present for people and enjoy the greatest gift of all, spending time with family and friends.

The day after Christmas, I started to advance the New Year's Eve show at the Lincoln Center in New York City with Al Jarreau. I found out that while we were in New York, Jerry put us all at the Plaza, one of the ritziest hotels in the city. First class all the way. And this time Lisa was coming with me. She was eighteen now but still cleared it with her parents, and she was coming to New York with me—New York City for New Year's Eve.

We flew out on the twenty-eighth for a rehearsal on the twenty-ninth and a load-in on the thirtieth. Two bands were actually using the Lincoln Center on New Year's—Jarreau was playing an early show, and the progressive band Devo was doing the midnight show. They figured that the Jarreau crowd, which was older and more sophisticated, would want to stay out late and go to an earlier show and parties after. We shared sound and lights with Devo and the early show was great with us, because we could do our show and still be done by ten thirty with minimal gear to load-out and still have the night to have a great time.

Lisa and I made our mind up to go to Times Square. Despite Red's doubts about how little fun that would be and warnings about pickpockets, off we went. It was Lisa's first time in the city, and it was awesome to share my

Al Jarreau Entourage.

world with her, especially New York.

The next day, we walked right across the street from the hotel to Central Park. We went to restaurants. We went shopping. Sharing that experience with Lisa was just incredible. We were totally in love, and she fit in well with the other people on the tour. Randy and Lisa became fast friends and actually were a lot alike. And it felt great to be able to share my life with Lisa.

1978 ended as fast as it came and looking ahead, I felt that 1979 was going to be even a bigger year. Fleetwood Mac was in the studio working on the record that would become *Tusk*. The tour was schedule for late 1979 with six weeks of rehearsals and the tour would last a year and a half or more.

The late great Al Jarreau (right) and Jerry Levin (left).

I was twenty-one years old and I felt like I was speeding on the freeway of life with no rearview mirror. Just dodging the cars in front of me leaning on the horn looking for the next exhilarating off-ramp.

CHAPTER TWENTY THREE

A VERY BUSY 1979, AND I MEET
RICKIE LEE JONES

SO, 1979 WAS HERE, THE LAST YEAR of the decade. 1978 was a good year; I worked a lot and saw no sign of slowing down. My now newfound management experience coupled with my already vast knowledge of lights and sound meant I was getting a lot of offers for work.

Most of the winter and spring in 1979, I did a lot of local shows. With my experience and success with Cal Jam 2, I was hired to do local stadium shows that seem to be happening every month. From Van Halen at the World Music festival to the Parliament Funkadelic's Funk Fest at the Los Angeles Coliseum and the Bee Gees at Dodger Stadium. The craziest one was a show called Skateboard

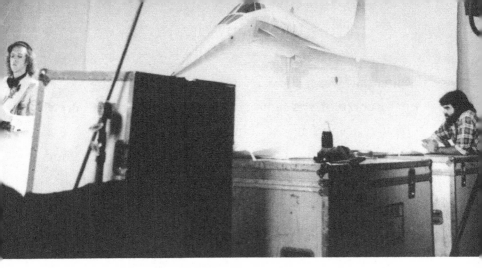

Me on the Bob Welch tour. Bob was the former
guitarist for Fleetwood Mac.

My good friend Dennis Mays
(Fleetwood Mac Sound engineer)
on the mound at Dodger Stadium
recording *Tusk*.

Christine McVie holding a
cardboard cutout of John McVie
at the *Tusk* video shoot at Dodger
Stadium. June 1979. John missed
the shoot while sailing his boat
to Polynesia.

Mania that was a show trying to capitalize on the Skateboard craze of the famous "Lords of Dog town" crew. Great concept that just didn't pan out.

It was keeping me very busy and making me good money. I even though picked up small short tours like The Moody Blues, Kenny Rodgers, and The Mac's old guitar player Bob Welch. I missed touring, I missed the fast-paced life and I mostly missed the camaraderie of being on a crew.

I knew Fleetwood Mac was finishing up the new record because in June I brought up some lights to Dodger Stadium that the band rented out to shoot a video using the University of Southern California marching band. It was for the song that was to become *Tusk*. It was great to see the band and crew and made me look forward to the tour.

At a Bruce Springsteen show in San Francisco in late 1978, I had run across Marc Brickman, a lighting and set designer extraordinaire. Marc started in the early 70s in a station wagon driving around doing shows with Bruce Springsteen. He rode the Springsteen wave into working and touring with many mega-artist like Pink Floyd, Paul McCartney, and many more throughout his life.

Marc told me that he was doing the lighting for an up-and-coming female singer by the name of Rickie Lee Jones. She was recording at one of Warner studios around Los Angeles, and Marc described her as a very talented and a very volatile artist. He told me she was one of those eccentric artists who was just amazing. "She's going to be a star"

Warner Brother Records planned small promotional tour with Rickie doing all small, 2,000- to 3,000-seat theaters to showcase their found sensation. The tour would play the Berkeley Theater in Berkeley, California. The Orpheum in Portland, and the Paramount in Seattle, all great classic venues perfect for an intimate night with any band.

Marc was brought on to oversee the set and lighting and create an overall feel for Rickie. His vision was to create an actual theater set behind her to make the experience like a stage show. I was intrigued by his excitement over this newcomer, and I was totally into his design ideas. The tour was a lot like Al Jarreau where we would use mostly what was in the theaters to cut down on truck space an allow us to do more.

Marc raved about Rickie and said we should go up to the studio and check her out sometime. To me that

Marc Brickman (blue jacket) with Bruce Springsteen 1972. Marc was and still is a good friend and part of my life.

was a bit odd. I never had been to an actual recording session to see a band; it was all about touring for me.

What I didn't realize at the time was this was Marc's stealthy way to introduce me to Rickie and see if there was a fit. Jerry and Marc were friends and discussed my expertise in theaters and what Jerry and I did on the Jarreau Tour. Marc felt I would be a value to the tour. Rickie was very hands on with her career and really wanted to know who was going to work with her.

I agreed with excitement and went up to studio where Rickie was working with two of their in-house producers, Lenny Waronker and Russ Titelman. The moment I walked into the studio; I had a good feeling about the whole thing. I knew some of the musicians in her band from the Al Jarreau days, a guitarist name Buzzy and Neil a keyboard player. They had a successful jazz band called Larsen Fieten managed by Jerry and they had opened for Jarreau a couple of times and played on his record. They were good guys, and amazingly talented musicians. Their playing, a cross between rock 'n' roll and jazz, had a great sound and feel. I took it as a good sign that they were also going to be in Rickie's touring band as well.

They brought me in to meet Rickie, and what can I say? She was Rickie—the beret, the black lace gloves, and the whole beatnik vibe. She had a very lazy yet direct way about her. It was a cool meet-and-greet—for a first time. From the Fleetwood Mac women I had experience working with female artists, so I knew I could work with her, and I think the rest of the people involved also were confident that I could work out.

Marc introduced us. "Hey Rickie, this is Leo. I'm bringing him out on the tour to help me." I reached out my hand and said, "it's a pleasure to meet you, Ms. Jones." She rolled her eyes as she grabbed my hand and said, "You're pretty young." I stood silent, not knowing what to say next, and then she said, "call me Rickie Lee, and thanks for helping out." "My pleasure, I'm looking forward to it." And that was my first of many conversations with Rickie Lee Jones, not knowing that in the future I would not only end up as her production manager but her tour manager as well.

I hung around in the studio for a while, listening to the band and catching up with Neil and Buzz. They were in the middle of tracking the finishing touches of a song called "Youngblood." They were trying to figure out the intro part, and they were having some trouble getting it to a place that satisfied them. Rickie was at the mixing board at this point, listening to the track played back, and Buzz was in the studio noodling around on his guitar and playing with the bass player. The bass player started playing this real funky bass line that was the intro for the track and Buzz started to play this sort-of reggae/funk riff with it. Rickie looked up from what she was doing as if she had been shocked by electricity. She shouted out, "That's it! That's the riff! Keep playing! She ran in there and sat at the piano, playing the riff and then playing against the riff.

The whole intro was born right there, right in front of me. It was so amazing and to this day when I hear that track it brings me back to that day in the studio. I think this was a turning point for me where I realized I really wanted to get more into the music side of things. It seemed fresh and more exciting. I guess you can say it hit the creative nerve that I didn't know existed.

Watching Rickie, I knew Marc was right. She was really something. She had an amazing grasp of the musical arrangements. She would tell each musician what to play and how to play it. If necessary, she would play each part on the piano, one by one.

Watching her and listening to her band was totally inspiring. It's the kind of experience that makes you want to be able to make music like that. By the end of the night I knew that I wanted to do the promotional tour not only for the cool design that Marc was working on but also for the music and future tours.

The next day, I called Mark, and let him know that I was in if he wanted me and just let me know when. They were right in the middle of making the record, so no one really knew when the tour would happen.

Meeting and hearing Rickie was a fantastic experience, and I figured that with such an eccentric and talented artist as Rickie, maybe it was OK for her to have weird quirks like having to meet all the people who were going to work on the tour. It was only later that I figured out what was really going on.

It seemed that Rickie and the entire band she had selected were addicts. It's really no secret now that Rickie had her problems, but back then, it wasn't well-known, and it could have really messed everything up if certain people knew about it. So, they had to know that the people they worked with were cool and could be trusted.

Weeks later, after the record was finished, I got a phone call from Marc. He told me that Rickie was going out on tour starting the first week of August and we needed to start thinking about rehearsals and the tour. He also told me that Obie Lights was doing the tour. I was excited.

Unfortunately, I also found out that another guy at Obie's, who wasn't well liked, was going to do the tour as well, and when I heard that, I was instantly afraid that it was going to be a looooong tour. He was an old-time rock and roll guy with a generally abrasive personality. Long hair. Bad attitude. Questionable personal hygiene. Anti-establishment. Very smart-alecky. Also, very smart. He had been with Obie forever, and I knew that there was going to be a power struggle. He didn't like the fact that Marc and I were so close because Marc needed help with lighting and sound mainly on the theatrical portion of the tour. I knew a lot about that type of touring and Obie's guy didn't like the fact that Marc asked me questions because I knew more.

Luckily, he didn't last long on the tour. About a week in, he developed a toothache, which he used as an out because he realized he just didn't fit on the tour.

Rickie did an amazing cover of the classic Four Tops track "Up on the Roof," so they had decided to call the tour the "Up on the Roof" tour. The stage manager/ production manager on the tour was a guy by the name of Dave. Dave worked with Marc before and was a good production manager. We all got to work and created Marc's design. It was genius! The stage was transformed to look like the top of a New York City building.

Set pieces at the front of the stage looked like a low brick wall. In the middle of the stage there was a skylight and a big roof fan and the band casually set up around the rooftop like they were just jamming. And the backdrop was the side of a building with a dimly lit Roi Tan Cigar advertisement on it. It was a beautiful effect—very evocative of a certain place and feeling. We set up all the lighting in rehearsals. Since we were going to be in theaters, we would hang the lights—no trusses or motors, just assimilate into the theater like a Broadway Play. Very elegant.

The whole tour was amazing. Rickie rocked it, the band was over-the-top great and most of all Warner Brothers knew they had a hit, so the money flowed in not only for Rickie but all of us as well.

Over the course of the tour I witnessed her doing some amazing things. The way she played her piano and her interplay with her phenomenally talented band was a joy to behold. The band was all very drug-dependent— they were all doing heavy drugs plus alcohol. But I gotta say that they never let it affect the show ... ever! Rickie was constantly on her game. Meanwhile the first radio single "Chuck E.'s In Love" was doing really well on the radio and was beginning to climb the charts. She was getting a lot of attention, with a lot of folks pegging her as the new Joni Mitchell with a rock 'n' roll edge.

It was just a little promotional tour that ran up the coast from Oakland to Seattle and down to LA. But that was good for me, because I found out I needed to be back in the middle of August to start working on Fleetwood Mac. So, everything was falling into place.

The first show was in Oakland. Everyone was a little nervous, of course, but it went fine, and Rickie and the band nailed it. Very controlled set. Short but great.

But then backstage before the next show, at the Berkeley Civic Theater, Marc was giving Rickie shit about the show being too short. Marc, the lighting designer for Springsteen who did four hour shows, was telling Rickie Lee the show had to be longer. "Give the people what they want ... more you."

The problem was, of course, Rickie was a new artist and she didn't have a lot of songs in her repertoire. She was doing a lot of covers, but still, that was stretching it. Marc was ribbing her a bit about how people had spent their good money on tickets. He was kidding around, but as always there is a lot of truth spoken in jest.

As usual, I watched a lot of that show standing at the light board with Marc. It got near the end of the show, and there was a lot of applause and Rickie went offstage. She came back on for her encore, when she played "Up on the Roof." But right before she started the song, she said, "You know, my lighting guy, Marc, works for Bruce Springsteen. And he was giving me shit earlier tonight about how Springsteen does four-hour shows and gives people value for their buck. So, the band and I decided that we're going to sit here and play every song we know." The crowd hooted and hollered. I looked at Marc, like, "Now you did it." He reached into his pocket, pulled out the vile of coke and said "Looks like it's going to be a long night."

And sure, enough they proceeded to perform one great R&B or jazz classic after another. And they kept playing and playing—one hour, then two—with the crowd just eating it up. It was incredible. Rickie's talent with that amazing band! Solo after solo, song after song, it became a private party.

Eventually Dave came up to Mark and me saying, "Dude, the union bill is going to be astronomical."

Marc said, "Look, I don't know what to tell you."

Being a promotional tour, Warner's was responsible for the cost of everything. I looked at Marc and Marc looked at me, we shrugged our shoulders, listened to the music and got high. Each night on the tour, Rickie would want to play longer and longer shows, but it wouldn't matter to us, we knew we were witnessing the birth of a superstar and were proud to be part of it.

We crossed the border into Vancouver and played the Queen Elizabeth Theater, a beautiful venue. Then on to Seattle, and Portland before heading for LA. By this time, she was getting pretty big, so she was booked into Los Angeles for three nights. L.A. was also a big deal because it's where all the Warner Brothers music executives were going to showcase Rickie to the news and entertainment press.

And, in fact, she nailed L.A. She brought everyone off their friggin' asses and on their feet. Standing ovations. Songs like "The Last Chance Texaco" were just amazing. Every day I became more enamored with what this woman was doing.

I knew she was going to continue her tour in the fall. I had to go out on tour with Fleetwood Mac, but I'll tell you, I was really seriously thinking about staying with Rickie. I think that if it had been anyone other than Fleetwood Mac pulling me away, I would have stayed.

Working with Rickie also introduced me into to the workings of record labels.

I made great contacts at Warner Brother Records and for year was handed all their new breaking artists and became their in-house tour manager.

The Warner Brothers era of Mo Ostin and team was an amazing time in music history never to be recreated, and it launched bands that will be heard forever.

Fleetwood Mac was on Warner's as well, so that also gave me more respect with The Mac.

Then the Phone call, the one I was waiting for. One word, *Tusk*!

CHAPTER TWENTY FOUR

TUSK

IT'S SEPTEMBER 1, 1980. Fleetwood Mac's playing the Hollywood Bowl. It's the last song of the night, the last song of the tour and like many nights before, the crew gathered offstage ten feet from the piano where Christine McVie was singing the enchanting words of "Song Bird." It's a song, she once told me, she wrote for her father.

I'm standing next to Mick Fleetwood, who every night would join his crew. We're all looking at the thousands of people waving their cigarette lighters to the song's mystic melody looking like fire flies caught in an impulsive wind.

Mick whispered, "look at that." He took a deep breath, whispering again. "You know Boys, I'm gonna miss this.

This shot is the last shot on stage for the Tusk tour 1980.

I'm really gonna miss this." Through my blurred vision from my tears of sadness and joy, I looked at Mick and I whispered. "Me too, Mick. Me too."

Even though "Song Bird" is off of the *Rumours* record, when I hear it, it always reminds me of *Tusk*. Every night It was the last song of the set for the hundreds of live *Tusk* shows.

Every night thousands of fans would grow silent and focus on that beautiful lit grand piano that accompanied Christine's silk voice singing, "And I love you, I love you, I love you, like never before." Then with the traditional "we love you and good night! London, Cleveland, Tokyo, Los Angeles" or wherever we were, the show was over.

The words came lovingly through the massive speakers

and everyone on the crew that said they weren't crying was lying. We all were.

As the night turned into morning the last truck door closed and pulled away from the Hollywood Bowl. Getting smaller and smaller until it was out of sight, we looked at each other in complete exhausted silence. It was over. The *Tusk* tour was officially over.

For Eighteen-months our massive sophisticated gypsy caravan was circumnavigating five of the world's continents performing one hundred and twelve shows for millions of devoted fans.

It was indescribable knowing that from this night on, the chances of all our *Tusk* family reuniting again was improbable and in fact impossible. We all gave each other one last hug, and were on our way.

Like many times in our lives, we would be on to our next tour ... on to our next family.

In music history, The *Tusk* project (record and tour) is a quintessential project. How could any band top itself and stay relevant after something so successful as *Rumours*; an album that became the soundtrack of a youth movement and a memoir tied to their most important encounters.

For Lindsey, it was easy to throw out all you know, all you have done, twist it and turn it one hundred and eighty degrees, and start over. Start over and just pray that your devoted and new followers believe in your new passionate revelation.

The vibe of *Tusk* took on its own life with the title song ironically named "Tusk." No longer a band with luscious pop flowing melodies and deep touching lyrics, *Tusk* was experimental, rebellious, bohemian, rough around the edges with a real fuck you attitude. The lyrics made you pay attention with the multiple messages from three dissimilar writing styles.

With Lindsey at the musical helm, even Stevie and Christine's songs had the layer of edge that brought out the odor of conflict and rebellion.

You either loved *Tusk* or hated it. There was no middle ground but if you had a good pair of headphones and some good drugs, it became your favorite record.

The song "Tusk" was actually a piece of music that we all had heard many times. In 1977, the schedule for press and other engagements away from the venue forced the band to miss sound checks. The vigorous schedule was also taking a toll on the band's stamina and mainly Stevie's voice. We needed to devise a way to check the sound levels and "tune" the venues to make sure the sound was perfect from every seat.

The road crew band played the afternoon sound check. Most techs on the crews were actually very good musicians. Most drum techs could play drums and most guitar techs could play guitar.

Crew bands were good but not good enough to get the actual sound dialed in. We had to come up with a scheme to make sure the sound engineers could get actual levels on the actual band before the downbeat of the first song.

Before the show started, and with thousands of screaming people in the now dark arena, a bit of music, "a riff" would be played to perfect the levels the road crew band had already set earlier in the day. Mick would play his drums, starting with the massive bass drum that made the walls shake. BOOM! BOOM! BOOM! BOOM! Then the gun fire sounding snare drum, POP! POP! POP! Then the tom toms and rest of the kit until he was playing a solid beat hitting all the drums and cymbals. The sound engineers in the front of the house and onstage would set their levels. With Mick's drums dialed in the sound engineer would give him the OK through the monitor talk back onstage so the crowd couldn't hear what we were doing.

"OK got it. John, the bass please." John would join Mick and play along with his beat and the rhythm section was set. "Got it John, thanks." "Chris, keys please." Christine would first layer in her Hammond B-3 Organ that was a key part of The Mac's sound, then one by one all the electric pianos and synthesizers. "OK got it. Guitars please." Lindsey would noodle in his complex fingering parts while layering in a bit of lead guitar with from his complex rig. To complete the process, through their vocal microphones each band member would then welcome the crowd to make sure the mics were working. From John, "Good evening." "Hello Nashville," or wherever from Christine. And Stevie's heartfelt, "Thanks for coming." After the sound engineers said, "OK we got it, let's do this," Mick would play one last long drum roll and the three-hour show began.

The mysterious stage lights would glow enough to reveal JC standing center stage, proudly delivering his nightly famous intro, "Ladies and Gentlemen, please, give a warm welcome to Fleetwood Mac" and like that the five of them took people on this magical journey.

That musical "riff," that piece of music that was used for the ingenious impromptu two-minute soundcheck, became the song "Tusk."

After hearing the almost completed song "Tusk" at the Dodger Stadium video shoot with a full USC marching band, it was apparent to me that the band and the songs on the new album were taking on a new sound and I was excited to hear what the rest of the songs were like. I found out it was a double album with over twenty-five songs with a mixture of Stevie, Christine and Lindsey's writing styles enhanced by high fidelity and modern recordings.

It was now mid-summer, and I was preparing to go out with Rickie Lee Jones when Curry called and said he got the green light to start thinking about the lighting for the new tour. Curry had been in and out of the studio and had a good idea of the direction and style of *Tusk*. We agreed to meet at the Village Recording Studios in West LA to sit and listen to the whole record.

One early perfect hot Los Angeles morning in 1979, I drove my Lotus to the Village to meet Curry to hear *Tusk* for the first time.

The Village Recorder was a classic studio where many bands and many, many big hit records were made. It was the old Masonic Temple hidden away in West Los Angeles, with a small green door on the side for artists to come and go with complete privacy.

The Mac leased and scheduled a six month lock out of the studio, but with the success of The Mac and where *Tusk* was headed, they used a brand-new Studio—Studio D—that Ken Caillat and Richard Dashut designed and built with the newest and most modern recording equipment. Even today in the high tech recording world many people try to emulate the procedures and sounds that The Mac made in Studio D for the *Tusk* record.

The *Tusk* sessions became quite complex with Lindsey taking the reins, recording and mixing a lot of the tracks at his home studio, which met with displeasure from the rest of the band. I give Mick Fleetwood credit for keeping things on track. His ongoing fa-

Ken Caillat and Richard Dashut

thering calmed the madness and he knew how to say the right thing at the right time to the right person to encourage them all to trust the undefined process.

Initially there were talks (that were killed by the accountants) that perhaps the band should purchase the Village to record *Tusk* and sell it when they were done. In hind sight it wasn't such a bad idea since after *Tusk* was done the total recording budget was more than double the value and the purchase price of the Village.

I arrived at the Village early in the morning and didn't expect to see any of the band, but John McVie was there on his way to his boat in Marina Del Rey. He greeted me and we chatted about the record and what he was up to now that the recording process was complete.

It was good to see John and my excitement about the tour was now in high gear. He asked me "did you hear the new record?" I said, "I had heard a little bit, but I'm here to listen to the rest of it." All he said was, "Well, it's different." He said Lindsey got involved in the mixing of the songs with Ken and Richard and took the music in another direction. "It rocks, it's not your Mother's Fleetwood Mac," he said, smiling.

I heard a bit of apprehension in his voice. I think even John wondered whether the band was going to be able to pull off the drastic change to its sound, but it was too late.

I sat in front of the massive audio mixing board with its thousands of knobs and enormous speakers in Studio D as the tape sped up hurling out the first notes of the album *Tusk*.

Over and Over, a slow ballad written by Christine McVie with her trademark voice and perfect three-part harmonies is the first song on the record. I immediately was blown away with the clarity and layers of sonic beauty. I asked for a legal pad and pencil to take notes that, to this day, I still have.

Some of my notes from 1979:

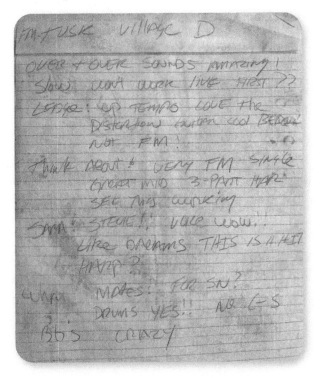

First page of my *Tusk* notes.

FM Tusk, village D

Over & Over: Sounds amazing! Slow. Won't work live too slow. First???

Ledge: Up tempo. Love the distortion, guitar cool brake down. Not FM!!

Think about: Very FM! Single, Great mid 3-part Har. See this working.

WHEN THE DEVIL SMILES, THE ANGELS FROWN

Sara: Stevie!! Voice wow! Like dreams, This is a hit! Harp? (meaning harpsichord, but was a tack piano)

What makes: For SN? (Lyrics for Stevie Nicks) *drums yes!! No c-s BG's* (no Christine and Stevie back ground vocals) *crazy!*

I kept writing note after note for song after song figuring it would help Curry and I find a direction not only for the lighting but a stage design.

Sitting next to Curry I was Suspended in time as we listened to all twenty songs. It was not what I expected and the one note that stood out the most that I wrote on the bottom of the page that was the defining difference between *Tusk* and ALL the other Fleetwood Mac records was:

Where the fuck is the lead guitar? There's no lead except on Sisters (Stevie's song Sisters of the moon). *So afraid?*

It for sure was a departure and to me *Tusk* lacked Balls! It was too artsy-fartsy for my taste and lacked the power, drive, and most of all it seemed like three solo records with the same rhythm section. Over time and listening to what The Mac did best, play live, I learned to love *Tusk*; it is one of my favorite records. You can hear *Tusk* a hundred times and every time you do you hear something new. Now that's a great record.

Looking back now I realize how fortunate I was to hear the songs before they were completely 100 percent finished and being involved with the conception of a project that would change the fabric of music history forever.

Curry finagled the mixes of *Tusk* on cassette tapes to take with us so we could study the songs even more and try to find a direction for the *Tusk* Tour.

Driving home I listened to all the songs again and in a smaller environment like a car *Tusk* sounded much different. Along with the schizophrenic style of the songs being the only common thread throughout the whole record was the power and connection of John McVie's bass with Mick Fleetwood's drums. I noticed that whenever there was kick drum or bass drum beat, there was a bass guitar note with it. Once again it was the amazing rhythm duo of John and Mick, forged from their youth going back to the street on London some thirty years earlier.

Ports "O" Call patio.

Every day for the next week or so I would either park my car down by the ocean or take my large but portable boom box down to Ports "O" Call restaurant in San Pedro that was right on the water at Los Angeles Harbor and listen to *Tusk*. I sat at my favorite out-of-the-way corner seat not to be disturbed and listened to *Tusk*.

I couldn't help but feel the conflict of the band through the music and was struggling to find the beauty in the record. Then like many moments in my life circumstance, fate, and destiny came sailing by and it hit me! This large ugly rusted ship that looked like it lacked love and care with its low rumble of big engines came slowly by. Even though it was unattractive and looking like something you'd never trust to be on, it glided by slowly with this mysterious graceful beauty, like a woman sneaking out of a room trying not to wake you after a good night. I was amazed. how could something so big and unattractive be so seductive and appealing? I realized at that moment that even ugliness has beauty and beauty could has ugliness! That was *Tusk*!

I listened to *Tusk* over and over and over again and to me it became very apparent. Embrace the differences of the music and the styles of Lindsey, Stevie, and Christine, and let it be what it is. Three diverse styles on one stage with the common thread of Mick and John.

I called Curry with a radical Idea. The concept I presented to Curry was to make it so that each band member ended up having their own stage, their own lights and their own world. I told him the ship story, and trying to contain my excitement, I went off like a sprinter that just heard the starting gun. "OK. So Curry, think about this! Instead of one big light rig why don't we create smaller identical light rigs over each of the band. This way, we could create all their looks separate and keep

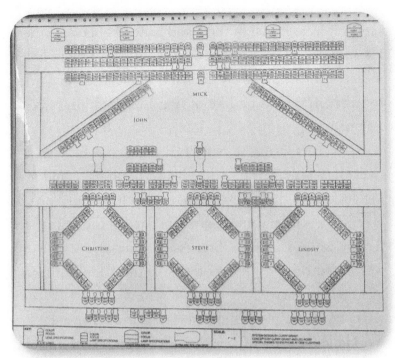

Tusk Light design.

Tusk light rig finished.

saturation over each of them and darkness between them for each of their songs. Then we would use a set of lights in between them and in the back to blend their worlds together. It would be like having four lighting systems on one tour!"

Each person in the band had their own little area—their own little world. With this scenario we could give each of the band their own light to match their persona. It was in line with the music of *Tusk*. Each of the main three writers' style, Christine, Stevie, and Lindsey, were so different and this enabled us to make them look different like their music.

For Sara we would light Stevie like it was her stage, her world blending Lindsey and Chris around her with solid colors for John and Mick representing the foundation of the band. When The Mac played "Not That Funny" or "What Makes You Think You're the One," we could light Lindsey's world and blend it with Stevie and Chris.

Using racks of lights behind the band we could keep the consistency of the older songs from the two previous records.

John didn't like a lot of light, so we kept it toned down for him, but for Mick, we set up special lights for his hands on the kit as well as his face. Mick, being the stoic figure, was always behind this massive pile of metal and wood called drums and we needed to find a way to bring him more out front and give him the props he deserved.

Since the hardware (rims and symbol, stands, etc.) on

the drum kit was all chrome, any lights we put on Mick tended to reflect and wash out anything behind it. Curry came up with this crazy-ass but genius idea to color all the chrome pieces of the drum hardware black so they would not reflect and bounce light to distract from the six-foot-five-inch bigger-than-life drummer. Paint all the hardware, every nut, bolt and screw black. Now you can't paint chrome, so we had to do a complicated process called ionization that cost a ton! But when we lit it, it didn't reflect a bit of light so you could see Mick without even seeing the drums if we didn't want you to. We had a set of lights overhead and in front and when lit all you saw was six-foot-five Mick Fleetwood.

Curry Liked the idea, so the next day I sketched it up and the concept of the light rig for *Tusk* was born.

During all this, Curry was thinking about the actual design of the *Tusk* Tour. When it came to color and feel Curry had an amazing grasp on what the band needed and what was best for them.

Besides JC, Curry had the longest legacy with The Mac. He was also living with Christine and was very close and in the inner circle of all the intimate and personal moments that forged the amazing music.

Christine McVie drove the art from the band's perspective and in fact had painted some old drops when the band was not so big. The famous moon with the tree backdrop from the Bob Welch era through *Rumours* was Christine's. Christine and the band got together with

Curry and decided they wanted some cool backdrops—
something pretty *avant garde* and different. They hired a
top-notch New York Theater set designer who came up
with a concept for abstract shapes and translucent mate-
rials that could make multiple looks with different lighting on it. We hired a friend of Curry and mine named
Larry Hitchcock who worked for FM Productions out
of San Francisco. FM Productions was owned by the legendary promoter Bill Graham. Larry had designed sets
for several large bands including the Grateful Dead, Rolling Stones, and Paul McCartney's Wings. Larry came up
with a cool design of translucent backdrops adorned with
sticks and circles and other abstract shapes. To make this
design work the drops could not be folded and had to be
wrinkle free every day. So, the design of roll drops was
implemented. To reveal each drop they were rolled down
lit from behind and back. The abstract material on the
drops would make different shapes and textures when lit
with different colors. So, we had four drops on huge for-
ty-foot-long rollers that were stored in massive construc-
tion tubes. They were the last items in the truck every
night and, unfortunately, very fragile.

Curry was looking for a way to light the band and
create silhouettes and create a mysterious vibe but not
see them from the front. The only lights that were bright
enough to create that affect were very bright follow spots.
The decision was made to build small cages that we would
hang onto the rear truss to hold a small spotlight and seat

for an operator. Every night, two local stage hands would climb the rear truss and run the follow spots. Up to this point, no other tour had rear follow spots on the truss close to the stage. The rear follow spot affect took off, and after *Tusk*, it became an industry standard that every band used.

The whole *Tusk* project was getting bigger. From the record promotion to the tour it was on a whole different level than anything the band had done before.

The design of the elaborate stage set-up was now dictated by the enormity of what The Mac had become.

On the stage, there was to be a hydraulic lift for Christine's piano, so as not to block her full body shot and showcase her more onstage. It was decided not to have her sit behind the piano anymore. They wanted her to stand up and be seen as much as Stevie to balance the stage. Besides the piano was only used for a couple of songs including "Song Bird," the last song of the set every night. We even brought an upright piano that rolled onto the other side of the stage, which Christine would use to play on "Sara," Stevie's tune, because it was a tack piano, and I mean, virtually a tack piano where thumb tacks were placed on the piano hammers to get that sharp and distinct sound for the song.

There was a huge drum riser to handle the now-massive drum kit. Even the stage itself had a bunch of pieces. There was a substage on each side that was three feet lower than the rest of the stage so that the guitar, key, and other techs could be offstage and not seen by the audience. Then just offstage on both sides, there were dressing room tents where Stevie and Christine could do their hair, makeup, and wardrobe changes, and inconspicuously indulge in the drugs that kept us all going.

As the whole thing came together in the production rehearsals, with the sound and the lights and the backdrops and the stage, it really started to look and feel great. It fit the vision of the band, and it matched the music that Lindsey and the rest of the band had assembled for *Tusk*.

At the end of September, we loaded the light rig into SIR, just to see how it worked. About a week later, we moved it over to WorldStage, along with the sound equipment and everything else. (Actually, at the time, it was called Zoetrope Studios because it had been bought by Francis Ford Coppola. In fact, right next door, Coppola was filming *One from the Heart* and actually recreated a portion of the Las Vegas Strip.

One day, I was leaving the studio. As I swung open the door, in came this person at a very quick pace, and BAM—we knocked into each other—things went flying everywhere. As the chaos subsided, there was Coppola on the floor next to me. At first, I didn't know who it was and immediately apologized and took responsibility for the collision. Then, to my amazement, I noticed that I had knocked over Francis Ford Coppola. Not sure what was going to happen, I went to help him up. He got up and actually apologized to me, saying he just wasn't looking. I took the opportunity to introduce myself, and he invited me to come and see the *One from the Heart* set.

Later that night, when I was done, I took him up on his offer and spent the rest of the night in awe, watching Coppola do his magic. Keep in mind, this was right around the time of the release of *Apocalypse Now*. He was on top of his game.

We ended up rehearsing the *Tusk* tour for a good month or so—spending probably $1,000 or $2,000 a day for this giant film stage. We brought in the whole sound system, as well, as all of the scenery way before the band to see how it would play off the lights and the overall look of the tour.

The tour was now at the level of the majors like the Rolling Stones, Beach Boys, and other large-scale tours with multiple trucks, buses, and very large crews.

JC and Trip, our main sound engineer, feared that this was too big for me to be the production/stage manager. JC recommend to the band that they bring in a production manager who had the experience to handle and coordinate a tour this big. I was insulted, and in my heart knew (or thought) I could do the job.

It didn't matter what I thought or felt the band decided and JC brought in Chris Lamb. I knew Chris from touring with Queen and a lot of the other shows that I had worked. Chris was an overall production manager with great experience and had tools that I didn't. He knew about budgets and mainly accountability for a tour this size. He also had a keen sense about coordination to move a tour of this size around. Just coordinating the daily union labor was huge undertaking and cost that could affect the bottom line.

Chris was a good friend of Trip's, and their combined experience was invaluable. I felt slated though. I was there from the start and felt like I was being demoted, and the jealousy set it hard. This is my tour! My band! Who the fuck do they think they are!

In hindsight, they had made the right decision to bring in Chris, and in fact, all the people that they did for all the jobs for the *Tusk* tour. It was a huge undertaking, and I never would have been able to make it happen. I just wasn't organized or experienced enough for a tour that had eleven full trucks, five tour buses (with over fifty crew members), and a private jet for the band.

Chris, on the other hand, knew his shit and had the experience with other large tours and shows and could get the job done. If I would have been deemed the production manager for the *Tusk* tour, my career in music would have been over. I would have failed and been banished into oblivion.

Chris and Trip were great. They had so much experience with bigger tours, and they took me under their wings and taught me a lot, always encouraging me. "You're great, Leo. Amazed how much you know for your age, Leo. Try it this way, do it that way." They allowed me to learn and grow and always included me in the major decisions of the tour so I could learn and grow.

I was humbled.

So, the crew heads were set. Chris was the production manager, Trip was head soundman, I was head electrician and lighting director, Curry ran lighting design, and my old friend Ray Lindsey was equipment/stage manager.

With the tour being so big with piano lifts, back drops, and staging, we needed a good head carpenter to put it all together every day—someone with a lot of skill, good on their feet and good with people. It was decided to hire my old friend Dave Richanbach—Shark Boy—for the job, not only because he was good with tools but because he was a good communicator and had done several of the Fleetwood Mac tours already. It was great for me because he and I would be first in and last out every day and night, and we know we could count on each other.

CHAPTER TWENTY FIVE

TUSK REHEARSALS

THE REHEARSALS WERE GOING GREAT, but the band was burnt out from producing the record. None of them really wanted to rehearse much or really be around each other. The crew would go in and tune up and be show ready for a rehearsal, and the band would come in, play maybe a set or a half a set, sit around and bullshit, then leave.

The anticipation of the release of *Tusk* and the tour to follow was epic, and the whole world was waiting and watching every move the band was making.

One day during rehearsals, we were all invited down to Hollywood Blvd. to watch the band receive their

Mick and John love pranks and shenanigans. This is one of my favorite shots that needs no explanation.

Hollywood star on the Walk of Fame. The Mac's star was perfectly placed smack dab in front of Fredrick's of Hollywood, the very sexy, sleazy lingerie store. Behind the band stood mannequins in garter belts and laced bras. The city of Los Angeles also declared it Fleetwood Mac day, and all the politicians who were just ugly failed actors were there in full force, vying for attention.

The next day, *People Magazine* showed up at rehearsals, doing a day in the life expose of Fleetwood Mac's band and crew. Being part of one of the biggest bands in the world, arrogance was at an all-time high. The resentments were starting to kick in, and all of us crew did whatever we could to derail the whole process by giving quirky answers and elaborating on complete nonsense. We made things so simple look like rocket science, and they bought into every bit of it. It didn't really matter, though, because at the end, they got the last laugh, and we all ended up on the cutting room floor.

We were in the rehearsal hall quite a while—it almost seemed like there was all the time in the world to prep and get the show down. Then, before we knew it, it got to be late October, and we were on our way to Idaho for the first show on the twenty-fifth. The Mac's first shows of every tour were always in out-of-the-way and obscure places. This was to avoid the press and media and give the band a chance to perfect the show and avoid bad reviews. We would find a city without an airport that the press just wouldn't fly to. We did, however, get the diehard one or two that would go to the ends of the Earth if that's where we were headed. Pocatello, Idaho was perfect, and it had a huge indoor/outdoor stadium with a huge footprint to accommodate the initial load-in and rehearsal.

Suddenly, it hit everyone. "Oh shit, we actually have a tour starting, and we have to do some shows now." So, the last four days of rehearsals, the eighteenth through the twenty-first, were mega-days where the band ran the set over and over and over. We also had a lot of last minute things we needed to take care of: things like spare lamps and screws bolts, little things that added up to a whole lot. We rehearsed one last time, and then the whole crew took a whole day to figure out the puzzle of the eleven truck pack, and the order of what went into the venue first, and the logistics of how the massive amounts of gear went in and out.

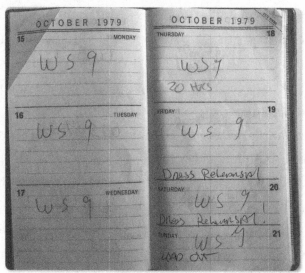

My day planner before computers. Long days, dress rehearsals, and load out.

This is where Chris was good. Down to the details, he had a vision of what we needed to do in order to make sure the show went up smoothly. It's an art. It really is.

During rehearsals, songs like "Sara" translated well. Lindsey did his stuff in the middle of the set. It was very rowdy and up-tempo. It was so unlike Fleetwood Mac. In certain songs, it translated, but in the end, it didn't matter because it was Fleetwood Mac. As long as they did the *Rumours* hits, and the white album hits, and a smattering of the older material, people were happy.

However, it became apparent during rehearsals that Fleetwood Mac was no longer a little family. Mainly because of my age, I had never really penetrated the band's innermost circle, but Curry had. He and Christine were together, so Curry went to the studio almost every night. Curry was as close as I ever got to the incestuous relationships of The Mac.

Fleetwood Mac was now a giant machine: lawyers and accountants, merchandising people, press and PR staff, ambience directors, even a masseuse and people to take care of pets on the road.

There was a time when the band was managing themselves with Mick and John at the helm. But now, there were rumblings of other people coming in to manage Stevie and Lindsey. The egos and attitudes were growing at a very fast pace. Stevie wasn't too hot on the new material. She mostly just went with it, but every once in a while, she would get into a rebellious, fighting mood. There was no way in the world that Lindsey was going to let Stevie have any control, especially with the music. In the beginning, the band only wanted Lindsey, and he had to convince them to bring Stevie along, and now Stevie was a driving force, and that was front and center.

For all of us who were there from the start and knew the dynamics, we knew that we all needed each other to make it right. Lindsey's production skills and aggressive style gave Stevie and Chris's songs space, room to breathe, and layers in tasteful parts that could be heard, enhancing the melodies to blend and wrap the lyrics around the music. Stevie and Chris wrote the songs that allowed Lindsey to do things no other band in history could do. It was the classic chicken-and-egg syndrome that was nothing without the solid rhythm section of Mick and John.

Call it circumstance, fate, destiny—five people with very diverse backgrounds, lifestyles, and amazing talent found each other and created a music style that has yet to be reproduced.

The tour routing was causing a lot of tension and drama. Looking at the itinerary, we were doing a lot of shows in a row, and it was going to be a real challenge mentally and physically on everyone from band to crew.

It affected the whole organization. To me, we were like this highly skilled sports team that, instead of playing hard to win and reach the levels we all achieved, we played to not lose, not fail, and just survive. There was fear, a fear of losing all we had gained and becoming irrelevant and inferior.

Fear is a tough emotion, and with The Mac, the fear manifested into anger, and once again, that underlying anger created that Fleetwood Mac magic onstage that could only be conceived by the five of them and will never be recreated.

JC was still the tour manager. And I think JC was struggling as much as a lot of us with Fleetwood Mac getting so big. He wasn't himself, and things that came naturally for JC to keep The Mac running like in the past were not as easy.

There were money people, accountants, lawyers, spouses looking over his shoulder auditing every move and forcing him to be accountable for every penny. The show grosses were so big that even the Internal Revenue Service were present every night to take their share.

For sure, that was not JC and not the way things were done in the past. We used to have this saying, "Fleetwood Mac problem; pour money on it, no problem."

JC was forced to be more diligent on the paperwork, and if there's one thing we all knew about JC, he did not get into rock 'n' roll to do more paperwork. It was decided to bring in a tour accountant, not only to do the tour budgets but to settle the shows every night. The business was changing, and money was taking the front seat over art, which was new to all of us, and it took a lot to get used to.

The band now had a private jet to get from city to city, so that all had to be coordinated. Just getting the drugs needed for the tour took the coordination skills of an octopus.

On the crew side of the tour, it now took a small army to set up, organize, and control our new massive operation. Each person in the band had his own tour coordinator or assistant with their own limo 24-7 from the time they got off the jet to the time the jet departed to the next city. Stevie and Chris had make-up people and wardrobe people. Our old friend from New Zealand, Wayne, was watching John McVie. A friend of Wayne's named Dennis was assigned to watch after Mick. Stevie had this guy named Dwayne. Lindsey, who was low-maintenance, had a guy by the name of Jet and Christine had another Dennis.

When the *Tusk* tour finally hit the road, what was once a thirteen-people tour in 1975 had become a 110-person traveling spectacle.

The little family vibe of what made The Mac so special was gone, and it was now a large, virtual corporation moving from city to city, grossing as much money as IBM or Coke.

All of us crew, security people, and assistants, with our orders and routines, fell into place to make the tour work.

Each band member had their own schedule and their own times. So, it was pretty much JC coordinating with each of the security team members to get the band where they needed to be.

Knowing that Stevie was always late, if we needed a venue call at six p.m., he would give Doug and Stevie a call time of four-thirty p.m. If John's call was at three, he would tell Wayne three because John was always on time. JC knew the band and their intricacies, and every night, the band would all end up being where they needed to be and on time.

At twenty-two years old, I was changing and still learning a lot about myself. Chris and Trip kept teaching me how to act and survive on the road with a tour that big. It wasn't easy, and the hardest part for me was getting over my own ego and my resurfacing youthful insecurity: no matter what happened, I had this feeling that I had to be the one who was right at all times, so as not to feel like a failure and feel inferior.

A lot of my feelings can be attributed to the drugs I was doing to comfort the negative feelings. But even after I got out of the drug scene, it took me many years to realize that I didn't always have to be right, and it was OK to keep learning and growing, and it was about being confident in what you had and trusting where you were going was going to be OK.

On *Tusk*, every day was an adventure. I was evolving with the business and learning a lot about eccentric people and their quirks and needs. The *Tusk* tour was full of abnormal situations and bizarre needs that were necessary to keep the tour moving. Even the backstage area was fitted for ambiance, not only for comfort, but for safety as well. Using ice buckets filled with ice would get the floor damp and wet. Several times Stevie, in her heels from her famous knee-high boots, almost fell, and that could have seriously hurt her, and the tour would have been over. It was decided to bring in refrigerators to all the dressing rooms to avoid accidents that could cause cancelations. Even though a cost, it was a small cost, verses the cost of cancelling shows.

The band also didn't want the backstage area to be plain, bland, and ugly like so many of those arenas were. It was decided to bring in the ambience director, Mike. Mike was working for Don Fox at Beaver Production, which was promoting most of the *Tusk* tour. Mike would make sure that every night the locker rooms and dressing rooms in the arenas and stadiums were comfortable (and ended up looking like a living room instead of a smelly locker room with cold floors and steel cages).

Mike would work with the local promoter to bring in drapery and couches and planters and lamps and pictures and whatever else it took to really make the place feel nice. He would transform these locker rooms into the best green rooms you would find in any theater.

Mike would be the first one up in the morning, announcing that today was Cabin Day or Hawaii Day or Mountain Day. And he would have a budget to transform the room. He also had carte blanche to trade tickets for items he needed to do his magic.

It almost became like a game with the band. Fitting out these rooms was not cheap—they spent a lot of money every day to make a cold, sterile shell of a room look like the Taj Mahal.

The logic for expenditures was becoming skewed. With tickets selling at fifty dollars apiece, the mantra became, "It's only a hundred tickets for this or two hundred tickets for that," so it seemed worth it, but in the end, as you will read, it all caught up with everyone.

Mike also did things that were very entertaining to keep the tour morale going and entertain the rest of us. Sometimes, as they walked into their *Tusk* atmosphere du jour, Mike would have some bizarre side show that no one would ever possibly think of.

One time in Texas, he gathered a bunch of us into the guy's dressing room for a daily spectacle. After a discussion with the six-foot-five Mick Fleetwood about his height and difficulties of being that tall, Mike thought it would be funny to expand on their conversation. On that fateful day in Texas, Mike had hired four, let's say "vertically challenged people," (little people) to dress up like cowboys with big cowboy hats to sing "Long Tall Texan" as Mick Fleetwood entered the dressing room. Imagine the sight of these four short cowboys surrounding Mick and coming up to only the top of his knees, serenading him.

Of course, the decadence included lots of drugs, mainly cocaine. There was so much of it around, and the distribution and coordination was a complex plan. The cocaine was hidden everywhere, including reverse topped small fire extinguishers where the top would unscrew in the opposite direction with the bottom filled with the powder. There were hidden spaces in road cases; mainly the stage pass case we called "Killer." It had a puzzle-type false back that, when figured out, led to an odorless chamber even the best drug canines couldn't detect.

Each of the security guards would be given a set of Heineken beer bottle caps. The caps were filled up with coke and placed on paper plates. When the band members were onstage, the plates full of cocaine-filled bottle caps were strategically placed in reach of each band member so any one of them could discreetly put a cap up to their nose, snort it up, and then toss the bottle cap. It was very inconspicuous, and only those of us on the inside knew this elaborate scheme.

Unlike the old family Fleetwood Mac days, where there was less crew and drugs were shared and flowed freely, the cocaine was now only for the band.

However, the security guards who were the guardians and gatekeepers of the "go powder" always took care of us who were responsible for getting The Mac to their monumental fame.

Wayno would bring a fresh plate of bottle caps out right at the end of the show right before the encore. He would always make sure that we (out in the middle of the arena at the sound and light boards) had a taste too. When the house lights came on, all the bottle tops would be fair game to the crew—first come, first served. Being closer to the plates, the band's road crew—those taking care of the changes while the show was on—had the first shot at the coveted plates.

If you ever see any old film or footage of the *Tusk* tour, you can see crew members actually diving toward these plates at the moment the house lights came up.

To simplify and be inconspicuous the code name "toot" was given to our legendary bottlecap initiative.

We even went as far as to print the acronym "GMAT" on the backstage passes, which stood for "give me a toot." It became a rally cry. If you happen to be wandering around backstage at a Fleetwood Mac show on the *Tusk* tour, you would have heard whispers or the subtle mumbles of "GMAT," and if you were holding, you'd pass some on.

We were off, and the *Tusk* tour was on its way.

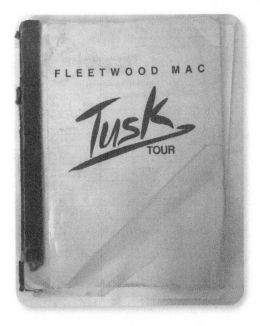

CHAPTER TWENTY SIX
TUSK HITS THE ROAD

BUILDING THE *TUSK* TOUR WAS A GRIND, but we did it and finally hit the road. The schematic of our lives was methodically laid out, and we were ready. The touring lifestyle was not one you acquired. Either you had it in you or you didn't. Some people had the mental and physical resilience to be on the road, but many became road casualties from the rigors of the road, with incapacitated dreams.

There were four legs booked. First, October through December in North America, then February in Japan. Then March, when we'd chase the spring sun in Australia and New Zealand and early summer end in Hawaii before

the summer European tour. The last leg was dedicated
to the Midwest and South, ending in Los Angeles at the
Hollywood Bowl.

I literally could write a whole book on this tour, and
may yet choose to do so. With my hundreds of journal
entries, photos, and stories from other crew members, the
Tusk story is one that could stand on its own. For this
book, there are a few poignant episodes on the *Tusk* tour
that are worth sharing.

For the first part
of the tour, we routed
through smaller markets
to make sure the ma-
chine was fine-tuned be-
fore we hit the northeast
doing cities like Boston,
Philadelphia, and New
York, where two-thirds

The Mini Dome at Idaho State
University, Pocatello Idaho, where
we started the Tusk tour.

of the United States population lived. Cities like Pocatello
and Ogden, Utah, were warm-up dates to refine the mistakes. The secondary cities like Salt Lake, Denver, and Al-
buquerque blurred by and were uneventful. Each show got
better and better, and we hit our stride, and the whole system—from load-in to show to load-out—was like a fined
tuned symphony.

The decision to film the two shows in St. Louis on
November fifth and sixth was made without consulting any of us on the crew. The dysfunctionality, lack of

communication, and greed was becoming apparent. The film producers made commitments to film at the Checker Dome, which was one of the most difficult venues in America to work. It didn't matter; the decision was made.

There were much easier and better places to film the show, but money was the factor. Lower local labor cost, venue costs, and lower travel expenses for the film crew dictated the decision to film in St. Louis. The decision was made by people who had never been on the road, nor had the expertise to find a better solution. Nevertheless, the date was booked, and the logistics were already in the works. Once again, the crew was asked to pull off a miracle, and we did. To supplement the rig and extra lights, labor and sound needed to film the show because of shooting at the Checker Dome drove the film shoot way over budget.

We finally hit the Northeast in full stride, going into New York for two sold out shows at Madison Square Gardens. The Mac attacked New York in full force , and everyone wanted to see The Mac, not only for the music, but for the spectacle around it too. The guest list ranged from politicians, to famous actors, to other rock 'n' roll stars, including Keith Richards and Ronny Wood from the Rolling Stones.

The most interesting guests were the New York elite types, like Andy Warhol, Timothy Leary, and the underbelly of the famed Studio 54 clan. After the first show Studio-54 hosted a record release party for the band and *Tusk*.

Many of us remember going to the party, but most of us (like me), remember very little after we got there and waking up the next morning wondering what day, month, and year it was.

To me, the most interesting thing that transpired that night was not onstage or even with the band. It was a moment of pride and acknowledgement that was uniting the gap between band and crew. With no loadout after opening night, our task was to just shut everything down and secure things for the night.

It was in the band's private dressing room where only the few elites would end up. The legendary story happened when our good friend and Lindsey's guitar tech, Ray, went into the dressing room to put away all the guitars and amps for the night.

In the dressing room, with all their intense sovereignty, were Keith Richards and Ronny Wood. Right in the middle of this soirée, a bunch of crew walked in to grab beverages and plan the aftershow events. "Glad you guys are here," Ray said as he hurried out the dressing room door. We didn't think much of it until later—when we heard the legendary story.

The story is better told from my dear friend Ray's book, *The Care and Feeding of Fleetwood Mac and Other Species.*

RAY: Every night I played "Go Your Own Way" onstage was a gas, but my favorite memory comes from the night a couple of Rolling Stones appeared at a gig. We were playing the first of two sold out nights in Madison Square Garden when halfway through the set, Keith Richards and Ron Wood appear beside me at my work area beside the stage. I knew Woody from his visits to our band house on Mulholland and made some room for the pair to stand by me with a clear view of the stage. I made sure their drinks were topped off and got back to work.

They were entertaining guests and had a great time checking out all the gear while taking in the show. Toward the end of the set, I strapped on my Ovation guitar to check the tuning and prepare for my entrance.

At first, Keith didn't seem to care much about the plastic bowl of a guitar around my neck until two things caught his eye. First, it had a capo high on the eighteenth fret, and secondly, it only had five strings. We had taken the low "E" string off because the root note of the chords I was playing was on the fifth string and the sixth wasn't needed.

Keith was famous among guitarists for playing in open tunings that chucked the superfluous low string as well. He was even more amused when I kept the guitar on and stepped around the pair to climb the steps and take my place onstage. It was an over-the-top NYC night at the Garden, and "Go Your Own Way" didn't disappoint. Once again, I happily rode the band's coattails for my five minutes of personal rock bliss.

When the song finished, I returned to my tuning station and noticed my two guests had disappeared. Twenty minutes later, the band finished their encores and left the stage for the last time. Since there was another show at the Garden the next night, the crew didn't have a lot to do. I headed to the dressing room to lock up my guitars and grab a beverage. I was drinking a beer with Lindsey when Keith appears from behind me, throws his arm around my shoulders, and bestows upon me classic Keith Richards incoherence, "That was fuckin' great, man." Woody hugged me from the other side and offered his own drunken words of admiration.

For a brief, priceless moment, I was the center of attention between the two Rolling Stones guitar players. Sensing it was time to redirect the focus back on my boss, I shared the story of Lindsey listening to "Street Fighting Man" at the Record Plant Bunkhouse in Mill Valley and getting the idea for the drums on one of his song. This pleased the two guitarists greatly, and the conversation veered back to Charlie Watts and old Stones records.

Ray playing "Go Your Own Way" at the Hollywood Bowl.

The dressing room was suddenly filled with crew guys not used to having free time after a show, so I excused myself and melted into their crowd.

New York came and went, and we wound our way through the United States like a whitewater river ending up at the Pacific Ocean in December doing shows in Los Angeles, San Diego, and finishing the first leg in San Francisco.

The newly proclaimed rock palace the Forum in Los Angeles was the place to play. Three nights immediately sold out, and after a token, smaller San Diego date, we had two more sold out shows at the Forum.

Mick Fleetwood was always thinking and wanted more for his fans, something special for the opening night at the Forum. His idea was to keep the crowd entertained non-stop—from when they came into the building until they left. This meant having some entertainment during the set change between The Mac's opener, Danny Douma, and The Mac. Mick had seen an escape artist whose name escapes me, but I think it was the Great Ronzonni. His routine was to be chained up in a straightjacket and locked into a small safe, and then escape within three minutes.

Danny finished his set, and the safe was brought out center to the front of the stage, along with Ronzonni the great and his female assistant. "Being chained and locked up, the Great Ronzonni will now escape and free himself!" said the beautiful assistant who was narrating the whole stunt. The trunk was shaking and moving while the assistant was narrating the dangers of lack of air, tight spaces, and the temperature inside the box. As we navigated around the box changing the set, we noticed that box was moving less and less, and the beautiful assistant was running out of dialogue and looking more and more concerned. Three minutes became five, five became seven, seven became ten, and there was no physical movement of the safe and no signs of life coming from the trunk. The Great Ronzonni assistant was now concerned and in tears. We all stood on the side of the stage with the band now ready to play and JC screaming at us, "What the fuck is going on?"

We pointed to the safe and said, "Not sure, but this doesn't look good."

JC made the decision to just get the box offstage, and the promoter rep Bill Reed went out with some small joke like: "Just kidding; let's give it up for the Great Ronzonni." With a forklift, we took the safe away, and The Mac hit the stage.

Backstage, with the safe in the tunnel, the assistant showed us the false door that revealed the trick. After removing the chains and prying open the trapdoor of the prop safe, we found an unconscious and Less-Than-Great-Ronzonni totally passed out with no signs of life. He was checked and, thank God, was alive. After a few taps and encouragement, "Hey, buddy, wake up. Come, on wake up," he took a few deep breaths and came to. We gave him some oxygen, which revived him, and handed him over to the paramedics. No one's sure what happened, and Ronzonni the Great was too embarrassed to want to discuss it. We chalked it up to another normal oddity in the world of Fleetwood Mac.

We finally hit the end of the decade. The 70s were dying off, and the 80s were looking good.

I couldn't think of a better place to end the first leg of the *Tusk* tour than in San Francisco. Three days at the Cow Palace, thirty minutes south of San Francisco. The shows were great, and we were all excited to be going home for the holidays.

The whole music scene in San Francisco was controlled, and pretty much owned, by the legendary promoter Bill Graham. The rumor was Bill wouldn't give The Mac the deal they wanted, and with the "new" people involved in the band's decision-making, Don Fox and Beaver Productions came into San Francisco to do the three shows.

Bill Graham was not amused, especially with all the support early in The Mac's career and all the money he paid them for the Day on the Green shows. It was like the Wild West when a young gunslinger would waltz into town guns a blazing, "Look out, people. There's a new sheriff in town."

We were excited to be in San Francisco, and with the crew being so large, we were put up at the Holiday Inn on Van Ness Avenue, while the band was the at the five-star Saint Francis Hotel in plush Union Square.

This was fodder for the ultimate Don Fox prank and revenge on his old friend JC.

Since 1972, JC had the reins and held them tightly. His harshness and inflexible attitude was purely to protect John, Chris, and Mick, and now Stevie and Lindsey. In the early days of Fleetwood Mac, JC spent most of the day dealing with the general public at hotels, airports, and restaurants, viewing his successful family as diverse freaks. The remainder of the day was dealing with promoters and venues getting the most he could out of them for the band.

He actually came from a very well established and well-to-do family that founded the Courage Ale Company. To rebel against the proper, English, traditional world he was raised up in, he ran off with Chicken Shack (Christine McVie's band before The Mac), and escaped to the circus of rock 'n' roll.

Don Fox and Trip Khalaf
in Hawaii 1979

When JC was ten years old, to teach him the value of hard work, his father got him a job at a poultry plant, dismembering and preparing the birds for processing. This left JC with not only a hate but a fear of chickens. His mistake was sharing this with

343

the crew and band. Over the years, people would mess with JC and sneak up behind him and cackle like a chicken to raise his tension.

Don Fox wanted to end the 70s with the ultimate prank on JC—a prank that he would never forget, and in fact, became a famous story in the annals of rock history.

Fox decided to inundate JC with his biggest fear: chickens. The plan: while we were all at the show for soundcheck and performance, he would fill JC's hotel room with live chickens. Not a couple of chickens, a lot of them.

Ray Compton, Fox's longtime confidant and loyal partner, tells the story from here.

Ray Compton:

Fox and I wanted to really get to JC. For the whole tour, he was busting our balls, and after the cowboy hat stupidity in Houston, we really wanted to fuck him over.

I remembered the whole chicken thing and knew we were in the right town to pull this off.

You see, Chinese people like to kill the chickens right before they eat them. They are fresher and taste better, so we knew we could get live chickens in Chinatown. So, I enlisted my local friend Pat Morrow, who was working with Journey, to help me pull this off. The idea was we would go to Chinatown and pick up live chickens and roosters to put them into JC's hotel room. We took my rental car and drove around all of Chinatown to get as many live chickens and roosters as we could. After we got the chickens and roosters, we pulled up to the back of the St. Francis Hotel with eight crates full. I paid off the bellman to use the freight service elevator to get up to the floor that JC's room was on. We also picked up corn feed, hey, and cognac to spread around in the drawers and cabinets that we opened around the room.

As the elevator doors opened, we were greeted by the maids on duty. They looked at us, startled and shocked, I just shouted, "Don't ask!" and continued on with the chickens and roosters.

We virtually turned JC's room into a small farm.

Fox's plan was to set up an end of tour party for the band and crew after the show to unveil his masterful plan and ultimate prank. No one knew about this, none of the crew, security guys, or the band.

For over eight hours, while the band was at soundcheck and then doing the show, the chickens and roosters were in JC's room shitting, pecking, poking, and screwing.

It was the perfect revenge to get back at JC for all the stunts that he had pulled over the whole tour. Fox made sure he rode back with JC in the same car but didn't actually go upstairs with him. According to Wayno, Christine's security person, when they got near his room, it was the odor and noise that was the first indication that something was up. When JC opened the door, he was out of his mind angry, and the room was a fucking mess. Shit was everywhere, and the smell was like being at a farm. JC yelled at the top of his lungs, "FOX! You're dead. You're a dead man!"

After a few minutes, me and Fox went up, and even Fox was in shock because he had no idea how far me and Pat took it. I mean, the room was trashed, and most of JC's personal items couldn't be replaced, and all the furniture in the hotel room was fucked up with holes and stains, unrepairable. Fox told JC, "Courage, I swear it wasn't supposed to be this bad," yelling at me, saying, "Ray, a few chickens, not a whole fucking farm!"

Well, the whole thing then turned and went a bad way for Fox. The whole entourage now knew and were up by JC's, witnessing the ongoing saga of JC vs. Fox. So, JC in his rage, started to shoo the chicken out the door into the hallway, and that was the cue for everyone else to jump in. Dennis Wilson of the Beach Boys, who was Christine McVie's boyfriend at the time, opened the window and was going to throw a chicken out until someone stopped him yelling, "Fuck, Dennis. Chickens don't fly." Then someone, I think it was Curry, started putting chickens onto the elevator and pushing the lobby button.

The Five Star St. Francis Hotel in San Francisco.

We searched high and low and this is the only shot we could find of the infamous chicken story at the St Francis Hotel.

So, there was some sort of Christmas party going on in the ballroom, and some tennis team for some cup was in the hotel, and the elevator door would open, and chickens and roosters would run out, and before we knew it, there were chickens all over the hotel and in Union Square. It was so funny; you see all these guys in suits and ties getting out of the elevator, and two chickens would follow them out, like they belonged.

The party lasted until morning, and by now, the hundreds of chickens and roosters were all over downtown, and the police were called.

We were asked to leave the hotel and, of course, were responsible for all the cleanup cost, which included moving guests to other properties and dealing with all of the animal rights groups.

In the end, it ended up costing a ton of money, and Fox had to pay it all, so JC got the last laugh. And I was in Fox's doghouse for the rest of my life.

A prank for the ages that today you could never get away with, but it was just another day in our life.

Most of the crew got to the St. Francis later after going to our hotel to prep for the party and the initial spectacle. I remember walking into the plush lobby and seeing the chickens and roosters, and we all looked at each other and said with a smile, "Fox." In the end, JC was a good sport, and the whole episode became one of the most famous rock 'n' roll stunts ever played.

We lost Ray Compton in the winter of 2018. Ray was an original member of the Knights of Rock and a brother, and I was so fortunate to get Ray's story in 2006, when we shot the original Knights of Rock piece.

Not only was Ray a great person and friend but an innovator who crafted many logistical and financial solutions that the music touring business still uses today.

So, the decade was over, and we all went home to try to assimilate back into normal life after chasing a feather in the wind. When I got back home to San Pedro, the saltwater air, my mother's lasagna, and other smells from my childhood were hitting me. They were a calming force when my mind was telling me I had to be here or had to be there or do this or that. I finally settled down in late January, about a week before we were off once again to Australia and Japan.

After we brought our own complete system to Australia and Japan in 1977, all the lighting and sound companies ramped up, vowing to never let a band like The Mac bring their own rig.

They became sophisticated very fast and now had everything, including instruments we could use instead of leasing a DC-8 to do the job.

Lots happened on that *Tusk* tour, but there's one famous event concerning a strange night in New Zealand. Read and believe what you want, but this is my firsthand recollection of being there when it happened.

The Australian tour went well and was planned with the normal magical animosity that was Fleetwood Mac. The tour was taking a toll on the band. The time zone changes, different cultures—even different local water—can affect even the strongest of people. Another factor was the drugs were different and what was being ingested may not have been as potent or pure.

We all knew that Lindsey wasn't one who really like touring and being ripped away from his norm, that was, his house and being in a studio. I saw him becoming more introverted and on edge; he wasn't hanging around as much. I also noticed Carol, his girlfriend, was more aloof, looking like an animal that was being stalked, trying not to become some other animal's dinner.

One crazy night in Wellington, New Zealand, I was backstage with Curry in the dressing rooms, and I saw Lindsey pacing, noodling his guitar as normal, but this night, he was a bit more aggressive. He stopped and asked Greg, his security person, to get JC. While waiting for JC, he shared a joint with Curry and was saying he had just had enough. It was a rant about everything—the travel, the food, the hotels, the shitty drugs, it's too hot, Stevie, John's drinking. It went on and on and on. It

Wellington Concert Poster

was obvious he wasn't in a good space, like a boxer winding up for a fight, ready to go apeshit.

When JC surfaced, Lindsey's face turned red with anger, and once again, JC was the target of the rage that was about to hit full force. Curry tapped my shoulder and pointed toward the door, and we both walked out.

The over 40,000 people didn't have a clue what they were in for, and honestly, neither did I. The band hit the stage, and I was out at the light board sitting with Curry, and it was obvious that Lindsey was out for blood. The guitars were getting louder and louder, and the notes were flying out like a jet in wild turbulence. Soft part of songs were overrun with harsh guitar sounds and notes were so deliberately off even a tone-deaf person would cringe.

Trip, the front of house sound engineer, looked over at Curry and me and threw his hands up into the air, surrendering to this new Fleetwood Mac anomaly. There were many band squabbles and fights, but never before had it negatively filtered into the magic space of the stage.

Then came "Rhiannon," Stevie's signature song. Stevie always started offstage and would enter from stage left. With her black veil and head down, Stevie would walk behind Lindsey right after the famous guitar intro. Tonight was different though. Lindsey faced the crowd, looked over his shoulder to see Stevie making her entrance, and began slowly stepping backwards, with every step reducing the space and room for Stevie to get by. She wasn't sure what to do, and this awkward moment became an ordeal. Stevie barely squeezed by, and with a look of "what the fuck, Lindsey" crackled the first words of Rhiannon.

The first verse was all over the place, with sounds and notes none of us never heard before. Then comes the beautiful soft three-part harmony chorus that sets up the solos and, "Rhiannnnnnnnon, Rhiannnnnnon," and it had wild guitar solos and notes that took any heart and soul out of the equation. Then, the deliberate, extra-long solo made Stevie stay crouched down waiting for the middle section of the song where all the lights, sound, and focus were on Stevie, while she mystically danced around in front of the large fans we had placed to make it look like she was flying. Mick, John, and Chris were lost, not knowing when to make the musical changes to all be in sync.

Finally, Lindsey tailed out of the solo into the slow section with Stevie dancing and where Lindsey would usually paint by notes to Stevie's beautiful movements onstage, but that night, the notes were loud and obtrusive. At this point, the stage was relatively dark, except for many different colors of lights from many angles, including the rear follow spots. I looked over at Lindsey and, OH FUCK! He threw his jacket over his head to mimic Stevie and started to dance around like her. "Curry!" I hissed, "are you seeing this?" I pointed to Lindsey. Curry reached for the faders for Lindsey's lights, and brought them down to zero and no more Lindsey. Well, we thought. I'm not sure if Lindsey knew he was in the dark or not, but he decided (with his new outfit) to walk over and get right into Stevie's light while she was dancing. Stevie looked up with a face of anger, and it was game on!

Throughout the rest of the set, there were sour and flat notes. During "Landslide," Lindsey was playing jazz notes, and in return, Stevie would either stop singing on all Lindsey's songs or sing purposely out of key.

Then came the last song of the set, "Go Your Own Way," the anthem inspired by Lindsey Buckingham and Stevie Nicks and used by the youth generations as an anthem for the love/hate relationship.

By this time, they both had enough, and it was a train wreck. Mick, John, and Chris, as solid as ever, just went along with it until the solo, where Stevie decided to dance and swirl and twirl center stage to draw attention away from Lindsey's solos. At the highlight of the solo, Lindsey came up behind Stevie and was jabbing the guitar neck into her lower back, stamping his feet and headbutting the back of Stevie's head. With fear in her eyes, Stevie took herself out of the equation and went to hide behind Christine at her keyboards. Lindsey followed but Christine's look of "don't you dare, motherfucker," scared Lindsey off like she had a gun. He went back to stage right to finish the solo and the set. At this point, I saw in Stevie's eyes the hesitation and uncertainty of what was going to happen next, but she knew she needed come out from behind Chris.

As the solo was ending, she was back center stage, keeping one eye on the crowd and the other on her biggest fear, Lindsey.

Lindsey finished the solo with rage and fury like none of us had ever witnessed, and after the snare, bass, keys, and guitar hit the last note, Lindsey ripped off the strap, took off his prized possession—a 1959 Les Paul guitar—and hurled it at Stevie. The guitar went flying through the air, like a missile heading to destroy its target. Stevie saw the guitar and luckily dodged it as it slid across the stage and landed right in front of Christine's keyboard rig.

Lindsey walked offstage as the rest of the band did a quick huddle to figure out how to address what the large stadium crowd had just witnessed.

I think it was Chris who said, "Thanks for coming, everyone." Stevie was too shaken up to say a word. John, who rarely came to the mic, said something, but knowing that he rarely spoke, the fader wasn't up; all I heard was, "It happens, and we'll be back."

All of us out in the front of the house tower just sat there in stunned silence as people hurled insults and wrapped us in a blanket of negativity.

We weren't backstage, but I heard that Lindsey went to his dressing room, packed up, and just left, but not before Christine tossed a drink into his face and tore him up.

Luckily, it was the last show of the Australia/New Zealand tour, and we were heading for Japan with a few days off to regroup and lick our wounds.

Lindsey was in the penalty box, and we weren't sure if we were heading to Japan or if Fleetwood Mac finally imploded and it was really over. Had it hit the point of no return?

Naaah, not The Mac. Just another day, another paranormal moment, and one of the nine lives of Fleetwood Mac. Things did calm down, but as far as I know, Lindsey never apologized. But that's Fleetwood Mac, the functioning, dysfunctional family making separate choices, not understanding that the choices were made for them by powers much stronger than their own. Fleetwood Mac would have ended a long time ago and never lasted if their fate and destiny was not preordained.

We hit Japan and then perfectly ended up in the much-needed tropical sun of Hawaii before the *Tusk* circus was on to Europe.

Being with Fleetwood Mac in Europe was always a good adventure. Being from the UK, the band cut their teeth on the continent following the Beatles path of Germany and all points south. It's unbelievable to think at one point that the old Mac was selling more records than the Beatles and there were hard-core fans who either loved the new Fleetwood Mac or hated them for abandoning their blues roots and becoming the quintessential pop band they had become.

Every European tour I did with The Mac, I grew—not only becoming more adaptable by learning and living within other cultures but gaining the experience of moving a large tour over multiple countries and borders. Before the European Union, touring Europe was very complex— multiple currencies, immigration, and borders. "OK, boys. We're at the border; wake up off the bus; bring your passports." This was right after you got to sleep after a long day, and sometimes, there were multiple border stops a night. The business was getting smarter though, and we, as always, figured out ways to use our stature to not beat the system but make our lives easier. It went from everyone off the bus to one guy with all the passports, a good rap, and a wad of local currencies to expedite our travel.

The Euro tour was mainly stadium shows and was a huge success. Only one cancelation from Mick and Lindsey, who thought they could keep up with Mick Jagger and Keith Richards one night. They tried but decided five minutes before a show in Germany that they were unable to make it through the set.

The little redheaded stepchild of rock 'n' roll was now a strong teenager flexing its muscles. Realizing the power in numbers, groups starting doubling and tripling up, combining efforts at the huge soccer stadiums all over Europe.

WHEN THE DEVIL SMILES, THE ANGELS FROWN

The summer of 1980, the epic tour was Santana, followed by Bob Marley, and then Fleetwood Mac. We combined forces, using the same staging, sound, and lights—crews even went as far as sharing the sacred ground of sharing musical instruments.

By 1979, Santana was already internationally recognized and could sell out stadiums on his own. Bob Marley was a force in Europe and gaining more momentum in North America, and the plan was to break him into Asia and Australia, which happened—but only after his unfortunate passing in 1981.

The tour was epic, not only in size but synergies. All the bands and crews got along, and it was a logistical and technical marvel. The experience and connections of our production manager, Chris, and his partner, Gerry, created this moving virtual city that transformed open fields and stadiums into temporary utopias that are here today and gone tomorrow. They were very long days with multiple set ups. While on the stage in Vienna, the stage in Kaiserslauten—the next stop on the tour—was being built and ready for us two days later. The synchronization was military without all the restriction—and plenty of cocaine to keep it moving.

The highlight to me was Bob Marley. Me, like most Americans, had heard about Marley but didn't experience the big bottom bass beats and quarter note hashing guitars with the Jamaican accents and message of love and peace. "Jah provides the rest, is this love, is this love, is this love that I'm feeling."

Mark Miller, this white Jewish kid out of New York, was Bob's production manager and had the task of organizing the lives of over thirty Rastafarians, with their love and need of ganga. It looked dysfunctional, but it ran well. Everyone knew where and when to be, and the shows were fucking amazing.

One night in Germany, Bob and his band hit the stage. I did my normal rounds to make sure the lights and stage were ready. Out of nowhere, all the band, background singers, and crew came onstage through every nook and cranny, and one by one, were tuning and checking levels. What amazed me was the nontraditional way they started their show—no introductions

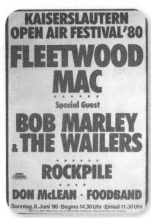

Fleetwood Mac and Bob Marley German concert poster.

or "are we ready?" No organization, just get out there and do it—180 degrees from how we did it with The Mac. The sweet smell of pot was everywhere, and what I thought was the smoke machines was just the blanket pot smoke from the band. One by one, they started to jam, and then there he was, Bob Marley. Bob was larger than life. There's artist, but then there's artist. Bob Marley had an energy, an aura, and a presence. I felt this calmness around the whole Marely ... all I could call it was "church."

This is the most iconic picture of the late great Bob Marley
taken by my friend, the incredible photographer Neal Preston

I sat on the huge subwoofer side fill that was there for
the necessary bass vibration the band needed. The first
song, "Natural Mystic," was electric—the whole band
moving in sync and the "I Threes," who were the background singers dressed in traditional, colorful, authentic
Jamaican dresses swaying in time with the drums and Peter Tosh's bass.

The next song was "Positive Vibration." Bob went to the
mic, and with his eyes closed sang, "Live if you want to live,
Rastaman, vibration yeah." Between the bass notes vibrating my body and the smell of pot and all the color, not only
onstage but in the crowd, I was somewhere I'd never been
before. Bob continued to sing the song, and in fact, did the
whole songs with his eyes closed, not missing a beat.

After the summer of 1980, reggae became a musical style that was etched into history, and its architect, Bob Marley, will never be forgotten.

I look back now and reflect on how fortunate I was to work with Bob Marley and to experience the growth of reggae—a true music pure and peaceful.

Later in life, like most children, mine got into reggae, and they were speaking to my friend Dennis Mays from the Fleetwood Mac family about it. Dennis said, "Ask your dad; we did a small summer tour with Marley back in the '80s." I didn't think I could become much cooler with my children, but I instantly did. Thanks, Bob!

CHAPTER TWENTY SEVEN
THE ANGELS AND DEVILS
IN EAST BERLIN

I WAS A TWENTY-TWO-YEAR-OLD KID with a much older soul during the *Tusk* European tour. Even though I had already been on the road for four years, I was still balancing the world of rock 'n' roll and my traditional Italian Catholic background, and at times, it was a very difficult thing.

Raised Old World Italian Catholic, you were taught the Ten Commandments, and without conditions, to honor your mother and father with the inherent promise to never disappoint or let them down.

It seemed that everything in the world of rock 'n' roll would break that promise and force me to live far outside the traditional Italian Catholic ways. I found myself living life in the fast lane, so as to be accepted by my peers and not become just another crewmember roadkill casualty.

Many times, I found myself doing things to stay relevant with my peers and then praying to God for forgiveness for forsaking everything I was taught as a boy.

Ahh, yes. Guilt!

I was great at hiding the guilt and a master at blending my strict traditions into my newfound rock 'n' roll life.

I remember one time in particular where all my resolve was tested. One second, I was that little Italian Catholic boy, and the next day I was a man.

On the *Tusk* tour, we were zigzagging through Europe, and in 1980, Germany had an east and a west, and the city of Berlin was split right down the middle. One side was Eastern Bloc and communist, and the west side was free with ties to the Western world.

The tours buses and trucks used to have to drive all the way around Communist Germany, which took a lot of time and was very inconvenient.

Other bands based in Europe, like Queen, Led Zeppelin, and The Who, preceded us travelling through Germany, and in fact, were starting to do shows in East Germany and the Eastern Bloc, so it was now easier for most of the bands to use this new shortcut.

In East Germany, we didn't have the luxury of stopping, so we would drive most of the day and night, being very cautious, minding the speed limits so as not to provoke any problems or attention.

There was a famous brothel in Berlin named Haus Von Tausend Nåchten (House of a Thousand Nights).

Brothels in East Germany in the late 70s and 80s were very taboo and underground, and some think that the House of a Thousand Nights was a government-run spy house to attract the elite Western gentlemen to gain access to secrets. Somehow, bands and crews driving through East Germany found themselves at Haus Von Tausend Nåchten.

On the evening of our historic drive through East Germany, the drivers called for a much-needed break, so we pulled up to our safe haven for what we thought was dinner and drinks. One by one, we got off the buses, walked down a dark alley to a red, lit door, and entered a very plush building.

There was this large foyer, and it was amazing! Darkly lit, dark purple velvet, red walls with blue and dim lights to accent the pictures of beautiful, naked women all around. We all looked at each other, realizing this wasn't just a dinner stop.

Once in the main hall, we were served food and drinks, and we all sat around and got comfortable in the grand foyer. I was amazed. One by one, beautiful women walked into the foyer and made themselves comfortable around all of us.

It wasn't that long before this that I was sitting at the Italian Catholic dinner table of my parents saying my

This is not the actual Brothel but almost exactly what it looked like.

prayers; radically different than sitting at the top brothel in East Berlin. I was terrified! In my upbringing, this was the work of the Devil, but in East Germany (and my new world of rock 'n' roll), it was totally acceptable and normal.

I was twenty-two fucking years old with world tours under my belt, and the angel and devil were brawling on my shoulders once again.

The angel, armed with my traditional values, was winning the battle, and I decided to sit this one out and not partake in the activities. Little by little, all the crew were heading off to their respective locations to enjoy the night.

One of the escorts for our trip across East Germany, and one of the more experienced guys (who asked to be anonymous) on the tour, was the catalyst for this experience. He was sitting with the madame, and they approached me and asked what was wrong and if I was OK. Knowing my age and how new this all was to me, the madame got me a drink and said, "Just relax; you don't have to do what you don't want to do."

One drink became two, three, four ... I was relaxed, confident, and before I knew it, her well-orchestrated plan was working. Now the devil, with his armament of alcohol, drugs, and beautiful women was kicking the angel's ass. I was all in with the devil's plan.

What normal twenty-two-year-old kid could resist? I was sitting there with three young, beautiful German girls who were right out of the pages of *Playboy* or *Penthouse*. Beautiful faces, perfect bodies, lingerie, the works: all ready to give me the night of my life!

My flesh overruled my spirit, and the battle was over. With so many gentle touches and nibbles, and the beautiful aroma of perfume and sex, my guilted mind didn't stand a chance.

I was escorted by not one, but two, of these beautiful Fräuleins to a room with a large, round bed draped with satin and lace; soft music played in the background.

My mind was on sex as the physical sensations took over like nothing I had ever felt before in my life. I remember through the haze still thinking, "This isn't right; these are women; you need to respect them, their bodies; these are someone's daughters; do they do this because they have to or want to?" Then, the physical sensations of body parts (from two beautiful women all over me again) overruled my mind. "It's fine; they're not being forced; they like you; you're doing nothing wrong." It was a total mind fuck!

I kept thinking about how disappointed my mother and father would be. What happens if one of these girls get pregnant? What about STD's? I mean, my head was all over the place.

Finally, after a while, I got to a place where I was too far gone and all was good. My mind and body connected and became one, and I was relaxed, and it was extraordinary. I was pretty high, not just on alcohol but adrenaline as well. I mean it was amazing ... fantastic, and I was finally OK with it ... Well, so, I thought.

Right in the middle of having sex with these two beautiful women, I was on my knees with one below me, laying on her stomach, and the other behind me, kissing my neck with her arms around me, pushing me to help her friend. The soft bodies of these two beautiful women were in motion with mine, and we were tangled up but still all moving in time.

I had a gold chain with a crucifix that my parents had brought me from their last trip to the Vatican. The crucifix was blessed by the Pope, and I wore it for protection.

If you look at this picture closely you will see the Crucifix that my mother gave me.

In the middle of having sex with the two women, the angel came back in full force. Every move I was

365

Tusk tour enterouge, 1980.

making caused the crucifix to fly up and hit me right in the face—like a clock clicking time ... one, two, one, two. Hitting me in the face like it was someone saying, "You know this isn't right," and the next moment, "Yeah, but if feels so good," ... "Yeah, but it still ain't right" ... "It's OK; this is your new life" ... "You're going to burn in Hell" ... "Just relax" ... "That doesn't make it right" ... "Yeah, but look at them; they're so beautiful." In the end, it all worked out. Afterwards, I lay there, exhausted but so satisfied, and for the moment, my mind and body were at peace, and the angel and the devil had reconciled and compromised.

It was now early in the morning; one by one, we all rallied back into the beautiful main foyer to depart and move on with the rest of the tour.

The way payment worked for this escapade was all drinks, food, and acts of ecstasy were tallied up and then prorated and split by the crew who participated. I never got a bill or was asked to pay my portion.

When I inquired, I was told, "No worries, the house took care of you."

I asked, "Why?" It seemed that the house madam, knowing my innocence and her amusement with my youthful situation, thought I was a virgin, so she was happy to take care of it.

I will never forget the Haus Von Tausend Nåchten in East Berlin, where the devil smiled and the angel frowned.

CHAPTER TWENTY EIGHT

TUSKED AND DONE AND
JAZZ REHAB LIFE LESSONS

AFTER WE *BLITZKRIEGED* THROUGH EUROPE and ended up back in North America, it was difficult to face more boring, mundane dates in secondary cities like Lakeland, Florida; Mobile, Alabama; and Omaha, Nebraska. All of us, band and crew, went through the motions just to get the tour over with. We were excited about two things: the Hollywood Bowl and being done with this fucking *Tusk* tour! It did finally end on the hot September night under the stars at the Hollywood Bowl.

For some, it ended harder and longer than others. With all the opulence and outrageous demands all the band members expressed on the tour, it was time to pay the

American Express bill, which was eighteen months out and grossed millions and millions of dollars from planning, rehearsals, and 112 dates. Merchandise sales alone was more than most bands would gross from live shows for five years.

The forensic accounting began, and when the dollars, nickels, and dimes were reconciled, each band member made only a little over $100,000. Eighteen months of hard touring and millions of miles of travel, and the band made less than me!

Of course, there were things like pot and cocaine that you couldn't have line items for that were substituted by things that were needed like sound, lights, travel, and salaries.

The blame needed to go somewhere, and the person nominated by the band was their most loyal friend and confidant, JC. The verdict came down, and it seemed that JC mismanaged the tour and spent more than the allotted budgets without approvals. He swallowed the sword and took it for his Fleetwood Mac family.

Raymond, Wayno, Curry, the other old guard, and I took offense to the way JC was treated, but by the time I heard and tried to reach out to JC, he was deported to Hawaii and spent many years in paradise, licking his wounds. Never once did any of us hear JC bad rap the band, the lawyers, anyone. He just faded away, and for him, not only was *Tusk* over, but for now, so was his time with Fleetwood Mac.

I always wondered what really went down every once in a while. On other tours or trips to the islands I spent time with JC, but it wasn't until much later in life (when he moved back to England) that we sat down and I got the true story of what happened and why. All I want to say about it is that it was good for all involved and for-

JC, Christine, and Stevie. JC has left us and we all miss him very much.

gotten. JC was taken care of and put the needs of the band in front of his own, and in turn, the band took care of him.

After the Hollywood Bowl and reconciling the *Tusk* tour, I was pretty burnt and rich. I made a lot of money, and we had expected a bonus from the band, but obviously that wasn't in the budget.

So, it's early September 1980, and I'm happy just sitting home and really not interested in doing anything, but as usual, the phone rang.

"Leo? its Jerry. Jarreau's got a new album out, and we're going to work it. The single drops next week, and first date is September 14. I need a production manager. You in?"

Jerry was a good friend and mentor to me, and as much as I wanted to say no, the Italian Catholic guilt thing hit. "Sure thing, Jerry. I'm in. Same guys? Is Red doing it?"

"Yep, Same cast of characters."

The tour was mainly in the Northeast with a week at the Uris Theater, which was also known as the Gershwin Theater on Broadway. That I was looking forward to. A week on Broadway!

I set up the tour, and since it was much, much smaller than the *Tusk* fiasco, I realized that this tour was going to be fun. Jerry allowed us to always be in nice hotels, and the load-ins were late in the morning. We got to fly and have hotel rooms every night and no fucking buses. Some preferred the buses, but not me. I loved having a bed every night with good meals and soaking up the culture wherever we put our heads down. I also loved the interactions with all the airline reps, flight attendants, and hotel front desk people. I entered the magical world of the doorman.

Red turned me on to the underworld and workings of the doorman connection. These were usually guys who grew up three minutes from the hotel, and with the snap of a finger, if you needed a reservation, a limo, drugs, a hooker, whatever, they could get it.

Al Jarreau stage passes. I toured with Al for over 15 years. There will never be another Al Jarreau.

We stayed at good hotels. Sometimes Hyatts or Hiltons, but Jerry had a network of small, out-of-the-way boutique hotels with posh rooms and privacy. With our usual Lincoln or Cadillac rent-a-car, we would pull up to these hotels and lay a C-note ($100 bill) in the hand of the doorman, saying, Take care of us, my man!" Needless to say, the rest of our stay was a breeze.

The shows were amazing! Jerry's plan of moving Jarreau out of jazz into the pop world, where there so much more money, was working. The single "Never Givin' Up" hit the pop radio charts, and Jarreau shows were selling out.

It's just what the doctor ordered for me, and I realized that I was making more money, doing less work, and having way more fun. It was my "jazz rehabilitation." Not only was my soul healing, I was gaining so much knowledge that laid the foundation for my future as a tour manager. My communication and street skills were getting sharper, and it came from my heart and a good space.

I learned that people just want to belong; they want to be a part of something and respected. I was looking deeper into things and connecting with people and realizing that they had a family, a mother, a father, children. Good, bad, or indifferent, they were hungry for positive interaction, especially from people like us (who they deemed special).

We weren't special; only fortunate, blessed, and given a gift. I learned how to use the gift afforded me to make positive change.

The Broadway shows were the highlight of the tour, and once again, being in New York in the winter before the holidays was a dream. Like everywhere we went, we fit right in. The Union crew loved us, and we were a breath of fresh air and a change from the normal six to eight month runs of what they deemed those "fucking headaches." You know you're loved when on the dark nights (no show scheduled), you were invited to one of their homes to have dinner and meet the family.

The tour and year wound down. We ended the tour with Jarreau doing a New Year's show in Oakland, California.

The next day, January 1, 1981, I went across the bay to San Francisco and walked the streets of North Beach (Little Italy), where my parents met and fell in love, and where I was born. I couldn't help but think that sixty years earlier my grandparents landed in the city looking for the American Dream and a better life for their children.

I sat in the park across the street from the large Italian church—St. Peter and Paul's—soaking in the odors of my youth, the fresh bread, the garlic, the smell of the wood breaks from the cable cars rubbing on the tracks arousing my subconscious memory. Then the angel appeared on my shoulder, and I was that innocent little boy, thinking how far my family had come from the farms of Northern Italy and the fishing villages of Sicily, including me, now sharing life with amazing artists who were literally changing the world. I said a quick prayer and wondered what I was to become.

Nineteen-eighty was an amazing year. I was twenty-three years old and ready for the future. I learned so much about life, and most of all, about myself. I was confident and was ready to take on the world.

Al Jarreau (right) with the great David Sanborn.

CHAPTER TWENTY NINE
OLD FRIENDS ARE GOLDEN

DURING THE *TUSK* TOUR, THE MAC had several opening acts. One in particular that was, and is, still near and dear to me is Christopher Cross. Chris came out of Austin, Texas, and has a male, angelic voice, and when you see him in person, you scratch your head mumbling something like, "That's not him, couldn't be him." That's because he had this large, athletic body; he doesn't *look* like anybody who could have this blessed, almost

Christopher Cross 1981

male soprano voice with an amazing dynamic range. He is also a very, very good guitar player and can rock when he wants and play those subtle, flowing melodies at the snap of a finger.

His song "Sailing" was climbing the charts and hit radio hard. The flowing guitar, coupled with soft verses and the huge hook of the chorus, made the listener float away to a magical space.

In the early '80s, MTV and videos were coming into play. Videos used to market music to Generation X, who like to get stimulation handed to them, were being produced faster than Ford was producing cars off their automotive plants. Bands were now negotiating large amounts of money from record labels and demanding a video, and the money would go out to any director who could either tell a good story or shock people with new digital technical effects that overshadowed the music. Some bands and their songs would have never made it without the MTV era ruining the music business.

Christopher had a problem. There was no way to really produce a video that could showcase his voice and be believable enough for anyone to accept that his voice matched his physical appearance. The decision was made to scrap all of the video plans and use the money in another way to market and promote this new, rising star.

Tim, Chris's manager, took a page out of the old school breaking-a-band plan. Get him in front of people, and let the music speak for itself. It wasn't that easy though. Sound, lights, tour buses, plus the gamble of selling tickets all created a very risky proposition. So, how could you get your artist in front of millions of people to showcase the music while keeping costs down? Open for a large artist like Fleetwood Mac and the Eagles, who both had the same audience for your style of music selling out massive stadiums with 50,000–100,000 people. Ten shows times 100,000 people = 1,000,000 people. If 10 percent of those people (100,000) buy the Christopher Cross record at twelve dollars per record = $1,200,000 dollars.

The brilliant idea was to use the unused video budget and buy Chris's way onto the tours and in front of millions of crossover fans. I believe it was the sum of $5,000 per show to the headliners, and Chris would use The Mac's lights, and our sound and stage, and some of his crew on our buses or for catering, and on and on and on. Our overhead was the same for The Mac and the Eagles, so the money coming in to them was pure profit.

Chris did twenty shows with The Mac and twenty with the Eagles, equaling $200,000. A true win-win and a brilliant scenario that has become industry standard.

During the *Tusk* tour, Christopher had some dates where he was the headliner. It was agreed that he could use a cut down version of The Mac's sound and lights, and we would all come along with the package. It was too small for Chris, our production manager, so I took over the role of production manager, not only to help Christopher but also to watch over our gear.

It was also a way for me to continue to grow my people management skills and learn I had to stay in control and sacrifice the party situations to be responsible.

Once, on a travel day, a delayed flight where time times road crew times alcohol/drug = mayhem, I finally poured the whole road crew onto the jet. As the unsettling of settling in took place, I went to back of the jet to talk to the flight attendants: to warn them I had a wild road crew and assure them they should have no problems. That was my initial motive, but after glancing at one of the most beautiful women I'd ever seen, my glance turned into a heart palpitating stare. My suave confidence kicked in, and I said, "Darlin'! What's your name?"

Inquisitive, afraid, apprehensive, and looking at me like I was an alien, she said, "Patricia."

"Patricia, My name is Leo, and I'm the production manager for Christopher Cross, these guys are my crew, and they're drunk, very drunk. They're nice, though, and I don't want you to worry, and there shouldn't be any problems, but if there are, come to me and only me."

My comments were true, sort of. I really knew that I was the only one who could handle any problems, but also, I didn't want any of the other guys to get in the way of me and this gorgeous six-foot brunette goddess with a mesmerizing smile who turned my arrogance to lust.

Once in flight, with all the crew passed out and passengers fed, Patricia and I sat in the back-jump seat and talked. She was from Denver, a hardworking single mother trying to make ends meet; I was the pirate, and once again the angel and devil were on my shoulders and in my head.

This time, the angel won, and at 30,000 feet, my ulterior motives of carnal exploration vanished, and we weren't man and women, just two people connecting—two people from extremely different worlds brought together by me taking advantage of my position of power and conceitedness. Patricia and I remained friends, and much later in life, reconnected in an even deeper and more spiritual way.

I was right on with what I saw in Christopher Cross, and it paid off. In 1981, his career took off, and I was asked to be the production manager for mainly promotional dates in the spring and for the 1981 summer tour.

The single for the song "Sailing" was on fire and crossed the Atlantic to England, and along with a promotional tour with radio and TV, there were shows at one of the most prestigious venues to play, the London Palladium.

At the same time, in 1981, Mick Fleetwood was working on a project aptly named "The Visitor." It was a project that took Mick and some of his fellow musician to Ghana, Africa, to record a record based around native drum beats and instruments played by local musicians. Some of The Mac's road crew, including his Italian drum tech, Tony Todaro, and my old friend Randy from the Jarreau days, with his mobile recording unit, were assisting Mick with the project.

After the project was recorded, they ended up in London to do the mix and finish the project at the Mill

WHEN THE DEVIL SMILES, THE ANGELS FROWN

Recording Studio that was owned by Led Zeppelin's Jimmy Page. As fate had it, we all ended up staying at the Blake—a long-term hotel. It was great to see Mick, Tony, and the gang and go to the studio to hear the new project. I felt like I was home, reconnecting with at least some of the family.

One night at the studio, Tony asked if I wanted to go with him on an errand. I said sure, not even thinking what it was. We took a train about forty-five minutes out of London to Frye Park. Tony told me Frye Park was the home of George Harrison of the Beatles. We met George's right-hand man confidant Terry at the door, and he gave Tony a small bag, and we were on our way. On the train back, I saw Tony was a bit uptight and fidgety and looking around.

I asked him, "What's up, brother?"

He said, "I'm just a bit uptight about carrying around a quarter ounce of cocaine in a foreign country."

With total panic, I said, "What! Are you fucking crazy?"

He said, "I thought I was only picking up a couple of grams!"

Not only was I afraid of getting busted but also mugged as well. The rest of the ride back, it felt like all eyes were on us.

When we got back to the studio, they were laying down guitar tracks for the song "Walk A Thin Line." As I sat in the control room listening to the song that was an old Mac track but also on the *Tusk* record as well, I heard the very familiar signature guitar sound of "While My Guitar Gently Weeps." NO! NO! It couldn't be! As I peered through the glass into the dark studio, there he was—Mick's ex-brother-in-law, George Harrison, playing his guitar with the feel that made the Beatles the Beatles. When the parts were laid down, George walked into the control room, and Mick introduced us. "George, this is Leo. He's one of our longtime crew."

George Harrison & Mick Fleetwood
Location: Studio In England Recording "The Visitor"
Date: Sometime In 1980

A picture from my good friend and Mac producer Richard Dashut. Mick and George in the studio. I'm glad Richard captured this moment. I was star struck.

George reached out his hand, saying "How are ya, pleasure."

"Nice to meet you," I said, shaking his hand, trying to be cool, like I wasn't ten feet off the floor. I was shaking hands with one of the fucking Beatles!

My whole life I'd been around the biggest rock stars and artists in the world, and I can honestly say that on that night, and in that moment, was the only time I was star-struck. Even later in life meeting Ringo and Paul, it wasn't the same as that night in London meeting George Harrison.

I also witnessed the eccentric, legendary, founder of Fleetwood Mac, Peter Green, who was in the studio playing and singing one of The Mac's first hits from 1969, "Rattlesnake Shake." It was a touching moment, witnessing Mick's sensitivity and handling of his fragile genius brother. Mick's words and actions of love and patience were slowly rebuilding Peter's confidence as he took his time to reflect back to when they were young with no worries. Over time, Mick brought back Peter's sound that was lost and buried, and was the catalyst for a style of guitar theory that influenced the best guitar players who changed the world.

Nineteen eighty-one was off to a great start. Thanks to being in Europe with great friends, like Christopher Cross and his band and crew, and then seeing some of my Fleetwood Mac family, my self-confidence was at an all-time high.

Andy Salmon (Christopher's bass player), Me, Rob Meurer (Christopher's Keyboard player) being tourists.

The Christopher Cross entourage trusted me, and in turn, I wanted to help them. That tour taught me a life lesson that I carried with me throughout my career. The gift of giving and sharing your experience with others is the best gift of all, not only for who you're sharing it with but for yourself. I felt good about myself, and my insecurity was melting away like snow when the sun came out on a warm day.

I spent most of 1981 with Christopher Cross, from the first record through the epic song "Arthur's Theme: Caught Between the Moon and New York City." I was not only happy to be involved with the creation of a talented, emerging artist like Christopher, but most of all, to have a good friend who to this day always remembers who helped him achieve his dreams.

It's always good to see Christopher and catch up, and we always part with the words he once wrote on a poster for me. "Hey, buddy! Old friends are golden." Yes, indeed, they are.

Thanks, Chris. Love you my brother.

As I was finishing up the Christopher Cross tour, Shark Boy called me and asked if I would help him on the Rolling Stones Tattoo You West Coast tour. The song "Start Me Up" zoomed up the charts, and the Stones extravaganza hit the road. Shark Boy was working for the Stones as the head electrician, supplying power for the show. I was excited to work with him and the Stones as well. Shark Boy and I would run power cables and distribution boxes for the stage, lights, sound, and dressing room compounds. We were first in and last out of every large stadium show on the tour that started in San Diego and ended in Seattle one month later. The tour was amazing; it paid well, and I figured it was another notch in my belt that had so many notches it was falling apart.

On October ninth and tenth in Los Angeles, at the Memorial Coliseum, a young, black guitar player hand-picked by the Rolling Stones hit the stage, opening for Mick Jagger and boys. He was a quiet, frail, skinny kid wearing underwear and a trench coat. His band was a bunch of misfits with odd moves and an undefined sound. He stepped up to the mic and said, "My name is Prince, and my band is The Revolution."

They started their first song with a heavy guitar lick and primal screams that went right into a funk groove. It was an odd paring when J. Geils and George Thorogood went on after this freaky Jimi-Hendrix-meets-Sly-Stone character. One thing I did notice: he could play the guitar. But it wasn't the style that the hardcore Stones fans wanted. After the first song, the boos were prevalent with people shouting not only obscenities but uncalled-for racial comments.

In 1981, the Stones fans were entitled, white, nontolerant biker types who were in no way going to accept anything this cutting edge and diverse. After a couple of songs, legendary promoter Bill Graham came onstage trying to calm things down and get the crowd to give this frightened new rocker a chance. The crowd just became more unruly with more racial and homophobic slurs.

It was during the third or fourth song when things started to fly up onto the stage. Garbage, food, clothing, shoes—anything that could be thrown—ended up onstage, and it started to look like a garbage dump. All of us were going onstage cleaning up the debris, and every time we thought we were getting ahead, there was more. It was useless trying to keep the stage clean, and soon bottles and cans started to hit the stage. The bass player got hit, and it was decided to pull the plug on young Prince out of fear that someone, mainly him, would get hurt.

Prince and his band came offstage with security all around them, shielding them from an ocean of garbage and laughter and loud applauses. My stomach was in knots, and my mind in disbelief. How in this day and age could people be so crude, vile, and repulsive to an artist?

Prince was distraught and decided not to play the second night and flew home. Jagger wouldn't have it and called the young rising star and told him to come back and said it was going to be OK. He also let Prince know he would go nowhere if he quit every time something was thrown at him or he was ridiculed.

We took a day off for a college football game, and the second show was scheduled for Sunday night in front of another 100,000 people. Prince took the stage after a conversation with Mick Jagger, who explained to him, "If you're going to be a headliner, you're going to have

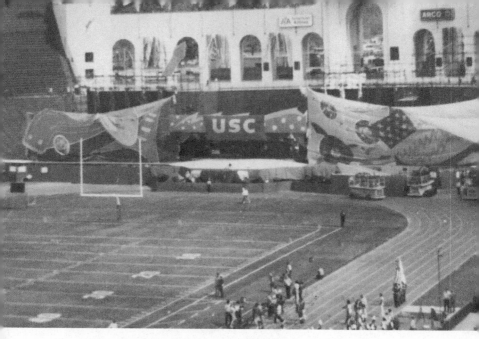

The Rolling Stones stage still set up During the USC game.
At the Los Angeles Coliseum 1981.

to deal with it and be prepared for the worse."

On this second night, there was the same rhetoric and slurs but less garbage, probably because for part of the show. Jagger and Richards stood on the side of the stage. soaking in this new protégé.

At one point onstage, Jagger told the Stones fans that they made a big mistake and Prince was going to be one of the biggest rock 'n' roll stars in history—and Jagger was right.

Prince went on to an acclaimed career, not only selling millions of records and sold out concerts but also paving the way for artists to break the bonds of slavery and be free of big record label servitude.

CHAPTER THIRTY

STEVIE NICKS. TAKE ONE

FOR SOME REASON, WHEN I TALK ABOUT my career,
I gloss over all my extraordinary experiences, moments,
and times spent with Stevie Nicks as a solo artist. Perhaps
because in my head and heart, it's hard to separate Stevie
from Fleetwood Mac? I've said before, Fleetwood Mac's
power as a whole is greater than the sum of each of them
as solo artist.

During *Tusk*, Stevie became a driving force and a
valuable commodity that was now being managed by
the Eagles famous manager, Irving Azoff, and his company, Frontline Management. The dysfunctional but
peaceful Fleetwood Mac was over, and the politics of

growth were too much for any one of them to handle.

During the Christopher Cross tour in the spring of 1981, I heard that Stevie was working with the acclaimed producer Jimmy Lovine on a solo project. At that time, Jimmy was producing artists such as John Lennon, Tom Petty, and Bruce Springsteen.

I liked Jimmy. He, like me, took a chance and showed up one Easter Sunday morning to work a recording session that no one wanted to do. The session happened to be John Lennon, and the rest is history.

Jimmy's vision was to bring the rock out of Stevie and turn her loose, and what better way to do that then have her work with rock 'n' roll royalty like Tom Petty? This fit well with Stevie because, at heart, she really wanted to be a rocker. Stevie was ready to stretch out and release her inner edginess.

The song "Stop Draggin' My Heart Around" was the recipe and remedy that matched Stevie's talent with the rock 'n' roll male fraternity that needed her sexy edge of pure strength. It was the perfect collaboration to set Stevie up as one of the world's most enduring rock stars.

With Jimmy and Shelly (Jimmy's amazing recording engineer) producing, coupled with her high-powered management team, every A-line artist was recruited and brought in to make the record Bella Donna: Roy Bitten from Springsteen's E-Street Band; Benmont Tench from the Heartbreakers; the Esteem drummer, Russ Kunkle;

Bobby Hall, Dylan's percussionist; and on guitar, the LA-based rocker Waddy Wachtel.

It was early August when I got the call from Curry about the short winter tour to promote Bella Donna and showcase Stevie's solo career to the world.

I asked who else from The Mac's crew was going to be involved. Curry said, "Uh, really no one. We're the only two. They want to stay away from the whole Fleetwood Mac thing. It's just you and me."

Curry and I were the only two that came out of the Mac camp to work with Stevie on her solo career.

Curry was locked in. Over the years, Stevie trusted Curry. With Curry, Stevie was comfortable and knew the show would look good and she wouldn't have to worry about that part of the project.

Curry also knew if I were the production manager, and with our history with Fleetwood Mac, that he would get what he needed to get the show right. I understood him, and he and I believed that with a new production manager Curry would have struggled, maybe even failed.

Curry also convinced management that I knew Stevie and what she needed on tour and I was the path of least resistance for Stevie to survive on the road. So, it was me and Curry, the two lone Fleetwood Mac family members on the Bella Donna Tour.

Curry also pointed out the pitfalls of doing the tour. "Leo, one thing to think about is how the rest of The Mac is going to see this. It could fuck up any future you may have with The Mac."

Curry was right. I could be viewed as an opportunist betraying the Fleetwood Mac family.

As always, I called my good friend and mentor Jerry for advice. "Hey, Jerry, it's Leo. How's it going?"

"Good what's up?"

"It's Stevie's solo tour! I've been asked to be the production manager, and you know the history." I poured my agonizing heart out to Jerry, and once again, the angel and devil on my shoulders offered their bipolar opinions of the seven virtues. Jerry, as always, had the best advice. "Call them! Call them and ask them."

"Call who?"

"The band! McVie, Mick, Chris, and Lindsey. Ask them if they care."

Once again, great advice from my old friend and mentor Jerry.

I picked up the phone to reach out to my old friends

and family, and mainly to the greatest rhythm section of all time, John and Mick.

I said a prayer, asking that what I was going to hear was what I wanted to hear, and hopefully, it was the truth. Mick was gracious. "Of course, Leo! no worries. We all want the best for Stevie." I never spoke to John McVie but did get a message saying that it didn't matter to him and never got a call from Christine or Lindsey, who I really felt wouldn't care. Looking back now, if you really analyze the situation, Stevie going solo was a huge advantage to The Mac. It was virtually impossible to talk about Stevie without referencing The Mac.

"Stevie Nicks of Fleetwood Mac has launched a solo career."

"Stevie Nicks of Fleetwood Mac has an album coming, a tour, a video."

The rest of the band was reaping the benefits of Stevie's massive appeal, and it translated into more sales, and they were home and not laboring on some tour.

So, I was in! And with some apprehension, excitement, and trepidation, I became the production manager for Stevie's Bella Donna Project.

A meeting was set up at Frontline Management Company with all the managers, accountants, and touring team members who would be running the tour. The road manager was named Harry Sandler. Harry was an established tour manager doing many big acts, mainly Springsteen. I knew of Harry and his excellent reputation and was excited to work with him.

Along with Harry was the tour accountant Bob Hurwitz. I knew Bob as the longtime tour accountant with the Eagles and was also happy to be working with him. Bob was a rare breed—a rock 'n' roll accountant with a heart. Then there was Curry and me. Howard, one of the partners in Frontline Management, walked in the room and right away made it be known that he was in control and the buck stopped with him. Looking right at me and Curry, he said, "First off, this isn't Fleetwood Mac, and we do things a lot differently hear at Frontline. Stevie Nicks of Fleetwood Mac and this Stevie Nicks are different. Two separate acts with two separate careers."

Howard made it very clear that we were not to go to Stevie for anything. "She needs to be an artist and not worry about career decisions. We do all that, and we're good at it, so come to us with any questions or problems."

We discussed how the tour would work. All logistics for sound, lights, gear, and crew would be handled by me, but through Harry, and then down to Bob, who controlled the overall tour profit and loss. All band and artist dealings would run through Harry, and we would meet or talk daily to discuss progress and pitfalls. No commitments for any expenditures were to be made unless Harry OK'd it. This was my first experience with the new world order for the rock 'n' roll "business."

The first part of the Bella Donna Tour was short and basically a series of shows to perfect the show live and get paid for it, leading up to a five-night stay at the Wilshire Theater to film an HBO special. The first show was back at the Houston Summit in Houston, Texas. Frontline realized that Houston was a huge market for The Mac, and that it would sell out, and the profits would be as large as Fleetwood Mac but not split five ways. The main objective was to break Stevie in as a solo artist, but Frontline was a master at making money and figuring out a way for people to pay and Stevie to profit from the promotional tour.

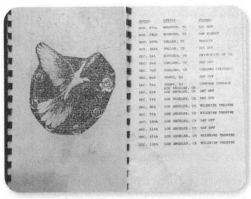

In 1981, with no computers, itineraries were very simple.

Curry and I met to start designing something that would be different for Stevie but not too far out that the set and lights would overshadow the band and the music. Curry was, and still is, an amazing designer, not only for look and feel, but technically as well. His idea for Stevie and Bella Donna was to feature Stevie downstage center and the band behind her on risers with the background singers offstage enough to isolate Stevie and highlight her. The band was a who's who of rock, all from A-line bands, and they needed to be highlighted, but in a way that it didn't intrude on the main event: Stevie.

The design ended up being very plain, with a series of multiple level risers elevating every player behind Stevie with all their heads being at the same height. A drummer sitting down next to a bass player created an image of instability and lack of continuity. So, Bob Glaub, the famous bass player for Jackson Browne, Linda Ronstadt, and many more, had a lower riser than his friend, the famous drummer for James Taylor and Linda Ronstadt, Russ Kunkle. Roy Bitton, with his grand piano far offstage sitting down, needed to be the same height as Benmont Tench standing behind his Hammond B-3 organ. Then, the amazing percussionist Bobby Hall, whose strong feminine presence keeping time standing behind her array of drums and toys, had to be the same height as her male counterparts.

It was important to Curry to try to make sure that everyone's heads were exactly the same height and the whole band looked uniform. I designed a set of risers that were adjustable. No riser was the same size or height, nothing

This is a close up of Stevie from the HBO Bella Donna video. If you search for it on YouTube you will see the genius of Curry Grant.

was uniform, and if the band or instruments changed, so would the risers.

On the stage left of Stevie was the high energy of the genius musical director Waddy Wachtel, who was a master of interacting with Stevie to enhance her performance. But, when it was needed, he gave her enough space so the world could see the new solo rock goddess.

Curry and I also worked with Waddy to perfect the sonic value of the show. It was important that the feel of the music was 100 percent right. Waddy made sure that the music wasn't only heard by the band, but that they felt it. Putting Russ's drums and Bob's bass close ensured that the low-end beats touched their souls. Then, on the stage floor right behind Stevie was Bob Glaub, the bass player, far enough away to not distract from Stevie but close enough to have the necessary feel with Russ the drummer. Then, from offstage right, came the strong voices and security of Sharon and Lori, Stevie's background singers and confidants.

Now that the stage was set, Curry needed to figure out what the style, look, and feel would be. He was leaning toward an art deco, classy vibe with a pink, black, and white motif. Curry and I met with Marty Culner, the director for the HBO video. Marty was a flamboyant, in-your-face guy with absolutely no subtleness. I immediately loved him because he was different and took chances. The day of the meeting was a typical hot summer day in Los Angeles, and Marty walked into the rehearsal hall with a full mink coat that you would only wear at a winter event in New York.

Marty's message was very clear: the light and set design were not to be for the live show but for the video. He would say, "Think about the close up, the edit piece. When you watch a video, it's a close-up, personal experience you can't get from a normal, live show. Think about cutting to the solos with the other band members and please, please, make sure we always have enough even light so the shots are consistent."

Curry and I got the message loud and clear, and we were very amenable to the plan to make Stevie herself the focal point and the main piece of scenery, not only for the shoot but for the live show as well.

So, we had the risers and decided to place pink art deco-type facings in front of each riser to light them and create a very soft separation between Stevie and the band. Curry's light design was to subtlety fill in the gaps between the band.

With The Mac, Stevie downstage center presence was balanced by Lindsey's magical animosity to her left and Christine's affirmative balance to her right, but it was becoming apparent that there was too much space, a hole—a void—in our set up. We needed a way to showcase Stevie but still have continuity onstage and make it look like a band.

Considering Marty's advice to think about the close-up shots, wide shots, and the rear shots, Curry said something that hit us both like a hammer over the head.

"What if we have a camera up with the rear follow spots for a high reverse shot?"

I said, "Then you would see the stage floor."

Then it hit us! The floor! The fucking floor! With light, color, and different patterns, we could change it and have multiple looks to accent the set.

We envisioned ourselves all over the arenas and theaters—at the sound and light boards, the balconies, and up in the less expensive seats where 80 percent of the people who come to a concert sit, looking down at the stage. With color and light, why not make the stage floor part of the set, a featured prop?

We decided on a consistent, seamless piece (to avoid Stevie tripping with her big-heeled boots) of off-white beige carpet that would blend the stage floor right up to the risers that flowed right into the backdrop. Perfect! The perfect solution! This allowed Curry to have a set of lights with the main purpose of creating pools of light that would not only fill the gaps between Stevie and the rest of the people onstage, but balance and counterbalance the look. This was the perfect solution that worked for the film and the live show. The carpet was the finishing touches of what became the everlasting image of Stevie Nick's Bella Donna video.

In the middle of the set design, I also had the responsibility of putting together the band's musical rehearsals, as well as finding a larger rehearsal hall for full production rehearsals. We leased out Studio Instrument Rentals on Sunset Boulevard for three weeks, first with the band and then with Stevie coming in for the last of the three weeks. It was relatively easy for me, but for Harry, managing the personalities of A-line band members from other superstar acts, with their own style and routine of touring, proved to be difficult. I noticed that there was a constant competition from a few of them who craved Stevie's attention, but as always, we got through it and it was on to full production rehearsals with sound, lights, staging, and crew.

Every crew person in the business wanted to be on this tour. It was the envy of the music industry. The crew I picked and adopted was amazing—a true rock star crew from top to bottom. I brought in Pete Townsend's guitar tech, Alan Rogan, from my first tour; the Eagles' bass guitar tech, Jage Jackson; keyboard and drums tech from Elton John, Steve Benjamin; and Carpenters from the Stones—the best of the best. We all got along really well and were excited to share not only new technologies and the different ways we did things, but most of all, this exciting experience we were all about to embark on. Ironically, I was both the production manager and the youngest on the crew.

On Monday, September 28, 1981, the well-incubated Bella Donna baby came out of the womb. The crew gathered as truck by truck showed up at the rehearsal soundstage with the band's instruments, sound, lights, and set pieces. With excitement and confidence, the rock star road crew was ready to tackle the task and show the world the new Stevie Nicks.

The schedule was two days to load and fine-tune the equipment. Lights, sets, and sound loaded in first, followed by the band's instruments, and then wardrobe.

On the third day, one by one, each band member showed up to have quality time with their tech and the sound guys. Remember, those were the days where digital was just a wrist watch and copious notes on reams of legal pads were needed for reference to repeat the proper setup from city to city.

By the end of the first week, the band and sound dialed in the music rehearsals without Stevie and the background singers. It didn't take long for all of us to realize that the band Waddy had put together was amazing—the best of the best who left their egos outside with one mission: to create an everlasting show for Stevie and the world.

The next three weeks of rehearsals created endless moments of magic and the swell and sensation of accomplishment ran through all our veins.

Harry, Bob, and I met daily to discuss logistics and budgets, and on Wednesday, November 25, the day before Thanksgiving, the last truck door closed and pulled away, heading to Houston, Texas, for the first gig of the Stevie Nicks Bella Donna Tour.

Even though so short, the Bella Donna Tour was a mixture of people from very different walks of life that felt like we'd all been together for years. On the crew side, no egos, attitudes, or squabbles. Everyone got along, and we all watched each other's backs. Harry did mention that on the band side there were rumblings of ego disease, and I wasn't surprised, given the amount of talent and eccentric attitudes of a group of musicians who had reached the level of success they achieved.

Houston to Dallas to Denver with stops in Oakland, Phoenix (Compton Terrace, a venue owned by Stevie's father Jess Nicks), and then San Diego before our five nights and the filming at the Wilshire Theater in Los Angeles. Phoenix was special.

I knew Stevie's father Jess Nicks from my time with The Mac. He was always nice to the crew and always made a point to thank us. Stevie's younger brother, Chris, was special, too, and in fact, he was a huge part of Stevie and Lindsey in the early days before they were with Fleetwood Mac.

At the Phoenix gig, Stevie was so gracious, and you could feel her excitement to be playing for her father.

At the start of the show, I escorted Jess Nicks onstage, and beaming with pride, he said, "Ladies and gentlemen, my daughter, Stevie Nicks." The band kicked in as I was walking him offstage, and Jess once again said, "Hey, Leo. Thank the crew for me."

Bella Donna was my kind of tour; with Stevie's fame came recognition that created power, and we wrote our own ticket. Being the production manager, every night, I had large suites with the whole crew getting upgrades.

Restaurants and bars comped drinks and meals, and we had the calculated rendezvous with the most attractive women in every town. It was monstrous. Since they couldn't be us, they wanted to be a part of us.

With the few dates and days off in between cities, we flew commercial airlines with hotels every night, so once again, I was at the top of my game, not only as a production manager, but interacting and validating myself with flight attendants, hotel staff, and people who were important to keep The Machine running.

We hit Los Angeles with full vengeance, ready to run over anything in our way. The Wilshire shows were the hottest ticket in town, and the press was everywhere.

After the San Diego show, we drove to Los Angeles for the early morning load-in. Even though the shoot was the last two nights, Marty and his team from HBO loaded in a day early to set up extra lights and cameras so we could setup around and make sure we had extra time to make any necessary changes.

As we all knew they would be, the LA shows were epic and flawless, with unbridled energy. The 2,000 people fortunate enough to score tickets for each show were treated to two hours of pure magic.

Stevie dug down deeply, pulling out her genuine, enchanting charm, and she took herself to new levels that I don't think will ever be recreated.

As the cameras were rolling on a cold night at the Wilshire Theater in Los Angeles, Stevie Nicks

This is one of my favorite pictures of Stevie Nicks with the
legendary photographer Neal Preston.

I was eighteen years old working a Fleetwood Mac show when Neal came
up to me at the light board and asked for more light on the stage so
he could get a particular shot. He probably expected the normal response:
"FUCK OFF." Instead, I made the stage brighter and
asked him, "is that enough?"

We've been friends ever since, working with many band and hundreds
of shows. His work speaks for itself. Thanks Neal. xxoo

My credit for the Bella Donna
HBO video. I was the tour
Production Manager and the
Stage Manager
or the Video as well.

402

The 1981 Stevie Nicks Bella Donna crew.

wrote her way into history as a woman working against the odds who became the unforgettable treasure the world has never forgotten. She was no longer Stevie Nicks of Fleetwood Mac. She was Stevie Nicks.

The short Bella Donna Tour was over, and right before Christmas, Curry called me and invited me to Marty's house to see a rough cut of the Stevie Nicks White Wing Dove concert. All I can remember is sitting on this big couch, looking at the huge monitor surrounded by huge speakers, watching something that was made in 1981 that millions still watch today.

I went into the holidays exhausted, but on the highest of highs. I learned a lot, made amazing new friends, and most of all, I grew. It was a true self-discovery. Not until much later in life did I realize that being the production

403

manager for the Bella Donna Tour meant my professional career and reputation had hit a new high. I was being recognized and was in demand.

Reflecting back, I think about the Led Zeppelin song "Going To California" where Robert Plant sings a line that says, "How can tomorrow ever follow today?" How could it? At twenty-four years old, I reached incredible highs; circumstance, destiny, and fate made me the hero in my own story, and I wasn't done yet.

CHAPTER THIRTY ONE

1982

IN THE WINTER OF 1982, I took some well-deserved rest and enjoyed being off the road. With little overhead and an abundance of income throughout 1981, I didn't need to work, but I liked doing local shows just to catch up with everyone and put a few bucks in my pocket.

In the spring, I started receiving calls about tours for the rest of the year—Rickie Lee Jones for the spring, a short Beach Boys tour in early summer, and then Fleetwood Mac was going to tour around their latest scheduled release: *Mirage*.

I kept in touch with The Mac gang. In order to eliminate distractions from the constant barrage of family and friends, they decided to go to a recording studio in a Chateau in France, far away from Parisian night life. I was surprised to hear that Stevie, with her solo career, would commit so much time to work with The Mac. Rumor had it that early on in the process they already had enough of each other and just wanted to lay down the basic tracks and get home.

The first and only leg of the tour was late summer through late fall; the time frame was variable, depending on how the record sold. Chris Lamb, the old production manager, was now the tour manager; he replaced JC. Given my success with Stevie's solo Bella Donna Tour, it was natural that I became the production manager, and all my fears of retribution and betrayal for touring with Stevie as a solo artist were unfounded.

Rickie Lee was working a record called *Pirates*. She spent a lot of time and money making the record, and Warner Records was 100 percent behind developing Rickie for a long-term career. With nothing more than an accounting firm that sucked the soul out of everything and no management, Warner's was calling the shots. They brought on a tour manager named Sal who was from the Van Halen family. They figured Rickie needed a familiar face, so they asked me to be the production manager. Sal, being an East Coast New Yorker, had a slick look—with a collar always up that matched his don't-worry-about-it attitude. It fit well with Rickie Lee and Sal, and I put together a streamlined, great band and crew. I brought in my production team from the Bella Donna and Mac tours, and Sal and Warner's put together a great band of Los Angeles musicians to compliment Rickie.

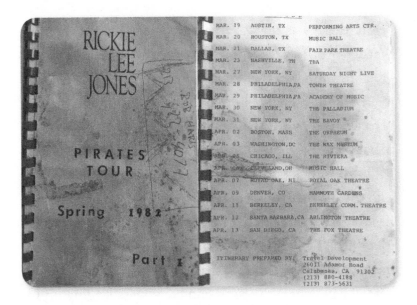

RICKIE LEE JONES
PIRATES TOUR
Spring 1982
Part 1

MAR. 19	AUSTIN, TX	PERFORMING ARTS CTR.
MAR. 20	HOUSTON, TX	MUSIC HALL
MAR. 21	DALLAS, TX	FAIR PARK THEATRE
MAR. 23	NASHVILLE, TN	TBA
MAR. 27	NEW YORK, NY	SATURDAY NIGHT LIVE
MAR. 28	PHILADELPHIA,PA	TOWER THEATRE
MAR. 29	PHILADELPHIA,PA	ACADEMY OF MUSIC
MAR. 30	NEW YORK, NY	THE PALLADIUM
MAR. 31	NEW YORK, NY	THE SAVOY
APR. 02	BOSTON, MASS	THE ORPHEUM
APR. 03	WASHINGTON,DC	THE WAX MUSEUM
APR. 05	CHICAGO, ILL	THE RIVIERA
APR. 06	CLEVELAND,OH	MUSIC HALL
APR. 07	ROYAL OAK, MI	ROYAL OAK THEATRE
APR. 09	DENVER, CO	MAMMOTH GARDENS
APR. 11	BERKELEY, CA	BERKELEY COMM. THEATRE
APR. 12	SANTA BARBARA,CA	ARLINGTON THEATRE
APR. 13	SAN DIEGO, CA	THE FOX THEATRE

ITINERARY PREPARED BY: Travel Development
26011 Adamor Road
Calabasas, CA 91302
(213) 880-4188
(213) 873-5631

In 1982, Rickie had a hard time handling stress, and to circumvent the stress, she turned to drugs. It's not my place to get into the details, but the tour struggled, and Rickie was constantly on edge. Carl, Rickie's representative at Warner's, was in the crosshairs of the daily barrage of Rickie's wrath.

It was a small tour with six crew members and me, so again, late load-ins, flying commercial, two rental cars, and hotels and a bed every night.

On the last night of rehearsals, Rickie called me over and said she had a problem. It was a medical problem around her addiction that needed immediate attention. I threw Rickie into my car to take her to the emergency room. I knew that when the doctors discovered her condition was drug related, they would be required to call local law enforcement. Given that the tour was about to begin, there was no way that could happen. I called the Warner Brothers rep to inform him of the situation.

"How much cash do you have on you, Leo?" he asked me. I told him I had a little under two grand, and he said, "Do whatever you can to get Rickie treated, but make sure they don't call the cops. Let me know where she ends up."

I drove Rickie to four different hospitals before finding a hospital in the Hollywood area which agreed to admit her. It cost $1,500 cash to the doctor to get Rickie admitted. I told Rickie I'd pick her up in the morning and we'd go from there. I called Bob with updates and went back to the rehearsal hall, where the band and crew were loading up for the tour that started in Austin Texas three days later. With rehearsals all done, I drove home, going over all the day's events and making a checklist in my head.

I woke up early in the morning to pick up Rickie from the hospital, and when I arrived, her room was empty and she was gone. I went to the nursing station to inquire, and they said after a small procedure, she slept a bit, pulled the IV out of her arm, got dressed, and left. The doctor came in and explained what was up.

He said "Physically, she's OK, but mentally she's in a bad way and really needs counseling." He wished me good luck and left the room. I called Bob with the update and learned she had already called him and said she was fine and going back to the hotel to rest. I was told to pick her up and bring her to the Warner offices for meetings. I agreed and was on my way.

As I pulled up to the Château Marmont on Sunset Blvd, there was a commotion and lots of police cars, news vans, and activity. I parked across the street and headed to the bungalow where Rickie was staying. As I came up the driveway, I saw the Los Angeles County coroner's van with a body bag in the back, and a sinking feeling came over me. OH FUCK! She finally did it; addiction finally took its toll.

I found my way to the bungalow and knocked on the door. No answer. I knocked again, no answer, and after a third time, Rickie answered the door with her small bag in hand, ready to go. With great relief, I grabbed her hand, and we walked the opposite direction of the chaos.

"What's up? What's going on?" she asked.

I said, "I don't know, but I need to get you to Warner's for a meeting." She thanked me for taking care of her and asked if everything was OK. I said yes and looked straight ahead at the road.

I needed to stop by the rehearsal hall before heading to Warner's to pick up something that was left behind. As I made it to the front desk, the news hit that John Belushi had overdosed and died at the Château Marmont. I was stunned and stood silently, knowing that the body in the coroners van was John Belushi.

I got back into the car, and looked at Rickie, and asked, "Did you see John Belushi at all last night?"

"No, Why?"

"He overdosed and died last night at the Château," I told her.

Rickie looked down and, in a low voice, said, "That's too bad, too bad." I brought Rickie into the Warner's building and left to pack and get ready to leave on the tour. On my drive home, I was sad, hurt, and mostly angry that someone so talented could be so tortured to go to the limit of self-destruction. Over the years, I began to realize that most talented people have that destructive side in them that also creates the talent that makes them great. But what a price. John Belushi was at the top of his game and one of the only entertainers in history to have a top TV show with *Saturday Night Live*, a top movie with *Animal House*, and *The Blues Brothers* at the top of the record charts all at the same time. You often hear, "Why? He had everything." He did have everything, but unless you're around it, you wouldn't understand: what drove his success was also his demise.

The tour hit all the major cities, including a stop at *Saturday Night Live*, where Rickie was banned from playing for pulling a stunt on her last appearance, when she had switched songs, forcing NBC to miss a commercial.

On that famous night in 1979, I was in the control room with Rickie's old Warner rep Bob, who was telling the new late-night show that if they ever wanted another

Warner artist again, they wouldn't cut Rickie off and go to a commercial break. I'm sure Bob was in fear for his life if Rickie was cut short.

I flew to Austin for the first date with the band and crew; Rickie would follow the next day. She was nowhere to be found and missed all her flights. She was finally located and put onto a private jet. Rickie showed up and immediately fired her wardrobe girl, had a physical altercation with Bob, and went onstage two

Boston Orpheum on top of the truck.
The 1982 Rickie Lee Jones Pirate tour crew. One of the best crews I ever put together from bands such as the Eagles, CSNY, Fleetwood Mac, and more.
Jage Jackson, Nick Storr, Tommy Beck, Me. Michale Cain and Tommy Covelli (David's Brother).
Vito's Cabana Club was a space on multiple tours where the crew would set up a lounge with chairs, table and a bar to hang in before, during, and after the show.

hours late at the brand-new Theater of Performing Arts at the University of Texas.

That was a prelude of things to come for the tour, and Rickie burnished her reputation as the new, edgy bad girl of rock 'n' roll.

The tour came and went, good friends and a good time, but my time with Rickie Lee Jones was done ... or so, I thought.

While prepping and advancing the Fleetwood Mac *Mirage* Tour, I picked up a one-month tour with the Beach Boys. It was a small West Coast tour for their twentieth anniversary, and I was on the light crew. Coming down from the Concord Pavilion in the East Bay of San Francisco in the middle of the night, down Highway 5, the old bus that was carrying the overcapacity crew caught on fire. Seemed the electrical system to the air conditioner unit shorted out. While all of us grabbed our bags and jumped off the bus, one of the crew grabbed a fire extinguisher and managed to put the fire out.

It was the middle of the night; there was no way to get another vehicle, so we decided to get back onto the bus and see if it would run so we could get to the last date at the Greek Theater in Los Angeles. The bus ran, but the smell in the back made it impossible to sit there, so we all huddled in the front lounge on top of each other, trying to get as much sleep as we could just to get to LA and do the last show.

At that show, Dennis Wilson created one of the most outrageous moments in Beach Boys history.

The Barry Manilow hit "I Write the Songs" was actually written by Bruce Johnston of the Beach Boys. During Bruce's introduction that night at the Greek Theater, Dennis wanted to make sure the crowd knew Bruce wrote the song and also that Barry, let's just say, wasn't sexually like the rest of us. Dennis was rambling on, telling the crowd that he always thought

1982 Beach Boys 20th Anniversary tour pass.

Barry was gay but he hadn't been sure, "But tonight, I'm here to tell you, Barry is a goddamn fag."

The crowd loved it, but it wasn't going over too well with Mike Love, the Beach Boy's front man. Mike went over to try to control Dennis and get on with the show. Dennis being Dennis, he took offense, and the fight began. The Boys' full-time tour manager, Jason, and a couple of the regulars, bear-hugged Dennis, and brought him backstage, and locked in him a dressing room, and he was replaced by the second drummer on the tour for the rest of the set.

As the set waned into the night, the encores were coming with the traditional final song "Fun Fun Fun." Dennis had calmed down and was told he could play if he promised not to do anything that would embarrass the band. The song began, and Dennis was hammering away, playing harder and harder as the song went on. We all noticed he had his eyes and his angst on Mike, and it was accelerating.

Then it happened: with Mike's back to Dennis, and at the crescendo, Dennis stood up, walked straight through his drums, jumped off the riser, and beelined to Mike. He grabbed him and took a swing that partially connected, and mayhem broke out. All the crew, Carl Wilson, and Al Jardine ran over to try to subdue the situation, but it was no use. Chaos erupted, and the Beach Boys twentieth anniversary show in Los Angeles ended. I stood in disbelief but learned later in life this was just another day in the life of the Beach Boys.

Much of my time on the Beach Boys tour was spent working on the new Fleetwood Mac tour. The album *Mirage* was released June 18, 1982, with lackluster reviews and was a stark contrast from *Tusk*. To me, the band had found the recipe to combine *Tusk* and *Rumours*. The opening track, "Love In Store," went back to the pop sensibility of Christine's infectious melodies, with her signature voice combined with Stevie and Lindsey's perfectly layered background vocals.

The first single to go to radio off *Mirage* was "Hold Me," a Christine McVie track that brought back the obvious sonic perfection of Lindsey's arrangements and the always-edgy recording schemes of Ken and Richard. The "Hold Me" video was shot in the desert in Southern California with Mick and John playing archaeologists looking for the rest of the band, who were in different obscure scenes.

The music industry was changing rapidly, the punk scene was becoming prevalent, and *Mirage* was panned as "just another Fleetwood Mac record." Over time, the *Mirage* record grew on people. There were departures with songs like "That's Alright" that made Stevie feel like she was young again, sitting on her grandfather's lap, singing country songs.

This is one of my favorite Fleetwood Mac Pictures.
Mirage is a very underrated record.

Warner Records decided that Stevie's song "Gypsy" would become the next single off *Mirage*. "Gypsy" is a strong song with great verses and a hooky chorus with amazing guitar parts and harmonies to ride out the tail end of the song.

Warner's also produced a video to accompany "Gypsy's" release. "Gypsy" was an ode to Stevie's past, waitressing tables and sleeping on the floor of her and

Lindsey's disheveled apartment on De Longpre Avenue in Hollywood. The song had been slated to be on Bella Donna. It was also a tribute to Robin Snyder, Stevie's best friend and vocal coach, who was dealing with leukemia. Robin was pregnant as well.

The video was a period piece throwing the band back to the Depression Era, when people were happy through their struggles. I was asked to bring large lights to Sunset and Gower Studios for the shoot. This wasn't just a rock 'n' roll video shoot; it resembled a full feature movie set up. The director, Russell Mulcahy, had many music videos to his credit and was known for beautiful transitions and layering of color. He went on to direct major films such as *Highlander* and TV shows like *Tales From The Crypt*.

Fleetwood Mac
Mirage tour pass.

This period piece video became the most expensive music video in history, with a budget that climbed over $1,000,000. The video was put into rotation on MTV, as well as the new adult MTV—called VH1—and sales of *Mirage* began increasing.

With all the videos and marketing that Warner's put into *Mirage*, the money for tour support was depleted. Tour support were funds that were given to bands to support a tour and promote the record. With the advent of the music video, it was more valuable to put out a video that hit millions and millions every hour instead of 20,000 people a day in over fifty cities around the world. That meant The Mac was on its own to pay and support the tour. It was decided to schedule only thirty shows on one North American leg and see how it went before committing to a world tour.

Rehearsals for the *Mirage* tour started in early August 1982. My old friend Raymond was the head stage tech/stage manager, and the normal cast of characters were there, like Tony, taking care of Mick, and Patrick, taking care of John. Wayno was heading up the security detail and had to handle a tour without his old friend and compadre JC. It was odd not to have JC around. With all the financial responsibility being on the band, Curry and I were forced to design around budgets instead of art. We went back to the art deco look, accompanied by small scenery pieces scattered around the stage. The lighting was the same rig as *Tusk,* with the addition of more rear follow spots. Being the production manager, I had a huge part in the profit and loss of the tour. My mind was also on quick ins and outs to keep the union labor cost down, as well as less crew and fewer buses and trucks on the road.

The tour was a typical arena tour with spatters of stadium shows with strong opening acts and was nothing to write home about, except for a few special events.

One special date was September 5, a show in the California desert called the US Festival.

This was shortly after the time that two young men from the San Jose, California, area took a risk, borrowed some money, and empowered mankind, changing the world forever by inventing the "personal computer."

Steve Jobs and his technical genius partner, Steve Wozniak, a.k.a. Woz, started a small company called Apple Computers. The world was ready to take information into their own hands, and Jobs and Woz were in the right place at the right time.

To celebrate taking Apple computers public (a move that made Jobs and Woz billionaires overnight), Woz wanted to throw a party with his favorite band, Fleetwood Mac. He also had a huge affection for Stevie.

Joining forces with the Bill Graham family, who never thought small and were masters at creating what is now known as Event-Based Entertainment, a three-day music festival in the desert of Southern California was born.

Fleetwood Mac was the headline on Sunday, September 5, 1982, and they became the first band to ever make $1,000,000 for a single show.

The only problem was the *Mirage* tour was booked and shows were on sale before the US festival date was solidified.

The tour started in Greensboro, North Carolina, on September 1, with Atlanta on September 3, and a stadium show on September 4 in Orland Florida.

The task put to the crew and me, mainly Raymond, was to figure out a way to play in Orlando the night of September 4 and load-in and be ready to play the US festival at eight p.m. on September 5 (on the other side of the United States), then rally back with the rest of the tour and crew in Lexington, Kentucky, on September 7 for a show. This was going to take a logistical miracle, but we were up for it. Bring it on!

From my detailed notes and journals that I wrote and somehow found, here is how we pulled off the challenge and task thrown at us.

August 15, 1982.

Note: Check with the band to see what songs they want to play at the festival. Set time? Special stuff? Pianos? Guitars? Tony, drums? Ray? Duplicate?

It was important to see what songs the band wanted to play for instrumentation, not only for band instruments but for sound and effects as well. The objective was to leave as much gear with the touring rig on the tour and in the trucks and bring less to San Bernardino. This would cut down on labor and cargo for air freight and fit into the hold of the private plane we needed to lease. It would also lessen any chance of gear breaking in transport to and from the festival. I needed to meet with Ray about exactly reproducing our complete stage so the band wouldn't know the difference. I wanted them to think we brought all their gear with us. I was pretty sure we needed to bring all the guitars. The more songs they were going to play,

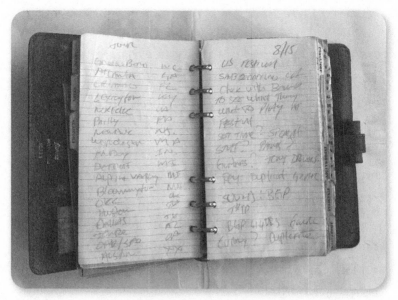

My Day Planner with my US festival Notes.

the more gear we needed to bring—or have reproduced there.

Note: Sound? BGP? (Bill Graham Presents) Trip?

The festival sound was the biggest sound system ever assembled, and we were hoping it was going to be Clair Brothers Audio, The Mac's touring audio company. If so, they would duplicate our system, including all the special effects we had on the tour.

Note: BGP. Lights? Generic? Curry? Do we get our rig since we are headlining? Duplicate?

I needed to check and see what the design was for the lights. Was BGP going to install one generic lighting system that all the bands would share? Since we were the headliner, BGP should duplicate our light rig, and everyone else should work around us.

Note: Crew? Transportation? Jet? How big?
Note: Wardrobe? Duffle, no cases, too big! New for the show?

Since the *Tusk* tour, the band's wardrobe and backstage ambience cases took up half of one truck, and there was no way we could bring or afford to bring any of the wardrobe cases with us. Plus, there was no time to airfreight them. I also made a note to see if anyone, mainly Stevie or Chris, wanted to have new outfits for the biggest show of their lives. In any case, we needed to figure this part out, and it wasn't going to be easy.

Note: Crew? Who? Need to leave someone with the crew.

How many of our touring crew did we need for the show? Did I need to bring stage carpenters for the risers and the flooring? Who was going to stay back with the crew that wasn't coming with us?

Note: OL t-bowl SB-fes Ken. Trucks, jetway sizes? Times crew? distance? Hotels BGP?

This was a note to figure all the logistical steps at all the stops, Orlando, San Bernardino, Lexington, Kentucky. What size trucks should we use: our forty-foot semis or smaller ones to get closer to the jet to load? What was the drive time from the stages to the airports and airports to the stages? Did we have crew at every stop? Did we have hotels upon arrival in San Bernardino?

Note: Passes? BGP Killer Who Wayno?

This note was about stage passes and credentials for

the stage. I was thinking being such a big festival with lots of staff and personnel, how we wanted to handle who was onstage when we were on and how we were going to control it. Wayno was our head of security and had the final decision on this.

Killer, ahh, Killer! Killer was a JC invention and the most important case on the tour. It was a small road box that carried all our stage passes and important documents, like contracts and personnel files. It was also the case that carried the tour's large stash of cocaine that was flown in, in large quantities. This was the only way to ensure that what the band was getting was real and pure and not cut with bogus filler that eradicated the euphoric high from the off-white, pure powder.

Killer had a hermetically sealed secret compartment that even the best trained drug sniffing canine's couldn't find. After mastering the removal of all the sliding drawers, there was a very thin two-layer false backing that held the cocaine. Once you had the first backing off, you had to be privy to the inner workings of Killer to get inside access to the second false backing, where the humidified sealed compartments were used not only for security, but freshness. Very few people knew about the inner workings of Killer.

It was essential for me to figure out if the plan was to carry enough or if the connection was going to supply it locally when we got to the desert.

Planning and pulling off the US Festival was as difficult as the short twenty-nine city tour, but it had to be done. I set up a series of individual and full crew meetings, and we put the plan in place, and it worked. There were many moving parts, but it was a true example of teamwork and ingenuity.

Being that the date had a $1,000,000 payday, we had a lot of flexibility, and the band trusted us to make sure that the most prestigious date in their history was going to be right.

Since his early days with the band, Curry always had input with the band's set list. That was because he was always in the front of the house at the lightboard and could gauge the flow, continuity, and success of the songs. Curry and the band gave us a setlist for the US Festival, and Raymond and Trip composed a list of equipment needed to do the show. Clair Brothers Audio did get the contract for the festival, so we were golden for sound; an exact replica of what Trip needed was going to be ready for The Mac at the festival. This even meant that Trip could send the settings of each channel; he could step right up to board and just mix the show.

Raymond had hired Mike Huber, a good friend, to be the gear guru of the band. Mike methodically drove around Southern California picking up gear to exactly reproduce the band's instruments, except for the few one of a kind pieces, like guitars and sound effects.

BGP decided to film the concert so the lighting had to be bright, and Curry collaborated with the film crew's director of photography and agreed on a mutual light design that worked for the live show as well as the film.

We decided to bring only essential crew: sound, band crew, one carpenter to handle risers and flooring (who would also assist me and double up as our backstage coordinator), and one lighting person to coordinate between the local lighting crew, and of course, Curry and all the wardrobe, makeup, and security teams. In total, the scaled-down entourage of twenty-one traveled to our US Festival adventure.

To pull this feat off, commercial air travel for the band and crew was out of the question, so we chartered a small, private, very deluxe DC-9 to pick us up in Orland, fly us to San Bernardino, and then on to Lexington, Kentucky. Chris had experience with the band Queen using private jets, and he picked this particular DC-9 for its large cargo holds and luxurious interior, which included a full galley with fresh food for the flight. It also didn't require long runways, so we were able to get into Ontario Airport, closer to the gig, instead of Los Angeles International. We were also able to use a private airport in Orlando that allowed us to pull right up to the jet with small trucks that we decided to use instead of our semitrucks. This saved time, aggravation, and money.

Reviewing the list of gear, there wasn't a lot we had to bring with us, but the gear took priority before any personal clothing or effects. We bought thick duffle bags for the essential wardrobe, and new outfits for Stevie and Christine were made and delivered to the gig. Each crew member was limited to only one carry-on that would fit inside the cabin, in case there was not enough room in the hold of the DC-9.

I circulated a piece of paper with columns and told each security person to get with their principal and find out the number of pieces each person was taking, as well as an estimated size and weight to prepare myself for the laborious conversations of: "Sorry, you can't take that; we don't have enough room." I also made them number each bag, too, so we could make a manifest list to track anything needed. Raymond and I combined the gear and personal list, and we calculated that we could fit everything on the DC-9.

September 4, 1982, we loaded into the Orlando Citrus Bowl with Loverboy as the opening act, but all our attention was on the logistics and excitement of the US festival. The show ran itself, and as the band showed up, so did their bags, and we loaded them into the small truck. Little by little, the truck was filling up and estimating the amount of gear on Raymond's list, I started to worry. Did we miscalculate? How the fuck is this all going to fit? It was too late to get another truck, so we had to make it work.

Pretty much everything got loaded into the small truck except the specialized guitars and instrument pieces that Mike in LA didn't get.

The truck was packed, ready to go, and the US Festival crew was rallying onto one bus—to follow the truck to the private airport to meet the band that had already left the venue.

With everyone on the bus, I made one last check, and Killer popped into my head. Oh shit! Something we overlooked. Killer. I ran to the production office and grabbed Killer, wheeled him to the bus, and threw him into the bus bay for the short ride to the airport.

We pulled up to the airport and onto the tarmac right next to the white with blue striped DC-9. We jumped out, and I was amazed to see how big the cargo holds of the jet actually were. With a collective sigh of relief, we began to load the jet. The pilot instructed us to load the heaviest equipment closer to the center of the jet by the wings. We understood, and it worked out perfectly.

When we landed in Ontario, the band would be going to the hotel, and we knew they would want their belongings first. Their bags were just the right weight size for the rear cargo hold and could be offloaded first. The heavier instruments fit perfectly right behind, and in front of the wings (and in less than thirty minutes) the jet was loaded, and we were ready to go—except for one thing.

I remembered Killer on the bus. Climbing the stairs onto the jet, with gold seat belts and thirty white leather seats, I tracked down Wayno.

"Hey buddy. Killer? Yes or no?"

"No, just leave it. I took care of it." So, Killer stayed on the bus to meet us in Lexington.

All buttoned up and ready to go, the sweaty, grimy

crew, tired from a long day of hot and humid work conditions, settled into predetermined space in the back of the jet, away from the band. I had set up towels and soap for all of us to at least clean up, eat and drink a bit, and rest for the upcoming, long day ahead of us.

The food and hospitality on the jet was as good as the décor, and with full bellies and some drinks to take the edge off, we all settled into our seats or onto the floor, winging our way to the Southern Californian desert.

At three a.m. we landed in the darkness of Ontario Airport in the Southern California desert. We were met by the BGP staff with limos (for the band) and two small trucks—one went to the hotel with luggage and the other took our gear to the gig. I also arranged a van to transport us backstage, where trailers with beds and showers were waiting.

We arrived at what felt like an oasis in the desert; the US Festival was a small city. It went on for miles and miles, and by the time we hit backstage, the colors of the Apple Computer logo with red, orange, yellow, purple, blue, and green created this mysterious, beautiful dreamscape like you were in the future.

The day's events were over, and Tom Petty & The Heartbreakers finished hours before, and the clean stage was ready for us. The lineup for Sunday, September 5 was the Grateful Dead, followed by Jerry Jeff Walker, then Jimmy Buffet & the Coral Refer Band, Jackson Browne, and finally Fleetwood Mac to finish the three-day extravaganza for over 350,000 people.

On a festival show, the headline band would set up first and sound check, then the opening bands would layer in front. After each band played, crews would systematically peel back their gear until the headliners gear was exposed and ready to go. That wasn't the case with US 1982. Every band was a headliner in their own right, so each band had control of the stage for their designated spots. BGP, being the ultimate premier professional promotion company, designed a stage big enough for the band behind the band onstage to set up on rolling risers, and as one band rolled off, the other would roll on and plug in and play.

We weren't scheduled to set up until late morning; that meant we could get some well-deserved rest. We off-loaded the truck and added to the pile of equipment that Mike brought, and we were ready to be lifted onstage when instructed.

Before laying our heads down, Raymond, being the ultimate professional (and paranoid of failure), wanted to check the gear being brought in to make sure everything we needed was there, in case we were missing something. We would have time to get it, so we wouldn't be running around like crazy the next day.

Mike did great, and everything was accounted for. It was dark with just a shimmer of light over the crowd, so it was impossible to see the colossal magnitude of the crowd and the festival.

We hit the trailers, and I was awakened around nine-thirty a.m. by the roar of the crowd as Bill Graham

The US Festival crowd as I walk up on the stage

introduced the Grateful Dead, saying something like, "There's nothing like breakfast with the Dead."

It was a perfect, warm Southern Californian morning, with blue skies and dry air that softens not only your skin but your mind as well. It was the perfect remedy to recover from the hastened pace of the show and travel from Orlando to Ontario.

Putting on a full-on stadium show with hundreds of thousands of people, then grabbing bits and pieces of it, on top of moving the entourage 3,000 miles in the middle of the night, was not normal. But then again, we weren't normal. We all shared the fear of living a mundane, boring nine-to-five life, and it drove us to do extraordinary things.

As I walked up the stairs to the stage, my legs wobbled, and I almost lost my balance. It was a sea of humanity as far as the eye could see. It was like a painting suddenly changing from black and white to color. The crowd was so big, it was impossible to focus on what was in front of you and the horizon at the same time.

All of this created by two visionaries who took a chance and brought power to the world with plastic boxes filled with electronics running codes of ones and zeros, empowering the curious imaginations and minds of chance-takers.

The day lingered on, and while waiting for our turn to set up, I worked on designing our escape to get us all back to what now seemed like the mundane, ho-hum tour.

The plan was to jump off the stage and bolt to the airport to try to avoid running into the large crowd trying to get out of the festival to return to their homes. This meant all of the gear, luggage, and things we brought with us needed to be ready to go right after the show. Hit and run! The Rolling Stones came up with a brilliant idea years ago, where they would put on a fifteen-minute fireworks show that the crowd would stay and watch, and that gave them time to get off the stage and out of the stadium, thus avoiding traffic.

The jet was ready, the pilots would be rested, the trucks and vans on this side were cool, Chris had the band; what was missing?

Raymond told us that during the traditional closing song, "Song Bird," with only Christine and the piano and two acoustic guitars for Lindsey and John, he could pack up all the items that were going back with us and be ready to go. Trip and our other sound engineers could have the local sound engineers finish the easy mix and be backstage, ready to depart. The band's luggage went from the hotel straight to the jet and would be loaded, and our luggage was in the van, ready to go.

While Jackson Browne was delighting the crowd with the many hits from his California sound, we were offstage setting up our gear to roll on when Jackson was done. Dialing in the sound levels, we were ready. We did our perfectly planned preshow sound check, where the band would come up and jam a bit while we got levels, and with that last drum roll from Mick, and with full vengeance on a perfectly warm beautiful night under the stars, Fleetwood Mac took themselves, along with hundreds of thousands of people, on a magical journey through time and space.

The show ended, and our well-crafted plan of getting out of the US Festival worked. We said our goodbyes to all the wonderful people who created the unforgettable memories of our US Festival experience, and because of the fireworks distraction and police escort, we soon found ourselves proudly resting in the back of our private DC-9. There were no words; we looked at each other and just smiled. Someone raised their hand, and we all high-fived, and I said, "Hey, who lives like us?"

Raymond smiled and said, "We do."

I wish I could say our US Festival ended without a hiccup, but it didn't. We landed, the band was on their way to their

Fleetwood Mac, legendary promoter Bill Graham, and Steve Wozniak, Co-Founder of Apple Computers.

hotel, and the trucks were there to pick up the gear, but there was only one bus. I asked where the other bus was, the bus that dropped us off.

Jim, the other bus driver, said, "Uh … we don't know."

I said, "What do you mean you don't know?"

Jim said, "After the driver dropped you off in Orlando, we haven't heard from him. There's another bus coming out for you now, and the office is trying to find the missing one."

We were so tired it didn't matter. We all just wanted to get to the hotel and spend a good couple of well-deserved days off, recharging our batteries.

Halfway to the hotel, I realized all our bags were on the bus, so none of us had clean clothes or our personal items. Then I jolted up.

"Oh fuck! Killer!" Killer was on the bus with all, and I mean all the band's cocaine. This was a problem.

I got to the hotel and immediately called Wayno to break the bad news. He said he had enough to get by, but it wasn't going to last.

Florida Coach, our bus company, called all authorities and gave them information to help locate the missing bus.

On September 9, we loaded into the Rupp Arena and went through our normal procedure; still no word on the bus. Wayno showed up and had to make a plan to find the necessary staple to get through the show until we could figure out what to do.

Finding local cocaine was dangerous and not a good idea because you never knew what it was cut with. Crooked business practices even infiltrated the local dealers, who would add bullshit additives to make a quarter ounce a half ounce to increase their profit. We needed to find something, and as showtime came close, we had no choice but to find something local to get us through. The Lexington show was promoted by Beaver, and Don Fox and Ray Compton were on it. The local caterer had a line on some local cocaine and just needed the money to go pick it up. Ray called Fox, and Fox came down and gave the caterer a wad of cash to go score the needed white powder.

As show time approached, there was still nothing, and calls were being made to find out what was going on. Around seven p.m., we got the call that the runner going to pick up the stash got busted and arrested. Now we had big problems. In trouble with the law, out a big wad of cash, and no cocaine for the band.

Showtime came, and everyone was on edge. Fox was angry and yelling at the caterers, feeling it was a scam and just a way to steal the money. That proved not to be true when two of Lexington's finest law enforcement officers showed up to discuss the situation. Seems the story was true, but luckily, the runner was busted with the cash before the buy and was so freaked out that she spilled her guts. Fox denied everything, saying, "Not me, not this band. Do you think we'd be stupid enough to give someone cash for a drug deal? We have too much to lose officers, not us."

It was now eight-thirty p.m., and the opening act was done, and it was time for The Mac to hit the stage. Eight-thirty p.m. became nine p.m., and the band gathered in the hallway outside the dressing rooms to get onstage. The tension was thick. I was out at the lightboard with Curry, who was on the headset. "Hey, Leo, they need you backstage."

As I got backstage, there was tension. The band was agitated. One said to the other.

"Fuck we don't need it; let's just play!" and the argument gained momentum.

Greg, who was now the security guard for Christine, was standing next to Christine, waiting for instructions with a smirk on his face. Just wanting to start the show and not liking Greg's smirk, John McVie confronted him, asking, "What's so fucking funny?"

I think the rugged schedule and travel of the US Festival pushed the normally passive John McVie, and he showed an aggressive side that I had never seen. A band squabble continued, with words hurling back and forth like a rock fight. John just took off, avoiding the wrath that the rest of the band and entourage was ready to put upon him.

It was game on, and what happened next will only be known by the people who were backstage in that Rupp Arena Hallway on September 9, 1982.

An hour later, the show finally began with Fleetwood Mac's magical animosity that once again gave the fans an unforgettable show.

The next day we got a call, the bus was found in a truck stop parking lot somewhere in Tennessee and was on its way to Norfolk.

At the Scope Arena in Norfolk, Virginia, we were reunited with our bus. I immediately went to the bus bay, and I closed my eyes as I slowly opened the bus bay. I opened my eyes, and with relief (like I saw my first child), there was Killer! Unopened and untouched, just as I left him on the tarmac in Orlando.

We snaked our way through the States, city after city and show after show, and in early October, we were back on the West Coast. After the Oakland show on October 3, heard that the devil's sweat, leukemia, had run its course on Robin, Stevie's best friend and confidant, and it was just a matter of time. Robin was seven months pregnant, and they took her baby boy, and with all the miracles from above, the baby was cancer-free. On October 5, 1982, Robin, the angel on Earth, departed this world and blessed the next with her amazing soul.

In my young life on the road, Robin taught me a great deal, not only about being on the road but about life. She mainly taught me the values of respect and tolerance for women on the road. Christie (Stevie's makeup person and other confidant), along with Robin and Stevie, were inseparable. They often told me, "Don't be the rest of those guys, Sugar Bear."

It was obvious Stevie was emotionally and physically shaken, but as always, with her supernatural talent coupled with shear emotion, Stevie hit a level that we all agreed we had never seen before. It was all captured on October 21 and 22 at the Los Angeles Forum, where The Mac and HBO captured the magic of Fleetwood Mac, and especially Stevie.

We completed the remaining twenty-seven shows, appropriately ending on Halloween in Austin, Texas. The tour was over, and there was not to be any more shows for the *Mirage* tour. No Europe, no Asia, no Australia, and in fact, no Mac shows for a very long time. The band had gotten back together just long enough to realize how much they really didn't want—or have—to work together.

Even though it was relatively short, it was a very hard tour, and we were all done. Chris, the tour manager, for sure was done. The tour was hard for him. He booked the Halloween party in a ballroom at a Howard Johnson's, that's how done he was; he just didn't care. At the party, I overheard Christine say, "JC would never do this to us—a fucking Howard Johnson's!" Then it hit me. Although JC was rough around the edges and crass, JC wasn't just a tour manager, he was part of The Mac. Without JC, The Mac wasn't the same, and it showed. He had their backs, and the love and dedication that he gave to the band was what was lacking on *Mirage*.

the SET   1982

B   SECOND HAND NEWS
A   The CHAIN
E *DON'T STOP!   • monitor
F   DREAMS   • monitor back
Em OH WELL!
Am RhIANNON
B   BROWN EYES
A *EYES OF THE WORLD
F   GYPSY
C   LOVE IN STORE
C   NOT THAT FUNNY (IS IT?)
    BRUSHES
  *LANDSLIDE
(A) Dm TUSK
F   SARA
Am*HOLD ME!
    YOU MAKE LOVIN' FUN
    SO AFRAID
    ~~BLUE LETTER~~
    GO YOU'RE OWN WAY
      ~ BLUE LETTER
A   SISTERS
    SONGBIRD

The Fleetwood Mac Mirage Tour set list from Ray's guitar world.
Notice the tunings on the left.

Reflecting back, I take back the sarcastic words I said back in 1982 when people asked me, "How was the tour?"

"Oh, you know, Just another fucking Fleetwood Mac Tour."

Now, when asked, "How was the *Mirage* tour in 1982?" I answer, "One of the best tours of my life!

CHAPTER THIRTY TWO
ONE WORD ... BETTE

DURING THE *MIRAGE* TOUR, my good friend and The Mac's stage monitor sound engineer, Chuck, told me that he had turned our good, mutual friend Jerry Levin onto a potential tour that he thought we should all do.

Years earlier, in 1978, Chuck was brought in to rescue the live scenes for the movie "The Rose," staring a young female artist named Bette Midler. In 1982, with her movie career flailing, Bette wanted to revisit her roots and go back on the road to live concerts.

Chuck got a call from Bette's longtime assistant, Bonnie. Chuck and Bonnie lived with each other for a stint, and she called him to see if he would be interested in tour

managing the upcoming tour. Chuck politely declined but offered his sound services, telling Bonnie, "Don't go with anyone else, other than my friend Jerry Levin."

Chuck, Jerry, and I all worked on the Al Jarreau Tour, and he suggested I call Jerry. I called Jerry, and he told me he just interviewed and got the tour director position and was going to call me.

Jerry said, "I think it's going to be one for the ages, Leo. It will be a tough one though; very theatrical with lots of moving parts. Right up your alley."

"OK Jerry, I'm in if you need me, when's it start?"

"Early December, going into 1983. There's going to be lots of rehearsals, so I'll need you early November."

"Great! Perfect, this Mac tour ends on Halloween."

"OK. Before I can hire you, we need to meet, and

you will have to meet with Bette, Bonnie, Bette's assistant, and Jerry Blatt, Bette's director. So, call me as soon as you get home."

I was back in Los Angeles on Monday, November 1, and went right from the airport to Jerry's house, and from there, we were going to the rehearsal space to meet my new potential employer.

Jerry knew I was out with The Mac and wanted to see how I looked and to make sure I wasn't one of The Mac tragedies strung out on cocaine. By this time in my life, I was pretty much done with drinking and drugs. I was sick and tired of waking up sick and tired.

With all the responsibility, I just didn't have time for it and besides, I loved what I did, and power became my new drug of choice.

Jerry was the tour producer. He was responsible for not only the tour but putting together the band and music. I was to be the production manager and handle all things production.

Jerry, who was always straightforward and honest with me, asked,

"How ya doing? You good?"

"Yeah, Jerry, I'm great."

"How was the tour?"

"Ah, you know, just another fucking Fleetwood Mac tour."

"You look good; you put on weight, I can tell you're off the shit."

"Yeah, done with it Jerry. Too much going on."

Jerry explained the tour to me, and plain and simple, it was going to be Bette's world of Gay Hollywood and rock 'n' roll on one tour.

"They want to tour with a Broadway show. Multiple shows in every city in old, rundown theaters in the worst parts of town. It's going to be difficult, and if I see you get high once, I'll let you go." I nodded in agreement. "Bill will be the front of house engineer, and Chuck will be doing monitors," Jerry said. "You will need to fill in the rest of the crew. I have a good idea who will be in the band but still need to audition a few positions."

We walked into Coles Rehearsal Hall in Santa Monica, and it was a full of people. Bette and Jerry Blatt, the director, were at the head of a long table with Bonnie at their side. Around the table was the flamboyant cast of characters handling scripts, wardrobe, design, and God knows what else. Then, there was Jerry and me. It was classic Sesame Street: "Which ones don't belong?"

Jerry Blatt started the meeting by welcoming all of us and thanking us for being involved in what is going to be a historic tour. Holding my yellow legal pad, I kicked Jerry under the table and whispered, "Does this mean I have the gig?"

Jerry Blatt continued. "The theme of the tour is Tour De Force, and it's revealing the new Bette Midler. Music plus extravagant sets with some old routines like the Doris De Lago and some new, kick ass rock 'n' roll numbers.

The idea is to play in the oldest, darkest theaters in the shitty parts of town to force the affluent fan base to come down so we can write around that in the scripts. I mean theaters that use to be porno houses ... closed ... we mean dirty." I looked at Bette, and she had that Bette Midler smile on her face, like a child eating ice cream.

Then Bette took the floor. "I really like the art of Andre Miripolsky. He's done a lot of work for Elton, and I like the way he uses color."

Then Jerry Levin said, "Perhaps, before we get started, let's go around the room and introduce ourselves, so we know who's who and doing what." Jerry Blatt and Bette agreed.

With her patented smile and her hands clasped together under her chin, Bette said. "Hi, I'm Bette, and I'm a diva." The roomed laughed again as Jerry Blatt chimed in a said, "Hello, I'm Jerry, and I'm also a diva."

Then, we all met the famous Bruce Valance, the head writer; costume designer extraordinaire, Bob De Mora; and Mary, his assistant; award-winning choreographer, Tony Basil; Franny, Bette's assistant and day-to-day handler; Bonnie, producer and Bette's partner in All Girls Productions; Bill, front of house sound engineer; and Chip, the lighting design-er. There were several more before coming to Jerry.

"I'm Jerry Levin, the tour director," and then there was me.

With pride and confidence, I blurted out, "My name is Leo, and I will be your production stage manager."

With all the pleasantries out of the way, we got down to business.

From the imprecise scribbles of my notes, Jerry Blatt continued, "Seedy, dirty, shitholes." At one point I remember him saying something along the lines of, "I want them to squirm in their tuxes."

Bruce mentioned he had a rough of the basic script but needed to fill in the music cues. It was a basic script that would be modified for each city to reflect the local news and trends and allow Bette to pester the local politicians and elite. The show was designed to be three hours long with the first half being two hours filled with up-tempo rock songs, like the Rolling Stones "Beast Of Burden" and Springsteen's "Pink Cadillac," followed by an intermission to sell drinks and merchandise. The one-hour finale would include the iconic ballad "The Rose."

As they went around the room, I was getting excited and realized this was not just an ordinary tour, and Jerry was right: it was a tour for the ages.

Bette Midler De Tour poster.

The meeting adjourned, and Jerry had set up a meeting for the tech side of the tour so we could fill in the holes for what we needed. Jerry also requested a copy of each scene and what possible set pieces and props would be needed, so we could get into the details like schedule, crew, trucks, and travel. Once again, my kind of tour. Because of multiple shows in each city, hotels every night, and commercial air—no long bus rides.

It didn't take long for Jerry to get the band into place. With all the years Jerry managed Al Jarreau, he worked with the best of the best musicians; Jarreau was so amazing some musicians would work for free. There was a long line of musical directors, like Barry Manilow and Luther Vandross, whose careers began in the small, gay bathhouses where Bette cut her teeth and cultivated a young, loyal fanbase that knew she was destined for success.

Jerry did his magic, and Bette Midler had her band. The accomplished keyboardist Bobby Lyle served as musical director, the rhythm section was Ricky Lawson on drums, Lenny Castro was on percussion, and the dapper "Pops" Popwell played bass. My old friend from the Rickie Lee Jones band Buzzy Fieten was on guitar, and Frank Zappa's multi-instrument-playing musical genius, Bobby Martin, was on all the other many instruments. Jerry auditioned and hired these amazing musicians not only for their musicianship but their ability to learn the music charts fast and be adaptable to the changes that Jerry had the foresight to see coming.

Along with the A-Line band were Bette's *The Harlettes*. Three hard-working background singers and dancers who carried the show, enhancing the vision of Bette and Jerry Blatt's Tour De Force circus.

Bette Midler De Tour Harlettes Katie Sagal (left)
Linda Hart (Center) Ula Hedwig
They were the hardest working people on the tour.

The Harlettes' Linda Hart, Eula Heartwig, and Katey Sagal put out nonstop energy and complimented the band and Bette's musical performances to round out the high-energy show. The show was taking shape, and as it came together, my excitement was intensifying, and I was once again that little teenager back in Long Beach, eager to take on the world.

Jerry gave me the scene synopsis and asked me to head the tech meeting. With my yellow legal pad and colored pencils in hand, I went for inspiration down to my favorite place on the water, Ports O' Call Village, where I sketched out a stage diagram, putting the band upstage with a barrier in front of them to create a large performing area for *Bette and The Harlettes.*

I wrote out scene by scene with a list of requirements for the shows—sound, lights, props set pieces, everything I could think of including quick change tents stage right and left where Bette could change during the quirky interludes for set changes.

The scenes were quite complex, and I was figuring out that we were going to need large set pieces, small set pieces, and set pieces that would have to fly in on pipes. Perhaps the most interesting scene was "Deloris Delago: The Toast of Chicago" that had *Bette and The Harlettes* in mermaid tails driving electronic wheelchairs to a choreographed performance (that included all of them on the floor lying but the audience still had to be able to see them). Man! How the fuck was I going to do this?

Act one, scene one was an opening where Bette would come onstage and greet her fans with *The Harlettes*. It was a number called "Don't Look Now" with comedic dialogue and music.

This number required Bette and *The Harlettes* to perform on the whole stage, which meant wired microphones were out of the question, and we needed to adopt the new technology of wireless microphones, using minitransmitters and receivers for complete mobility and for them to hear themselves. The stage needed to be cleared of speakers. We were going to have to adapt what is now commonly known as "in ears" a wireless monitor system, so Bette and *The Harlettes* could hear themselves, each other, and the music.

My concern was the amount of radio channels needed to pull off the tour. I added a note to meet with Bill and Chuck to discuss the sound.

Being that the tour wasn't a normal rock 'n' roll tour, it was necessary to look at companies that were more familiar with theatrical type shows and smaller profile speakers and lighting for the theater. Knowing what I was up against, I also knew I needed the right crew—good on their feet and with theatrical experience.

The key positions for lighting and props would have to be on their game with the rapid changes I anticipated. For lighting, we hired Erick Eastland from the Jarreau team. Erick's biggest quality was his ability to work with people with a good sense of seeing problems before they would happen, and most of all, liaising with Chip the lighting designer (who was very artistic but didn't have a technical bone in his body). I needed a light company and crew that understood the workings of a traditional theater counterweight fly system and who understood the psychology of a theatrical union stagehand.

The last key position was the head carpenter who would be responsible for all the set pieces, props, and most of all, working with the local union carpenter to work the counterweight system for the pipes that would hold all of our gear. I hired Nick Storr. Nick was from San Pedro, and I got him a job at Obie Lighting, where he worked his way up the ladder to becoming a lead and crew chief himself. Nick was perfect for the job and the tour. He fit in well and was a master at using tools and fixing things that I knew were going to break down on the tour.

Rather than a traditional lighting company, I decided to go with TVI, a lighting company that had expertise with theater productions. We also went with Maryland Sound, an upstart sound company and had a variety of smaller sound cabinets that fit into all of the venues we were going to play. Within two weeks of the first meeting, all the things were in place to plan rehearsals.

The tour routing was taking shape, and as Jerry Levin worked with the agents picking dates and venues, I called the theater managers to see what we needed to do to make the tour work in each theater.

First was the Northwest with stops in Portland, Seattle, Vancouver, San Francisco, and ending on New Year's Eve at the Universal Amphitheater in Los Angeles. Each city was multiple nights with one load-in and rehearsal day and a minimum stay of five performances.

In San Francisco, we chose the dilapidated Golden Gate Theater on Market and Taylor Streets in the heart of the Tenderloin District, where only hookers and derelicts hung out. The Golden Gate Theater was perfect for Bette's and Jerry Blatt's plan to bring the rich and affluent to the most hardened and seedy part of town. The script would have Bette saying, "Oh, look at the front row, the rich and famous, The who's who of Frisco! Good to see you in this part of town, at least for a show."

After talking with the Golden Gate Theater's manager, and not getting the information I needed other than "good luck," I told Jerry Levin in order to be 100 percent

449

certain that this show was going to work as planned that Bill Darlington and me, the head sound person, should go visit and advance the theaters on this first run and also to meet with the union heads to give them a thorough document that I would create with blueprints, drawings, and descriptions of the show. We could also take pictures for reference for the changes that we all knew were going to happen in rehearsals.

At first Jerry said no, it's not necessary. "Leo, you've done this a million times; you can do this; it's not that difficult."

As the tour director, Jerry was responsible for the profit and loss of the tour, and he was concerned that the costs were already getting out of control, with our gay counterparts ordering costumes and extravagant props to match what Bruce wrote into the script. Bill and I tag-teamed Jerry and convinced him it was imperative that we did the advance. I promised Jerry I'd keep the cost down and was pretty sure we could advance Vancouver, Portland, Seattle, and San Francisco into one day. Of course, I was lying and just trying to convince him. He finally agreed, and I set up the advance trip. To my surprise, when I set up the advance trip, all the flights lined up. If we spent ninety minutes at each venue, and even with broken down taxis and traffic, we did all four cities in one day, with the last being the Golden Gate Theater in San Francisco at eight p.m. We spent the night in San Francisco and flew home the next morning with a very good idea of what we were up against. The advance trip paid off—not only because we knew what we were up against but because the unions took us seriously, figuring that if we took the time to make the trip and advance it with them, we were for real and not just another show coming in to ruin their week.

We decided on the Wilshire Theater for three weeks of full technical rehearsals before heading up to the great Northwest with the Tour De Force. The show came together in rehearsals but not without some tension. There was a transition period for gay Hollywood and rock 'n' roll to figure out how to work together.

From their past tours with Bette, Bill and Chuck were invaluable, and they shared their experience dealing with Bette's predominantly gay team: be patient, don't react, think it through, and most of all, listen ... Listen to them, they know what they're doing.

The rest of the rock 'n' roll crew and I viewed them with apprehension because they were not like us. I felt the division and lack of continuity. Chuck and Bill saw it and knew something needed to be done.

They pulled the crew aside, and Chuck said, "You guys have to realize, you're not all that different from them; they're people just like us, guys."

Then Bill chimed in, saying, "They just like different things, and it's not a choice; they were born that way."

After the meeting, and the more we all worked with Bette's crew, seeing their amazing talents, the division

Bill Darlington (on the right). Bill has golden ears. He can make an AM car radio sound good. He had the most experience seeing both sides of rock n roll and gay Hollywood on the Bette Midler tour.

My long-time good friend and fellow Knight of Rock Chuck Hull. We've done many tours together and now enjoy sharing our story.

wall came crumbling down, and from then on, we were one team with one goal: put on a show for the ages that no one would ever forget.

The full tech rehearsals were tough. But all great things are tough, and if they weren't, everyone would be doing them. The changes in running order, scripts, costumes, sets, props, and mainly choreography were many and intense. *The Harlettes* had long days of dancing and singing: with repetition becomes perfection. The new technologies of wireless microphones and in-ear monitors actually worked out, and happy accidents were abundant.

For the Deloris DeLago mermaid scene, we designed forty-foot-wide by eight-foot-high mirrors that needed to fly in and tilt, so when Bette and *The Harlettes* were wriggling around on the floor, they could be seen by the audience. The challenge was to tilt the mirrors at forty-five degrees with the bottom of the mirrors being pulled up. We connected the mylar (a light, soft, reflective material) mirrors together, so the rigid set of mirrors could move as one. We had ordered two small electric motors to actuate the mirrors and create the tilt. We installed the mirrors and motors, and it didn't work. The middle would bend, and motors couldn't handle the weight. It was a disaster.

Nick decided to make sure the mirrors were secure, so for safety, he had wires hooked up to the top and bottom of each mirror, with two pipes side by side. The pipes had to fly together, or the mirrors would bend and break.

Dropping the two pipes down to the stage to check the motors, the front pipe came in, and the back pipe accidentally stopped, and the mirrors tilted forty-five degrees. Nick screamed, "Stop!" Not for only safety reasons, but we found our simple solution: to tilt the mirrors.

Tech rehearsals were over, and we hit the road with the Tour De Force. Opening night was in Portland, Or-egon, on December 9, 1982, at the Paramount Theater. We loaded in on December 8 for a dress rehearsal run-through of the show. There were a few little things we were still working through that needed attention. We ran through the show once without Bette to make sure that things were 100 percent. This was not only for us but to eliminate any possible stress for Bette, who had a history of losing it even when things were all good.

After the run-through, we had a company meeting to discuss notes, and the only thing not ready to go were the fake palm trees that would live on the backs of the wheel-chairs for the Deloris De Lago scene.

I asked Nick, "What's up with the palm trees?"

Jerry Blatt jumped in, saying that he changed the design, and they weren't delivered on time, and we could get them shipped up as soon as possible. "OK. We all good with that?" We all agreed, and I said, "OK, let's set up for the top of the show, and I'll call Bonnie and let her know to bring down the diva."

The Devine Miss M. showed up, and we had a pre-rehearsal meeting, and went through the script for final changes, and set places for the top of the show. Bonnie gave us the heads-up that Bette was nervous, saying, "She hasn't been on a live stage in a long time, and she's realizing (unlike the movies where you can retake), she has to be on."

The rehearsal was going well, but Bette insisted that we stop for sound problems and blocking issues with *The Harlettes.* Jerry Blatt kept insisting that we run the show to get the running time and pacing down, and he would keep notes, and we could fix it from there. This didn't sit well with Bette, but she powered through the rehearsal until we hit the Deloris DeLago scene.

The band played the interlude as she and *The Harlettes* went to the quick-change tents to transform into the four mermaids sitting in electric wheelchairs. As the lights came up and everyone was ready for the scene, Bette screamed at the top of her lungs, "STOP! STOP! Where are the fucking palm trees?" She wheeled herself to center stage as Jerry Blatt explained, "They were redesigned and aren't ready yet. They will probably be here tomorrow. Don't worry about that; let's keep going." The argument ensued, and we were about to witness the wrath of Bette Midler we had been promised we would ultimately see.

Bette is the ultimate professional and looking back, all she wanted was the best for her fans and to give them the best show she could. After all, it was her name on the marquee, and after her movie career took a turn for the worse, the pressure was on to make this first live tour in years be a hit—not only for her fans but for the press as well. The whole world was watching, and it had to be right.

Bette carried on with angst until we hit intermission, and she bolted to her dressing room. Franny (the key wardrobe person) and Jerry Blatt followed her.

I asked, "Hey, Jerry, need me in there?"

"Nah, I got this," he said, looking like he'd been through this a million times. I instructed everyone, "Set up the top of Act Two."

As I walked over by the sound monitor board, Chuck called me over with this huge grin. Bette had taken her wireless microphone with her to the dressing room and left it on so we could now hear the conversation, or should I say be entertained by the dialogue, between Jerry Blatt, Franny, Bonnie, and Bette.

It was obvious that Bette was just very nervous, and most of what she was bellowing out was just to get the warranted stress off her chest. The whole entourage was soon huddled around the sound board, and we all, and I mean *all*, got ripped by the Devine one. Everything from I hate the hotel, to she sings flat, the bands too loud, Jerry Levin hates me, I'm too fat, and on and on and on. Every time she would get down on someone, we would point and laugh, waiting to see who was next. Franny, an older woman who'd been with Bette forever was the only one who would or could speak her mind to Bette. Franny was straight and to the point, "You're just nervous, honey. Stop being so dramatic!" Jerry Blatt addressed the fabricated problems, and Bonnie, God bless her, used her own calm demeanor to calm Bette down and bring normalcy back to the situation.

It was one of those happy accidents that once again came our way. Right before opening night, onstage at the monitor at the Paramount Theater in Portland, Oregon, we bonded—embracing each other—and became one entourage. Band, cast, crew, male, female, gay, straight, all together bending over in laughter with love

Bette Midler De Tour pass.

and tears of exhilaration, ready to show the world Bette Midler's Tour De Force.

Bonnie and Franny's magic finally calmed Bette down and gave her the strength to go back out, and we all scurried back to our places, trying to pretend like nothing happened, keeping our secret from Bette. We finished rehearsals and were ready for opening night. The palm trees did arrive the next day, and all was right with the world, and it was on with the show.

We traveled from Portland to Seattle to Vancouver to San Francisco with a sold-out show Christmas Eve at the Goldengate Theater. Santa Claus was right in the middle of the audience, and no one took responsibility for hiring him. I guess he was just a Bette fan.

We loaded out Christmas day with enough time to catch our six a.m. Western Airlines flight to Los Angeles. Looking out the window of the Boeing 727, I was reflecting on how fortunate I was and was excited to spend Christmas with my family but also had my mind on the five Universal Amphitheater shows and the rest of the tour in 1983 that included a long stint at the famous Radio City Music Hall in New York City.

Christmas was a welcomed break with family, friends, and great food, and I mostly enjoyed the rest, even though short. Los Angeles was waiting for the return of the Devine Ms. M, and what better way to welcome her than five days during the finale of 1982, culminating with a New Year's Eve show at the Universal Amphitheater. We loaded in December 27, and with the new script in hand and some grit and polish, we were all ready to take on Los Angeles. The shows, mainly the New Year's Eve show, were epic. The whole entourage—Bette, *The Harlettes*, the band, and us (the crew) were now an unstoppable, well-oiled

WHEN THE DEVIL SMILES, THE ANGELS FROWN

machine, night by night performing flawless shows with amazing reviews. Bette Midler was back home, with her roots in music resurrecting her career.

The divisions between gay Hollywood and rock 'n' roll at the onset of the tour were now nonexistent, just a distant illusion. We were one family with all our guards down, working together with a huge sense of pride, knowing we all had our own part in this historic endeavor.

The tour picked up in late January after some well-deserved time off. We opened in Dallas, then on through the south at the legendary Fox Theater in Atlanta before making a left turn to head to the Northeast to play some of the iconic theaters that were constructed when America was just an infant: the Academy of Music in Philadelphia, the Boston Opera House, and on to the legendary Radio City Music Hall in New York City.

Philly went as planned, with the city of brotherly love living up to its reputation, but Boston was a different story. We hit Boston during a stagehand union strike and work stoppage against the promoter. With possible picket lines and the fear of union solidarity boycotting the shows, we had to make a decision: to play or not play. With the power and intervention of the Devine Miss M., it all worked out. Jerry Levin, Jerry Blatt, Bette, and I all met in Bette's suite to discuss whether to cross the lines and play Boston or reschedule. The promoter was demanding we play and said if we canceled, all rescheduling cost would be on us. Overhearing the discussion from the other room, Franny, Bette's assistant, walked in and asked about the problem.

We explained it to Franny, and with a very calm but confident tone, she said, "Let me see if I can help." Franny picked up the phone and called her brother, who happened to be the business manager for the stagehand union in Boston where she grew up. Franny calmly explained the situation to her brother, and within ten minutes, there was going to be a Bette Midler show in Boston. It was a temporary solution that I feel solved the labor issues in Boston after we moved on to New York.

Call it luck, karma, fate, or what you want, the Tour De Force was on a roll, and I thought nothing was going to stop us now. But just as life has its way of convincing us we have choices, when in reality the choices are made for us, I got a phone call. Stevie Nicks had just completed her second solo record and was going on a six-month tour, starting in April, with a show at the second US Festival, a few weeks before the first date of the tour. I had no hesitation about my decision to leave the Bette Midler tour early, and I committed to Stevie's Wild Heart Tour, which would begin in a few months.

Firing on all cylinders with faultless confidence, we pulled into New York for our lengthy engagement at Radio City Music Hall. *The Harlettes*, band, crew, and writers—all of us—had one common goal: to slay that largest of dragons, New York and its threatening press corp.

We decided to load-in a day early and rehearse all the

moves before the actual show day.

Jerry had chosen to put the whole entourage at the five-star Parker Meridian Hotel that was an easy walk to the venue. This would eliminate all ground transportation and travel costs; locating us in the heart of Manhattan around the clubs and restaurants made the entourage happy. We rented a ballroom for the script read through and rehearsal, and it was apparent that Bette was very nervous and preoccupied by the guest list containing the biggest of the big stars, such as Liz Taylor, Cher, Barbara Streisand, Sly Stallone, and many, many more. We all questioned the decision for Bette to see the list, but Jerry Blatt's insistence that it drove Bette to perfection overruled all common sense.

On opening night, with only hours to go and everything ready, Jerry Blatt mentioned to me that the pink floor for the opening act of the show was dirty, and from the balcony, it really looked bad. I mentioned it to the tour carpenter, Nick, and he and the local union crew initiated a cleaning detail and scrubbed the floor to its original, new state.

With a thirty-minute hold for the New York elite, the show finally began, and we were on our way with the Tour De Force at Radio City Music Hall. All was good until the script hit the first dance number, and it was obvious that something was very wrong. *Bette and the Harlettes* were having trouble with their feet gripping the floor that was now like being on ice. With the cleaning and scrubbing of the floor, Nick and the union crew scrubbed off all the nonskid layer that was on top of the dance floor. Oh fuck! Now what?

As we stood stage right contemplating the emergency, the Radio City head carpenter, who had obviously faced this before, came up with the plan to mop the stage with hot water and coke, and that would act as a nonskid. While Bette was singing the Stones' track "Beast Of Burden," Jerry Blatt walked up behind me and

Bette Midler De Tour
Radio City Music
Hall 1983.

said, "Good. You're here. I need a five-minute dialogue piece for Bette to do. What can we put in right now?"

Jerry thumbed through the script and said, "Tell her to do the New York section now instead of in the second act. That's about seven minutes long." The plan was to move Bette as far down in front of the stage with a stool and close the main curtain as Nick and the crew applied the hot water and coke to the pink dance floor. I went to the quick-change tent and let Franny know to get the outfit for the New York monologue ready as I explained the plan to her. Barry, the head band tech, alerted the band and *The Harlettes* that after the New York dialogue, we'd go back to the show as planned.

With "Beast of Burden" winding down, and with the microphone in one hand and the mic stand over her shoulder, step by step, Bette headed our way, and with every step, her intensity grew and grew. Just as she reached the presidium like an Olympic Javelin athlete, Bette heaved the mic stand with full force in my general direction. She was now screaming with complete rage, so I put my arm around Bette to direct her to the quick change while giving her the new plan.

"What the fuck, Leo! What the fuck happened?"

Knowing it would take too long to explain, I wanted to get to the new plan saying, "Listen, we're fixing it, but you need to put the New York monologue in now and go as far downstage as you can."

"I look like a fool! Did you know who's here? Fucking Liz Taylor's in the fifth row!"

I told her, a bit forcefully, "Bette, Bette, listen to me; you need to go as far downstage as you can and do the New York monologue." She was still screaming at the top of her lungs. The last thing I remember was ripping open the quick-change tent and then coming to, lying on my back with Franny, Jerry Blatt, and the stagehands around me laughing.

The passion and power of a right cross from Bette Midler floored me and took me out. It was a punch or one of vengeance but one of nerves or frustration. I got up, and my first reaction was to make sure that Bette did what we had planned. Jerry Blatt assured me that Bette was good and the plan was working. Being the ultimate pro, she did understand and took her time with the monologue and pacing to make sure Nick had the time he needed to get the floor right.

I understood and was never angry and knew it was a part of the job, and to me it was over and like it never happened. It was opening night, and it was Bette's name was on the marquee—not mine—and shows and moments like an opening at New York's Radio City Music Hall can diversely alter and affect the course of an artist's career, with long-term ramifications.

Bette and I never spoke about the incident until many years later when we ran across each other. We both agreed we were locked into the moment of the high-pressure show. I told her she had a mean right cross, she said, "You deserved it," and we both had a laugh about opening night of the Tour De Force at Radio City Music Hall.

The tour peaked at Radio City, and rightly so. Playing at that iconic venue with a very high-profile show was a once in a lifetime experience. We hit other great venues and some where you scratched your head mumbling, "What the fuck are we doing here?" One of those places was Merrillville, Indiana, at the Holidome that was a huge Holiday Inn with a pool in the middle and a good-size theater on the back of the property. It was central to Chicago, Indianapolis, and all the cites in between. People from all around would come see a show and spend the night and make an event around whatever was playing. It was very successful and perfect for Bruce and his script-writing team.

For us, it was seven nights of Holiday Inn bliss where everything smelt like chlorine from the giant pool.

With the lack of urban activities like clubs, restaurants, and gay establishments to occupy everyone's attention, we were left to entertain ourselves. It was stealth bonding with straight, gay, black, white, male, and female hanging until before the show when we went on the prowl to find innocent victims to bring into our bizarre reality. Being a predominantly gay crowd, it was much easier for gay brothers to score their temporary prey as we, the hardcore rock 'n' rollers, sat by and watched the circus unfold right in front of us.

In the spirit of shear boredom, good fun, and our new friendships, we created the "sex police." The sex police's objective was to break up any potential hookups or disrupt hookups that were in play. With our gay brothers in full game mode, using their slick looks and convincing dialogue to score, the sex police would swoop in, and it wasn't long before the predator and its kill would be in the pool.

After shows, if they were crafty enough to get by the sex police and partake in activities in their rooms, an intervention with an emergency key from the front desk, or even a rappel from the balcony above, was the tactic of choice. Every morning, the sex police would circulate a full written report on all homosexual and heterosexual episodes. No one was safe and off-limits from the sex police. The times were different then.

It was all in good fun, and we were one big happy family sharing an extraordinary journey. It was all going so well, until one day, a cold bug and flu seem to hit the entourage, and it was running around the tour. It hit so hard that people were being sent home, and others on the road were confined to their rooms.

It was Bill, our sound engineer, who noticed that is was mostly our gay brothers who were being affected by this virus, and one who had been sent home was now deathly ill and in the hospital.

Then we got the devastating news that he had passed, and it wasn't just a common cold but a disease that was named gay-related immune deficiencies (GRID). It was explained to us that it was a disease that was like a contractible cancer but mainly affecting the gay population.

We all panicked, not knowing if we contracted it. We had shared drinks, hugs, and had physical contact with our gay brothers who were being attacked by this horrible new disease.

Jerry Levin made some calls to get information to try to ease all of our fears on what was now a tour filled with very frightened people.

With as much information as was available, Jerry sat us all down and explained that this was a virus that attacked the immune system, which compromised the body's ability to fight off infections and common illnesses, like a cold and the flu. The virus would manifest in pneumonia; the body couldn't fight it and would ultimately just shut down. It seemed to be only affecting the gays, and they weren't sure how it was being transmitted.

That's all they knew, so for the time being, no body contact, no sharing drinks or food, and no sex. The doctors were telling us until we knew more to refrain from all contact, and it would be a good idea if there was no sexual activity at all. Paranoia spread around the tour, and morale hit bottom. There was contemplation of cancelling the tour, but with only a few cities left, we decided to finish it off.

One by one, more of the gay entourage, including Jerry Blatt's boyfriend, Sean, got ill and flew home terminally ill to pass away.

What were once hugs of love and affection became just mere, simple gestures and touches to keep from contracting this unknown virus terrorizing us all.

In 1983, sex, drugs, and rock 'n' roll died, and the new world order of acquired immunodeficiency syndrome with its fearsome acronym, AIDS, reared its ugly reality, and we all realized that the horror of tomorrow was already here—and there was nothing we could do about it.

The tour was financially successful, and even with the dark cloud of AIDS all around, more dates were being added well into 1983. Al Jarreau was breaking a new record that would demand all of Jerry Levin's time, so he advised Bonnie that he would not be returning to the tour. The reality was Jerry just wasn't having a good time and was done with the tour and with Bette.

There were others departing the tour as well, including me, going back with Stevie on her Wild Heart Tour. I also told Bonnie, and the news hit her pretty hard. Jerry leaving was bad enough, but now Jerry and I, the two main key players on the tour were departing. I explained to Bonnie that if the roles were reversed and I had the history with Bette that I had with Stevie, Bette would expect the same. Bonnie agreed and just asked me to assist her in finding someone I trusted to take my place. I gave her three very qualified recommendations, and they went with one of them.

I thought it was strange that day that we all received a tour bonus for the 1982–83 Tour De Force. I thought Bette would have been pissed or hurt that I was not returning but figured, oh well, maybe I wasn't that important or loved by the Devine one. It was wasn't until years later I found out how important I really was.

It was Thanksgiving Day at my parent's house, and my family was sitting around when Bette came on the TV. My father pointed and said, "Hey, that's the crazy lady that came to the house one night looking for you. What'd you do to her? She sure was mad."

With a look of shear confusion, I shook my head and said, "What are you talking about, Dad?"

"It was late one night, and she came to the door, screaming and banging on the door looking for you. She was cursing up a storm. I told her, "Lady, I work on the docks, and you have a filthier mouth than a longshoreman and slammed the door on her.""

Sometimes when I say I did the Bette Midler De Tour in 1982-83, people google and this picture comes up and I'm not in it.
The story goes like this.

Jerry called me on the radio to come take the picture. I was in the middle of a horrendous labor dispute to settle the show and I couldn't leave the meeting so I missed the picture.

This was an amazing tour with amazing people through an amazing time in history.

And yes, I was there!

My mother said, "Yeah, it was pretty late, too; it scared me. Is she an old girlfriend or something?" My sisters laughed and told them: "That's Bette Midler; she's an actress and singer that Leo used to work with." I never substantiated this story until one day when I ran across Bette working in her garden on my way to a Fleetwood Mac meeting at Christine McVie's house; Bette was her neighbor.

We sat and talked about the punch and the tour and my father. She remembered the punch but not the trip to San Pedro.

I ran across Bonnie years later, and it seemed she never told Bette I was leaving the tour because she felt that Jerry Levin leaving was enough and if she learned I was leaving it may have been too much. So Bonnie waited until production rehearsals to let Bette know I went back to work for Stevie and told Bette she needed to applaud my loyalty. Neither of them remembered running down to my parent's house, but anyone who knew my parents knows it's something they would never fabricate. The whole episode brings a smile to my face, and I realized that Bette did care, and I was a big part of her musical comeback.

CHAPTER THIRTY THREE

STEVIE NICKS, TAKE TWO

I IMMEDIATELY JUMPED FROM the Bette Midler tour right into Stevie's second solo tour, Wild Heart.

I was looking forward to getting back out with Stevie, so I thought. My intention here is not a bitch session or pouring out sour grapes, and I mean no disrespect to anyone. It's just my truth on how I saw the music business changing and where it was heading. My journals and notes are not quite as tame as what follows.

When I reflect back on the Stevie Nicks Wild Heart Tour, I realize that the early '80s was when the music industry started its metamorphoses from art and creativity to money and greed.

It had a lot to do with the Music Television Channel (MTV) that was in full force, using gimmicks to expose so-called artist to millions of people with the flick of a switch. They would create and use imagery and eye candy (rather than good music) to seduce the youth into believing that creativity was easy and anyone could do it. It also created a whole new financial model as a way to promote artists that cost much less than touring and instantaneously reached more people.

People professing to have talent, with not an artistic fiber in their body, found a way to get their greedy, self-serving lives where they didn't belong, and they brought along their lawyers. And where there are lawyers, there are accountants.

This new generation coming into its own was coined Generation X, and were brought up with instant gratification habits, and craved the desire to experience pleasure or fulfillment without delay. They found their way into the touring side of the music business, and the managers bought into their thought process and schemes.

This new Gen X were a different breed. Like a shark to blood, they smelled money, and they would sell their own mothers for

These are the tour itineraries. I love that Stevie's has design and flare and Joe's is just a marker.

a percentage of the potential large revenues that were on the horizon, but most of all, it validated them. They were important; they were noticed.

For Wild Heart, the tour setup started as normal, with Harry Sandler back as the tour manager, Curry on design, and me production and Frontline management.

The new addition to the team was a young, sharply dressed, fast walking, fast talking tour accountant named Neil. He had this suave arrogance around him with stylish shirts, smart ties, and slicked back hair and a 70s porn mustache.

Neil wasn't a bad guy, but he just wasn't one of us— not a music guy, even though he thought he was. He had one thing and only one thing on his mind—profit, and it didn't matter who he had to run over, disregard, disrespect, or ignore to make it. That was his job, and he did it well.

The more money Stevie made, the more the managers made, so they paid top dollars to these new accountants to drive up the profits, even at the cost of an artist being at their best. Art was just another four-letter word to all these parasites who had used their car salesman tactics to trick the artist that it was all about them, all the while sucking them dry. Statistics show that the majority of artist/manager relationships end horribly, with many hurt feelings.

For the first time in my life, I saw the foundation of this huge wall being built between the bands and crews. It was being built strongly to never fall, and I didn't like it.

They had no respect for the crew and believed we were lucky to have a job, and that anyone could do what we did.

This new regime of touring accountants were mainly young, college educated hotshots, and while they were at their frat houses having life handed to them, most of us were on the road working long twenty-hour days, breaking these bands and building the music business that they had no respect for and were destroying.

Reflecting back, I realize I couldn't expect them to sympathize with what crews were going through without experiencing it themselves. If you ever had twenty-hour workdays seven days in a row and had to take a thirty-hour bus ride, you'd never say to any road crew "deal with it."

Once again, at the first meeting, Howard, the managing partner of Frontline, walked in with the same bullshit from the Bella Donna Tour, reminding us again that this isn't Fleetwood Mac, and the bullshit of Stevie being bigger than Fleetwood Mac, and this is Stevie Nicks, and they are two separate acts with two separate careers and blah, blah, blah.

I believe there had always been this deep-rooted anger at Frontline, and they felt disrespected because they were unable to manage the whole Fleetwood Mac band, and it was more apparent this time, and it seemed that Neil, the new accountant, bought into the indignant Frontline philosophy and brought it right onto this tour.

We discussed the new record and how the tour would work. Same as the first tour: the schedule, logistics, sound, lights, gear, and the crew would be handled by me but through Harry and then down to Neil, who controlled the overall tour profit and loss. All band and artist contracts would run through Harry, and we would meet or talk daily to discuss progress and pitfalls. All expenditures were to be given to Neil and Harry, who would OK them, and then they were passed to the new big accounting firm for process and payments. Rock 'n' roll business.

After the meeting concluded, Neil asked if he and I could meet. He was obviously coached about my experiences with The Mac and was fishing for information. We discussed how things ran with The Mac, and who did what, and Stevie's likes and dislikes on the road, and what was ahead. I let him know that Stevie was a person of habit, and she knows what she likes and doesn't like, and if she's uncomfortable the tour just won't work, she will get sick and the shows will suck.

He then went into a monologue on how he was going to try to change Stevie's touring habits on the road, including late-night flights and eliminating the megaroom service bills that fueled her late-night camaraderie gatherings with all the other women on the road. He even mentioned putting Stevie on a tour bus, which I immediately laughed off. Stevie loathed buses, and I believe to this day never toured on one.

I turned away and just rolled my eyes, thinking how Stevie was going to eat Neil alive; he represented everything Stevie hated about being on the road and the music industry in general.

Along on the tour as an opening act was guitarist extraordinaire Joe Walsh, who's solo career and work as the Eagles guitar player already notched him into rock 'n' roll history. He was also the king of pranks, with legendary antics like carrying a chainsaw on the road to remodel hotel rooms.

As well as opening for Stevie, Joe would be doing his own solo shows on Stevie's day off. It was decided that some of the crew, including me as Joe's production manager, would double duty and use the gear from Stevie's show to do the solo shows for Joe. We were all paid more to handle Joe's solo tour, and it was a win-win for all involved.

Frontline brought in the Eagles tour manager, Richard Fernandez, to manage Joe's tour. He was a soft-spoken, seasoned professional I knew from the time when The Mac opened for the Eagles. I was excited to work with Richard.

So, with Stevie being from Fleetwood Mac and Joe being from the Eagles, the "rock star crew" was a mixture of guys who worked for two of the largest bands on the planet, and we had no shortage of ideas and touring techniques.

The most impactful change was the collision of entertainment and technology. In 1983, the large home computers that were basically electronic terminals for holding text were coming around. Apple had the Apple One and Apple Two, but other companies were seeing the need for computers that you could carry around—and that could talk to each other over phone lines.

Neil called a meeting one day at the office to introduce "a new way we're going to do things." He handed us all a small Radio Shack TRS-80 portable computer. It was the size of a magazine with the thickness of a candy box. Along with the computer came two rubber cups that connected the computer to a phone handset. Using the static digital symphony that a fax machine used, we were able to make the computers talk to each other over a traditional phone line. I sat in amazement as, during the demonstration, I was communicating directly with Neil, Harry, and others on a one-on-one basis. The computers had enough storage to hold about 100 pages of text, so you could prepare a document and send it through the phone lines. The system was called IMC, and we all had numbers as our identities. I was IMC077.

I still have my Radio Shack TRS-80.

Once again, rock 'n' roll was on the cutting edge of human progress, and I was at ground zero.

Since the tour was going to be over eight months long and having a band like on the Bella Donna Tour would be financially and logistically impossible, the search and auditions for a new band became a priority. For two weeks, every great player from around the world came through Studio Instrument Rentals in Hollywood vying for one of the coveted spots in Stevie's band.

We coordinated the production rehearsals, but first there was the US Festival Two in 1983, a few weeks before the tour started. Joe Walsh was also going to do the US Festival, so we decided to go to Salt Lake City and Las Vegas to warm up both bands before heading back to the Southern California desert for the second US Festival.

Curry and I met to start the discussions designing something that would be different for Stevie but not so different than Bella Donna. Curry was, and still is, an amazing designer, not only for look and feel but technically as well. His idea for Stevie's Wild Heart was similar to Bella Donna and to still feature Stevie downstage center and the band behind her on risers with the background singers offstage.

Waddy Wachtel was back as the music director; he played stage left of Stevie. His high energy enhanced Stevie's performance. Then, as before, Sharon and Lori were offstage right—Stevie's background singers and confidants. The band rounded out with a combination of new artists like Wizard, a soulful African American bass player from Atlanta; Liberty DeVito, the bashing high energy drummer from Billy Joel's band; Benmont Tench from the Heartbreakers on keys; and Bobby Hall, back on percussion. Since it was a yearlong tour and some of the band had to return to their principal gigs, we had a revolving door of artistry coming and going at any given time.

Now that the stage was set, Curry needed to figure out what the style, look, and feel would be. We both knew that, being a small tour there were budget constraints, so digging back to our theater days, I told Curry we should think about renting a classic drop from a light opera or Broadway play. I called an old friend from my Long Beach days, and he turned me onto the Grosh Scenery House that stored old drops from hundreds of plays.

Curry and I drove to Grosh and went through hundreds of pictures and drops, and finally settled on a classic backdrop of the flower marketplace from the show Flower Drum Song. It was perfect—large painted columns with translucent material that when lit gave us multiple looks we could use throughout the set.

So, we had the risers and the backdrop, and Curry was designing the lights to subtlety fill in the gaps. Thinking about Bella Donna again, and the less expensive seats higher up in the arena, I realized 80 percent of the people would be looking down at the stage so why not make the stage floor part of the set. Blend the stage floor into the risers that flowed right into the backdrop. Perfect! The perfect solution! Now, what were we going to design? Curry and I put our creative, budget-conscious minds together to figure out the finishing touches of what became the everlasting images of Stevie Nick's Wild Heart Tour.

Driving home, I was racking my brain for a direction for the finishing touches that would achieve the ultimate goal—where your heart and mind reconcile and reach a place of ecstasy.

Again, the ocean has always been inspiration for me. Maybe it's in my blood, handed down from my ancestors; maybe it's my upbringing, subconsciously feeling the ocean air my whole life. But once again, I turned to the ocean for help. Usually, I went to the local restaurant Ports O' Call in San Pedro and sat along the harbor's edge drinking red wine and breathing in the damp air. But that night, I wanted something different. I decided to go to Long Beach and visit the Queen Mary. The Queen Mary came to Long Beach in 1967, and as I child, my father would take my family there, not only as an outing, but so he could reexperience his love for the ocean liners that he had captained as a younger man.

As I wandered around the Queen Mary that night, strolling to the top deck and into Sir Winston's for dinner, I was taken aback by the pageantry of the elegance of what first class looked like back in the Industrial Age, when the efforts of quality and pride made a difference.

The maître d' informed me that they were all booked, and the first seating available was at least ninety minutes. With nowhere to go, I decided to go to the observation bar that was at the other end of the ship. As I was walking along the deck, it hit me. I realized that the décor of the Queen Mary was exactly like Stevie's Bella Donna set—same décor, style, even the colors. I sat at the bar, ordered dark Myers rum and pineapple (my favorite drink at the time), and sketched and made notes of the ambiance I was immersed in on a napkin. The sconce lamps, the window frames, anything I saw engulfed me. I closed my eyes and literally went back in time, and when I opened them, I was looking down on the floor, and there it was! The art deco floor with pearl inlays, large slabs of marble separated by shiny brass borders. It was perfect—just what the Wild Heart set needed! What time was it? Where was I? Drink after drink, sketch after sketch, I lost all sense of time and space and was somewhere I'd never been before.

I went home and sketched up the set and added my version of the art deco floor. Center, where Stevie stood, I imagined a big black and white circle with offsetting pieces—to her right, black and white offsetting triangles—to

Art Deco floor for the Stevie
Nicks Wild Heart tour.

Art Deco floor at the observation bar
on board the Queen Mary I.

her left, offsetting black and white horizontal lines. Realizing that the white on the floor would change color,
depending on the color of the light that hit it (and black
always being black), Curry could balance or counterbalance the front of the risers and the backdrop with color
and have virtually thousands of different looks.

I excitedly called Curry and told him I got it and was
on my way to see him. With a few tweaks and modifica-
tions, the floor became a cross between art deco and an
abstract Aztec piece, and we were ready to show the idea
to Stevie and management. What was coined as the Aztec Landing Strip was approved, and the Wild Heart Tour
had its stage, lights, and set.

I brought in most of the crew that was on the Bella
Donna Tour to try to keep things consistent. Some were
available and some weren't, but it was another rock star
crew from top to bottom. Once again, Alan Rogan, the
guitar tech for Pete Townsend of The Who, was back
to handle Waddy and Joe, and he brought a few of his
English crew brothers also. We also had Steve Benjamin,
Elton John's keyboard tech and Jage Jackson, the Eagles
guitar tech, so once again, the crew was some of the best
in the business.

In late May 1983, with the band and crew in place, we
hit the road for the Stevie Nicks/Joe Walsh tour. The first
two shows in Salt Lake City and Las Vegas shows were
uninspiring, to say the least, but necessary to tune up both
bands for performances at the US Festival.

It was Memorial Day, Monday, May 30, and Joe Walsh and Stevie Nicks were slotted to play right before David Bowie, who was the headliner. Joe was originally scheduled for Sunday but was moved to Monday to accommodate the addition of Quite Riot to Heavy Metal Sunday. Plus, Joe wasn't really heavy metal and didn't belong on the Sunday Metal Show.

US Festival 83 passes. I was there with Stevie Nicks and Joe Walsh.

It was a good way for everyone to feel each other out before heading back to Coppala's Zoetrope Studios for three weeks of production rehearsals for the tour.

Since Walsh was touring with Stevie, we brought one truck and loaded in both bands. Joe was scheduled to play midafternoon on the thirtieth. We wanted to do something special for an introduction, so we planned to have one of Glenn Fry's (another member of the Eagles) road crew act like he was drunk and go onstage saying, "The drinking man's musician, Joe Walsh." I was nominated to escort him off the stage to make it look realistic, and I wondered how many people would believe that a drunk fan got onstage, with all the security, at one of the largest events in history. It was immortalized in 2017, when edited into the *History of the Eagles* documentary.

Joe and his band kicked ass in a high-powered rock show with guitar anthem hits culminating with the iconic

Rocky Mountain way with Joe's insane talk box speaker tube in his mouth where he actually made his guitar talk. After the show, we all felt amazing, with intensity running through our veins. Somehow, we got fire insurance while living in Hell, and we could write our own ticket to paradise.

That was the Joe Walsh tour, a small group of road warriors running around the

Me at the US Festival 1983
I was watching TV one day and the history of the Eagles was on. The section where they talk about Joe Walsh included a clip from the festival where I was escorting a drunk fan off stage. The truth is it wasn't a drunk fan but one of Glen Fry's road guys playing a prank on Joe.

country between the Stevie shows, just playing music and having fun. It was a release for me to get away from the high-pressure and laborious tasks of Stevie's tour. It was obvious that the Walsh dates would be much more fun and less stress than the Stevie dates, even though it was like doing two tours at the same time.

At the US Festival in 1983, we loaded Walsh off the stage and positioned Stevie on to do her set right before Bowie.

The most exciting thing to me about the festival was seeing the band U2. Earlier in the year, I was invited to one of the night clubs on Sunset Strip to see this new four-piece band out of Ireland, and I was happy to see they were invited to play the US Festival in the middle of the day. Bono, the lead singer of U2, wowed the crowd

WHEN THE DEVIL SMILES, THE ANGELS FROWN

by climbing to the top of the sound tower, pulling out an Irish and an American flag, and claiming that U2 had arrived and was not going anywhere for many years to come. We were all excited to see U2 and made sure we were on site by midday to see them play, and they didn't disappoint us or the massive crowd. It was obvious that U2 was here to stay, and for a long time.

At sunset of the third day of the US Festival, with the fans enduring the heat of the California desert, Stevie Nicks hit the stage and once again, took herself to a new high playing Fleetwood Mac songs and her own solo songs from Bella Donna and the new Wild Heart.

Joe Walsh and Stevie Nick's performances at the US Festival was a prelude to what was to come for the summer and fall of 1983. We were all excited and ready to get into rehearsals and get this summer tour on the road. I was ready and confident, and nothing was going to get in my way. But as they say, the best laid plans …

Rock 'n' roll, this once beautiful, pure musical experience with a shining halo was now fading and cracking, and the halo was being pushed forward over her eyes by the horns of the devil, those dishonest people with self-centered motives seducing her with false hopes for their own gain.

As predicted, the management team, other than Harry, didn't know Stevie, and their thought process was counter to everything that made Stevie who she was. Stevie was, and still is, a creature of habit. She knows what she wants and needs in order to sustain not only life on the road but also her career. It's plain and simple: keep Stevie happy and comfortable, and she will perform and blow people away and continue to grow and prosper. She needed her posse around her, and money wasn't an issue or a priority.

Neil was the ultimate pro at maximizing a band's money. On other tours he did with younger bands that never had the guidance to develop and create a sustainable career, it was all about the cash—a grab-all-you-can-now attitude because there may be no tomorrow.

In rehearsals, unwarranted scrutiny of every dime being spent began forming this dark cloud of negativity, and more time was being spent on the massive amounts of request forms and triplicate diatribes of explanations then on getting the things we needed to put on a good show.

One day, it came to a head. With a full crew of production, riggers, sound, lights, band techs, and set carpenters, we were a crew of over twenty. We needed three tour buses. One early bus carried the riggers, carpenters, and production crew that were first in early and last out every night. Then the sound and light guys were on the second bus, followed by the third bus with band techs for both bands; these guys came in late and left early so they didn't have to wait around for the rest of us to be done.

Being on the road was tough with long hours, and the three buses were needed to maximize precious sleep—each crew could follow their necessary schedule without waking up the others. It was the way it worked and how things were done.

It was hard for someone who has never been on a crew to understand the rigors of being on the road and how the bus life worked.

Neil approached me one day and said, "Management wants the crew in two buses to reduce cost," and I had to make it work. They also wanted us to double up on hotel rooms on the nights off. At first, I thought he was joking. I told him it would be a big imposition on all of us and hurt the tour, but he didn't care and said, "Just deal with it, and make it happen."

I met the crew and broke the bad news, and it didn't go over too well. The crew, made up of the best of the best in the business, didn't like it. The biggest concern was that if we gave in on these two issues there would be more, and we were right. More money had to be made to validate the accountant's existence, and unfortunately, it was at the expense of the crew.

So, there we were, crammed into two buses, but we didn't have to share rooms because of Joe Walsh's demand that his crew not be treated like slaves, so he picked up the cost of single rooms for the both crews.

In rehearsals before the tour even started, I had the uneasy feeling about the tour and the direction it was going. Nevertheless, we pushed through, but I started to rebel and push back on monetary requests that were going to affect the crew. I was spending money without approvals and really didn't care because I knew in my heart what was right.

In mid-June, with two buses and three full forty-foot trucks of gear, we hit the road.

The negative, abrasive attitudes, all based around money, intensified with daily arguments between Neil and me while Harry tried being the peacemaker. I was hearing it constantly: "The union labor bills are too high. There's too much catering. Do we really need this? Do we really need that?" It hit a point where it just wasn't going to work, and something had to change.

It was either Neil or me. It wasn't personal. I like Neil as a person, but we just had a different way of doing things, and unfortunately, we worked for the same people, and they really couldn't give a fuck about what the Fleetwood Mac guy thought; they knew who was making them the money.

It was just a huge difference of style: my Fleetwood Mac style of touring was to get it done and ensure everyone was respected and treated fairly; Neil's style was to make the most money for your client (who was really Frontline, not Stevie) at whatever expense, cost, or discomfort it created. The tour management was toxic and irreconcilable, and there had to be a change.

Management decided I was being spread too thinly, managing both Joe Walsh and Stevie's tours. Howard was told by Neil he was afraid things on the tour were falling through the cracks because I was overworked. Looking back now with a clearer vision and reflection, that was actually true. I was in way over my head. It was a lot for one person to handle, so the decision was made to bring in another overall production manager for the tour and Stevie. I would continue to be the production manager for Joe Walsh and the stage manager for Stevie.

I really had no say in the decision and had a choice to go along with it or resign. I went along with the plan. In hindsight, it was a good idea, although my ego was bent and mangled.

Most of my production duties with Stevie stayed the same, and I didn't have to deal with all the back-stage dressing room and travel matters, and most of all, I didn't have to deal that much with Neil anymore.

Ironically, the production manager brought in was also named Leo and a good friend. I welcomed and supported "the new Leo," and right or wrong, everyone found their place—just to make it work.

The tour limped along through the hot summer with lackluster reviews. Knowing Stevie like I did, I felt and knew in my heart she was ready to get back with Fleetwood Mac. It was the way the tour was being executed—completely opposite of the way The Mac toured, with all the comforts that made being on the road easier and palatable. The catering and backstage ambiance was substandard, and the band and crew were complaining daily about the horrible food and lousy treatment on the tour. I frequently heard, "This isn't like the last tour," and management just didn't care.

With all the drama, and to keep the tour going, Stevie was being shielded from it all and isolated from the entourage, and I noticed that it just wasn't fun for her to be on the road. She continued having her nightly ritual gathering with all the women on the road in her suites, with late nights and massive room service bills.

On one occasion, Neil approached the background singers about the room service bills and accused them of taking advantage of Stevie's kindness and generosity. With no hesitation, they vented to Stevie.

I was summoned to her dressing room, and Stevie went nuclear on Neil and me, letting us know to never question anything she wanted or needed on the road.

"I don't like it, and it better stop. I want this to be more like Fleetwood Mac, Leo, you know this!" I sat in silence, taking the heat, and in Neil's defense, he took the brunt and said it was all him and I had nothing to do with it.

In my opinion, the subconscious negativity on the tour, coupled with the pressure of being the only principal that was usually shared by the five Mac members, was too much for Stevie.

The Wild Heart Tour started in May 1983, and sixty shows later, it ended November 24 in Columbia, South Carolina. Sure, they made Stevie money, and lots of it, but at the expense of hardworking people who still cared about the music, the art, and Stevie.

For me, the tour was a successful failure. I was still learning a lot about myself and figuring out how I was going to approach the future. Touring the United States was getting mundane and boring, and I wanted more.

The music business was now being run by so-called business people with not a bit of heart or soul. Notes became numbers that were dictating the future direction of creativity, and dreamers, believers with confidence and passion, were being told, "No, you can't do that; it costs too much, and there's no return on the investment."

What I learned from the Wild Heart Tour helped me later in life as I became a tour manager/director and was responsible for budgets: behind every number in a spreadsheet is an emotion, a person with a personal experience.

Plain and simple, put money into the budget to fly a hard-working crew if the routing has a thirty-hour bus ride. If there's not enough money to do the tour right, it's better you don't do it than half-ass it and shatter any hope for a sustainable career for the artist.

Music, the beacon of light and hope is still present, but where there's light, there are always shadows.

CHAPTER THIRTY FOUR

1984. THE END OF THE WORLD
AND THE START OF MINE

IT WAS THE YEAR THE WORLD WAS SUPPOSED TO END, but for me, I was just getting going. My confidence was at an all-time high, and I felt literally nothing could hold me back.

I knew I needed some down time but really didn't want to stop the momentum of not only keeping busy but making money. The dollars were rolling in—and I mean rolling. My father, given I really wasn't home much, decided to parlay the house into apartment units, so I contributed some cash for the renovation, and soon we owned a six-unit apartment complex in lower San Pedro.

All the winter tours were staffed and booked, so it was a perfect time to take a little break. Being back in LA and just doing local shows was a blessing in disguise, and I needed the rest.

A bunch of us wayward road crew members decided to rent a four bedroom house up on the point in the beach section of San Pedro. The house was owned by one of my old teachers from San Pedro High School, and knowing we all made good money and paid cash, he gave us a good rate. Lisa was my full-time girlfriend by then, and while we were all on tour, the ladies took care of the house. Life was good, just doing local shows and occasional small tours, waiting for what would happen next.

It was late spring when again my old friend Jerry Levin called.

"Hey, Leo, what's up?"

"Just hanging, Jerry, what's new?"

"Didn't you work with Rickie Lee Jones?"

"Yep, sure did."

"OK, so Pat and I are now managing her, and she's working on a new record followed by a tour to promote it. You wanna do it with us?"

"Yeah, what do you need? A production manager?"

"No, more of a day-to-day guy to help her finish the record and a tour manager to put the tour together. We need to put together the whole thing: band, crew, set design, everything. It would be good for you. You can get into management and be a tour manager, and I think you're ready for it."

I was ready for it, and it was the next step for me, not only in my career but for my ego as well.

"It sounds great, Jerry! I'm in. When's it start?"

"Come up to the office next week, and we'll talk about pay and the whole project."

Thinking about going into management and taking my career to the next level excited me. I knew I had all the skills to pull it off. Production wasn't a challenge anymore, and I needed something new to feel complete.

There was another major deal in my life at the time: Lisa was pregnant. For years, we'd had an off and on relationship, with me being on the road and her at home. We had a don't-kiss, don't-tell relationship.

After my first five years of sex, drugs, and rock 'n' roll, I didn't partake as much as most guys on the road did. Not only did I have a lot of responsibility, but I was taught that you can do a million things right, but the first time you fuck up, no one remembers all the good you did. They just remember the times they saw you drinking and womanizing. So don't ever give them something to go back to.

At first, I told Lisa, "No way. We're not keeping the baby."

I was afraid and insecure and also selfish. But after thinking about it more, and having conversations with good friends and family, and considering my new direction entering the world of management, I started to feel more confident about being a father and was warming up to the idea. Lisa said it didn't matter what I said or did, she was going to have the baby. So we decided to have the baby.

Nineteen eighty-four wasn't the end of the world, but for sure, the start of a new one for me. At a young age, I had managed to accomplish a lot, and it would have been easy to sit back and be complacent, but that wasn't in my insecure makeup. The blessed curse of the fear of rejection and not being accepted was driving me, just like all the great superstar artists I had been working for. The need for always wanting more was good for me ,and I was fortunate to have this negative become the biggest positive in my life.

At the meeting with Jerry and Pat, they told me that Rickie was completely clean and sober. She got clean and sober on her own with no ther-

Rickie Lee Jones album The Magazine.

apy and was feisty as ever. She also was in a relationship with a struggling actor named Greg who was with her 24-7; the two of them were planning a wedding.

The record was the last of her Warner deal and was being produced by the famed producer James Newton Howard. The band included all the characters in my circle from the past: Buzz Fieten, Neil Larson, Nathan East (fresh from Hong Kong), Lenny Castro, and on and on and on. The expenditures were getting up there, and Warner's had asked Pat to keep an eye on gear rentals and hiring outside musicians whose day rates were exorbitant.

In the middle of the meeting, Rickie burst in the room. Pat greeted her. "Hey Rickie! How's it going?"

Rickie's problem of the day was that she had just been informed by Carl, her Warner A&R person, that the cost of the record was escalating, and in order to stay on track with the release date, she needed to get it finished.

Pat let her know he would handle it; he told her, "Don't worry; when it's done it's done."

Then Pat said, "Rickie, you remember Leo, don't you? We're bringing Leo on as your day-to-day, and he will manage the tour."

Rickie abruptly got into Pat's face. "He will, will he? Do I have a say in this, Pat? I mean, what if I don't want Leo to manage the tour? Are you making decisions for me again without my approval, Pat?"

We all sat stunned, and I had no idea how to react, so I just got up and said, "I'll give you guys a minute."

Pat explained to Rickie that since she and I had history, he just assumed it was OK to bring me on. Rickie smiled and looked over at me and said, "Sit down, Leo. This isn't about you. Of course you're OK. It's just the fact that decisions shouldn't be made without me, Pat!"

For a second, I thought it was all over for me. Relieved to discover it wasn't, I walked over and gave Rickie a hug and told her I'd see her at the studio in the next couple of days. She said great and that she had some good ideas for the new tour and couldn't wait to share. Before I left the office, Pat and Jerry's new female assistant, Shirley, gave me a box with files for the whole project so I could review them.

Driving home, I realized that Pat and Rickie weren't going to make it. Pat was a very calculated manager who always had a plan. and judging by Al Jarreau's career, he could pull it off if the artist was willing to trust, listen, and follow instructions. That wasn't Rickie Lee. She was unmanageable, and her suspicious nature led her to believe that everyone was out to take advantage of her. She had very few sustainable relationships. I felt fortunate that I was one, but I also knew that this was going to be a wild ride. To some, mainly her fans, Rickie Lee Jones was a blessing; to others, she was a curse.

I went through the mammoth box of papers that Shirley gave me and organized my approach of how I was going to attack this beast. Using my history of working with Rickie, I knew for sure that I always needed to have an answer for her questions. If you didn't, she would pounce onto you with painful interrogations.

I decided to go up to the studio only after I had a good grasp on the whole situation. I called Creative Artist Agency, Rickie's agent, and Carl at Warner Records to set up a meeting with James Newton Howard, the record producer. I knew at that time that he had the most intimate interactive relationship with Rickie, and I hoped that he could, and would, give me the overall snapshot of what was the reality.

Unlike most, I loved being in the studio, although I wasn't stuck there for months at a time. Watching the process of making a record is magic, and those who have the opportunity to be a part of it are fortunate.

The day I arrived, the last bit of instrument tracking was being done, and just like back in 1979, there was Buzzy Feiten layering in an enchanted lead guitar part on the song "Juke Box Fury" that no one else on the planet could do. With the cordial hellos and a bit of tension, I sat and listened to the song that would become a single. James said, "Let's catch up before you leave." Rickie hadn't arrived yet but was due momentarily.

Rickie walked in and introduced me to Greg, her fiancé. He was a good-looking, unassuming, normal guy. Rickie looked happy, and I was shocked; I had never seen this sensitive side of her. She was a totally different person around Greg. I thought to myself, "Who the hell are you, and what did you do with Rickie Lee Jones?" It was good to see a soft side of Rickie that I'd never seen before.

We went into the lounge, and Rickie had a list of what she wanted to talk about. It was well organized, and I remember how intense she was while we discussed everything about the record project. It was obvious that she was in complete control and knew what she wanted.

Rickie was passionate about her new record *Magazine*, which was a collection of work about Rickie's upbringing and a reconciliation of how she became who she was. The music is filled with deep, lyrical content and with movie soundtrack music, accompanying the tales of her family and estranged relationship with her father. The record takes you on a journey of why and how she became the female musical prodigy Rickie Lee. "I want people to feel the music and have it take them away, like a play. All the band onstage will have a part, a script that we can act out between songs." Her conviction and the strength of words went straight to my heart and took me back to Long Beach, where the teenager got bit by the magic of the theater. "I want backdrops, props, sound effects, everything." As I took notes, I scribbled on my legal pad, "This is going to be great!"

"Have you heard the record yet?" she asked me. "It's not mixed, but you can get an idea."

I said, "No, not yet. Just bits and pieces."

"James, can you make Leo a cassette?" James pointed to the studio engineer as we sat and listened to Buzzy and he continued to lay down his captivating solo.

I listened to rough mixes of the record a few times, and I understood even more Rickie's vision of the live show. As always, Jerry was doing his magic by putting together a band that would fit Rickie's vision. I met with Pat and Jerry to discuss the meeting I had with Rickie and told Jerry it wasn't going to be an easy task to get great musicians that could also act and remember lines. We met with CAA, the tour booker, to see about size venues and what the tour would gross. This was to make sure we could be both creatively and financially successful. CAA said medium-sized theaters—2,000–4,000 seats—one night in each city. Also, the money dictated that we would have a small crew with one crew bus and only one truck. This was a problem—a big one. How were we going to fulfill Rickie's vision with all the limitations ahead of us?

As Jerry worked on the band, I needed to start thinking about a crackerjack crew that could double up on jobs and improvise every day. I also needed to think about a designer who could maximize a stage design with multiple looks in the confines of one truck that also had to carry sound, lights, and band gear.

Over the next few weeks, while also keeping track of the progress at the studio, I set up meetings with several designers who I had worked with over the years. I wanted my old friend Marc Brickman, who was Rickie's longtime friend and designer, but unfortunately, he was too busy with his main act, Bruce Springsteen, and his new act, Pink Floyd. Marc had several recommendations, and Jerry had a few as well. I went to my old friend Shark Boy to inquire if he would come out as the tour carpenter and handle the sets. He had taken a job at Apple coordinating their events and was set. It was a dream job that I don't blame him for not wanting to leave. He recommended I speak to Larry Hitchcock, who was one of the mainstays at Bill Grahams FM productions and who had a theatrical background, as well as a rock background designing sets for the Rolling Stones, Bob Dylan, and more.

I drove up to San Francisco and met with Larry, and we listened to Rickie's rough mixes and discussed the possibilities. Our conversations went from design to how could we leverage technology and still be creative at the same time. I liked the direction Larry was going.

Rickie Lee Jones album The Magazine set. You can see the white panels that we projected on.

Sometime after the San Francisco trip, I was driving and noticed a reflection on my windshield. It was the image of a street sign, and as the car moved, the image did as well. It was like a movie. That was it—an image! Shine an image on material. If we had a plain white drop, we could use a slide projector to shine images and virtually have hundreds of images for each of the ideas we wanted to portray. I called Larry with the idea, and he said one of his and Sharon's strengths was photography. Over the course of the next week, Larry and Sharon expanded the vision with a set of white drops of all different shapes and sizes that would be placed around the stage. Then, with a series of synchronized slide projectors, we could create multiple looks, using photos and images based around the parts of the shows and songs. All that this required was two small hampers of soft goods and one medium-sized case of slide projectors; this would virtually replace one full truck of set pieces. The next piece of the puzzle was set and so was what would be the rest of the imagery. Larry drew up a sketch of the generic stage with risers for the drums and keyboards with the piano stage right. We presented the design to Pat, and Jerry and got the approval to present to Rickie.

We all met with Rickie at the office to present the idea, and Jerry was going to give Rickie a list of players that he thought would fit the requirements for the show. I noticed a lot of familiar names on the list, including the bass player George Hawkins from the Loggins and Messina days. Jerry also found a young female background singer who had dance chops named Vonda Shepard. Vonda had been in the LA circuit playing with various bands while trying to launch her own career. Some of the normal go-to guys like Buzzy were making so much recording and creating royalty streams for themselves, they no longer wanted to tour. The next step was to set up auditions to pick a band.

I presented the stage and set idea to Rickie, and she got it! She understood that she could have a number of looks and scenes. One idea she came up with was to use the famous ink blots that Dr. Herman Rorschach used in his psychology practice to measure the unconscious thought process of one's brain. We left the meeting with a plan in place and enough information for me to start putting together a crew.

It was now early summer, and the *Magazine* record was done and scheduled for release on September 27, 1984. The tour was tentatively slated to start in October, with one month of rehearsals. Putting the crew together was going to be easy. Just like me moving up into management and tour management, I felt Nick Storr, who was the carpenter for the Bette Midler and Stevie Nicks tours, was ready to become a good production manager. Erick Eastland was a natural to be the lighting designer and head up the lighting crew. For sound, Jerry and I went with Lars Brograd, a tall, handsome Danish man with sensibility to mix sound. He also had the temperament to work with difficult artists like Rod Stewart and Diana Ross. We also felt with his pedigree that Rickie wouldn't question his ability. The rest of the crew—Jeff Chonis and Doug Lacy—were seasoned vets who we paid extra to double up on jobs to reduce payroll and space on the bus. Nick would be the carpenter, along with his production manager duties.

The band was a mixture of seasoned veterans with George Hawkins on bass, Mike White on drums, Mark Morgan on keyboards, and a young new and up-and-coming guitar player, James Harrah. Vonda Shepard rounded out the band with her strong voice, good looks, and amazing stage presence.

Production rehearsal was intense. Larry and Sharon brought in copied images, as well as original images that they shot. There were also set pieces like a large window to demonstrate an exterior of a house and a cargo net for a wharf and dock feel. There was also a round circle with white material that various images could be projected onto.

Rickie was very involved with every area of the show: the music, the sound, the set, and the lights. Between advancing the travel and shows, I spent most of my days mediating problems between Rickie and just about everybody. If it wasn't the band about music, it was with Larry and Sharon about images. One night, Erick missed a light cue at the top of the show, and Rickie stopped the rehearsals, screaming at the top of her lungs, "What the fuck, Erick! Are you ever going to get this right?"

Erick came from behind his light board in the audience, and came to the front of the stage, and screamed back, "Rickie, this is hard to do when I feel like there's a knife at my throat for every fucking cue!"

Rickie replied, "The knife is on my throat! Not yours, motherfucker! It's my name on the marquee, not yours! You fuck up and they're not going to say 'Erick sucked.' It's me who'll take all the shit!"

I let the argument continue, knowing that they both needed to find their boundaries until enough was enough.

"OK, everyone," I said. "Let's take a thirty-minute break."

I pulled Rickie aside and said, "You're right, Rickie, you're right." I knew it would be the only way to calm her down. I then approached Erick and explained to him that Rickie was stressed and not to take it personally. "Her whole career is riding on this record, and that's a lot of stress for her."

Erick got it and humbled himself and did the right thing by apologizing to Rickie, saying he understood, and that all was good in Coolville again.

The closer we got to the first date, the more intense Rickie got. Everyone understood and learned to lean on each other for support. In the most ironic way, Rickie made herself the demon, the adversary, and focal point, and this bonded the band and crew together.

The show was spectacular, with its high-tech scenery, music, and the unique story line narrated by Rickie and acted out by the band. At one point, George (the bass player) played Rickie's father in the war, and Vonda interacted with Rickie as a younger version of herself.

The show opened with Van Morrison's band theme song "Gloria," that was Rickie's alter ego in the show. The set twisted and turned through Rickie's youth and career, with her past hits as well as the new message of the *Magazine* record.

At the end of the show, with Rickie softly lit behind her grand piano, she recited the final lines:

On a stage somewhere, in my future time, in my father's past, and always, Gloria is present. Gloria's hair is blonde, not black, and there is a shadow behind her, and I see foreboding harm.

We were ready. The show was polished, and with one truck, one star bus for Rickie, Greg, and me (and any band member who wanted to travel with Rickie), a bus for the band, and a bus for the crew, we hit the road.

The first shows were in the Midwest, with a couple of smaller cities first to stay away from the press (the old Mac trick). Then we hit Chicago and wound our way back to finish in Los Angeles right before the holidays.

With so much rehearsal, it was like we had been on the road for years. Rickie was still a bit abrasive, and there was still tension between her and the band. I would invite some of the band to travel on Rickie's bus but got no takers. I found myself hanging with Rickie and Greg, listening to them plan their future.

Lisa was due to have the baby sometime in late November, and I made plans to have Gary "Red" Geller come out and relieve me on the road. Since this was Lisa's first, we were hoping that maybe the baby would be late and be born after the first leg of the tour in early December.

We finished the Bismark Theater show in Chicago the night of November 16, and Rickie told Vonda that she wanted her to ride on her bus. I informed Vonda, and she didn't want to do it. She had all kinds of excuses: all her stuff was on the other bus, she wasn't feeling well, she didn't want to get Rickie sick. The buses rolled, and Rickie asked, "Where is Vonda?"

I explained to her that Vonda wasn't feeling well and had stayed on the other bus, but she would ride with Rickie when she was feeling better. Rickie wasn't stupid. She figured it out, and all her anger was suddenly aimed at me. She raged about every little thing that was on her mind that she could think about. I finally had enough, and we got into it and hashed out a lot of frustration that we'd both been holding in. After about three hours, and hundreds of miles, Rickie got up and went into her state room in the back of the bus. I sat up in front, exhausted from the evening. Rickie came through the door and said, "Oh yeah, one more thing. I think Lisa's in labor." I just blew it off, grabbed a blanket, and passed out on the couch.

I was woken up by my old friend, the bus driver Bob Williams, saying I was needed at the front door of the bus right away. While I slept, we had stopped in Minneapolis. As I stumbled down the stairs, there was a hotel concierge from the Hyatt Regency, saying, "Mr. Rossi! Come on! Come on! You have to go! Your wife is in labor! There's a car ready to take you to the airport, and if you hurry, you can make the next flight."

I grabbed a quick bag, and jumped into the car, and was whisked off to the airport. I barely made my Northwest Airlines flight that ended up being the longest flight of my life. I wasn't sure what to expect when I got to Los Angeles but was sure that there would be someone there to meet me. The flight went on and on and on, and it was like time was standing still. When we finally landed, of course there wasn't a gate, so we sat on the runway for another thirty minutes. I couldn't sit still, and started to get angry, and caught myself when I knew there was nothing I could do about it.

When we finally hit the gate, knowing my situation, the flight attendants opened the cabin door and got me off the jet. At the top of the jetway, there were four signs with my name on them. It seems several people set up a car to get me to the hospital. One of the drivers came up to me and said, "I have a small car and can get you there faster."

I said, "Let's go," and ran through the airport to see if I could make my child's birth.

When I got to the hospital and up to the maternity floor, I looked down the hallway and watched as they rolled Lisa across the hallway into a room with my firstborn son, who we named Ryan Dino Rossi. He was born November 17, 1984, at 12:46 p.m., and I missed his birth by the amount of time we sat on the fucking runway waiting for a gate, and it's something Ryan jokingly never lets me forget.

My head was racing; there I was, holding my newborn son with my girlfriend (we weren't married yet) and wondering, "How did Rickie know? How did she know Lisa was going to go into labor?"

I called the hotel to make sure that Red was OK and settled in. The show went off fine, and they were just getting onto the bus to drive for a day off in Columbus, Ohio. I gave Red the hospital room phone number and let him know it was OK to call me anytime he needed to. I also let him know I would be back out in a couple of days when Lisa was settled in back at home.

We checked out of the hospital the next day, and I brought Lisa and Ryan to a new two-bedroom condo I bought in San Pedro. My new little family settled in, not far from both sides of the family, in case Lisa needed help.

It was midday, and the phone rang, and it was Red.

"Leo?"

"Hey Red, what's up?"

"We have a problem. George rode on Rickie's bus last night, and he got high with Greg. Rickie is fucking pissed!" Rickie and Greg were sober for over a year, and with one moment of indiscretion with George, and it was all out the door. Rickie wanted George gone and was crazily angry at Greg.

That night, we were at home, and I was holding my new son when the phone rang. It was Rickie. She congratulated me on the birth and went right into the Greg and George situation. I listened to Rickie vent, and when I finally got a word in, I told her that I was heading back out and would meet up with her in Columbus the next night and just let it be for now. I would come out and sort it out. After we hung up, I realized I had to get back out there and leave my family behind. Lisa had planned to meet me with Ryan when the tour hit San Francisco.

To Red's relief, I was back. He had his hands full, and I didn't really expect anyone could just jump onto this tour and take control. The rest of the tour went off without a hitch, and at the ripe old age of two and a half weeks, my son Ryan was on tour in the city where I was born— San Francisco. Ryan, Lisa, and I lived a lot of firsts—first restaurant, first hotel, first shopping spree, and first concert. After San Francisco, we hit Santa Barbara for one show before ending the first part of the tour in Los Angeles at the Universal Amphitheater.

The rigors of the road were taking its toll on Rickie Lee, and at the show in Santa Barbara, in the middle of the set, Rickie launched a tirade into the crowd because she felt they weren't getting into her performance.

"Hey, listen. I'm not a fucking radio," she said, pointing at the crowd in anger.

The crowd responded with applause and cheers, and that was enough to get things back on track to finish the show. The next night at the Universal Amphitheater went as planned and without drama, but the following night, the last at Universal and with the tour winding down, she did it again. I was in the house at the sound board when Rickie launched another tirade at the crowd. She was wrong! Dead wrong! The sophisticated LA crowd was mesmerized and totally stunned at how good her performance was. I walked rapidly backstage, and in the hallway under the stage, there was Rickie.

"I fucking hate this, Leo! They just fucking sit there with no respect." As she started to pace, she continued the rant. "We're working our asses off out there, and they just fucking sit there!"

"Listen to me." I said. "I'm out there! I'm out in the house! The fans are loving it, Rickie! Your performance is so good they're silently soaking it all in. You have to trust me on this one; I'm not lying to you. They've never seen anything like this, so get out there and finish them off, and we're done for the year." She turned and walked back onstage to loud applause and the band vamping a groove track. I made her take off her jacket and put on her trademark beret to make it look like a costume change. I went back to the sound board and sat with Lars; he hugged me and winked. Later, Lars told me he was listening through his headphone over Rickie's wireless mic and heard the whole ordeal backstage.

Rickie sat down at the piano and continued the show with one of the best performances I'd ever seen her do. "Chuck E's In Love" to "Juke Box Fury" to "Last Chance Texaco"; song by song, she stepped it up.

During the last song, with Rickie at the grand piano, Erick had one blue light from the back and a dim spotlight from the front as Rickie glided into "After Hours," the last song that was a ballad from her first record. The crowd was dead silent, like Rickie was in a theater with not a soul in sight. Not giving them any time to applaud, Rickie broke into her final "Gloria" dialogue and walked off the stage to a roaring standing ovation. She hugged me as I pushed her back out onstage to take her final bow, and then the band and crew all gathered around her to share the love.

And like that, it was over: the show, the tour, and 1984.

CHAPTER THIRTY FIVE

1985, DIVAS, JAZZ, AND
FREQUENT FLYER MILES

THE HOLIDAYS OF 1984 WERE UPON ME, and with all
the fatherhood responsibilities splitting time with my
rock 'n' roll lifestyle, I found something that I loved more
than being on the road. I was always great at multitasking
and the responsibilities of being a father were much more
rewarding. I found myself feeling guilty for sometimes ig-
noring my duties of a tour manager to soak up my family,
as if I was cheating on my mistress, rock 'n' roll.

The last week of the Rickie Lee Jones *North American
Magazine Tour*, Jerry and Pat had said there were serious offers for Rickie to tour Australia in February. Figuring we would be in that part of the world anyway, we

knew Japan, Hong Kong, and the new emerging market of Singapore would also be in consideration. The enticing thought of going back to Hong Kong got me excited, and Japan was always on the top of my list of places to tour.

Between Christmas and New Year's, Rickie's manager, Pat Rains, called me and asked if we could meet. I drove up to their offices on Sunset Blvd. Jerry, Pat, and I sat in Jerry's office.

"Well, Leo," Pat started. "The Far East Tour is on."

"Great," I replied. "When is it?"

"It starts in early February. We also have three cities in Japan and Hong Kong in consideration, and they look good as well."

"Wow! That's pretty soon; we better get a jump on things."

"Well, there's another thing," Pat continued, "Rickie and me, and the company (looking at Jerry), are parting ways."

"Parting ways?" I asked.

"Yeah, it's just too much and not worth it for us to continue to work with her. Al's record has crossed over to the pop charts, and we need to really put all our focus there. We don't want to just drop her, so we'd like you to do the tour. You don't have to, but it would really help us."

I looked at Jerry to try to get a feel for what he was thinking. He said, "Just do it, Leo. And right after that, I need you to take Jarreau to Europe in April."

"OK, I'll do it. How's Rickie with all this?"

Walking over to pick up a box with all the Rickie files, Pat said, "She's good with it, and I think she's glad we're parting."

As I knew from the start, Pat and Rickie were too different, and it wasn't going to work.

Pat went on, "We will still assist you, but here is Owen Sloan's (Rickie's attorney) phone number. He'll mange the deals, and if I were you, I'd talk to him about a new deal since you'll be doing more work." I grabbed the box of files and drove back home to ponder the situation, Of course I was going to do it, not only for Pat and Jerry but for the tour. Going back to Asia and Australia! Who wouldn't want to do that? I also was thinking about the band and the crew and couldn't leave them to fend for themselves in the complicated land of Rickie Lee Jones.

In early January, I reached out to Rickie to check in and see how she was doing. She sounded great and was excited about the upcoming Far East Tour. We talked about the separation between her and Pat, and her story was quite different. She said she fired Pat because he just didn't understand her and she didn't feel the amount of money he was making was worth it. She asked me to call Owen to make sure we were on track with the tour. I had a knot in the pit of my stomach, and my gut was telling me it was just a matter of time before I became Pat and Jerry, so I might as well enjoy it and make the best of it.

Owen asked me to come up to discuss the tour and meet the new young promoter, Richard MacDonald from Australia. As many times as I'd been to Australia, I'd never heard of Richard or his company, Bottomline Touring, and this made me a bit nervous about being in Australia and not getting paid and being stranded with a full entourage. Owen showed me the deal, and it was a good deal, and more money to Rickie than I expected. I told Owen I needed a couple of things: roundtrip airlines tickets and travel expenses for the whole entourage to get us home if Bottomline didn't pay the balance. I suggested the airline ticket scenario knowing that if we received airline tickets instead of money, the taxes to Rickie would be less.

Soon Richard, the Australian promoter, walked in. Richard was a reserved younger guy and looked quite nervous. As we got into the deal, he looked at me and said. "Leo, my partner Mark Pope says hello."

I smiled with relief and said, "Ahh, Mark's your partner on this?"

"Yes, and he's looking forward to working with you." Mark was a good production manager and was on both Fleetwood Mac tours with me, and we remain good friends. This made me much more relaxed. Then Richard said, "Also, Peter Edmunds will be your day-to-day person for the tour." Peter, also known as "Skip" was another dear friend from my Australian past, and to this day, is a good friend and confidant.

"That's great to hear, Richard. I'm looking forward to working with both of them." So, it was obvious that Richard and Bottomline were legitimate and there would be no problems, but it was agreed that travel would be paid for upfront by Bottomline, mainly for taxes. So, right off the bat, I made Rickie 30 percent more by avoiding paying taxes on income that would have gone to travel anyway.

My next hurdle was the foreign work—visas for all the countries. In setting up any tour, it's customary to gather all information, including passport and social security numbers, for the whole entourage. For Australia (that ironically was founded as an island prison for England), you couldn't have a felony or any blemish on your record to get into the country. I gathered all the passports, and with the contract in hand, went to the Australian Consulate to obtain the visas. By then, it was mid-January, and the tour was scheduled to depart on February 3. The consulate told me it was impossible to get the visas with only ten working days.

OK, now what?

Remembering that Owen had an Australian accent, I called him and spewed out the dilemma. He said, "Just stay there, and don't worry."

Within twenty minutes of my call to Owen, a young Australian man come through the door.

"Mr. Rossi?"

"Yes, that's me."

"Please come with me." I was ushered into the office

of the Australian ambassador to the United States. The ambassador was a good friend of Owen's and instructed his people to take care of our visas. We sat and chatted, and literally within thirty minutes, I had all the passports, except one with all our work visas attached.

The person doing the work whispered to the ambassador, who then told me, "We do have one problem, though. One of your crew has a felony for drunk driving, but give me a day or so, and I will work it out." I thanked him and went on my way back to San Pedro, excited about the tour. My excitement was stopped dead in its track as I entered the house and picked up Ryan, and I realized how much I was going to miss him while on the tour.

I set up the last bits and pieces of the tour using my brand-new Apple Macintosh computer that my good friend Shark Boy had sent me. I knew a lot about the mac, and its new little companion, the mouse. It wasn't released to the public yet, and some of us were lucky enough to pay our dues with Apple to get the prerelease of this historic piece of plastic and glass that changed the world. I stayed up for two days straight after the box showed up at my door.

I sat with Nick and Erik as we drew up the stage and light plots for the contract rider for the tour. The only equipment

My Boarding pass To Japan, once again on the best airline ever, Pan Am.

brought by us for the tour was the slide machines and white screens and specialty guitars and instruments we couldn't rent in Asia and Australia. All our band equipment was set up by Yamaha Music, who Rickie endorsed.

We were ready and on February 2, 1985, I kissed Ryan and Lisa goodbye and headed to the airport to once again sit in my Pan American first-class seat next to Rickie Lee Jones on our way to Tokyo. Her boyfriend, Greg, decided not to come along, and it felt to me like Rickie wasn't pleased about that decision. But the truth is, we had a hard schedule with press, record label meetings, and shows, and it was best Greg didn't come.

After we landed, I scheduled one day of rest for the band as the crew got the gear together and prepped for the tour. In the meantime, I met with the Warner Record Japan team, which had a full two days of press events, meetings, and photo shoots. Rickie was great and on her game. She gave 100 percent with no complaints other than a bit of jet lag. The highlight was the entourage's invitation from the record company to a very traditional Japanese dinner at a very exclusive restaurant.

The Japanese shows went well with the exception of the language barrier and the audience understanding the dialogue in the show. I recommended to Rickie that for the remainder of the Asian shows that we leave out a lot of the dialogue and just play the music. She agreed, and we adjusted the set knowing we would get back to it when we hit Australia. The last night in Osaka, and on our way to Hong Kong, I noticed that Rickie was a bit on edge and not herself. I confronted her and asked if she was tired and if there was anything I could do before we hit Hong Kong the next day. I told her I knew Hong Kong well. She asked me to see if there was a place she could look at wedding rings because she and Greg were talking about getting married. I said of course. "No problem, Rickie. Leave it to me."

We flew into Hong Kong on February 13 with one day off before the show on the fourteenth. It was good to be back but bittersweet knowing we had less that forty-eight hours to spend in the Pearl of the Pacific. The morning of the fourteenth, I called Teresa Carpio, who was a Chinese singer actress that was a child prodigy and grew into an Asian sensation. In the winter of 1983 on one of Jerry Levin's eccentric projects that only he could find, I had the opportunity to spend three months in the magical city of Hong Kong producing a magic show with music for Teresa. Teresa gave me the name of a jeweler who was able to hook Rickie up with what she needed. She seemed happy, but I sensed a bit of apprehension with her decision.

We did the show in Hong Kong, and the next day, we departed Hong Kong for Melbourne, Australia, with only one day off and two shows a night at the Palais Theater. In advancing the tour, I knew with all the travel and scheduling of press, meet and greets, and shows that this is where the tour was going to get tough, but after Melbourne, we had a few days off to relax and charge our batteries in the Australian summer.

If you're not familiar with the Eastern Hemisphere, it's impossible to know how long the flights are from ma-jor city to major city, even though looking so closely on a map, the flight from Tokyo to Hong Kong is almost as far as Los Angeles to Tokyo.

The flight from Hong Kong to Australia was a bit under nine hours, and all the long-distance flights in a short amount of time take a toll on one's body. With this touring schedule and three long flights in a two-week span everybody, mainly Rickie, need- ed some down time. We found that time on the western shores of Australia in Perth. Mark and Richard had set up a yacht to

Rickie Lee Jones on the beach at Rottnest Island.

take us to the famous Rottnest Island, which at the time was barren, with beautiful white, quiet sand beaches. The whole entourage went on this four-hour cruise, lying in the sun and getting away from the grinding schedule of the tour. It was well deserved and just the thing we all needed before heading back to the east coast of Australia and then back home.

With ten days left on the tour and the band and crew running on all cylinders, I was anxious to get home. Jerry called me and informed me that the Al Jarreau Tour in Europe was now in March, and we would be leaving LA on March 15 with the first stop in Spain. I was excited but also bummed knowing that I would be leaving Ryan and Lisa again. It was a lot on Lisa, to say the least, but also hard on me—being away from my new son. I voiced my concern to Jerry, and he suggested that since we were flying and using the trains that I bring Ryan and Lisa along on the tour. He also mentioned that George Hawkins was playing bass and bringing his wife, Josie, and daughter, Molly, as well. I got excited and called Lisa, and she agreed that would be great. So we planned to do the tour, and right after the tour was done, spend some time in Italy with my cousin Giovanni and the family.

Ten more days on this tour, back home for two weeks, advance the Jarreau Tour and on to Europe with my new family. Life was good. Real good … so I thought.

When we hit Sydney, I was in my hotel room when Rickie called and needed to see me right away.

"Leo, I need to cancel the rest of the dates!"

"OK, Rickie. Why?"

"That asshole Greg, he fucking blew off the wedding; he said he's not ready to get married!" I didn't know what to say and just sat and listened.

"What the fuck! I bought the rings, picked out a dress!"

"Maybe he just needs some time, Rickie."

"I just wanna go home! NOW!"

I explained to her it wasn't that that easy and would cost her a ton on money. "You really don't want to cancel Rickie. You really don't. We only have a few more shows, and then you can go home and sort this out. I'm sure it will be fine. It's a big step for both of you; he's probably just nervous."

I calmed her down the best I could and went back to my room to call Owen to let him know what was going on. He asked me to figure what the cancelation would actually cost. I told him the shows were sold out and we would not only be responsible for refunds but all the advertising, promotion, and commitments to all the promoter con-tractors and to the band and crew as well.

"Too much, Owen, to say nothing about what it will do to her career. It will ruin her."

Rickie ultimately decided not to cancel and finished the tour. The final week of the tour was tough, but we made it through.

I don't have it in my heart to put into words and write what happened that week. It will only be shared by the special few of us on the tour who took the brunt of the situation. In the strangest way, everyone went the extra mile to try to help Rickie get through her pain and disappointment.

The day before going back to the US, Rickie asked me to try to find her a place to get away, where she could be alone and no one would know her or find her. "I just want to vanish off the face of the Earth, be by myself, and reflect and write a little," she said.

I chose the island of Bora Bora in Marquesas French Polynesia, in the middle of the Pacific Ocean, which had daily direct flights from Sydney. Back in 1984, Bora Bora was not as inhabited by the Western world and was still very remote. Rickie liked the idea.

The next day, as we all prepared to board our flights back to the US, I had breakfast with Rickie and set up her ride to the airport for her trip to what I felt was to find herself. We talked about her future and what was next for her. One thing for sure, I knew I wasn't going to be in those plans. I'm sure it was a mutual decision. I knew when Rickie looked back in time, I would always be associated with one of the worse times in her life.

"What do you think I should do Leo? What's next?"

Trying to be as honest as I could I said, "The music business is changing, Rickie. The younger generation doesn't seem to care about songs. It seems they are relating more to fads and trends like Madonna and Prince. Maybe you should think about collaborating with a younger artist and share your experience, your talent." She looked at me with that Rickie Lee look when she was ready to explode. I knew I was in for it, and bracing myself for the barrage of the women scorned, she tapped her fingers on the table, looked at me, and said, "Is the car out front?"

I nodded yes. She got up slowly, grabbed her bag, and just walked away.

I sat silently. My heart wanted to go after Rickie for reconciliation and resolution, but my mind was declaring its freedom from what I knew had no chance of existing. My time with Rickie Lee Jones was done.

Some say if you learn from a bad situation, it becomes a good one. That was the case for me and all my time with Rickie. She taught me so much, not only about the business but about life, things that I use every day.

I hear about Rickie every now and then and just smile. I reflect how lucky I was to work with one of the true iconic women in rock 'n' roll. To you, RLJ!

I only had eight days to advance and depart for the Al Jarreau European tour. It was great to get home and see Ryan and Lisa, and I was excited that they were going on the tour with me.

We were flying into London, and onto the north of Spain, and on from there. On the Jarreau Tour, there was no first class like the Rickie tour, but being with Ryan and Lisa it was OK because we had a row to ourselves.

Lisa and Ryan's Jarreau Tour Pass.

The tour was amazing, with some of the most talented musicians around Jarreau, who could make his voice mimic any instrument or sound.

He was more popular in Europe than he was in the US, so the shows were bigger and in larger venues, and we were playing the large European jazz festivals, including the granddaddy of festivals, Montreux, in Lake Geneva, Switzerland. We zigzagged around the continent through Spain, Portugal, Italy, Belgium, France, and once again, we found ourselves bussing through communist East Germany, where we were held at the border to verify that Ryan's and Molly's (George's daugh-

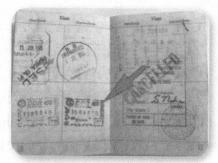

Passport with the DDR (East German) stamps. We almost had to leave the children there.

ter) passports were legitimate and we weren't smuggling children out of East Germany.

Being a production manager again was a relief with less pressure and drama than being a tour manager, and I was in Heaven. Having my family there was a blessing, too, and actually quite easy. Ryan didn't require much other than a cheap stroller and a small breast pump.

In the middle of the tour, Jerry called me into the production office to let me know that Warner Records Los Angeles was trying to get ahold of me. They had another temperamental female artist climbing the charts, and they needed my expertise.

It was a week before Easter, and the tour ended so Lisa, Ryan, and I took our side trip to Italy to visit my cousin Gian Luigi, who is my age and lived with us for a year while we were in high school. Lisa and I were still not married and tried to get married in a church in Repia, where my father was baptized. The priest denied my request and bribe because we didn't have our birth certificates and we had a baby. On Easter Sunday, we were wakened by church bells ringing and spent the rest of the day immersed with my Italian family and a traditional Easter feast.

With heavy hearts and fresh perspectives on life, we flew home to continue our new life, balancing the wild pace of the music business and parenthood. With the new positions and responsibilities, I was making much more money than before. It was time to get out of the condo and buy a bigger house with a yard for Ryan. I also figured it would give Lisa something to work and focus on as I continued to tour to support us.

Upon my return to Los Angeles, I returned the call to Warner Records and spoke with Michael Ostin, who is the son of the famous Mo Ostin. Mo was responsible for most of the bands in the classic rock era, and Michael was the heir apparent. His goal was to break in the emerging artist and rebuild the Warner roster. Michael invited me up to a meeting to discuss a lega-cy artist with a record zooming up the charts. As I sat around the table with all the high brass and tastemak-ers, I knew this was a big deal. After that meeting, I took the position, and that decision was another in the long line of decisions that would affect the next three years—and my life forever.

Of all the women artists I've had the pleasure of working with over the years, there is one who hits my heart every time I hear her name: Yvette Marie Stevens. You may not know her by that name but by the name that describes who she became: Chaka Khan.

From my early days with The Mac, I learned how to work with women on the road. It's completely different than touring with only men.

You have to be aware of your language and your sometimes immature male behavior. Women on the road didn't take lightly to the groupie scene of men taking advantage of women who go to desperate measures just to meet the band.

I learned to understand that on the road, the differences between men and women intensify. Some of the strangest, most confusing times were when it was that time of the month. If there were a group of women on the road, that time of the month became a daily occurrence.

I was fortunate to work with great female artist like Stevie Nicks, Christine McVie, Rickie Lee Jones, Bette Midler, Diana Ross, and also many, many background singers and support women who had the hearts and ears of the headlining stars.

They were all talented, and some of their deep insecurities and fears of rejection drove them to greatness. Often this led to excessive use of drugs and stimulants to ease the pain of their insecurity and deal with the rigors of life on the road.

Being very insecure myself while growing up, I guess I could relate to their feelings, and to be quite honest, Stevie and Christine were a perfect training ground for me to learn the skill of working with the women on the road.

I scored a lot of tours because of my ability to identify the problems women would have on the road and be ready for most road blocks that were flung into the path of a woman on tour.

I first met Chaka on the road with The Who in 1976 with her new band, Rufus. They were the opening act for one of the most iconic rock 'n' roll bands in history.

Rufus was the quintessential funk band that had the Anglo white music fan paying attention to strong backbeats with heavy bass,

Chaka Khan with Rufus opening for The Who 1976.

great melodies, and most of all, a beautiful, strong female vocalist with a powerful voice.

Chaka was born to sing. I've been close to many superstar female singers, but in my opinion, none of them compare to the raw, natural, deep talent that Chaka possesses. She can scale the octave chart with ease, and her dynamic range and power is nonhuman and is signature. If you hear Chaka, you know it's Chaka without laying eyes on her.

With technology and the internet, anyone can read the truths and untruths about their favorite artist. It's no secret that along the way there were substance abuse problems that Chaka dealt with. I won't get into details on the abuse, that's between me and Chaka, and I honor and respect my relationship with her enough not to cross the line of loyalty.

Chaka Khan's I Feel For You 1984.

In 1984, with the hit record "I Feel For You" racing up the charts, Warner Records, remembering my success working with the same issues with Rickie Lee Jones, wanted me to assist them with their new solo female sensation, Chaka Khan. Sitting in that meeting with all the big Warner brass, and remembering Chaka with her band Rufus back to The Who days in 1976, I emphatically said, "Of course. I would be honored."

Turns out I knew some of the guys in the band. Michael, Chaka's new music director, who I worked with on Rickie Lee Jones, heard I was coming onboard and gave me a call.

We spoke, and he gave me the lay of the land for the new project and his perceptions of what he thought the challenges might be with the new Chaka tour. He said, "It's a lot like Rickie Lee: family background issues, and the huge pressure, and fear of failing," he said.

I met with Chaka soon after, and we immediately hit it off. She was drenched with soul, and I felt the power of her words as she described her dreams to me. She realized things were getting to a level that she couldn't ever imagine, and she was questioning if she could achieve on her own without her security blanket of Rufus. Her biggest fear was failing and going back to small venues and small record sales, not knowing what the future would bring her.

After meeting Chaka, and with her approval, I met with her manager, Burt, who I really liked. Burt's claim to fame was that he was the Beatle's agent for the 1964–65 tour and had a license plate on his car that said, "Star Maker." A big, burly man who was all about business,

Burt told me, "I know you're good at what you do. Warner's is very happy you're onboard as the tour manager; all I expect from you is to keep her healthy so she works hard and don't take my job."

I laughed until I realized he was serious.

Burt was a good manager and really gave the touring reigns to me. We had a good relationship; he made the deals, and I made them happen.

While tour managing Rickie Lee, I figured if I put her in high-end situations with five-star hotels and first-class flights, she would act accordingly. It was the fear of feeling inferior in a high-class environment that made her want to be sober and work harder. She didn't want to fall back into her past of three-star style touring.

Unfortunately, this plan was a Band-Aid and worked as long as the record stayed hot, and the tour dates sold out, and funds were available to keep up that lifestyle. Once the record—along with the crowd—died, the lack of funds dictated that we went right back to three- and four-star accommodations, and things went back to normal.

The idea was the same for Chaka: elevate her to the elite status, and she will act elite.

Burt and Warner's bought off on the plan, and the 1984 Chaka Khan I Feel For You Tour was on its way.

In my three years with Chaka, we did two world tours with hundreds of shows all around the world, including playing for the troops overseas. She loved to sing and perform, sometimes doing eight, nine shows a week. Chaka was a hard worker and never complained about the demands that it takes when you have a huge hit record on the charts worldwide.

One night, we finished a long European run with an award show in Belgium and were on our way back to New York when I received a phone call letting me know that when we landed I was to bring Chaka right to the Power Station Studio to record backgrounds for Russ Titelman, who was producing Stevie Windwood's track "Higher Love," a song that was originally written for Chaka.

We landed with a car waiting to take us to the studio where Chaka, with her Chaka energy, nailed the background part that became the signature of the song. I sat in the control room of the studio and watched Chaka do what not very many people can do.

I ran into Russ one day later in life, and we reminisced about the Higher Love sessions, and I laughed when he told me that out of the many takes Chaka did that day, the first take she sang was the best and one he ended up using on the final mix. That was Chaka! A pure talent.

I can write a whole book on my years with Chaka, and one day, I may—but one night in 1987 particularly stands out as a night I will never forget.

Near the end of the tour, when the *I Feel For You* record cycle was fading away, we were forced to lower our standards and go back to

Chaka Khan 1985 tour pass. I was so tired of making new ones we started using aluminum.

the four- and sometimes three-star style of touring. I saw that it was starting to take its toll on Chaka and some of the substance abuse was creeping back into her life. We had a couple of dates in New York City, where Chaka resided and was her stomping grounds. I got a call from a touring buddy of mine who was out with Etta James, and they were doing a private show at the Sounds Of Brazil (SOBs) club in Manhattan. I asked Chaka if she wanted to go and see Etta, and Chaka said, "Of course. I would love to see Etta." It was all set up, and these two giants of the R&B world were going to meet at the venue.

When we arrived at the hotel where she was staying, I saw that Chaka's brother was there waiting. For many artists, family can become a trigger, and they can derail the artist just by being around. In the lobby, I told her brother that we were going to see Etta, and asked him to please make sure Chaka was ready around seven thirty, and told him if he wanted to come I would love to have him join us; this was a way that I could keep an eye on Chaka.

Seven thirty rolled around and then eight, and no Chaka. I called the room, no answer. I went to the front desk and got a key to her room to see what the deal was. I knocked; no answer.

I opened the door, "Hey, CK, you here?" I heard a radio playing and walked back to the bedroom to see what was up. My heart was beating for the fear of what all tour managers fear when working with artists like Chaka and Rickie.

She was there, sleeping, and as I surveyed the room, I knew instantly she wasn't going to make the show.

Disappointed, I locked up the suite, went to the lobby, and told the front desk please no visitors and asked them to leave a message for me if she left with anyone. Off I went with some of the band to see Etta James.

We arrived at the venue and went backstage to see the band, and of course, the legendary Etta. We were all backstage, and I noticed Etta looking for Chaka. When she didn't see her, she walked slowly back into her dressing room, shaking her head. That was my cue to at least let Etta know that Chaka wasn't showing up. I knocked on the door jam, and introduced myself, and let Etta know that Chaka didn't make it.

"She OK?" Etta asked. I was caught off guard and not prepared with an answer but didn't feel it was my place to divulge the truth. My thoughts were scrambled trying to think of something to say, and it just came out, "Yeah, she's OK, just been a hard run, and she just needed to catch up on some sleep." Etta instantly picked up on my awkward and insincere words, rolled her eyes, and shook her head, and said, "She's fucked up, ain't she?" I was slow to answer.

This was Etta James, one of the women of color who kicked open the door for people like Chaka.

At that moment, I decided to tell her the truth because I really felt in my heart Etta deserved the truth. I said, "Yes, unfortunately, she met up with some of her family, and she's ... she's ..." Shrugging my shoulders; I couldn't get the rest out.

"Oh well, just hold on tight, son," she told me.

I should have just left well enough alone, but again, I felt Etta deserved more. Turns out I was wrong! I said, "It really hurts me to see her hurt herself like she does. I can only imagine what she could be if she just cleaned up. I wish I could do more."

Etta turned sharply with a look of anger I wasn't ready for. "Who the hell do you think you are? You're not God! She's going to do what she's meant to do ... like me, like Billie (Holiday). She's Chaka because of what she does, and that makes her who she is. You take that away from her, she's just Yvette, another nigga singer."

She continued, "If you're so concerned, stop making the money that's fucking her up. Take the money away, and then maybe she'll clean up.

"You're just afraid, and I understand. Yeah, she may die; she may live. But I tell you what, if she does die, make sure it's not on your watch." With that, Etta said, "Oh well, give her my love." She turned around and slowly walked away.

I was mentally and physically shaken by this whole interaction. So much so I just left without seeing the show and walked all the way back to the hotel.

The next day the tour continued, and Chaka came out of it as normally as could be. Just another episode ... a bump in the road. She asked, "How was the show?"

"Great," I said. "Etta sends her love." I turned away, hearing Etta's words "on your watch."

We finished the dates, and in fact, did some co-head-line shows with my old friend Al Jarreau. The shows were great. Chaka got worse personally but still managed to be as great professionally as she was every night.

The tour ended in the Mid-west. It was finally over, and Chaka was to be in New York two days later to record the song "End Of A Love Affair" for a new record she was working on. The session was with a full fifty-piece orchestra and being

Etta and Chaka finally did the duet in 1987.

produced by my friend Russ, who was one of the premier, in-house producers for Warner Brothers.

I was told by Burt to give Chaka a fair amount of cash and put her onto a plane to New York. I told Burt it was bad idea to let her travel alone and she really should be chaperoned back to New York.

He insisted, "No, it's OK. The tour is over; she will be fine. Come on home."

Later, I found out that Burt's fears of me taking over surfaced after he heard praises from Warner's, and he was just protecting his interest. I can understand how he could feel that and really don't blame him.

On the early morning of Chaka's recording session, I was home in Los Angeles, and my phone rang.

It was Russ, "Hey, Leo, where's CK?"

"Not sure Russ. I didn't fly with her; I put her on a plane to New York a couple of days ago. Did you call Burt?"

"I'll do that next."

As the day went on, more calls. No Chaka. The recording session was canceled, and for two weeks, calls were coming in with everyone looking for Chaka—the most urgent, her mother with a maternal fear in her voice every time we spoke.

"Has she called! Have you heard anything?" She was upset with me that I didn't fly with Chaka to make sure she got home safely. I apologized and realized that in my heart I should have just gotten her home no matter what. The sense of failure weighed tons on my shoulders, and I felt responsible and was praying for a positive outcome. For years, I had remorse about the decision not to fly home with CK, and it affected my decisions on future tours. Go with your gut, no matter the outcome or cost.

One day I got the call. Chaka was found. I choose not to share the details, but I can say I was relieved when I heard she had been found and was being taken care of.

For those two agonizing weeks Etta's words of "not on your watch" haunted me to the point that I knew my time with Chaka was over.

The next two albums did okay, but not nearly as well as *I Feel For You*. Chaka settled her way into history as a premier artist struggling with addiction but coming out on the other side OK.

Burt and Chaka soon parted ways, and Chaka's little sister, Tammy, took over the management duties. That made me happy. Tammy always was there for Chaka, and it comforted me that she was in good hands with such a wonderful person.

My time with CK was amazing, and I will never forget the night I was put into my place, learning an important lesson. When you think you know it all, you really don't. And sometimes you get put in your place by a legend like Etta James.

Me and the incredible and talented Evette Marie
Stevens, aka Chaka Khan.

CHAPTER THIRTY SIX
1988 BACK WITH THE MAC AND SOMETHING COMPLETELY DIFFERENT

DURING MY THREE YEARS WITH CHAKA, my personal life held some significant changes. In June of 1986, Lisa and I had our second son, Tristan Ryan Rossi, and following Tristan, my third son, Shain Anthony Rossi. The family was growing and shrinking at the same time.

On October 18, 1987, I lost my mother to cancer. There are no words for the loss of love ones. I wish we had her around for a few more years, but I also see my friends living through

The Rossi Boys: Shain, Ryan, Channing, (born 1989), Tristan.

the horror of parents aging and deteriorating and realize that is something I could never do. I also realize that the loss of my mother was just a prelude for things to come and gave me the tools to handle the worst, most ultimate pain that would be in my future.

I was actually in Hawaii helping Shark Boy produce the entertainment for the Apple convention when I got the call to come home because it was just a matter of time before she was off to her next journey. What the family didn't know was that my mother and I spoke many times about what to do.

"Mom, if I'm on the road, what do you want me to do?" In her loving voice, and always thinking about others before herself, she said, "You don't need to be here. What can you do about it? Do what you need to do, son. I'll be fine."

After the call from my sister, I took a long walk on the Maui beach and reflected on what was to come. A world without a mother is something you think about, but when it actually happens, you can never be prepared. Out of love people will say words of love, and comfort, and those words, they all sound the same, but all those words never seemed to ease my pain.

My mother, God bless her, held on for another two days. I got home and went to the hospital that night. I saw her lying peacefully in the hospital bed. I was shattered and spewed out all the mess that was in my head, confessing my drug addiction and asking forgiveness for all the holidays and times I missed by being on the road.

Even though I knew she was close, I know she heard me by the little squeeze of my hand. Little did I know that my father was in the corner, and he said, "She waited for you, son ... She waited for you." I held my father as I cried like never before. On October 18 at 4:16 a.m., with all of us around, my mother took her last breath and peacefully went away.

It was 1988, and for once in my life, I had no plans or tours on the books and figured it would be a good time to regroup and get my family life in order—a bigger house for the boys and huge backyard for swing sets, baseball, and soccer. Ryan came home from preschool wanting to play soccer. Being it was the world's game, and with my travels around the world, I thought it was a great idea, so we signed him up. Like a duck to water, Ryan loved it!

I kept in touch with The Mac gang and the new record, *Tango In the Night*, was picking up. They were on their third single; the first single was "Big Love," Lindsey's song that showcased his fast-paced, Travis picking style. The second single was a Stevie track, "Seven Wonders," followed by Christine McVie's track "Little Lies" that eclipsed the Fleetwood Mac sound. After the release of "Little Lies," the record took off.

The most interesting part of the Tango tour was that JC was back. After his *Tusk* Tour exile to Hawaii and missing the *Mirage* tour in 1982, JC was back as the tour manager. The tour director was Doug Casper, who was Stevie's tour manager for her solo tours.

In December, while in San Francisco, I went to the Cow Palace to see the show and the band. JC pulled me aside and asked me if I was ready to get back on the road. The question blindsided me, and I blurted out, "HELL YEAH!"

"The band wants to make a change with Doug. Things have gotten too close between him and Stevie, and it's created some uncomfortable situations." I told JC I was interested and to let me know if I could help.

The tour was scheduled to pick back up in mid-May and go to the end of June in Europe. I hung out backstage at the sound and light boards, and went to the dressing rooms after the show, where Mick approached me. "I hear you may be back?"

I smiled and said, "Sure, if you guys will have me."

JC called me right before Christmas and said I was in, and after New Year's, we'd meet and go over the tour so I could start advancing the dates. Fleetwood Mac was

Tim Wooley, tour accountant (left) and Timmy "Fat Bear" McCarthy (right). Tim handing me the hotel bill with the handling charges for over 200 pieces of luggage.

not your typical tour; it took time and effort to coordinate the private jets, ground transportation, and hotels for an entourage of fifty traveling with the band. The band

WHEN THE DEVIL SMILES, THE ANGELS FROWN

hired my old friend Timmy "Fat Bear" McCarthy just to handle the compliment of over 200 pieces of luggage.

I jumped in headfirst, and with long days and longer nights (daytime in Europe), spent hours on the phone. Email was, by then, a more stable solution that made things easier. I set up a space in the garage of our new four bedroom house so I didn't wake up the family while booking the Fleetwood Mac Shake The Cage European Tour.

Already on the tour were the normal cast of characters, Wayno, Dennis, and Mitch (Lando) on security. Barbara and Kim assisted Stevie with wardrobe and makeup, and the comic relief of Peter Baynes took care of Mick Fleetwood. Of course, Sharon, Lori, and Lynn sang background along with a bevy of support musicians on and offstage.

The obvious difference was no Lindsey Buckingham on guitar or vocals. Lindsey just didn't want to tour, and at a band meeting where things got heated, an altercation ensued and Lindsey quit. The Mac was in demand, and with dates already booked decided to tour without Lindsey.

Rick Vito (left), Billy Burnette (right).

It took two players to replace Lindsey. An old friend of The Mac, Billy Burnette played rhythm guitar and sang Lindsey's vocal parts, and Rick Vito covered all the lead guitar parts that were necessary

for The Mac's sound. In addition to being the tour director, I was also responsible for Billy and Rick (who didn't
have or really need a security person).

Winter became spring, and with a month of rehearsals,
we were ready to go. With first-class flights and five-star
hotels, it was still difficult to move around the band, and
buses were out of the question.

In the '80s, travel in Europe was always challenge.
Hotels were not like hotels in the US, and airports were
always on the outskirts of town, but the train stations
were always dead center and never more than five to ten
minutes from all the nice hotels in each city. The band
loved the fact that, on a whim, I had an idea to call British
Rail and Deutsche Bahn Rail to inquire about chartering
private trains for us to travel through Europe. I asked for
eight cars, one for each band member, one car for the support staff, a luggage car, and finally a diner/bar car in the
middle of the train.

Because it was The Mac, both companies were excited
to assist me with this clever idea, and it was the first of
many times I chartered trains in Europe.

I was excited to be back with The Mac and on the
road, but it was hard leaving home and my family. I set
up nannies to help Lisa, and both families were there to
support her while I wasn't home.

The first leg was ten days in England, first stopping
in Birmingham and then on to London for six shows at
the Wembley Arena. Over the course of the tour, we hit

Scandinavia (including Sweden), then six shows in Germany, including a hit-and-run to East Berlin that, in 1988, was still under the communist regime. We then hit Holland and back to London for three more shows at Wembley, on to Dublin, and we finally ended at the Maine Road Soccer Stadium in Manchester, England.

Even without Lindsey, the shows sold out, and everywhere we went, we were treated like royalty. Tango In The Night had run its course, and the band needed some well-deserved rest.

The plan was to take a break and go into the studio without Lindsey, and with Billy and Rick, make a record to be released in 1989, followed by a tour in 1990–1991. Just as I got back in the game, I was on hiatus. I was excited to get back home to the family and had enough money saved to take some time off to figure out what was next.

My connections with Apple were getting stronger, and the money I was earning was really affording me the opportunity to get deeper into the computer world. Apple would send me their newest computers, and they put me in their early adopter program. It also became an addiction because information was power, and power was something I love!

My reputation with computers in the music industry led to a phone call from Frontline Management, which still managed the Eagles at the time. Frontline was now into the merchandise business and started Facility Merchandise Industries (FMI) to sell tour merchandise and pocket the money instead of giving it to third parties. Not only were they facilitating their artists, they were also representing venues and stadiums.

They knew my expertise in the computer world and wanted to know if I'd be interested in creating a new computerized inventory system for their new crown jewel venue, Dodger Stadium. The job entailed product in and out and tracking sales and mainly reordering merchandise. The software requirements were way over my head, but I knew the hardware and knew I could find a developer to make the inventory tracking software. I was working with the flamboyant younger brother of music mogul Irving Azoff, Ron. Ron was a great guy with good energy, and when you worked with Ron, there was never a dull moment.

It was a perfect opportunity to stay home for a while and do something new. I eagerly took on the consulting gig for FMI, which meant an office at the stadium and fucking traffic every day. I loved the homestands when the Dodgers played at the stadium.

The gig was great! I made a deal where Apple got season tickets in trade for all the computers for all the office and the satellite merchandise stands. I also implemented the Dodgers first mail order catalog that mailed out to their season ticket holder list. With a limited budget, I used an old friend, Rich Rachman, as an art director to lay out the catalog and used my son and children of friends as models with hats, tees, and anything with Dodgers on it that would sell.

When the Dodgers won the World Series in 1988, the catalog mail order sales went from a mere $23,000 in 1987 to over two million in 1988—a huge success. A huge success that I didn't get a piece of or bonus from.

I spent the entirety of 1988 at Dodger Stadium, working not only with the merchandise but helping with promotions, which meant working with my fellow Pisan Tommy LaSorda, the over-the-top Dodger manager.

It was amazing, with full access to the press club, and good food and conversations. I befriended all the sports writers and radio and TV hosts and their staffs. Jay Lucas was one of the main public relation people (and we remain friends to this day), and I brought him on as tour manager in 2015 for Brian Wilson of the Beach Boys.

I learned about baseball in 1988, sitting with the scouts and players like ex-Dodger Al Downing, who had the postgame radio show and who was, and probably is, one of the smartest men in baseball. Baseball players are very similar to musicians and artists: sacrificing most of their youth, missing dances, parties, and family and social gatherings to achieve the highest level of their profession.

My World Series pass.

During the World Series with the Dodgers playing the Oakland Athletics, late in the game, the Dodgers were down and, like a movie script, Kirk Gibson limps to the plate. I was in the office but decided to go out on the concourse to see the end of the game. I had my head turned, and like a surreal scene that was created ,I heard the crack of the bat and actually felt the energy and the air move from the gasp of the 56,000 people inhaling as Kirk hit the ball out of the park. It was pandemonium. It was like being back at a huge stadium rock concert during the encore. I soaked it all in and watched the gauntlet of emotion as he rounded third with the whole stadium waiting for him to step on home plate. Another magical moment that now, more than ever, I understand I had the good fortune to be at.

To me, the sports business was easy. You had a legacy product with a built-in audience to whom you knew you could sell. Unlike a record that you only hoped and prayed would be successful, the Dodgers could do no wrong.

My World Series clubhouse pass. Very few of these were issued.

It was so easy for anyone in the music business to latch on to the sports world like FMI did and break the bank.

The World Series was so successful, and Ron and the other guys couldn't keep up with the demand for World Series tees and sweat shirts. As soon as they fell off the truck they were sold, and cash was flying. Even with the new computerized inventory system, the reconciliation was a mess, and in the end, there was money unaccounted for. I believe there was no bad doing or theft, but just an unmanageable situation with poor planning.

Bob Graziano (a Pedro kid), the vice president of finance, and Barry Stockhammer, vice president of marketing pulled me into a meeting and asked if I would work through 1989. That was the Dodgers one hundredth anniversary. They also wanted to develop a concept for a gift shop located above home plate, high in the sky, named Top of the Park.

I was enjoying working at Dodger Stadium but was getting the jones to get back into music and maybe get back on the road. It was in my blood, and even though I enjoyed staying home with the boys, the road kept calling me back.

I stayed in touch with The Mac, and they were on schedule to release their new record. *Behind The Mask* came out April 1990, and the tour was to begin before the release date in March 1990 in Australia.

The Dodgers offered me a full-time job that I really wasn't interested in because I knew I wanted to go back with The Mac for the next tour. The Dodgers operated by hiring people for key spots and bringing in overzealous interns who were eager to work for the team, for no pay, to do the brunt of the work.

Out of respect, I took a look at the offer from the Dodgers, and just as I expected, the annual salary was less than two months of what I made with The Mac.

In the summer of 1989, after I received my World Series ring, I was done with the Dodgers. It was an amazing experience working with good people who became life-long friends. It was a dream job for others but not for me.

On May 18, 1989, our fourth son, Channing Christopher Rossi, was born. It was a difficult pregnancy, so Lisa and I gave up on having a girl but were unsuccessful in getting her tubes tied because the hospital couldn't find the consent forms. My family was growing, and I was excited about the future and the upcoming tour, but in the back of my mind, I knew that someday I would have to get off the road and raise my boys.

In the fall of 1989, JC and the new tour accountant, Bob "The Dude Man" Cayne, and I began work on the Fleetwood Mac Behind The Mask World Tour.

CHAPTER THIRTY SEVEN
BEHIND THE MASK. THE END
OF THE ROAD

A NEW DECADE WAS HERE, bringing the last of the millennium. I reflect back now and see how much my life had changed in less than fifteen years. My career was established, I was a father, and most of all, I realized I did it on my own terms. I was thirty-two years old and never had a straight job. I was confident and fearless, but always in the back of my mind, I knew that I needed to find a way to make the kind of living I was used to—but stay home and raise my family. I made a decision that this would be my last tour, so I needed to make as much as I could to handle the transition that I knew was ahead of me.

The normal cast of characters were back. Curry was at the helm of the design again, and the band wanted something bigger and less traditional than the other tours. Billy Burnett and Rick Vito were back with Lindsey, still on the sideline working his solo career.

The *Behind the Mask* record was an up-tempo Mac record that opened with another Christine McVie pop hit, "Skies The Limit," with Stevie and Billy and Rick's new sound of layered vocals.

Fleetwood Mac
Behind The Mask
tour pass.

Billy and Rick had great voices that were different than Lindsey's but worked with the songs that they cowrote.

The other big difference was Richard Dashut and Ken Caillat were no longer producing. They were replaced by my old friend Greg LaDanyi who had success with Jackson Browne and Don Henley of the Eagles solo projects. Greg had a style of pop rock sensibility that worked with the new writing structure of The Mac. Rick Vito was a bluesman with more of a style of Peter Green's Fleetwood Mac back in the '60s but could rock 'n' roll when called to the task. Billy, on the other hand, came from rock 'n' roll royalty. He was one of the next generations of the Rocky and Dorsey Burnett rockabilly trio that was Elvis Presley's main influence. Billy was a rocker through and through. From the young age of eight years old, when he released his first record as a child star, he ran fast and hard and never stopped. Late nights and late afternoons were his norm, but he always was on his game when he hit a stage.

Billy's song "In The Back Of My Mind" was perfect for an intro for the live shows, with its dark, driving drum beats and ethereal guitar parts below enchanting vocals from Chris, Stevie, Billy, and Rick.

Curry, working with Alan Branton, who was another LA set designer, brilliantly decided that the show would start with the lighting truss tilted down like a pyramid revealing the top of the roof. The roof of the stage was covered with four huge, colorful masks lit from behind. The house lights went down, and the low-end rumble of the subwoofer speakers

The Behind The Mask stage.

that ran the width under the stage shook people to their core. Slowly recorded music would layer in like a Bach fugue while the band snuck into their places, and then, as the live music replaced the recorded tracks, the lighting truss would rise revealing the band onstage. The opening had a lot of coordination and moving parts; it was different for the band but was a spectacular way to start the concert.

Not being in production, I was fortunate enough to

share it with the adoring fans over the 101 shows we did on the tour, and it never got old.

The entourage for the tour was bigger than all of the previous Mac tours. With the large sets and expanded sound, it was a large crew that was headed up by Michael Grassley. Mike was a rigger out of the infamous Disney camp who turned production manager. With the moving structure, he brought in Roy Bickle, another Disney Rigger extraordinaire, to ensure the rig was safe and secure. It was an amazing crew with the best of the best from the old Mac team and the rest of the industry.

I quickly realized that moving over seventy people around the world was going to be a momentous task. We needed a system. JC and I adopted the team concept. The "A-team" would be headed up by him and the accountant "Dude Man" Bob Cayne. Stevie's wardrobe and makeup team was headed up by Kim Brakely and Barbara Buck, and Timmy "Fat Bear" would handle dressing rooms and bags and the rest of the ten member A-Team."

The "B-team" would be the guys in the band headed up by each of their security persons. All coordination was done through the security detail and never did I speak to a band member directly. Each security person had control of their principal. Then the "C-Team"—Christine and Stevie, with their support family—Stevie's confidants Liza Edwards and Johnny Starbuck ran Stevie's day-to-day. Christine was now being handled by Wayno, who also ran the venue security along with Mike Grassley.

Every day, I would follow up, and be last to the gig, and pick up the slack, and daily there was something that was left behind. At the end of the show, each security detail had their car and their driver, and were on their own to get back to the hotel.

Under your door every night, Timmy would slide the "day sheet" that you'd follow with all the hotel and venue information, addresses, phone numbers, departure and arrival times, and other pertinent information for the day.

This logistics were designed to avoid any conflict between the band members (who were all very different) having to wait on each other in a car or hotel lobby. I coordinated these six little tours that worked as one, and even though it was very expensive, it was the only way that the tour would have worked.

The first stop was Australia, and we needed a way to get the entourage down under. With the band and their immediate support, we needed twenty first-class seats, an additional twenty-five business class seats, and a bunch of coach seats. I called all my travel agent connections to research the cost for all the air travel. I also inquired about hotel and internal transportation cost. Bob Cayne had meetings with the promoters to pick up the travel cost in order to reduce the income and foreign taxes, but the promoter declined and wanted no part of the tax evasion plan that the Australian government was now aware of.

In 1990, my brother Joe was working for United Airlines as a customer service representative at Los Angeles

International Airport. He had mentioned to me that United was flying the brand-new 747-400s directly from LA to Sydney, and the jets were amazing. He also got me a contact and set up a meeting for me to meet United sales to see about purchasing the tickets directly.

It was also decided that Mike and I would fly down to Australia to advance the tour, meet with the promoter and sound and light companies, and advance the hotels. In my meeting with United, I told them if they comped us two business class tickets for our advance trip, we would use them. They agreed, and we were on our way.

We landed in Sydney and made our way to the Four Seasons Hotel where again our rooms were comped in hopes that they would get the lucrative business of the Fleetwood Mac tour.

I was up early in the fall Sydney morning taking a walk, and there was a billboard, and side by side was an ad for the Fleetwood Mac show and another for United's new 747-400 LA to Sydney. The light bulb in my head went off: PROMOTION!

I somehow connected with Peter Green, who was the vice president of sales for United Airlines Australia. We discussed a promotion idea I came up with where United would sponsor the tour and comp us all the air travel LA-SYD-LA, and in exchange, The Mac would give a full-page ad in the tour program, banners at all of the shows, and their logo on the tickets. Peter said he would run it up the ladder at United and see what was possible.

We ended up getting all our airfare covered, but only after we agreed to one of the most creative deals that Peter came up with. Not only did United get all the promotional exposure, Peter crafted a program where he reached out to all the travel agents in Australia and created a contest where if you sold an agreed amount of United Transpacific Air, you would get free tickets to a show and a backstage meet and greet with the band. The top grossing agent would get a private dinner with a couple of the band members.

The United Airlines promotion deal we made. It was a win/win for everyone.

For The Mac, it was money for literally nothing, and they agreed, and I went back to the US with a deal of a lifetime for the band. For the crew who was flying coach, we worked a deal where they would get two coach seats per crew member to have a bit more room to stretch out.

I made a deal to take a small commission off the amount I saved the band. It was my goal to make as much as I could to make sure I had enough money for my upcoming career change.

With rehearsals right around the corner the band and crew were set and JC, Bob, and I were meeting daily to keep placing pieces of the puzzle together.

Between managing the tour of one of the biggest rock 'n' roll bands in history, I was on a soccer field or preschool event living my schizophrenic life. I would sit with the other parents and just wonder what it would be like if they realized what my other life was like.

One minute a soccer dad and the next minute the tour director for Fleetwood Mac. That was my bipolar life, a life with the rite of passage where a goal from my son was as good as any great guitar solo.

Rehearsals came and went, and the show was fine-tuned and ready to go. We had a cut down version of the set, lights, and sound to avoid extensive shipping charges. We were also doing stadium and festival shows where the set wouldn't work anyway.

It was like a fine dinner that took a lot of time to prepare, and now it was ready to serve for all to enjoy. On the United 747-400, almost all of the seats were occupied by Fleetwood Mac personnel or a United executive. I sat in business class with Curry and the other support team as the pilot came on the speakers, "Ladies and gentlemen, this is your pilot, and we'd like to thank you for being some of the first to be flying on United's 747-400 to Sydney." He went on and on about the jet the flight plan and then, "We would also like to welcome the Fleetwood Mac tour on board, and we're happy to have them on board the friendly skies." Everyone on the jet applauded, and moments later, we roared down the runway, and the massive 747-400 jet slowly pointed her nose to the sky and south to Australia. I reminisced about how far I'd come, thinking back thirteen years when I was taking off in a DC-8 cargo jet, going to Australia with Fleetwood Mac.

The Australian tour was a month long with thirteen shows through the typical cities of Brisbane, Melbourne, Adelaide, Perth on the sunny western coast, and Sydney. Being that this was first leg of the world tour, everyone, band and crew, was feeling each other out. Like most tours, small cliques of like-minded people were formed, and infatuations and romances were beginning to form.

Because of the romantic atmosphere and sexiness of being on the road and on tour, it was very common that what was intended to be the simple, innocent, "We're just good friends" ended up awkwardly. There were many unexpected rendezvous with soft walking people sneaking out of rooms while I was making rounds, helping Timmy with the delivery of day sheets early in the morning. With Easter in Sydney, most of the entourage, including me, flew their families in to join the tour. This put a strain on the support staff, mainly the security staff, who worked overtime to keep up with both the shows on the tour, as well as all of the added sightseeing and extra needs.

With the last Australian show behind us, the band, crew, and families all packed up and headed home to get ready for the first North American leg of the tour.

Touring the States is much different than touring internationally. It's a much faster pace with fewer days off. The travel and movement is the most difficult part of the tour. Packing bags and getting in and out of cars, vans, and hotels takes its toll, and the show becomes the easiest part of the day.

With the amount of people on the tour and buses not an option, it made more sense to charter a jet than to use commercial flights. The only problem was finding a jet that could handle the full complement of the entourage. I needed a jet that could handle twenty-five to thirty people. Air Charter in 1990 was not as developed and accessible as today, and finding a jet that would fit our needs proved to be more difficult than I had imagined. Back

The Behind The Mask MGM Boeing 727 touring jet.

in 1987 with Chaka, I flew on the specialty airline MGM Air. MGM was made up of three Boeing 727s that had all first-class seats with a spacious interior and a set of four seat suites in the rear of the jet for people traveling together. It was a luxurious experience that ran from Los Angeles to New York with gourmet food and service, including a limo to pick you up and drop you off when you landed. It cost a tad more than first class on the traditional airlines. The MGM 727s were the perfect jets for the tour.

On a whim, I drove to the MGM terminal on the southside of the runways at LAX. Explaining my situation to the reservation counter, I was led to the back offices, where I met the director of operations. "My name is Leo, and I'm the road manager for the band Fleetwood Mac. I'd like to charter your jet."

The director just laughed.

"No, I'm serious. I'm looking for a jet for the Fleetwood Mac tour." Seeing I was serious, I now had his attention. We sat and discussed the possibility, and over the course of the next two hours, we had a plan that was going to be presented to the MGM management.

Two days later, I received the call, and we had a jet. The deal was an all-inclusive deal where MGM would have to pay for the fuel, takeoff, landing, and airport fees, based on the itinerary.

I said, "I'm sure we can work it out, please hold the space from May 25 to August 3," which was the first leg of the tour.

Looking at the tour and the way it was booked, the shows were in the four quadrants: north, south, east, and west of the US. Some cities, especially in the Northeast, were close together and required short flights. Talking to

Timmy about the bags and moves, we discussed the cargo holds and baggage limitations for the tour. In one of our conversations, Timmy said, "Too bad we can't just stay at one hotel and drive."

BING! There was that light bulb again.

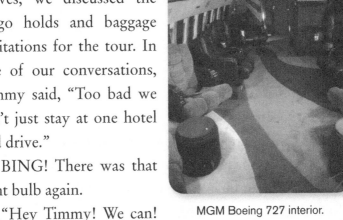

MGM Boeing 727 interior.

"Hey Timmy! We can! Let's just use the jet as a bus!" And the hub concept was invented.

The hub concept would cost a bit more but was worth it. In each quadrant, we would find a city that had a good hotel that was close to an airport (preferably a private one) that would be open twenty-four hours and use it as our home base. This way we could check in a hotel, unpack, and make ourselves at home and fly to and back from whatever city the show was at.

For the Northeast, we chose Philadelphia—the Four Seasons five-star hotel, a fifteen-minute travel time to the airport with a private terminal to handle a jet as large as a 727. From Philly, we could hit-and-run Boston, New York, Buffalo, Washington, DC, Hartford, and all of the cities in between. We checked into the Philly Four Seasons on July 9 and checked out August 3, hubbing ten cities. It was the perfect solution for the tour.

This is how a typical day of the hub concept worked on the Fleetwood Mac Behind The Mask Tour in 1990:

I would get up early in the morning and check the weather where we were and where we were going. If it looked like the weather was going to impact the day, we would adjust the schedule.

The security team and support staff would meet to discuss the day and movements and confirm the schedule.

We would have staggered times for departure based on each of the principal band members. The ladies would always need more time than the men, so we would give them different times for lobby calls and limo departures. The objective was to get the band onto the jet within thirty minutes of each other to avoid delays.

I would call the pilots to discuss the flight plan and contacted the flight base operator (FBO) on both sides— departure and arrival—to make sure they were ready for the jet and the band. Most of the time, the limos were allowed to drive right up to the stairs of the jet. I would also call the head flight attendant to make sure catering was ready for both flights.

If you were lucky enough to be on the Fleetwood Mac Behind The Mask tour, This is what a typical show day would have been like:

A day in the life on the road.

A band member would wake up and prepare for the day in the hub city.

The band depart the hotel lobby and walk ten feet to

their limo to the airport, usually around two p.m.

The limos would pull right up to the stairs of the jet, and the band would board.

Food and drinks were available before takeoff as everyone settled in for the flight.

The jet would take off for an average flight of an hour.

The jet would land, and the limos would pull up to the stairs.

The A-Team would jump right off into a van and hustle to the venue for setup.

Security would delay the limos fifteen minutes to give the A-Team time to get to the venue.

The limos would depart FBO with the band from the airport and drive to the venue.

We typically would arrive at the venue by five-thirty p.m., and the band would prepare for the show

Showtime was either seven-thirty or eight and lasted two and a half hours.

After the show, the band would come offstage, and cool down, and change (typically forty-five minutes).

The limos pulled up backstage only feet from the band's dressing rooms and would drive off to the airport.

The limo would pull up feet from the stairs, and the band would board the jet.

The band would be served drinks and dinner as the support team loaded the jet and waited for the A-Team.

The jet would depart the show city, typically around twelve-thirty a.m. to one a.m.

The jet would land in the hub city around two a.m.

The limos would pick up the band ten feet from the jet stairs in the hub city.

The limos would drive back to the hotel and drop off in the lobby.

By two-thirty a.m., the band members were back in their rooms.

At three a.m., the security staff and support would quickly meet, and Timmy and I would deliver day sheets for the next day.

We were one happy family living a life only others could dream about. The tour ran like clockwork and rarely (other than some weather incidents or air traffic delays) was there any problems. Thirty-two shows in seventy days with no major hiccups and no drama other than one cancellation, due to the passing of Christine McVie's father.

On the days off during the first North American leg, I was busy advancing the European tour that started in Belgium. The tour was fifteen shows in thirty days, mainly in Germany and on the continent of Europe. The first part of the tour was in Belgium and Holland, and then on to England and Ireland, followed by Scandinavia, and down into Germany and Italy before a private show for United Airlines in Paris.

I made a deal to use the MGM 727, making multiple stops to get most of us over to Europe. We left Los Angeles, flew to New York to pick up the East Coast people, then went on to St. John's Newfoundland, Canada, then to Reykjavik, Iceland, then Shannon, Ireland, and finally landed in Paris.

Like the Euro tour in 1988, I decided to charter trains again. Deutsche Bahn Rail in Germany really set us up this time, giving us an older train, including a very luxurious parlor car used by the Third Reich in World War Two. This fascinated all the guys on the tour, but the women were not amused and wanted nothing

I can't seem to find any pictures of the inside of the train but this is pretty close to what it looked like.

to do with it. On September 15, we had a show way up in the Alps of Switzerland. It was in a town square in a small city named Locarno. We started the day in Austria, where we had played the night before. The morning of the fifteenth, we jumped onto the train and headed to Locarno to do the show, and then, right after the show, we would head south through the Alps to Italy. We were fortunate that there was a station literally one mile from the stage in Locarno.

The show was magical, and I was amazed that over 20,000 people from all over Switzerland made the trek to Locarno to see The Mac. It was like we were in a make-believe city that Disney had built for us to play in.

After the show, we jumped into the cars for the short ride to the train station to board the train to Italy. The band settled in, and most of us ended up in the parlor car to go over the day and plan for the next.

It was a warm September night in Central Europe with a full moon, and we were on our own private train, winding our way through the Alps. Every night, when the band had settled in, Timmy, most of the support team, and I would end up in the luggage car where we could open the large cargo door, and some of them could smoke pot and just chill and reflect on the day.

That particular night, we found ourselves in one of the most beautiful parts of the world, the Alps. The train routes took us to remote parts that were off the beaten track. We rapidly whipped by small cities and towns, and one minute later, we were looking up at the bright white snow-topped mountains that didn't even look real but more like an animation. We all just sat on the luggage with the fresh air hitting us and refreshing ourselves to be ready for the next day. I fell asleep, and when I awoke, it was daylight with the sun kissing me good morning. We were descending into the flatlands of Italy, heading to Modena, where we would lose the train and reunite with the 727 to finish off the European tour. An enchanted night I have never forgotten, and even today when taxing moments bring me down, I sometimes find myself thinking about the night in the luggage car, and things get better. Timmy, Peter, and Wayno are no longer with us and have gone to the great gig in the sky, but I know they are looking down, smiling with me, as I share with you a day in our blessed life back in 1990.

We hubbed the Italian dates out of Rome, staying at the Crowne Plaza across the street from the Pantheon. The hotel's location was perfect with a roof top pool and larger rooms that weren't common in Europe. Before the Rome date we had a hit-and-run in Milan. September 18 was just another typical hub day until we got to the jet, and the pilots informed me there was a wildcat strike for the aircraft fuelers.

We were twenty-sixth in line for fuel and scheduled for late that night. We had enough fuel to get to Milan, but getting back would be too risky, and refueling in Milan wasn't an option. Bob the tour accountant and I put our heads together. Driving would take too long and flying one way to Milan and spending the night would disrupt the flow and be very costly, and besides, there were no hotel rooms available in Milan anyway.

In my broken Italian, I asked the flight base operator manager if there was any possible way we could get to the front of the line to get fueled up. He said he would check, and I asked to use the phone to call JC. I explained the problem to JC. Luckily, the A-Team decided to take a train excursion that day and get to Milan early, so at least JC was already in Milan to manage that side of things.

JC said, "It's sold out, so do whatever you can to get here, and we will figure out the rest later."

It was getting late, and we needed to figure out a plan. The six-hour drive put us in Milan around nine p.m., which was doable, but if we were going to do it, we needed to make a decision.

The FBO manager came back with another Italian gentlemen who said this was his cousin and he could get our jet fueled pretty quickly by a private vendor, but it would cost us more.

"*Quanto costre?*" I asked him.

He spouted out a number of Italian lire, and I looked Bob who said "about ten grand."

"*Mezza* (half)," I said.

He spouted another number, and I looked at Bob again. "Five grand and change."

"*Quando?*" I asked.

With his hands in the air, he said loudly, "*Propiro adesso.* (Right now.)" I shook his hand, and Bob and I went back to the jet to get the money. Since it was so much money, we decided to bring Wayno with us for protection and also to witness the transaction, in case anyone asked.

Being Italian and knowing my people, we paid half the money up front and the balance when the pilots told us we were fueled. Sure enough, within ten minutes, a fuel truck pulled up and filled up our tanks, and we were ready to go. I met my *paisanos* at the bottom of the steps with the balance of the cash, and we were on our way to Milan.

We pulled it off, and it was the most economical way to get to Milan. Buses and hotels would have cost more, and cancelation was not an option.

Bob laughed at my negotiation skills and said, "You went from ten grand to five in a blink of an eye; not bad for ten seconds of work, Rossi."

From Rome, we had one more show in Paris. United Airlines opened its European hub in Paris and wanted to sponsor the tour. Flying commercial wasn't feasible for this tour, but I still wanted to help United. We negotiated a deal where we did a pri-

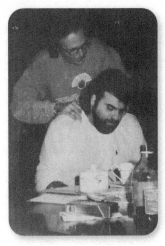

Johnny Starbuck, Stevie's security person, de-stressing me in the dressing room in Milan.

vate show for just all the European travel agents, and in return, United gave each band member a credit card with $50,000 of credit on it, good for life. They also picked up our tour budget for two days.

The show for United Airlines in Paris was successful, and on the flight back to London, I had a special dinner for the band on the 727.

John McVie seemed a bit agitated and asked, "Who's paying for this?" Lying through my teeth, I said MGM (the charter company) picked it up. He was poking through his food and wasn't amused.

John had been requesting English pork pies to be on the jet for the whole tour, and for some reason, it didn't happen. It was one of those legendary John McVie nights where he was a bit beyond himself.

We were all buttoned up ready to go, and Wayno said, "McVie wants to see you, and he ain't too happy."

"What's up John," I asked.

In his John McVie soft-spoken voice, he said, "Am I in this fucking band?"

"Yes, I'm sure you are, John."

"Then why can't I get what I want! Everybody else gets what they want, why can't I? Chris has her fucking Champaign, Mick his fucking beer, Stevie whatever she fucking wants, why can't I get a fucking pork pie?"

"I'll go check on it, John," I said. Usually once we took off, he would fall asleep and that would be the end of it, but not tonight. He went on and on and on about the fucking pork pies.

Now, one thing about John McVie is if you pranked him and got him, he loved it, even if things didn't turn out like he wanted. It was one of those nights where I wanted to get him and get him bad. I had an idea to get him pork pies, not just a few—but a hundred. I wanted to have 100 pork pies in his hotel room when we got back to the St. James Palace where we were staying. How was I going to do this? Easy.

I went to the cockpit with the pilots and had them radio the FBO and had the FBO call David Werner, the head concierge at the St. James, who I knew would get the pork pies. About fifteen minutes before landing in London, the pilots received the message that the deed was done. There were 100 traditional English pork pies in John McVie's room, awaiting his arrival.

The whole flight, John kept on and on and on about it, and I just went about my business, which included letting everyone know about the prank and to be in the lobby after we got to the hotel. We landed in London, and this night, we traveled to the hotel all in one bus rather than the normal fleet of limos.

We got to the hotel, and everyone went their separate ways, except those who wanted to see the result of the pork pie prank. We sat and sat, waiting for McVie, and finally the elevator door opened, and there was a raging John McVie, carrying a gaggle of pork pies, screaming and yelling.

"Where's Rossi, that Italian, Dego wop! I'm going to kill him!"

Oh fuck, did I go too far? Did I drive John McVie past the point of no return? He saw me and was heading right toward me, and Wayno intercepted him and put his large body between us.

John was incensed. "What the fuck? You think this is funny?"

Wayno said, "Calm down, John. It's just a joke!"

I said, "You wanted your fucking pork pies, you got 'em, McVie!"

He then shouted, "Yeah, but where's the fucking mustard? You can't eat pork pies without mustard, Rossi!" I was stunned silent. He got me, and the joke was on me. We all laughed and went to the bar and had pork pies and beer. And yes, mustard.

Stevie comforting me after the pork pie incident. People always ask
me "is Stevie as nice as she seems?" I say, "Yes, whatever
you've heard or have been told, multiply it by one hundred...
And that's Stevie Nicks!"

With the European tour done and a one month break,
we had one more US leg with thirty shows left. The plan
was to end the tour with two shows at the Fabulous Forum in Los Angeles.

In October 1990, I knew I needed to find a way to
stay home and make a living and raise the children. The
entertainment industry and technology companies were
on a collision course; all the taped assets were convert-
ing to digital. Records were replaced by CDs, and vid-
eotape VHS was being converted to digital and could be
played on computers from compact disc read-only memory (CD-ROMS), and there was this new up-and-coming
technology digital versatile disc (DVD).

During the break, Shark Boy invited me up to Apple

to see the new digital video technology that would become Apple's QuickTime. It was revolutionary and in its infancy, and Apple was interested how the entertainment industry early adopters could assist them in making sure what they were building was viable. For two days, I was immersed in long think tanks, answering questions about what we would do with this new technology. I left Apple with a prereleased new laptop and a set of tools to work with this new format.

The last leg of the Behind The Mask Tour started in Florida and headed north back to the Northeast, up into the coldest parts of the winter in Canadian cities and to Seattle, then down the West Coast to Oakland and Los Angeles.

In Seattle, we were told that Lindsey would be joining us on the tour in Oakland and Los Angeles to do a couple of songs with the band. We, mainly the old guard, were excited that Lindsey was going to join us.

The tour was running like clockwork, and the hubbing concept had proven to be the right decision for this particular tour.

In mid-November, we found out that Lisa was pregnant again—our fifth child. She came out to visit to share the news and celebrate what was for sure to be our last child. Boy or girl, we were done. To celebrate the pregnancy, Christine McVie, Wayno, Lisa, and I went out to dinner. Near the end of the dinner, Christine, in a very heartfelt manner, told Lisa and me that of all her accomplishments, what she regretted the most was the fact that she never had a child. She and Stevie were so wrapped up in not only their careers but Mick, John, and Lindsey that they felt obligated to not stop the fast moving, hugely successful Mac machine and take time out to have children and start a family. It was ironic and sad to see that women who would carry the children unlike the men in Fleetwood Mac never had children.

Near the end of the dinner, Christine took a ruby ring off her finger and placed it on Lisa's saying, "If a boy or a girl, it would make me happy if you gave my name to one of the child's names. The miracle appeared six months after the tour ended, on May 20, 1991; a baby girl, Khiara Christine Rossi.

Khiara Christine Rossi. My Angel. My Rock. A son is a Son until he takes a wife, A daughter's your daughter for the rest of your life.

We decided to stay at the Four Seasons in San Francisco for the Oakland show on December 7. I set up a suite for Lindsey and was excited to see him. The front desk called me, and I met him in the lobby upon his arrival. With a hug I said, "Hey LB! So good to see you!" I gave him his transportation and info for the stay and told him if he needed anything, just give me a call.

At the sound check, it was decided that he would come out and do "Landslide" with Stevie, and that was it. Everyone was sensitive not only to Lindsey's feelings but to Rick and Billy as well. All of us old guard knew to have the five of them back onstage together was going to be epic and lead to the rumors of reunions and discount how far The Mac had come without him.

Lindsey walked onto the stage with his slow, confident swagger, guitar in hand, like a king who had been away from his castle returning from a battle. He hugged Stevie and gathered in front of the drum kit with Mick, John, and Chris. Billy seemed not to be phased and joined the reunion, while Rick seemed preoccupied with his own thoughts. After the soundcheck, the normal, calm backstage of a tour on its one hundredth show was now buzzing with anticipation for the reunion. Most of the crew on the tour never had the fortune to see the magic of the five of them together but immediately understood why The Mac was The Mac. Even a slow acoustic ballad like "Landslide" portrayed the chemistry and presence of Lindsey and Stevie.

The show started and with "Landslide" being in the middle of the set, I knew the crowd was going to go off.

Stevie finished "Gold Dust Woman" and went to a quick wardrobe change for "Landslide" as the rest of the band played "I Loved Another Woman," an old Fleetwood Mac blues song from the '60s featuring Rick Vito on guitar.

I went to Lindsey's dressing room and knocked on the door, "Hey LB, it's time. You ready?"

The door opened, and there he was in his grey shark-skin suite, white shirt, skinny tie, and his guitar in hand. JC met us in the hallway, flashlight in hand. "Wow, man, look at you. Good to have you here, Lindsey. You ready?"

"Yep, I'm ready," he said as we walked toward the stage.

The song ended, and the stage went to black, and I walked Lindsey up the stairs. Stevie came out of the quick-change tent, looking over with her inviting Mona Lisa/Stevie smile, and on cue, Lindsey and Stevie just naturally walked out onto the stage, and Buckingham Nicks was together again.

Slowly, the lights came up, and at first, the crowd didn't know who it was, and then, like a swelling river that burst its banks, the applause was deafening. Lindsey, hugging his guitar in one hand and Stevie in the other, took a bit of bow and walked Stevie to the microphone centerstage. Lindsey gave her a kiss and took his position at the stage left mic, like he had done thousands of times in the past.

"This a simple song, and I'd like to dedicate it to Buckingham Nicks," Stevie said, looking at Lindsey. "I hope that someday he'll find it in his heart to spend some time with me and play some music with me again."

The song came and went with Christine's piano solo in the middle. Onstage, reunited, were three of The Mac, and hand in hand, they slowly walked together off the stage. Everyone there, the fans, the crew, the ushers, all witnessed an enchanted moment in music history.

We decided to stay the night in San Francisco and keep everyone together to land into Los Angeles, go straight to the Forum and do the show, and then everyone could go home. Lindsey flew with the band on the private 727, and it was discussed and decided to have Lindsey play "Landslide" and his song "Go Your Own Way" at the end of the set. They all sat on the jet with an acoustic guitar and went over the new arrangement and vocal parts. I sat with Johnny Starbuck, Timmy, and Wayno in awe, seeing that last night was going to be topped by tonight.

It had already gotten to the press that Lindsey was back; the local LA radio stations were all over it. We arrived at the Forum, and the crew had the stage set up with enough gear to have Lindsey join in for "Go Your Own Way." Even our old brother Ray Lindsey, fresh off a Def Leopard tour, was there to share this special moment. It was decided that all three guitar players would be onstage. Billy would play the acoustic rhythm part, and Rick would double up on the lead guitar, but Lindsey was going to sing the lead vocal part. The first run-through of the song at sound check was like the version the band had been doing all year that was purposely not like Lindsey's version. During the the second run through, Lindsey took control, standing in front of Mick's drums, looking at John as if to say, "Bring that bass over here, and kick my ass, motherfucker.

Lindsey downbeat started the song as Billy's offbeat of the acoustic counterpart blended in. Lindsey then took control, looking at John and Mick, saying, "Party time is over, boys," forcing them to step up the tempo that made the song sore to heights it hadn't all year.

The vocals kicked in, and once again, Stevie and Lindsey locked eyes with the words, "If I could, I'd give you my world, but you won't take it from me."

The magical animosity that no one else could create was in the air and took the song from just notes and words to making people feel the emotions that they could all relate to.

Then there was the solo—the solo like only Lindsey could play with his finger-picking style hitting multiple strings like he had six fingers.

"Go Your Own Way's" crescendo came crashing to the end, and then there was silence, dead silence. Everyone had been stunned into disbelief by what they had just witnessed. With one person applauding from the audience, it finally hit everyone, which launched into a series of whooping, cheers, and whistles.

December 8, 1990, at eight p.m., the house lights went out for the final time of the tour. The show started and wound its way to "Landslide" with Stevie and Lindsey showing no signs of letting up from where they left off the night before.

"Did you like that?" Stevie asked the rapturous crowd. "Well, maybe we can get him to come back out." I'll never forget that line. Did Stevie mean tonight or with The Mac?

The end of the show was here, with "Go Your Own Way" as the last song before the encores. The crew went through their setup, and Lindsey came out and plain and simply made Fleetwood Mac the legendary band they had always been.

Fleetwood Mac's power as a whole was greater than the sum of its parts, and it needed all five of them with their complex combination of love, animosity, family, and talent to transcend the norm to touch people, triggering their emotions making them feel alive.

During the solo of "Go Your Own Way," the Forum floors and walls were vibrating like an earthquake had hit. It was something we had seen on Mac tours in the past but not recently on the Behind The Mask Tour.

Rick and Billy were great. Rick Vito, to this day, is still one of the best guitar players I have ever worked with, and Billy Burnett had writing ability and amazing vocals that fit perfectly with Chris and Stevie. They both had the confidence to do what a lot of musicians wouldn't do: make a superstar band better.

As the band walked off the stage, I stood with Bob Cayne at the top of the stairs. The crowd was once again deafening. He shouted, "Well, dude man, it's over; the tour is over. What a way to end it, huh? We reconcile the numbers next week and put her to bed."

Just then, Rick Vito walked by, looked at me, handed me his guitar, and said, "Well, there's two and a half years of my life gone." He, like the rest of us, knew it was over.

The final bow at the Forum in Los
Angeles, December 8, 1990 with Lindsey
on stage. Everyone knew the magic
was back.

Lindsey was back, and this version of Fleetwood Mac was done.

With Lindsey playing the last two dates, the Fleetwood Mac magic was back—not only for the current fans, but the ones not yet born.

The crew was loading out as I put the last band member, John McVie, into his limo home. I walked around, saying goodbye to the crew with the sound of the load-out, slamming cases, and smelled diesel fumes from the trucks picking up the gear for the very last time.

The tour was over, and it felt like just another end of a long day on the road. It really didn't hit me until I looked out the window and I saw I was under the Vincent Thomas Bridge that was the icon for San Pedro and the gate to the Pacific Ocean. I rolled down the window, took a deep breath, and smelled the familiar odor of fish and cargo.

I was home, where it all began. I now had four sons, a daughter on the way, and no idea what was next, but I knew in my heart, mind, and soul that the road and me needed to part ways and be together no more.

At that moment, the angels were smiling, and the devil frowned.

EPILOGUE

EVERY MORNING, I WAKE UP, and it's Saturday.

Simplicity, happiness, gratitude, and peace are no longer just words but my way of life.

Do I miss my past? Who wouldn't—the adrenaline rush of the crowd when the band hits the stage, the lights shining in my eyes, the sound pounds my chest, and most of all, the camaraderie that made that life something very special?

In the first thirty-three years of my life, I lived ten lifetimes and survived them all. I became a citizen of the world, moving side by side with creative revolutionaries who rescued a civilization, using music to create cultural awareness.

My blessed life ultimately became a curse because I was constantly chasing that feeling, that rush of going warp ten with my soul on fire. I lived a life others could only dream about.

I often asked myself how could tomorrow ever be as good as today. What's next? Don't blink, or you'll miss out and be one of them, one of the normal folks, one of the nine-to-fivers.

I was adopted by a freak show, one that stole the dreams of a normal youth and blurred the lines between pain, joy, fantasy, and reality.

Looking back, I can honestly say I wouldn't change a thing. I've had many families with lifetime friendships; I traveled to the ends of the Earth visiting places I never imagined and may never go to again.

After the 1990 Fleetwood Mac tour, married to Lisa with four sons and soon a daughter, I knew that changes were needed, and with the fear of having to grow up, I hit speed bumps on the road to paradise.

I thought change was possible, but soon it became obvious it wasn't, and fate decided it was best for my family to jump in line at the all-you-can-eat buffet of excitement.

With my confidence, calmness, and years of experience managing the chaotic world of being on the road, I plotted a course to raise my family in this fast-changing world.

I found myself teaching technology to entertainment and entertainment to technology.

From my past with The Mac and Apple, I understood both industries and was able to articulate how to digitally enhance and reissue the artist's old content, not only to give it a new polished life but also create new profits ... large profits.

The two mammoth industries melded together with one common factor—money. Lots of money.

I found the secret sauce to support the family and keep living my exciting entertainment lifestyle while being a stay-at-home father.

I was lucky ... and luck happens when opportunity and preparation meet, and there I was, at the crossroads with both staring me right in the eyes.

I was never afraid. I was young, confident, and I didn't know the word "failure" because I believed there was nothing to lose.

I believed I was Teflon, unbreakable, only to realize that there were small cracks that became large fissures, which later in life would need attention and repair.

The hardships of life came my way fast and furious, bringing with them the struggles and pressures of raising five children with a mother now diagnosed with bipolar disorder and substance addiction, but most of all, dealing with my own insecurities of not failing at any cost.

Yes, there were holes in the dyke, but being blessed with the experiences of my past had taught me patience, knowledge, and flexibility. I had enough fingers and toes to stop the leaks and save the village.

I rode the entertainment technology tsunami, building a record label, managing bands, and with the help of good friends and family was fortunate to share the world I knew so well with my children and once again live the life that I wanted.

We went from having more money than we needed to having food and a Christmas tree left on our front porch by the church. We struggled, loved, learned, and grew together through the good times and bad. And we survived.

I landed on my feet, and now have children who grew to leave the nest and who are my proudest accomplishments.

With the unorthodox lifestyle of being raised in the wraps of a rock 'n' roll security blanket and dealing with their mother's misfortunes, my children learned patience and compassion, and were slow to judge others, but most of all, they viewed things as they can be and not as they are. I am them, and they are me.

In the literary world, two of the great seven stories are going home and being reborn. So true to form in my fractured fairytale life, I did exactly that, I was reborn back on the road home to my world of rock 'n' roll.

Much older, with even more wisdom and patience, I jumped into the deep end and spent 2006–2016 on the road with old friends and "classic rock" artists who just wouldn't go away, draining every last drop out of their illustrious careers.

Bands on fiftieth anniversary tours that were a joke to all of us years ago became common occurrences, and we still managed to maintain the integrity of the past by refusing to let the new, Millennial-entitled business process beat us.

I finally relented when music became numbers instead of notes and knew there was no going back. Even a dull blade with enough force can make a deep cut.

In 2011, fate and destiny called again, changing my life forever. My world was turned upside down with the loss of my oldest son, Ryan (at twenty-seven years old), to the evils of cancer—but not before using his own music career to start 20K Watts, a foundation helping less fortunate children in third world countries, replacing kerosene lamps with solar and providing water filters for fresh water. Ryan never doubted he could, or would, make a positive change in the world.

Life will never be the same without Ryan here, and I just pray it gets easier.

Over time, Lisa and I drifted apart, and there I was, standing all alone with this confusing excitement—looking for answers and wondering what was next.

I knew I was done making millions for millionaires who would be the richest people in the graveyard lying in their coffins next to dead presidents.

When I'm gone and the world moves on, and like my son Ryan, I don't want to be remembered for what bands I worked with or how much money I made, how nicely I dressed, or what car I drove.

My expertise, experience, and energy are better suited for charity to help people in need in a deeply divided world. I wish to be remembered for what I did with what I was blessed with and to carry on Ryan's dream, helping impoverished children grow healthy and strong to make positive, everlasting change.

I've had a blessed life. Sure, there's been ups and some downs, and along the way, there was always a higher power in my pocket that I knew was there but sometimes ignored.

Now, right now in my life, I realize it's important not to try so hard to control my future but to accept that whatever is in store for me is meant to be. I live for today. I live for today because I don't know what will happen tomorrow.

I wake up every day taking one step at a time and letting fate determine my destiny.

Our dreams are our gifts to the world.

This is the actual blanket my mother knitted for me in 1976, the one that got thrown off the roof and ended up in traffic on Hermosa Avenue.

It reminds me of home where my story began and the starting place for all my dreams that came true.

My home was not a place but a feeling, a feeling of comfort and love that gave me a great life.

ACKNOWLEDGMENTS

ABOVE ALL, THANK YOU, GOD, for giving me a great life that until recently I took for granted. A life that I know now was given to me to help others in need of His word.

My children: Ryan, Tristan, Shain, Channing, and Khiara. You are my world and I love you all.

Ryan, I'm Just Lovin' It!

Lisa, thank you for the motivation and five beautiful children who are what they are because of you.

My brothers and sisters and the Russo and Rossi families for their unconditional love and support throughout my life. My children and I would be nothing without all of you. Vi amo tutti!

Phillis (Rossi) and Craig Peterson: What can I say but thank you, thank you, thank you!

My parents, Dino and Mary Rossi: You were perfect, and even though you're not here on Earth, you are with me every day.

To my Fleetwood Mac family: Ray Lindsey, Curry Grant, Dave "Shark Boy" Richanbach, Ron "Rhyno" Penny, Mark Drale, Kenny D'Alesandro, Patrick Byrne, Tony Todaro, Dennis Mays, Chuck Hull, Trip Khalaf, Jim Devenny, Chris Lamb, Bobby O'Neal, Bob "Dudeman" Cayne, Wayne "Wayno" Cody RIP, John Courage (JC) RIP, Timmy "Fat Bear" McCarthy RIP, Jim Barnes, Mike Grassley RIP, Marty Hom, and ALL the other amazing crew and technicians throughout my whole time with the Mac. We will always be family.

Fleetwood Mac: Mick Fleetwood, John McVie, Christine McVie, Stevie Nicks, and Lindsey Buckingham. Thank you for taking a chance on a young kid and bringing him along with you on a magical journey. Also: Rick Vito, Billy Burnette, Sharon Celani, Lori Perry Nicks, Robin Snyder RIP, and Christie Alsbury Lindsey. I love you all.

Also: Gary "Red" Geller, Randy Ezratty, Bill Darlington, Marc Brickman (you're one of a kind!), Andre Augustine, Lars Brogard, David Covelli, Ray Compton RIP, Mike McGill, Chuck Alvarez, Brad Liszt, Steve Moris Jeffery Foskett, "Swifty," Timmy and Tara and Tim Foster. Katy Lindsey, Katey Sagal, Mike Droke, Gerry Brown, Mitzi Spallas, Tim Lamb, Jay Lucas, Donald Jacobelly, all the Brewers, Ray Deeter, Nick Storr, Jay Shanker, Nancy Seely, Coach Teora (thanks for throwing me out of gym class), Mary Schlatter,

Richard Demar, Dave Lynch, John Matera (blanket photo), Andy Fiamengo (loaded bases with two outs!), and everyone who knows they should be in here I overlooked. You know who you are.

Alan Rogan: Rest in peace, our old friend, and take it easy on everyone up there, will ya!

Thank you: Chaka Khan; Rickie Lee Jones; Bette Midler; Al Jarreau RIP; Jeff Lynne and ELO; Christopher Cross; The Beach Boys Brian Wilson, Al Jardine, Mike Love, and David Marks; Billy Idol; John, Julie, and Bob Fogerty; Neil Young; Ms. Diana Ross; and the hundreds of band members, background singers, and support I've had the pleasure to work, tour, and share the world with.

George Hawkins RIP: You're my Brudda!

Jerry Levin: You're a father, a brother, and most of all a great friend. I would have nothing without your guidance and expertise, not only in the music business but in life. We've done a lot together and have come a long way since that cold night in Long Beach way back in 1974. Let's write PortTown!! Meff

Curry Grant: From the night in Long Beach in 1975 when you saved my life from the falling trusses through all the amazing collaborations with all the artist over the years, I can't thank you enough for sharing your vision and talents with a young kid that I know tested your patience. I always said if you look up lighting designer in the dictionary it says: Curry Grant! Love you my brother!

The amazing Neal Preston for all his photos. You are

the eyes of the world of rock 'n' roll. Your work is epic, timeless, and above all historic. Hundreds of years from now people will be able to relive the "classic rock" era because of your talents—the world will share it forever!

My literary team: My publishing manager Polly Letofsky. My amazing editors Bobby Haas and Jennifer Zellinger, you make my words jump off the pages. My layout and book designer Victoria Wolf. Herb Zimmer for the many printouts of the manuscript.

Larry Heimgartner: thanks for teaching me how to express myself through writing and allowing me to do something I thought I'd never do.

Gino, Kelly, Tony, Wendy, and the whole Cutri family at Raffaello's for feeding me and being there every step of the way through this book process.

The 20K Watts team: Bri Erger, Juan Baez, Dylan Chase and Saul Frausto. Like Ryan said, "We can't save them all but have to save as many as we can to save the right ones who will become the leaders who will influence and enhance the lives of millions more, so Just Love It!

I'm sure there are so many more people I might have forgotten. If I did, please forgive me, but you know who you are and how much I love you all.

Last but not least, Patricia Montour, thank you for inspiring and empowering me with your endless love and support. You opened the door to the cage so I could fly again.

Made in the USA
Las Vegas, NV
25 May 2024

90365481R00343